TAKING◆SIDES

Clashing Views on Controversial

Issues in Mass Media and Society

EIGHTH EDITION

Selected, Edited, and with Introductions by

Alison Alexander
University of Georgia

and

Jarice Hanson
Quinnipiac University

McGraw-Hill/Dushkin
A Division of The McGraw-Hill Companies

Photo Acknowledgment
Cover image: © PhotoDisc, Inc.

Cover Art Acknowledgment
Charles Vitelli

Library of Congress Cataloging-in-Publication Data
Main entry under title:
Taking sides: clashing views on controversial issues in mass media and society/selected, edited,
and with introductions by Alison Alexander and Jarice Hanson.—8th ed.
Includes bibliographical references and index.
1. Mass media. 2. Information services. I. Alexander, Alison, comp.II. Hanson, Jarice, comp.
302.23
0-07-304402-4
94-31766

Printed on Recycled Paper

h
13.10.06

TAKING SIDES

TAKING SIDES

Clashing Views on Controversial

Issues in Mass Media
and Society

Preface

Comprehension without critical evaluation is impossible.

—Friedrich Hegel (1770-1831)
German philosopher

Mass communication is one of the most popular college majors in the country, which perhaps reflects a belief in the importance of communications systems as well as a desire to work within the communications industry. This book, which contains 36 selections presented in a pro and con format, addresses 18 different controversial issues in mass communications and society. The purpose of this volume, and indeed of any course that deals with the social impact of media, is to create a literate consumer of media—someone who can walk the fine line between a naive acceptance of all media and a cynical disregard for any positive benefits that they may offer.

The media today reflect the evolution of a nation that has increasingly seized on the need and desire for more leisure time. Technological developments have increased our range of choices—from the number of broadcast or cable channels we can select to the publications we can read that cater specifically to our individual interests and needs. New and improving technologies allow us to choose when and where to see a film (through the magic of the VCR), to create our preferred acoustical environment (by stereo, CD, or portable headphones), and to communicate over distances instantly (by means of computers and electronic mail). Because these many forms of media extend our capacities to consume media content, the study of mass media and society is the investigation of some of our most common daily activities. Since many of the issues in this volume are often in the news (or even are the news!), you may already have opinions on them. We encourage you to read the selections and discuss the issues with an open mind. Even if you do not initially agree with a position or do not even understand how it is possible to make the opposing argument, give it a try. We believe that thinking seriously about mass media is an important goal.

Plan of the book   This book is primarily designed for students in an introductory course in mass communication (sometimes called introduction to mass media or introduction to mass media and society). The issues are such that they can be easily incorporated into any media course regardless of how it is organized—thematically, chronologically, or by medium. The 36 selectionsm have been taken from a variety of sources and were chosen because of their usefulness in defending a position and for their accessibility to students.

Each issue in this volume has an issue *introduction*, which sets the stage for the debate as it is argued in the YES and NO selections. Each issue concludes with a *postscript* that makes some final observations about the selections, points the way to other questions related to the issue, and offers suggestions for further reading on the issue. The introductions and postscripts do not preempt what is the reader's own task: to achieve a critical and informed view of the issues at stake. In reading an issue and forming your own opinion you should not feel confined to adopt one or the other of the positions presented. Some readers may see important points on both sides of an issue and may construct for themselves a new and creative approach. Such an approach might incorporate the best of both sides, or it might provide an entirely new vantage point for understanding. Relevant Internet site addresses (URLs) that may prove useful as starting points for further research are provided on the *On the Internet* page that accompanies each part opener. At the back of the book is a listing of all the *contributors to this volume*, which will give you additional information on the communication scholars, practitioners, policymakers, and media critics whose views are debated here.

Changes to this edition   This eighth edition represents a considerable revision. There are 6 completely new issues: Issue 12: *Should Freedom of Speech Ever be Restricted?* Issue 13: *Should the FCC Liberalize Ownership Rules?* Issue 14: *Is Economics the Bottom Line in the Newsrooms of Today?* Issue 15: *Do the Media Introduce Us to New Ways of Thinking about Things?* Issue 16: *Can the Music Industry Survive, Despite Technologies that Facilitate Downloading?* Issue 18: *Is the Information Society Better Than What We've Known?* In addition, for Issue 1: *Are American Values Shaped by the Mass Media?* the No-side selection has been replaced to bring a fresh perspective to the debate. For Issue 9: *Is Negative Campaigning Bad for the American Political Process?* both the Yes- and No-side selections have been replaced with updated material. For Issue 10: *Do the Media have a Liberal Bias?* The No-side selection has been replaced.

A word to the instructor   An *Instructor's Manual With Test Questions* (multiple-choice and essay) is available through the publisher for the instructor using *Taking Sides* in the classroom. And a general guidebook, *Using Taking Sides in the Classroom*, which discusses methods and techniques for integrating the pro-con approach into any classroom setting, is also available. An online version of *Using Taking Sides in the Classroom* and a correspondence service for Taking Sides adopters can be found at http://www.dushkin.com/usingts/.
   Taking Sides: Clashing Views on Controversial Issues in Mass Media and Society is only one title in the Taking Sides series. If you are interested in seeing the table of contents for any of the other titles, please visit the Taking Sides Website at http://www.dushkin.com/takingsides.

Acknowledgments   We wish to acknowledge the encouragement, support, and detail given to this project. We bid farewell to Theodore Knight and the many individuals at McGraw-Hill/Dushkin in Connecticut. We thank Nichole Altman for the care given to this project at the new location of McGraw-Hill/Dushkin in Iowa. We would also like to thank Keisha Hoerrner for her help with this project and for her work on the Instructor's Manual.

We would also like to thank Ho-Ling (Haley) Kao and Cheryl Christopher at the University of Georgia for their valuable assistance. Finally, we would like to thank our families and friends (Frank, James, Katie, James Jr., and Torie) for their patience and understanding during the period in which we prepared this book.

Alison Alexander
University of Georgia

Jarice Hanson
Quinnipiac University

Contents In Brief

Contents

PART 2   MEDIA ETHICS   92

on the way in which advertisers seek to control magazine content and, thus, go beyond persuasion and information into the realm of influencing the content of other media.

PART 3   MEDIA AND POLITICS   154

Erik Bucy and Kimberly Gregson examine the conditions under which individuals feel psychologically engaged with a political system through participating in direct interaction with candidates for an office. They examine political radio, tv, electronic town forums, and the use of the Internet as ways of increasing a special type of *space* for particiaption. Diane Owen is far more critical of what really happens in teh different media contexts; she agrees that political radio has been the most successful forum for like-minded citizens to agree with political views, but she takes a far more pessimistic view of how different media formats have actually contributed to quality interactions, or better understanding of political issues.

Mass communication scholars examine the truth behind the assumption that negative campaigning has a negative impact on deemed negative ads fairly worthless and that such ads increased negativity about campaigns. Other potential consequences such as cynicism, efficacy, and apathy were not found. Politicial advertising scholars report on the lessons of their studies of negative campaign advertising. Negative ads, they argue, are more memorable. They help voters make distinctions between candidates; they influence voters. But not all negative ads are useful, and the authors help us make the distinction. Despite the revulsion that pervades public opinion toward negative ads, these authors argue that they are helpful to voters.

Journalist Bernard Goldberg looks at the common phrase, "the media elite have a liberal bias," and gives examples of the way coverage becomes slanted, depending upon the reporter's or anchor's perception of the subject's political stance. Journalist James Wolcott examines the impact of Fox television network's conservative approach, as evidenced by the news programs that feature right-wing pundits and pro-Republican views. He contends that Fox's news and public affairs coverage attained the highest ratings when appealing to the "angry white male."

PART 4   REGULATION   220

Author Michael A. Banks explains that as more people turn to libraries for Internet access, libraries and communities have been forced to come to grips with the conflict between freedom of speech and objectional material on the World Wide Web and in Usenet newsgroups. He adds that software filters are tools that help librarians keep inappropriate materials out of the library. The American Civil Liberties Union (ACLU) concludes that mandatory blocking software in libraries is both inappropriate and unconstitutional. Blocking censors valuable speech and gives librarians, educators, and parents a false sense of security when providing minors with Internet access, argues the ACLU.

Law Professor Eugene Volokh examines several situations in which absolute freedom of speech would very likely conflict with the precedents that have been set in the realm of creating "hostile environment law." For example, if any offensive speech or images were transmitted in a public arena, the law would side with the more conservative approach toward restricting speech or images that would offend certain people, or that would create an uncomfortable atmosphere. Two media consulting firms collaborated on a survey of rock radio listeners to discover what might be offensive to them. The results, taken from the perspective of the audience who listens to rock, created an argument for restricting government involvement in censoring content, and a clear preference for allowing individuals to choose what they hear, or requiring parental involvement in the cases of radio content and audiences of children.

Federal Communications Commission (FCC) Chairman Michael K. Powell in testimony before the Senate Committee on Commerce, Science and Transportation outlined the FCC proposal to relax ownership rules. He cites changes in the marketplace and argues that these changes will benefit the public interest through protecting viewpoint diversity, enhancing competition, and fostering localism. University professor McChesney and *The Nation* correspondent Nichols explore the unprecedented public outcry over the relaxation of ownership rules. Concern about the impact of consolidation crosses traditional political lines and reflects an increasing concern within the American public that media have become defined by commercial and corporate concerns.

PART 5   MEDIA BUSINESS   282

Daniel Sutter, Associate Professor of Economics at the University of Oklahoma, takes a unique approach to the study of the driving forces behind the production of news. He postulates three important forces: audience demand, ownership bias, and journalist socialization. Posing a liberal cartel as a rationale for news bias, he demonstrates the economic consequensces of such a postion. The Project for Excellence in Journalism produces an annual report on American Journalism. In evaluating the major trends in content, economics, ownership, and investment, they conclude that many forces are creating a transformation in journalism. Theses forces include fragmentation of audiences, variable journalistic standards, convergence of media, and economic forces. No single factor is the bottom line in the newsrooms of today.

Author James Wolcott examines the world of web logs (blogs) and calls them the "most vivifying, talent-swapping, socializing breakthrough in popular journalism…" As the newest form of jounalistic speech, he sees the exchange of ideas as a backlash to the commercialism of traditional media, and he applauds the blog form as the best thing to happen to print journalism since the 18th century. Jesse Suneblick criticizes traditional print media for becoming so conservative, and discusses the plight of the editorial illustrator, who, today, can't sell truly innovative, creative artwork because the owners of print media want non-offensive images that encourage audiences not to think or question the content of images.

Author Kevin Kelly provides a brief history of music as it changed from live performer to recorded work. Stating that the most significant change has been the change from analog to digital recording, Kelly looks optimistically toward a future of music in which there will be greater varieties of music for discriminating fans. In a Senate Hearing to assess the matter of whether digitally recorded music could be protected by copyright, Senators Orrin Hatch and Patrick Leahy, and Napster Interim Chairman, Hank Barry, discuss the problems of trying to protect original ownership in a age of digital duplicaton.

PART 6   THE INFORMATION SOCIETY   346

Journalist Simson Garfinkel discusses how today's technology has the potential
to destroy our privacy. He makes the case that the government and individuals
could take steps to protect themselves against privacy abuse, particularly by
returning to the groundwork set by the government in the 1970s and by
educating people on how to avoid privacy traps. *Forbes* reporter Adam L.
Penenberg discusses his own experiences with an Internet detective agency,
and he explains how easy it is for companies to get unauthorized access to
personal information. He specifically describes how much, and where, personal
information is kept and the lack of safeguards in our current system.

Technology Review senior editor Wade Roush reflects on the way we currently
use the architecture of the web. She outlines the likely scenario for the future of
the Internet, with global networks connected to "smart nodes" which will be
able to store all of our files, and allow us to access them from remote sites with
only small, hand-held devices. The improvements in technology will then lead
to a more dynamic use of the web, and will make the Internet more-user
friendly, as well as more secure. Author Matthew Robinson warns that no
matter what technologies we have available, human beings seem interested in
fewer subjects and know even less about politics and current events. He warns
that even though we may call it an "information" society, there is evidence to
suggest that we actually know less than in earlier years. His examples are
humorous as well as sobering.

Introduction

Ways of Thinking About Mass Media and Society

Alison Alexander
Jarice Hanson

Media are everywhere in our industrialized world today. It is likely that anyone reading this book has access to more forms of media than their grandparents could have ever dreamed of. Many readers are probably adept at multitasking—a term unheard of when this book series began. With access to telephones (both land and cell), radio, tv, films, CDs, videotapes, DVDs, personal computers and the Internet— which has the ability to transfer any of the messages formerly confined to the discrete forms just mentioned, our sense of our world, and our relationship to it, has become a complex web of real messages as well as mediated messages.

Media are often scapegoats for the problems of society. Sometimes, the relationship of social issues and media seem too obvious *not* to have some connection. For example, violence in the media may be a reflection of society, or, as some critics claim, violence in the media makes it seem that violence in society is the norm. But in reality, an important reason the media is so often blamed for social problems is because the media are so pervasive. Their very ubiquity gives them the status that makes them seem more influential than they actually are. If one were to look at the statistics on violence in the United States, it would be possible to see that there are fewer violent acts today than in recent history—but because of violences depicted in the media, through reportage or fictional representation, violence appears more prevalent.

There are many approaches to investigating the relationships that are suggested by media and society. From an organizational perspective, the producers of media must find content and distribution forms that will be profitable, and therefore, they have a unique outlook on the audience as consumers. From the perspective of the creative artist, the profit motive may be important, but the exploration of the unique communicative power of the media may be paramount. The audience also, has different use patterns, such as desires for information or entertainment, and demonstrates a variety of choices in content offered to them. Whether the media reflect society, or shape society, has a lot to do with the dynamic interaction of many of these different components.

To complicate maters, even our terms and definitions have evolved. The "mass" media have changed in recent years. Not long ago, "mass" media referred to messages that were created by large organizations for broad, heterogeneous audiences. This concept no longer suffices for the contemporary media environments. While the "mass" media still exist in the forms of radio, television, film, and general interest newspapers and magazines, many media forms today are hybrids of "mass" and "personal" media technologies that open a new realm of understanding about how audiences process the meaning of the messages. Digital technologies and distribution forms have created many opportunities for merging (or *converging*) media. Time-shifting, memory, storage of information, and truth all play important roles in the use of Internet communication, and call our attention to aspects of the communicative process that need fresh examination.

Still, most of the new services and forms of media rely, in part, on the major mass media distribution forms and technologies of television, radio, film, and print. The challenge, then, is to understand how individuals in society use media in a variety of formats and contexts, and how they make sense of the messages they take from the content of those media forms.

As we look at U.S. history, we can see that almost every form of media was first subject to some type of regulation by the government, or by the media industry itself. This has changed over the years, so that we now have a virtually unregulated media environment in which the responsibility for the content of media no longer rests with higher authorities. We, as consumers, are asked to be critical of that media which we consume. This requires that we be educated consumers, rather than relying on standards and practices of industry, or government intervention into questionable content. While this may not seem like a big problem for adult consumers, the questions and answers become more difficult when we consider how children use the media to form judgments, form opinions, or seek information.

The growing media landscape is changing our habits. The average American still spends over three hours a day viewing television, and in the average home the television is on for over seven hours a day. Politics and political processes have changed, in part, due to the way politicians use the media to reach voters. A proliferation of television channels has resulted from the popularity of cable, but does cable offer anything different from broadcast television? Videocassettes deliver feature-length films to the home, changing the traditional practice of viewing film in a public place, and video distribution via the Internet is now a practical option for anyone with transmission lines large enough to download large files. The recording industry is still reeling over the impact of MP3 and free software that allows consumers to sample, buy, or steal music on line. Communications is now a multibillion-dollar industry and the third fastest-growing industry in America. From these and other simple examples, it is clear that the media have changed American society, but our understanding of how and why remains incomplete.

Dynamics of Interaction

In recent years, the proliferation of new forms of media have changed on a global scale. In the U.S., 98% of homes have at least one traditional wired-telephone, while cell phone use continues to rise. Still, there are places in the world where traditional wired-phone lines may be limited, or where access to telephones is rare. There are some countries that have more cell phone use, per capita, than people in North America. In the U.S., over 98% of the population has access to at least one television set, but in some parts of the world, televisions are still viewed communally, or viewed only at certain hours of the day. The use of home computers and the Internet has grown annually in the U.S., with a majority of home computer users accessing their messages over high speed systems. And yet, less than half of the people of the world have access to the Web. These figures demonstrate that the global media environment is still far from equitable, and they suggest that different cultures may use the media in different ways.

But apart from questions of access and available content, many fundamental questions about the power of media remain the same. How do audiences use the media available to them? How do message senders produce meaning? How much of the meaning of any message is produced by the audience? One increasingly important question for discussion is how do additional uses of media change our interpersonal environments and human interactions?

In the early years of the 21st century, many of the institutions we have come to depend upon are undergoing massive changes. The recording industry is perhaps one of the most rapidly changing fields, with micro-radio, web-streaming, and subscription services offering different alternatives for message distribution. We have branched from the ethical and legal issues of music downloading to issues of copyright ownership and peer-to-peer file transfer protocols. Many of the industries that you've grown up with are undergoing massive changes due to new ownership rules, competition, and industry change. We can expect to continue to see threats and challenges to our traditional media systems in the future. Even the ubiquitous personal computer could become obsolete with personal desk assistants (PDAs) offering cheaper, more portable forms of computing, and the ability to store information at remote locations.

Progress in Media Research

Much of media research has been in search of theory. Theory is an organized, commonsense refinement of everyday thinking; it is an attempt to establish a systematic view of a phenomenon in order to better understand that phenomenon. Theory is tested against reality to establish whether or not it is a good explanation. For example, a researcher might notice that what is covered by news outlets is very similar to what citizens say are the important issues of the day. From such observations comes agenda setting (the notion that the media confers importance on the topics it covers, directing public attention to what is considered important).

Much of the early media research was produced to answer questions of print media because print has long been regarded a permanent record of history and events. The ability of newspapers and books to shape and influence public opinion was regarded as a necessity to the founding of new forms of governments—including the U.S. government. But the bias of the medium carried certain restrictions with it. Print media was limited to those individuals who could read. The relationships of information control and the power of these forms of communication to influence readers contributed to a belief that reporting should be objective and fair and that a multiple number of viewpoints should be available to readers.

The principles that emerged from this relationship were addressed in an often–quoted statement attributed to Thomas Jefferson, who wrote, "Were it left to me to decide whether we should have a government without newspapers, or newspapers without a government, I should not hesitate a moment to prefer the latter." But the next sentence in Jefferson's statement is equally as important, and often omitted from quotations. "But I should mean that every man should receive those papers and be capable of reading them."

Today, media research on the relationships of media senders, the channels of communication, and the receivers of messages is not enough. Consumers must realize that "media literacy" is an important concept as well. People can no longer take for granted that the media exist primarily to provide news, information, and entertainment. They must be more attuned to what media content says about them as individuals and as members of a society. By integrating these various cultural components, the public can better criticize the regulations or lack of regulation that permits media industries to function the way they do. People must realize that individuals may read or understand media content in different ways, and that different cultures act as important components of understanding messages, as well as controlling access to some forms of media.

The use of social science data to explore the effects of media on audiences strongly emphasized psychological and sociological schools of thought. It did not take long to move from the "magic bullet theory"—which proposed that media had a direct and immediate effect on the receivers of the message, and the same message intended by the senders was the same when it was "shot" into the receiver, to other ideas of limited, or even indirect means of influencing the audience.

Media research has shifted from addressing specifically effects–oriented paradigms to exploring the nature of the institutions of media production themselves, as well as examining the unique characteristics of each form of media. What most researchers agree upon today, is that the best way to understand the power and impact of media is to look at context specific situations to better understand the dynamics involved in the use of media and the importance of the content.

Still, there are many approaches to media research, from a variety of interdisciplinary fields: psychology, sociology, linguistics, art, comparative literature, economics, political science, and more. What each of these avenues of inquiry have in common is that they all tend to focus attention on individuals, families, or other social groups; society in general; and culture in the broad sense. All of the interpretations frame meaning and investigate their subjects within institutional frameworks that are specific to any nation and/or culture.

Today's researchers question the notions of past theories and models as well as definitions of *mass* and *society*, and now place much of the emphasis of media dynamics in the perspective of global information exchange. A major controversy erupted in the early 1970s when many Third World countries disagreed with principles that sought to reify the industrialized nations' media. The New World Information Order (NWIO) perspective advanced the importance of the economic and social benefits of industrialized countries, and it noted that emerging nations had different priorities that reflected indigenous cultures, which were sometimes at odds with Western notions of a free press. The Third World countries' concern dealt with power as imposed upon a nation from outside, using media as a vehicle for cultural dependency and imperialism.

Many of the questions for media researchers in the 21st century deal with the continued fragmentation of the audience, caused by greater choice of channels and technologies for both traditional, and new communication purposes. The power of some of these technologies to reach virtually any place on the globe within fractions of a second will continue to pose questions of access to media, and the meaning of the messages transmitted. As individuals become more dependent upon the Internet for communication purposes, the sense of audience will further be changed as individual users choose what they want to receive, pay for, and keep. For all of these reasons, the field of media research is rich, growing, and challenging.

Questions for Consideration

In addressing the issues in this book, it is important to consider some recurring questions:

1. Are the media unifying or fragmenting? Does media content help the socialization process or does it create anxiety or inaccurate portrayals of the world? Do people feel powerless because they have little ability to shape the messages of media?
2. How are our basic institutions changing as we use media in new, and different ways? Do media support or undermine our political processes? Do they change what we think of when we claim to live in a "democracy"? Do media operate in the public interest, or do media serve the rich and powerful corporations' quest for profit? Can the media do both simultaneously?
3. Whose interests do the media represent? Do audiences actively work toward integrating media messages with their own experiences? How do new media technologies change our traditional ways of communicating? Are they leading us to a world in which interpersonal communication is radically altered because we rely on information systems to replace many traditional behaviors?

Summary

We live in a media-rich environment where almost everybody has access to some forms of media, and some choices in content. As new technologies and services are developed, are they responding to the problems that previous media researchers and the public have detected? Over time, individuals have improved their ability to unravel the complex set of interactions that ties the media and society together, but they need to continue to question past results, new practices and technologies, and their own evaluative measures. When people critically examine the world around them—a world often presented by the media—they can more fully understand and enjoy the way they relate as individuals, as members of groups, and as members of a society.

On the Internet . . .

The Center for Media Education

The Center for Media Education (CME) is a national, nonprofit organization dedicated to improving the quality of electronic media, especially on the behalf of children and families. This site discusses such topics as the effect of television violence, online advertising, media images, and new technologies.

http://www.cme.org

Communication Studies: General Communication Resources

An encyclopedic resource related to a host of mass communication issues, this site is maintained by the University of Iowa's Department of Communication Studies. It provides excellent links covering advertising, cultural studies, digital media, film, gender issues, and media studies.

http://www.uiowa.edu/~commstud/resources/general.html

Kaiser Family Foundation

The Kaiser Family Foundation site provides articles on a broad range of television topics, including the V-chip, sexual messages, and programs about AIDS. From the home page, go to "select a topic" and choose television.

http://www.kff.org

Writer's Guild of America

The Writer's Guild of America is the union for media entertainment writers. The nonmember areas of this site offer useful information for aspiring writers. There is also an excellent links section.

http://www.wga.org

PART 1

Mass Media's Role in Society

*D*o *media merely reflect the social attitudes and concerns of our times, or are they also able to construct, legitimate, and reinforce the social realities, behaviors, attitudes, and images of others? Do they operate to maintain existing power structures, or are they a pluralistic representation of diverse views? The ways media help us to shape a sense of reality are complex. Should concern be directed toward vulnerable populations such as children? If we truly have a variety of information sources and content to choose from, perhaps we can assume that distorted images are balanced with realistic ones. But is this truly the media scenario in which we live? Questions about the place of media within society—and within what many call the information age—cannot be ignored.*

- Are American Values Shaped by the Mass Media?
- Is Television Harmful for Children?
- Is Emphasis on Body Image in the Media Harmful to Females Only?
- Do African American Stereotypes Still Dominate Entertainment Television?

ISSUE 1

Are American Values Shaped by the Mass Media?

YES: Herbert I. Schiller, *The Mind Managers.* (Beacon Press, 1973)

NO: Horace Newcomb and Paul M. Hirsch, from "Television as a Cultural Forum: Implications for Research," *Quarterly Review of Film Studies* (Summer 1983)

ISSUE SUMMARY

YES: Critical scholar of modern mass media, Professor Schiller, argues that mass media institutions are key elements of the modern capitalistic world order. Media, he argues, produce economic profits and the ideology necessary to sustain a world system of exploitative divisions of social and financial resources. It is the job of the citizenry to understand the myths which act to sustain this existing state of power relationships.

NO: Professors of communication Horace Newcomb and Paul M. Hirsch in their classic article counter that television serves as a site of negotiation for cultural issues, images, and ideas. Viewer selections from among institutional choices is a negotiation process as viewers select from a wide set of approaches to issues and ideas.

Can the media fundamentally reshape a culture? Americans are increasingly part of a culture in which information and ideas are electronically disseminated. Are media simply the conduit, the information channel, through which these ideas flow? None of the authors above would agree with that simplistic description. But they do disagree significantly on the way media influences society. Stop a moment and consider: what are the ways you feel media influence society? Groups within our society? And yourself? Currently in mass communication research, two vastly different perspectives on the impact of media on society exist. The critical/cultural perspective is advocated by Schiller, the pluralistic perspective by Newcomb and Hirsch. These articles are classic statements of the disagreements between these perspectives.

Schiller outlines the five myths that structure media content and manipulate consciousness. These myths function to reproduce the status quo and maintain existing social power structures. Despite changes in technologies and practices, Schiller argues that the ideological core of media messages remains the same. He is not alone in his concern that electronic media are negatively influencing our society. There are a number of mass communication scholars from the critical and cultural perspectives who are concerned that the power of media to shape attitude and opinions, paired with the power of media organizations to craft messages, will inevitably result in a recreation of current power structures, which inequitably divide social resources.

Newcomb and Hirsch offer the opposite interpretation. They assert that television operates as a cultural forum and is central to the process of public thinking. It is in the stories that media tell, that the nation creates, recreates and maintains its sense of self. In part, the effects of mass media on American values may be explained by examining the limits and effectiveness of popular pluralism, and the processes by which that pluralism is created and maintained. Communication, according to Newcomb and Hirsch, is dependent on shared meaning. Television is dependent upon pluralism more than many other forms of discourse. So one must consider how television is implicated in the creation of patterns of interpretation and the maintenance of sharing that defines pluralism as an effective cultural norm.

The media are so pervasive it is hard to believe they do not have important effects. Alternatively, many people do not believe that the media have personally influenced them to buy products or have harmed them, nor do they believe that the media hold a place of "prime importance" in shaping their lives. In everyday experience, many people do not consider the media as having an observable impact on them or on those around them. However, to understand how the media may shape the attitudes of individuals and of society, and how media may shape culture itself, requires that the reader stand back from his or her personal experiences in order to analyze the arguments presented on each side of this debate.

In the first selection, Schiller argues that U.S. media, through their "taken for granted" myths help structure the practices and meanings around which society takes shape. Ideology is not imposed but is systematically preferred by certain features of television, whereas other oppositional ideas are ignored or domesticated. Schiller was a powerful proponent of the theory that media is structured by the economic conditions under which it operates.

In the second selection, Newcomb and Hirsch advance a cultural forum model to understand the place of television in our society. Multiple meanings are key in understanding how television operates to provide a forum for the featuring of issues and ideas, and providing therefore a forum wherein those issues become a focus of cultural concern. Rather than concentrating on the fears of media's influence upon society, Newcomb and Hirsch push us to examine their functions.

Herbert I. Schiller  **YES**

The Mind Managers

Introduction

America's media managers create, process, refine, and preside over the circulation of images and information which determine our beliefs and attitudes and, ultimately, our behavior. When they deliberately produce messages that do not correspond to the realities of social existence, the media managers become mind managers. Messages that intentionally create a false sense of reality and produce a consciousness that cannot comprehend or wilfully rejects the actual conditions of life, personal or social, are manipulative messages.

Manipulation of human minds, according to Paulo Freire, "is an instrument of conquest." It is one of the means by which "the dominant elites try to conform the masses to their objectives.[1] By using myths which explain, justify, and sometimes even glamorize the prevailing conditions of existence, manipulators secure popular support for a social order that is not in the majority's long-term real interest. When manipulation is successful, alternative social arrangements remain unconsidered....

The permanent division of the society into two broad categories of "winners" and "losers" arises and persists as a result of the maintenance, recognition, and, indeed, sanctification of the system of private ownership of productive property and the extension of the ownership principle to all other aspects of human existence. The general acceptance of this arrangement for carrying on social activity makes it inevitable that some prosper, consolidate their success, and join the dominant shapers and molders of the community. The others, the majority, work on as mere conformists, the disadvantaged, and the manipulated; they are manipulated especially to continue to participate, if not wholeheartedly, at least positively, in the established routines. The system gives them a return adequate to achieve some marks of economic status, and manipulation leads them to hope that they might turn these routines to greater personal advantage for themselves or their children.

It is not surprising that manipulation, as an instrument of control, should reach its highest development in the United States. In America, more than anywhere else, the favorable conditions we have briefly noted permit a large fraction of the population to escape total suppression and thereby become potential actors in the historical process. Manipulation allows the appearance of active engagement while denying many of the material and *all* of the psychic benefits of genuine involvement....

The means of manipulation are many, but, clearly, control of the informational and ideational apparatus at all levels is essential. This is secured by the operation of a simple rule of the market economy. Ownership and control of the mass media, like all other forms of property, is available to those with capital. Inevitably, radio- and television-station ownership, newspaper and magazine proprietorship, movie-making, and book publishing are largely in the hands of corporate chains and media conglomerates. The apparatus is thus ready to assume an active and dominant role in the manipulative process.

My intention is to identify some of these conditioning forces and to reveal the means by which they conceal their presence, deny their influence, or exercise directional control under auspices plat superficially appear benign and/or natural. The search for these "hidden processes," along with their subtle mechanics, should not be mistaken for a more common kind of investigation—the exposé of clandestine activities. Conspiracy is neither invoked nor considered in these pages. Though the idea of mind management lends itself easily to such an approach, the comprehensive conditioning carried on throughout American society today does not require, and actually cannot be understood in, such terms....

Manipulation and the Packaged Consciousness

Five Myths That Structure Content

1. The Myth of Individualism and Personal Choice   Manipulation's greatest triumph, most observable in the United States, is to have taken advantage of the special historical circumstances of Western development to perpetrate as truth a definition of freedom cast in individualistic terms. This enables the concept to serve a double function. It protects the ownership of productive private property while simultaneously offering itself as the guardian of the individual's well-being, suggesting, if not insisting, that the latter is unattainable without the existence of the former. Upon this central construct an entire scaffolding of manipulation is erected. What accounts for the strength of this powerful notion?

...The identification of personal choice with human freedom can be seen arising side-by-side with seventeenth-century individualism, both products of the emerging market economy.[2]

For several hundred years individual proprietorship, allied with technological improvement, increased output and thereby bestowed great importance on personal independence in the industrial and political processes. The view that freedom is a personal matter, and that the individual's rights supersede the group's and provide the basis for social organization, gained credibility with the rise of material rewards and leisure time. Note, however, that these conditions were not distributed evenly among all classes of Western society and that they did not begin to exist in the rest of the world....

In the newly settled United States, few restraints impeded the imposition of an individualistic private entrepreneurial system and its accompanying myths of personal choice and individual freedom. Both enterprise and myth found a hospitable setting. The growth of the former and consolidation of the latter were inevitable. How far the process has been carried is evident today in the easy public acceptance of the giant multinational private corporation as an example of individual endeavor....

Privatism in every sphere of life is considered normal. The American life style, from its most minor detail to its most deeply felt beliefs and practices, reflects an exclusively self-centered outlook, which is in turn an accurate image of the structure of the economy itself. The American dream includes a personal means of transportation, a single-family home, the proprietor-operated business. Such other institutions as a competitive health system are obvious, if not natural, features of the privately organized economy....

Though individual freedom and personal choice are its most powerful mythic defenses, the system of private ownership and production requires and creates additional constructs, along with the techniques to transmit them. These notions either rationalize its existence and promise a great future, or divert attention from its searing inadequacies and conceal the possibilities of new departures for human development. Some of these constructs and techniques are not exclusive to the privatistic industrial order, and can be applied in any social system intent on maintaining its dominion. Other myths, and the means of circulating them, are closely associated with the specific characteristics of this social system.

2. The Myth of Neutrality   For manipulation to be most effective, evidence of its presence should be nonexistent. When the manipulated believe things are the way they are naturally and inevitably, manipulation is successful. In short, manipulation requires a false reality that is a continuous denial of its existence.

It is essential, therefore, that people who are manipulated believe in the neutrality of their key social institutions. They must believe that government, the media, education, and science are beyond the clash of conflicting social interests. Government, and the national government in particular, remains the centerpiece of the neutrality myth. This myth presupposes belief in the basic integrity and nonpartisanship of government in general and of its constituent parts—Congress, the judiciary, and the Presidency. Corruption, deceit, and knavery, when they occur from time to time, are seen to be the result of human weakness. The institutions themselves are beyond reproach. The fundamental soundness of the overall system is assured by the well-designed instrumentalities that comprise the whole.

The Presidency, for instance, is beyond the reach of special interests, according to this mythology. The first and most extreme manipulative use of the Presidency, therefore, is to claim the nonpartisanship of the office, and to seem to withdraw it from clamorous conflict....

The chief executive, though the most important, is but one of many governmental departments that seek to present themselves as neutral agents, embracing no objectives but the general welfare, and serving everyone impartially and disinterestedly. For half a century all the media joined in propagating the myth of the FBI as a nonpolitical and highly effective agency of law enforcement. In fact, the Bureau has been used continuously to intimidate and coerce social critics.

The mass media, too, are supposed to be neutral. Departures from even-handedness in news reportage are admitted but, the press assure us, result from human error and cannot be interpreted as flaws in the basically sound institutions of information dissemination. That the media (press, periodicals, radio, and television) are almost without exception business enterprises, receiving their revenues from commercial sales of time or space, seems to create no problems for those who defend the objectivity and integrity of the informational services.[3]...

Science, which more than any other intellectual activity has been integrated into the corporate economy, continues also to insist on its value-free neutrality. Unwilling to consider the implications of the sources of its funding, the directions of its research, the applications of its theories, and the character of the paradigms it creates, science promotes the notion of its insulation from the social forces that affect all other ongoing activities in the nation.

The system of schooling, from the elementary through the university level, is also, according to the manipulators, devoid of deliberate ideological purpose. Still, the product must reflect the teaching: it is astonishing how large a proportion of the graduates at each stage continue, despite all the ballyhoo about the counterculture, to believe in and observe the competitive ethic of business enterprise.

Wherever one looks in the social sphere, neutrality and objectivity are invoked to describe the functioning of value-laden and purposeful activities which lend support to the prevailing institutional system. Essential to the everyday maintenance of the control system is the carefully nurtured myth that no special groups or views have a preponderant influence on the country's important decision-making processes....

3. The Myth of Unchanging Human Nature   Human expectations can be the lubricant of social change. When human expectations are low, passivity prevails. There can, of course, be various kinds of images in anyone's mind concerning political, social, economic, and personal realities. The common denominator of all such imagery, however, is the view people have of human nature. What human nature is seen to be ultimately affects the way human beings behave, not because they must act as they do but because they believe they are expected to act that way....

It is predictable that in the United States a theory that emphasizes the aggressive side of human behavior and the unchangeability of human nature would find approval, permeate most work and thought, and be circulated widely by the mass media. Certainly, an economy that is built on and rewards private ownership and individual acquisition, and is subject to the personal and social conflicts these arrangements impose, can be expected to be gratified with an explanation that legitimizes its operative principles. How reassuring to consider these conflictful relationships inherent in the human condition rather than imposed by social circumstance! This outlook fits nicely too with the antiideological stance the system projects. It induces a "scientific" and "objective" approach to the human condition rigorously measuring human microbehavior in all its depravities, and for the most part ignoring the broader and less measurable social parameters.

Daily TV programming, for example, with its quota of half a dozen murders per hour, is rationalized easily by media controllers as an effort to give the people what they want. Too bad, they shrug, if human nature demands eighteen hours daily of mayhem and slaughter....

Fortune finds it cheering, for "example, that some American social scientists are again emphasizing "the intractability of human nature" in their explanations of social phenomena. "The orthodox view of environment as the all-important influence on people's behavior," it reports, "is yielding to a new awareness of the role of hereditary factors: enthusiasm for schemes to reform society by remolding men is giving way to a healthy appreciation of the basic intractability of human nature."[4]

The net social effects of the thesis that human nature is at fault are further disorientation, total inability to recognize the causes of malaise—much less to take any steps to overcome it—and, of most consequence, continued adherence to the *status quo*....

It is to prevent social action (and it is immaterial whether the intent is articulated or not) that so much publicity and attention are devoted to every pessimistic appraisal of human potential. If we are doomed forever by our inheritance, there is not much to be done about it. But there is a good reason and a good market for undervaluing human capability. An entrenched social system depends on keeping the popular and, especially, the "enlightened" mind unsure and doubtful about its human prospects....

This does not necessitate ignoring history. On the contrary, endless recitation of what happened in the past accompanies assertions about how much change is occurring under our very noses. But these are invariably *physical* changes—new means of transportation, air conditioning, space rockets, packaged foods. Mind managers dwell on these matters but carefully refrain from considering changes in social relationships or in the institutional structures that undergird the economy.

Every conceivable kind of futuristic device is canvassed and blueprinted. Yet those who will use these wonder items will apparently continue to be married, raise children in suburban homes, work for private companies, vote for a President in a two-party system and pay a large portion of their incomes for defense, law and order, and superhighways. The world, except for some glamorous surface redecorations, will remain as it is; basic relationships will not change, because they, like human nature, are allegedly unchangeable. As for those parts of the world that have undergone far-reaching social rearrangements, reports of these transformations, if there are any, emphasize the defects, problems, and crises, which are seized upon with relish by domestic consciousness manipulators....

4. The Myth of the Absence of Social Conflict ...Consciousness controllers, in their presentation of the domestic scene, deny absolutely the presence of social conflict. On the face of it, this seems an impossible task. After all, violence is "as American as apple pie." Not only in fact but in fantasy: in films, on TV, and over the radio, the daily quota of violent scenarios offered the public is staggering. How is this carnival of conflict reconcilable with the media managers' intent to present an image of social harmony? The contradiction is easily resolved.

As presented by the national message-making apparatus, conflict is almost always an *individual* matter, in its manifestations and in its origin. The social roots of conflict just do not exist for the cultural-informational managers. True, there are "good guys" and "bad guys," but, except for such ritualized situations as westerns, which are recognized as scenarios of the past, role identification is divorced from significant social categories.

Black, brown, yellow, red, and other ethnic Americans have always fared poorly in the manufactured cultural imagery. Still, these are minorities which all segments of the white population have exploited in varying degrees. As for the great social division in the nation, between worker and owner, with rare exceptions it has been left unexamined. Attention is diverted elsewhere—generally toward the problems of the upward-striving middle segment of the population, that category with which everyone is supposed to identify....

Elite control requires omission or distortion of social reality. Honest examination and discussion of social conflict can only deepen and intensify resistance to social inequity. Economically powerful groups and companies quickly get edgy when attention is called to exploitative practices in which they are engaged. *Variety*'s television editor, Les Brown, described such an incident. Coca-Cola Food Company and the Florida Fruit and Vegetable Association reacted sharply to a TV documentary, "Migrant," which centered on migrant fruit pickers in Florida. Brown wrote that "the miracle of *Migrant* was that it was televised at all." Warnings were sent to NBC not to show the program because it was "biased." Cuts in the film were demanded, and at least one was made. Finally, after the showing, "Coca-Cola shifted all its network billings to CBS and ABC."[5]

On a strictly commercial level, the presentation of social issues creates uneasiness in mass audiences, or so the audience researchers believe. To be safe, to hold onto as large a public as possible, sponsors are always eager to eliminate potentially "controversial" program material.

The entertainments and cultural products that have been most successful in the United States, those that have received the warmest support and publicity from the communications system, are invariably movies, TV programs, books, and mass entertainments (i.e., Disneyland) which may offer more than a fair quota of violence but never take up *social* conflict....

5. The Myth of Media Pluralism   Personal choice exercised in an environment of cultural-information diversity is the image, circulated worldwide, of the condition of life in America. This view is also internalized in the belief structure of a large majority of Americans, which makes them particularly susceptible to thoroughgoing manipulation. It is, therefore, one of the central myths upon which mind management flourishes. Choice and diversity, though separate concepts, are in fact inseparable; choice is unattainable in any real sense without diversity. If real options are nonexistent, choosing is either meaningless or manipulative. It is manipulative when accompanied by the illusion that the choice is meaningful.

Though it cannot be verified, the odds are that the illusion of informational choice is more pervasive in the United States than anywhere else in the world. The illusion is sustained by a willingness, deliberately maintained by information controllers, to mistake *abundance of media for diversity of content*....

The fact of the matter is that, except for a rather small and highly selective segment of the population who know what they are looking for and can therefore take advantage of the massive communications flow, most Americans are basically, though unconsciously, trapped in what amounts to a no-choice informational bind. Variety of opinion on foreign and domestic news or, for that matter, local community business, hardly exists in the media. This results essentially from the inherent identity of interests, material and ideological, of property-holders (in this case, the private owners of the communications media), and from the monopolistic character of the communications industry in general.

The limiting effects of monopoly are in need of no explanation, and communications monopolies restrict informational choice wherever they operate. They offer one version of reality—their own. In this category fall most of the nation's newspapers, magazines, and films, which are produced by national or regional communications conglomerates. The number of American cities in which competing newspapers circulate has shrunk to a handful.

While there is a competition of sorts for audiences among the three major TV networks, two conditions determine the limits of the variety presented. Though each network struggles gamely to attract as large an audience as possible, it imitates its two rivals in program format and content. If ABC is successful with a western serial, CBS and NBC will in all likelihood "compete" with "shoot-'em-ups" in the same time slot. Besides, each of the three national networks is part of, or is itself, an enormous communications business, with the drives and motivations of any other profit-seeking enterprise. This means that diversity in the informational-entertainment sector exists only in the sense that there are a number of superficially different versions of the main categories of program. For example, there are several talk shows on late-night TV; there may be half a dozen private-eye, western, or law-and-order TV serials to "choose from" in prime time; there are three network news commentators with different personalities who offer essentially identical information. One can switch the radio dial and get round-the-clock news from one or, at most, two news services; or one can hear Top 40 popular songs played by "competing" disc jockeys.

Though no single program, performer, commentator, or informational bit is necessarily identical to its competitors, *there is no significant qualitative difference*. Just as a supermarket offers six identical soaps in different colors and a drugstore sells a variety of brands of aspirin at different prices, disc jockeys play the same records between personalized advertisements for different commodities....

Yet it is this condition of communicational pluralism, empty as it is of real diversity, which affords great strength to the prevailing system of consciousness-packaging. The multichannel communications flow creates confidence in, and lends credibility to, the notion of free informational choice. Meanwhile, its main effect is to provide continuous reinforcement of the *sta-*

tus quo. Similar stimuli, emanating from apparently diverse sources, envelop the listener/viewer/reader in a message/image environment that ordinarily seems uncontrolled, relatively free, and quite natural. How could it be otherwise with such an abundance of programs and transmitters? Corporate profit-seeking, the main objective of conglomeratized communications, however real and ultimately determining, is an invisible abstraction to the consumers of the cultural images. And one thing is certain: the media do not call their audiences' attention to its existence or its mode of operation....

The fundamental similarity of the informational material and cultural messages that each of the mass media independently transmits makes it necessary to view the communications system as a totality. The media are mutually and continuously reinforcing. Since they operate according to commercial rules, rely on advertising, and are tied tightly to the corporate economy, both in their own structure and in their relationships with sponsors, the media constitute an industry, not an aggregation of independent, freewheeling informational entrepreneurs, each offering a highly individualistic product. By need and by design, the images and messages they purvey are, with few exceptions, constructed to achieve similar objectives, which are, simply put, profitability and the affirmation and maintenance of the private-ownership consumer society.

Consequently, research directed at discovering the impact of a single TV program or movie, or even an entire category of stimuli, such as "violence on TV" can often be fruitless. Who can justifiably claim that TV violence is inducing delinquent juvenile behavior when violence is endemic to all mass communications channels? Who can suggest that any single category of programming is producing male chauvinist or racist behavior when stimuli and imagery carrying such sentiments flow unceasingly through all the channels of transmission?

It is generally agreed that television is the most powerful medium; certainly its influence as a purveyor of the system's values cannot be overstated. All the same, television, no matter how powerful, itself depends on the absence of dissonant stimuli in the other media. Each of the informational channels makes its unique contribution, but the result is the same—the consolidation of the *status quo.*

Notes

1. Paulo Freire, *Pedagogy of the Oppressed* (New York: Herder and Herder, 1971), p. 144.
2. C. B. MacPherson, *The Political Theory of Possessive Individualism* (Oxford: Clarendon Press, 1962).
3. Henry Luce, the founder of *Time, Life, Fortune, Sports Illustrated*, and other mass circulation magazines, knew otherwise. He told his staff at *Time*: "The alleged journalistic objectivity, a claim that a writer presents facts without applying any value judgment to them [is] modem usage—and that is strictly a phony. It is that that I had to renounce and denounce. So when we say the hell with objectivity, that is what we are talking about." W. A. Swanberg, *Luce and His Empire* (New York: Charles Scribner's Sons, 1972), p. 331.
4. "The Social Engineers Retreat Under Fire," *Fortune*, October 1972, p. 3.
5. Les Brown, *Television: The Business Behind The Box* (New York: Harcourt, Brace Jovanovich, 1971), pp. 196–203.

NO ⬅

Horace Newcomb
and Paul M. Hirsch

Television as a Cultural Forum

$\mathbf{A}$ cultural basis for the analysis and criticism of television is, for us, the bridge between a concern for television as a communications medium, central to contemporary society, and television as aesthetic object, the expressive medium that, through its storytelling functions, unites and examines a culture. The shortcomings of each of these approaches taken alone are manifold.

The first is based primarily in a concern for understanding specific messages that may have specific effects, and grounds its analysis in "communication" narrowly defined. Complexities of image, style, resonance, narrativity, history, metaphor, and so on are reduced in favor of that content that can be more precisely, some say more objectively, described. The content categories are not allowed to emerge from the text, as is the case in naturalistic observation and in textual analysis. Rather they are predefined in order to be measured more easily. The incidence of certain content categories may be cited as significant, or their "effects" more clearly correlated with some behavior. This concern for measuring is, of course, the result of conceiving television in one way rather than another, as "communication" rather than as "art."

The narrowest versions of this form of analysis need not concern us here. It is to the best versions that we must look, to those that do admit to a range of aesthetic expression and something of a variety of reception. Even when we examine these closely, however, we see that they often assume a monolithic "meaning" in television content. The concern is for "dominant" messages embedded in the pleasant disguise of fictional entertainment, and the concern of the researcher is often that the control of these messages is, more than anything else, a complex sort of political control. The critique that emerges, then, is consciously or unconsciously a critique of the society that is transmitting and maintaining the dominant ideology with the assistance, again conscious or unconscious, of those who control communications technologies and businesses. (Ironically, this perspective does not depend on political perspective or persuasion. It is held by groups on the "right" who see American values being subverted, as well as by those on the "left" who see American values being imposed.)

Such a position assumes that the audience shares or "gets" the same messages and their meanings as the researcher finds. At times, like the literary critic, the researcher assumes this on the basis of superior insight, technique, or sensibility. In a more "scientific" manner the researcher may seek to establish a correlation between the discovered messages and the understanding of the audience. Rarely, however, does the message analyst allow for the possibility that the audience, while sharing this one meaning, may create many others that have not been examined, asked about, or controlled for.

The television "critic" on the other hand, often basing his work on the analysis of literature or film, succeeds in calling attention to the distinctive qualities of the medium, to the special nature of television fiction. But this approach all too often ignores important questions of production and reception. Intent on correcting what it takes to be a skewed interest in such matters, it often avoids the "business" of television and its "technology." These critics, much like their counterparts in the social sciences, usually assume that viewers should understand programs in the way the critic does, or that the audience is incapable of properly evaluating the entertaining work and should accept the critic's superior judgment.

The differences between the two views of what television is and does rest, in part, on the now familiar distinction between transportation and ritual views of communication processes. The social scientific, or communication theory model outlined above (and we do not claim that it is an exhaustive description) rests most thoroughly on the transportation view. As articulated by James Carey, this model holds that communication is a "process of transmitting messages at a distance for the purpose of control. The archetypal case of communication then is persuasion, attitude change, behavior modification, socialization through the transmission of information, influence, or conditioning."[1]

The more "literary" or "aesthetically based" approach leans toward, but hardly comes to terms with, ritual models of communication. As put by Carey, the ritual view sees communication "not directed toward the extension of messages in space but the maintenance of society in time; not the act of imparting information but the representation of shared beliefs."[2]

Carey also cuts through the middle of these definitions with a more succinct one of his own: "Communication is a symbolic process whereby reality is produced, maintained, repaired, and transformed."[3] It is in the attempt to amplify this basic observation that we present a cultural basis for the analysis of television. We hardly suggest that such an approach is entirely new, or that others are unaware of or do not share many of our assumptions. On the contrary, we find a growing awareness in many disciplines of the nature of symbolic thought, communication, and action, and we see attempts to understand television emerging rapidly from this body of shared concerns.[4]

◦❦◦

Our own model for television is grounded in an examination of the cultural role of entertainment and parallels this with a close analysis of television program content in all its various textual levels and forms. We focus on the collective, cultural view of the social construction and negotiation of reality, on the creation of what Carey refers to as "public thought."[5] It is not difficult to see television as central to this process of public thinking. As Hirsch has pointed out,[6] it is now our national medium, replacing those media—film, radio, picture magazines, newspapers—that once served a similar function. Those who create for such media are, in the words of anthropologist Marshall Sahlins, "hucksters of the symbol."[7] They are cultural *bricoleurs*, seeking and creating new meaning in the combination of cultural elements with embedded significance. They respond to real events, changes in social structure and organization, and to shifts in attitude and value. They also respond to technological shift, the coming of cable or the use of videotape recorders. We think it is clear that the television producer should be added to Sahlins's list of "hucksters." They work in precisely the manner he describes, as do television writers and, to a lesser extent, directors and actors. So too do programmers and network executives who must make decisions about the programs they purchase, develop, and air. At each step of this complicated process they function as cultural interpreters.

Similar notions have often been outlined by scholars of popular culture focusing on the formal characteristics of popular entertainment.[8] To those insights cultural theory adds the possibility of matching formal analysis with cultural and social practice. The best theoretical explanation for this link is suggested to us in the continuing work of anthropologist Victor Turner. This work focuses on cultural ritual and reminds us that ritual must be seen as process rather than as product, a notion not often applied to the study of television, yet crucial to an adequate understanding of the medium.

Specifically we make use of one aspect of Turner's analysis, his view of the *liminal* stage of the ritual process. This is the "in between" stage, when one is neither totally in nor out of society. It is a stage of license, when rules may be broken or bent, when roles may be reversed, when categories may be overturned. Its essence, suggests Turner,

> is to be found in its release from normal constraints, making possible the deconstruction of the "uninteresting" constructions of common sense, the "meaningfulness of ordinary life,"... into cultural units which may then be reconstructed in novel ways, some of them bizarre to the point of monstrosity.... Liminality is the domain of the "interesting" or of "uncommon sense."[9]

Turner does not limit this observation to traditional societies engaged in the *practice* of ritual. He also applies his views to postindustrial, complex societies. In doing so he finds the liminal domain in the arts—all of them.[10] "The dismemberment of ritual has... provided the opportunity of theatre in the high culture and carnival at the folk level. A multiplicity of desacralized performative genres have assumed, prismatically, the task of plural cultural reflexivity."[11] In short, contemporary cultures examine themselves through their arts, much as traditional societies do via the experience of ritual. Ritual and the arts offer a metalanguage, a way of understanding who and what we are, how values and attitudes are adjusted, how meaning shifts.

In contributing to this process, particularly in American society, where its role is central, television fulfills what Fiske and Hartley refer to as the "bardic function" of contemporary societies.[12] In its role as central cultural medium it presents a multiplicity of meanings rather than a monolithic dominant point of view. It often focuses on our most prevalent concerns, our deepest dilemmas. Our most traditional views, those that are repressive and reactionary, as well as those that are subversive and emancipatory, are upheld, examined, maintained, and transformed. The emphasis is on process rather than product, on discussion rather than indoctrination, on contradiction and confusion rather than coherence. It is with this view that we turn to an analysis of the texts of television that demonstrates and supports the conception of television as a cultural forum.

❧❦❧

This new perspective requires that we revise some of our notions regarding television analysis, criticism, and research. The function of the creator as *bricoleur*, taken from Sahlins, is again indicated and clarified. The focus on "uncommon sense," on the freedom afforded by the idea of television as a liminal realm helps us to understand the reliance on and interest in forms, plots, and character types that are not at all familiar in our lived experience. The skewed demography of the world of television is not quite so bizarre and repressive once we admit that it is the realm in which we allow our monsters to come out and play, our dreams to be wrought into pictures, our fantasies transformed into plot structures. Cowboys, detectives, bionic men, and great green hulks; fatherly physicians, glamorous female detectives, and tightly knit families living out the pain of the Great Depression; all these become part of the dramatic logic of public thought.

Shows such as *Fantasy Island* and *Love Boat*, difficult to account for within traditional critical systems except as examples of trivia and romance, are easily understood. Islands and boats are among the most fitting liminal metaphors, as Homer, Bacon, Shakespeare, and Melville, among others, have recognized. So, too, are the worlds of the Western and the detective story. With this view we can see the "bizarre" world of situation comedy as a means of deconstructing the world of "common sense" in which all, or most, of us live and work. It also enables us to explain such strange phenomena as game shows and late night talk fests. In short, almost any version of the television text functions as a forum in which important cultural topics may be considered. We illustrate this not with a contemporary program where problems almost always appear on the surface of the show, but with an episode of *Father Knows Best* from the early 1960s. We begin by noting that *FKB* is often cited as an innocuous series, constructed around unstinting paeans to American middle-class virtues and blissfully ignorant of social conflict. In short, it is precisely the sort of television program that reproduces dominant ideology by lulling its audience into a dream world where the status quo is the only status.

In the episode in question Betty Anderson, the older daughter in the family, breaks a great many rules by deciding that she will become an engineer. Over great protest, she is given an internship with a surveying crew as part of a high school "career education" program. But the head of the surveying crew, a young college student, drives her away with taunts and insensitivity. She walks off the job on the first day. Later in the week the young man comes to the Anderson home where Jim Anderson chides him with fatherly anger. The young man apologizes and Betty, overhearing him from the other room, runs upstairs, changes clothes, and comes down. The show ends with their flirtation underway.

Traditional ideological criticism, conducted from the communications or the textual analysis perspective, would remark on the way in which social conflict is ultimately subordinated in this dramatic structure to the personal, the emotional. Commentary would focus on the way in which the questioning of the role structure is shifted away from the world of work to the domestic arena. The emphasis would be on the conclusion of the episode in which Betty's real problem of identity and sex-role, and society's problem of sex-role discrimination, is bound by a more traditional conflict and thereby defused, contained, and redirected. Such a reading is possible, indeed accurate.

We would point out, however, that our emotional sympathy is with Betty throughout this episode. Nowhere does the text instruct the viewer that her concerns are unnatural, no matter how unnaturally they may be framed by other members of the cast. Every argument that can be made for a strong feminist perspective is condensed into the brief, half-hour presentation. The concept of the cultural forum, then, offers a different interpretation. We suggest that in popular culture generally, in television specifically, the raising of questions is as important as the answering of them. That is, it is equally important that an audience be introduced to the problems surrounding sex-role discrimination as it is to conclude the episode in a traditional manner. Indeed, it would be startling to think that mainstream texts in mass society would overtly challenge dominant ideas. But this hardly prevents the oppositional ideas from appearing. Put another way, we argue that television does not present firm ideological conclusions—despite its *formal* conclusions—so much as it *comments on* ideological problems. The conflicts we see in television drama, embedded in familiar and nonthreatening frames, are conflicts ongoing in American social experience and cultural history. In a few cases we might see strong perspectives that argue for the absolute correctness of one point of view or another. But for the most part the rhetoric of television drama is a rhetoric of discussion. Shows such as *All in the Family*, or *The Defenders*, or *Gunsmoke*, which raise the forum/discussion to an intense and obvious level, often make best use of the medium and become highly successful. We see statements *about* the issues and it should be clear that ideological positions can be balanced within the forum by others from a different perspective.

We recognize, of course, that this variety works for the most part within the limits of American monopoly-capitalism and within the range of American pluralism. It is an effective pluralistic forum only insofar as American political pluralism is or can be.[13] We also note, however, that one of the primary functions of the popular culture forum, the television forum, is to monitor the limits and the effectiveness of this pluralism, perhaps the only "public" forum in which this role is performed. As content shifts and attracts the attention of groups and individuals, criticism and reform can be initiated. We will have more to say on this topic shortly.

Our intention here is hardly to argue for the richness of *Father Knows Best* as a television text or as social commentary. Indeed, in our view, any emphasis on individual episodes, series, or even genres, misses the central point of the forum concept. While each of these units can and does present its audiences with incredibly mixed ideas, it is television as a whole system that presents a mass audience with the range and variety of ideas and ideologies inherent in American culture. In order to fully understand the role of television in that culture, we must examine a variety of analytical foci and, finally, see them as parts of a greater whole.

We can, for instance, concentrate on a single episode of television content, as we have done in our example. In our view most television shows offer something of this range of complexity. Not every one of them treats social problems of such immediacy, but submerged in any episode are assumptions about who and what we are. Conflicting viewpoints of social issues are, in fact, the elements that structure most television programs.

At the series level this complexity is heightened. In spite of notions to the contrary, most television shows do change over time. Stanley Cavell has recently suggested that this serial nature of television is perhaps its defining characteristic.[14] By contrast we see that feature only as a primary aspect of the rhetoric of television, one that shifts meaning and shades ideology as series develop. Even a series such as *The Brady Bunch* dealt with ever more complex issues merely because the children, on whom the show focused, grew older. In other cases, shows such as *The Waltons* shifted in content and meaning because they represented shifts in historical time. As the series moved out of the period of the Great Depression, through World War II, and into the postwar period, its tone and emphasis shifted too. In some cases, of course, this sort of change is structured into the show from the beginning, even when the appearance is that of static, undeveloping nature. In *All in the Family* the possibility of change and Archie's resistance to it form the central dramatic problem and offer the central opportunity for dramatic richness, a richness that has developed over many years until the character we now see bears little resemblance to the one we met in the beginning. This is also true of *M*A*S*H*, although there the structured conflicts have more to do with framing than with character development. In *M*A*S*H* we are caught in an antiwar rhetoric that cannot end a war. A truly radical alternative, a desertion or an insurrection, would end the series. But it would also end the "discussion" of this issue. We remain trapped, like American culture in its historical reality, with a dream and the rhetoric of peace and with a bitter experience that denies them.

The model of the forum extends beyond the use of the series with attention to genre. One tendency of genre studies has been to focus on similarities within forms, to indicate the ways in which all Westerns, situation comedies, detective shows, and so on are alike. Clearly, however, it is in the economic interests of producers to build on audience familiarity with generic patterns and instill novelty into those generically based presentations. Truly innovative forms that use the generic base as a foundation are likely to be among the more successful shows. This also means that the shows, despite generic similarity, will carry individual rhetorical slants. As a result, while shows like *M*A*S*H*, *The Mary Tyler Moore Show*, and *All in the Family* may all treat similar issues, those issues will have different meanings because of the variations in character, tone, history, style, and so on, despite a general "liberal" tone. Other shows, minus that tone, will clash in varying degrees. The notion that they are all, in some sense, "situation comedies" does not adequately explain the treatment of ideas within them.

This hardly diminishes the strength of generic variation as yet another version of differences within the forum. The rhetoric of the soap opera *pattern* is different from that of the situation comedy and that of the detective show. Thus, when similar topics are treated within different generic frames another level of "discussion" is at work.

It is for this reason that we find it important to examine strips of television programming, "flow" as Raymond Williams refers to it.[15] Within these flow strips we may find opposing ideas abutting one another. We may find opposing treatments of the same ideas. And we will certainly find a viewing behavior that is more akin to actual experience than that found when concentrating on the individual show, the series, or the genre. The forum model, then, has led us into a new exploration of the definition of the television text. We are now examining the "viewing strip" as a potential text and are discovering that in the range of options offered by any given evening's television, the forum is indeed a more accurate model of what goes on *within* television than any other that we know of. By taping entire weeks of television content, and tracing various potential strips in the body of that week, we can construct a huge range of potential "texts" that may have been seen by individual viewers.

Each level of text—the strip as text, the television week, the television day —is compounded yet again by the history of the medium. Our hypothesis is that we might track the history of America's social discussions of the past three decades by examining the multiple rhetorics of television during that period. Given the problematic state of television archiving, a careful study of that hypothesis presents an enormous difficulty. It is, nevertheless, an exciting prospect.

✦❦❦✦

Clearly, our emphasis is on the treatment of issues, on rhetoric. We recognize the validity of analytical structures that emphasize television's skewed demographic patterns, its particular social aberrations, or other "unrealistic distortions" of the world of experience. But we also recognize that in order to make sense of those structures and patterns researchers return again and again to the "meaning" of that television world, to the processes and problems of interpretation. In our view this practice is hardly limited to those of us who study television. It is also open to audiences who view it each evening and to professionals who create for the medium.

The goal of every producer is to create the difference that makes a differ-ence, to maintain an audience with sufficient reference to the known and rec-ognized, but to move ahead into something that distinguishes his show for the program buyer, the scheduler, and most importantly, for the mass audi-ence. As recent work by Newcomb and Alley shows,[16] the goal of many pro-ducers, the most successful and powerful ones, is also to include personal ideas in their work, to use television as all artists use their media, as means of personal expression. Given this goal it is possible to examine the work of indi-vidual producers as other units of analysis and to compare the work of differ-ent producers as expressions within the forum. We need only think of the work of Quinn Martin and Jack Webb, or to contrast their work with that of Norman Lear or Gary Marshall, to recognize the individuality at work within television making. Choices by producers to work in certain generic forms, to express certain political, moral, and ethical attitudes, to explore certain socio-cultural topics, all affect the nature of the ultimate "flow text" of television seen by viewers and assure a range of variations within that text.

The existence of this variation is borne out by varying responses among those who view television. A degree of this variance occurs among profes-sional television critics who like and dislike shows for different reasons. But because television critics, certainly in American journalistic situations, are more alike than different in many ways, a more important indicator of the range of responses is that found among "ordinary" viewers, or the disagree-ments implied by audience acceptance and enthusiasm for program material soundly disavowed by professional critics. Work by Himmleweit in England[17] and Neuman in America[18] indicates that individual viewers do function as "critics," do make important distinctions, and are able, under certain circum-stances, to articulate the bases for their judgments. While this work is just beginning, it is still possible to suggest from anecdotal evidence that people agree and disagree with television for a variety of reasons. They find in televi-sion texts representations of and challenges to their own ideas, and must somehow come to terms with what is there.

If disagreements cut too deeply into the value structure of the individ-ual, if television threatens the sense of cultural security, the individual may take steps to engage the medium at the level of personal action. Most often this occurs in the form of letters to the network or to local stations, and again, the pattern is not new to television. It has occurred with every other mass medium in modern industrial society.

Nor is it merely the formation of groups or the expression of personal points of view that indicates the working of a forum. It is the range of response, the directly contradictory readings of the medium, that cue us to its multiple meanings. Groups may object to the same programs, for example, for entirely opposing reasons. In *Charlie's Angels* feminists may find yet another example of sexist repression, while fundamentalist religious groups may find examples of moral decay expressed in the sexual freedom, the personal appearance, or the "unfeminine" behavior of the protagonists. Other viewers doubtless find the expression of meaningful liberation of women. At this level, the point is hardly that one group is "right" and another "wrong," much less that one is "right" while the other is "left." Individuals and groups are, for many reasons, involved in making their own meanings from the television text.

This variation in interpretive strategies can be related to suggestions made by Stuart Hall in his influential essay, "Encoding and Decoding in the Television Discourse."[19] There he suggests three basic modes of interpretation, corresponding to the interpreter's political stance within the social structure. The interpretation may be "dominant," accepting the prevailing ideological structure. It may be "oppositional," rejecting the basic aspects of the structure. Or it may be "negotiated," creating a sort of personal synthesis. As later work by some of Hall's colleagues suggests, however, it quickly becomes necessary to expand the range of possible interpretations.[20] Following these suggestions to a radical extreme it might be possible to argue that every individual interpretation of television content could, in some way, be "different." Clearly, however, communication is dependent on a greater degree of shared meanings, and expressions of popular entertainment are perhaps even more dependent on the shared level than many other forms of discourse. Our concern then is for the ways in which interpretation is negotiated in society. Special interest groups that focus, at times, on television provide us with readily available resources for the study of interpretive practices.

We see these groups as representative of metaphoric "fault lines" in American society. Television is the terrain in which the faults are expressed and worked out. In studying the groups, their rhetoric, the issues on which they focus, their tactics, their forms of organization, we hope to demonstrate that the idea of the "forum" is more than a metaphor in its own right. In forming special interest groups, or in using such groups to speak about television, citizens actually enter the forum. Television shoves them toward action, toward expression of ideas and values. At this level the model of "television as a cultural forum" enables us to examine "the sociology of interpretation."

Here much attention needs to be given to the historical aspects of this form of activity. How has the definition of issues changed over time? How has that change correlated with change in the television texts? These are important questions which, while difficult to study, are crucial to a full understanding of the role of television in culture. It is primarily through this sort of study that we will be able to define much more precisely the limits of the forum, for groups form monitoring devices that alert us to shortcomings not only in the world of television representation, but to the world of political experience as well. We know, for example, that because of heightened concern on the part of special interest groups, and responses from the creative and institutional communities of television industries, the "fictional" population of black citizens now roughly equals that of the actual population. Regardless of whether such a match is "good" or "necessary," regardless of the nature of the depiction of blacks on television, this indicates that the forum extends beyond the screen. The issue of violence, also deserving close study, is more mixed, varying from year to year. The influence of groups, of individuals, of studies, of the terrible consequences of murder and assassination, however, cannot be denied. Television does not exist in a realm of its own, cut off from the influence of citizens. Our aim is to discover, as precisely as possible, the ways in which the varied worlds interact.

Throughout this kind of analysis, then, it is necessary to cite a range of varied responses to the texts of television. Using the viewing "strip" as the appropriate text of television, and recognizing that it is filled with varied topics and approaches to those topics, we begin to think of the television viewer as a *bricoleur* who matches the creator in the making of meanings. Bringing values and attitudes, a universe of personal experiences and concerns, to the texts, the viewer selects, examines, acknowledges, and makes texts of his or her own.[21] If we conceive of special interest groups as representatives of *patterns* of cultural attitude and response, we have a potent source of study.

On the production end of this process, in addition to the work of individual producers, we must examine the role of network executives who must purchase and program television content. They, too, are cultural interpreters, intent on "reading" the culture through its relation to the "market." Executives who head and staff the internal censor agencies of each network, the offices of Broadcast Standards or Standards and Practices, are in a similar position. Perhaps as much as any individual or group they present us with a source of rich material for analysis. They are actively engaged in gauging cultural values. Their own research, the assumptions and the findings, needs to be re-analyzed for cultural implications, as does the work of the programmers. In determining who is doing what, with whom, at what times, they are interpreting social behavior in America and assigning it meaning. They are using television as a cultural litmus that can be applied in defining such problematic concepts as "childhood," "family," "maturity," and "appropriate." With the Standards and Practices offices, they interpret *and* define the permissible and the "normal." But their interpretations of behavior open to us as many questions as answers, and an appropriate overview, a new model of television is necessary in order to best understand their work and ours.

This new model of "television as a cultural forum" fits the experience of television more accurately than others we have seen applied. Our assumption is that it opens a range of new questions and calls for re-analysis of older findings from both the textual-critical approach and the mass communications research perspective. Ultimately the new model is a simple one. It recognizes the range of interpretation of television content that is now admitted even by those analysts most concerned with television's presentation and maintenance of dominant ideological messages and meanings. But it differs from those perspectives because it does not see this as surprising or unusual. For the most part, that is what central storytelling systems do in all societies. We are far more concerned with the ways in which television contributes to change than with mapping the obvious ways in which it maintains dominant viewpoints. Most research on television, most textual analysis, has assumed that the medium is thin, repetitive, similar, nearly identical in textual formation, easily defined, described, and explained. The variety of response on the part of audiences has been received, as a result of this view, as extraordinary, an astonishing "discovery."

We begin with the observation, based on careful textual analysis, that television is dense, rich, and complex rather than impoverished. Any selection, any cut, any set of questions that is extracted from that text must somehow account for that density, must account for what is *not* studied or measured, for the opposing meanings, for the answering images and symbols. Audiences appear to make meaning by selecting that which touches experience and personal history. The range of responses then should be taken as commonplace rather than as unexpected. But research and critical analysis cannot afford so personal a view. Rather, they must somehow define and describe the inventory that makes possible the multiple meanings extracted by audiences, creators, and network decision makers.

Our model is based on the assumption and observation that only so rich a text could attract a mass audience in a complex culture. The forum offers a perspective that is as complex, as contradictory and confused, as much in process as American culture is in experience. Its texture matches that of our daily experiences. If we can understand it better, then perhaps we will better understand the world we live in, the actions that we must take in order to live there.

Notes

1. James Carey, "A Cultural Approach to Communications," *Communications 2* (December 1975).
2. Ibid.
3. James Carey, "Culture and Communications," *Communications Research* (April 1975).
4. See Roger Silverstone, *The Message of Television: Myth and Narrative in Contemporary Culture* (London: Heinemann, 1981), on structural and narrative analysis; John Fiske and John Hartley, *Reading Television* (London: Methuen, 1978), on the semiotic and cultural bases for the analysis of television; David Thorburn, *The Story Machine* (Oxford University Press: forthcoming), on the aesthetics of television; Himmleweit, Hilda et al., "The Audience as Critic: An Approach to the Study of Entertainment," in *The Entertainment Functions of Television,* ed. Percy Tannenbaum (New York: Lawrence Eribaum Associates, 1980) and W. Russel Neuman, "Television and American Culture: The Mass Medium and the Pluralist Audience," *Public Opinion Quarterly,* 46: 4 (Winter 1982), pp. 471–87, on the role of the audience as critic; Todd Gitlin, "Prime Time Ideology: The Hegemonic Process in Television Entertainment," *Social Problems* 26:3 (1979), and Douglas Kelnner, "TV, Ideology, and Emancipatory Popular Culture," *Socialist Review* 45 (May–June, 1979), on hegemony and new applications of critical theory; James T. Lull, "The Social Uses of Television," *Human Communications Research* 7:3 (1980), and "Family Communication Patterns and the Social Uses of Television," *Communications Research* 7: 3 (1979), and Tim Meyer, Paul Traudt, and James Anderson, Non-Traditional Mass Communication Research Methods: Observational Case Studies of Media Use

in Natural Settings, *Communication Yearbook IV*, ed. Dan Nimmo (New Brunswick, N.J.: Transaction Books), on audience ethnography and symbolic interactionism; and, most importantly, the ongoing work of The Center for Contemporary Cultural Studies at Birmingham University, England, most recently published in *Culture, Media, Language*, ed. Stuart Hall et al. (London: Hutchinson, in association with The Center for Contemporary Cultural Studies, 1980), on the interaction of culture and textual analysis from a thoughtful political perspective.

5. Carey, 1976.
6. Paul Hirsch, "The Role of Popular Culture and Television in Contemporary Society," *Television: The Critical View*, ed. Horace Newcomb (New York: Oxford University Press, 1979, 1982).
7. Marshall Sahlins, *Culture and Practical Reason* (Chicago: University of Chicago Press, 1976), p. 217.
8. John Cawelti, *Adventure, Mystery, and Romance* (Chicago: University of Chicago Press, 1976), and David Thorburn, "Television Melodrama," *Television: The Critical View* (New York: Oxford University Press, 1979, 1982).
9. Victor Turner, "Process, System, and Symbol: A New Anthropological Synthesis," *Daedalus* (Summer 1977), p. 68.
10. In various works Turner uses both the terms "liminal" and "liminoid" to refer to works of imagination and entertainment in contemporary culture. The latter term is used to clearly mark the distinction between events that have distinct behavioral consequences and those that do not. As Turner suggests, the consequences of entertainment in contemporary culture are hardly as profound as those of the liminal stage of ritual in traditional culture. We are aware of this basic distinction but use the former term in order to avoid a fuller explanation of the neologism. See Turner, "Afterword," to *The Reversible World*, Barbara Babcock, ed. (Ithaca: Cornell University Press, 1979), and "Liminal to Liminoid, in Play, Flow, and Ritual: An Essay in Comparative Symbology," *Rice University Studies*, 60:3 (1974).
11. Turner, 1977, p. 73.
12. Fiske and Hartley, 1978, p. 85.
13. We are indebted to Prof. Mary Douglas for encouraging this observation. At the presentation of these ideas at the New York Institute for the Humanities seminar on "The Mass Production of Mythology," she checked our enthusiasm for a pluralistic model of television by stating accurately and succinctly, "there are pluralisms and pluralisms." This comment led us to consider more thoroughly the means by which the forum and responses to it function as a tool with which to monitor the quality of pluralism in American social life, including its entertainments. The observation added a much needed component to our planned historical analysis.
14. Stanley Cavell, "The Fact of Television," *Daedalus* 3: 4 (Fall 1982).
15. Raymond Williams, *Television, Technology and Cultural Form* (New York: Schocken, 1971), p. 86 ff.

16. Horace Newcomb and Robert Alley, *The Television Producer as Artist in American Commercial Television* (New York: Oxford University Press, 1983).
17. Ibid.
18. Ibid.
19. Stuart Hall, "Encoding and Decoding in the Television Discourse," *Culture, Media, Language* (London: Hutchinson, in association with The Center for Contemporary Cultural Studies, 1980).
20. See Dave Morley and Charlotte Brunsdon, *Everyday Television: "Nationwide"* (London: British Film Institute, 1978), and Morley, "Subjects, Readers, Texts," in *Culture, Media, Language.*
21. We are indebted to Louis Black and Eric Michaels of the Radio-TV-Film department of the University of Texas-Austin for calling this aspect of televiewing to Newcomb's attention. It creates a much desired balance to Sahlin's view of the creator as *bricoleur* and indicates yet another matter in which the forum model enhances our ability to account for more aspects of the television experience. See, especially, Eric Michaels, *TV Tribes*, unpublished Ph.D. dissertation, University of Texas-Austin. 1982.

POSTSCRIPT

Are American Values Shaped by the Mass Media?

Television is pervasive in American life. Yet the influence of television on society is difficult to ascertain. Although these issues are as hotly debated today as they were when these articles were written, a number of things have changed since then. Newcomb and Hirsch have noted that with the passing of the network era, the notion that television serves as a site of negotiation for cultural issues, images, and ideas has shifted. The development of multiple channels now undercuts the dominance of the "big three" network era. Now the "viewing strip" is so complex as to be almost impossible to identify. The negotiation process may be much more complex than ever, as viewers select from an ever-widening set of approaches to issues and ideas. The cultural negotiation is perhaps more limited, because choices are more diverse. Similarly, alterations in programming strategies, particularly the creation of niche programming, may strain the notion of an ideological core of myths that structure content as advanced by Schiller. Yet many argue that all this additional programming is simply "more of the same." Others disagree, arguing that specialized channels and additional electronic options like the Internet open up spaces for "contested meanings" that challenge the dominant hegemonic reality. For a different take on the ways in which production of media content is influenced by corporate ownership, see Issue 14 on economics and media content.

Yet some effects of television have been dramatically illustrated. The media were instrumental in bringing together the entire nation to mourn and to respond to the events of September 11, 2001. Television's ability to bring events to millions of viewers may mean that television itself is a factor in determining events. For example, television has reshaped American politics, but it may have little influence on how people actually vote. Television is now the primary source of news for most Americans. It has also altered the ways in which Americans spend their time, ranking third behind sleep and work.

For more from Horace Newcomb, see his edited book *Television: The Critical View*, 6th ed. (Oxford University Press, 2000). Herbert Schiller was the author of several books, including *Corporate Inc, Information Inequality,* and *Networks of Power*. Authors such as Neil Postman also suggest that media shapes American values, by changing the nature of public discourse. Postman argues in *Amusing Ourselves to Death* (Viking Penguin, 1985) that television promotes triviality by speaking in only one voice—the voice of entertainment. Thus he maintains that television is transforming American culture into show business, to the detriment of rational public discourse.

ISSUE 2

Is Television Harmful for Children?

YES: **W. James Potter,** from *On Media Violence* (Sage Publications, 1999)

NO: **Jib Fowles,** from *The Case for Television Violence* (Sage Publications, 1999)

ISSUE SUMMARY

YES: W. James Potter, a professor of communication, examines existing research in the area of children and television violence. Such research is extensive and covers a variety of theoretical and methodological areas. He examines the nature of the impact of television on children and concludes that strong evidence exists for harmful effects.

NO: Jib Fowles, a professor of communication, finds the research on children and television violence less convincing. Despite the number of studies, he believes that the overall conclusions are unwarranted. Fowles finds that the influence is small, lab results are artificial, and fieldwork is inconclusive. In short, he finds television violence research flawed and unable to prove a linkage between violent images and harm to children.

Youths now have access to more violent images than at any other time in United States history, and these images are available in a diverse array of electronic sources: television, movies, video games, and music. Does such graphic, immediate, and pervasive imagery influence children's behavior and ultimately the level of violence in society? Is media a powerful force that can no longer be considered mere entertainment? Or, are Americans as a society overreacting, using media as a scapegoat for the concern over seemingly hopeless social problems?

In April 1999, after a series of similar school shootings, Columbine High School in Littleton, Colorado, was forever etched in our memory. The shootings there raised, in the most dramatic way possible, questions of how America had come to this tragedy. Did media play a role? Many would argue yes and would point to reenactments of video games, fashion choices from recent movies, imitative behaviors, and Internet discussions. Others would point to the long history of mental illness and social isolation of the perpetrators as more proximate causes.

Is media violence a threat to society? Those who would answer affirmatively might point to the content of children's viewing, arguing that it is a significant part of the socialization process and decrying the stereotypes, violence, and mindlessness of much of television fare. Others might argue that there are other negative consequences intrinsic to television viewing: the common daily fare of television themes, particularly a perception of the world as a scary place. Many would maintain that there are millions of people who watch television with no discernable negative consequences. Furthermore, they might say that there is a constellation of negative influences that seem to appear in violent individuals, a lack of proof, and an absurdity of thinking that television entertainment harms people.

Researchers began to study the impact of television on children early in television history by asking who watches, how much, and why. They analyzed what children see on television and how the content influences their cognitive development, school achievement, family interaction, social behaviors, and general attitudes and opinions. This is a large and complex social issue, so even extensive research has not provided final answers to all the questions that concerned parents and educators, professional mass communicators, and legislators have raised.

W. James Potter asserts that decades of research have led to several strong conclusions: violence is a public health problem and evidence is there to support the risks of exposure and discern the most susceptible individuals. Moreover, violent portrayals are pervasive; exposure leads to negative effects, both immediately and over the long term; and certain types of portrayals and certain types of viewers maximize the probability of negative effects. Jib Fowles disagrees. The evidence just is not that strong, he asserts, and the impact is very small when it does occur. He criticizes the methods of laboratory, field, and correlational research. Why, he asks, are such small effects considered so worthy of concern? His suspicion is that the scapegoating of media allows politicians, businesspeople, and society in general to feel they are tackling a problem without really taking any of the steps necessary to promote fundamental change.

W. James Potter  **YES**

On Media Violence

Overview and Introduction

Violence in American society is a public health problem. Although most people have never witnessed an act of serious violence in person, we are all constantly reminded of its presence by the media. The media constantly report news about individual violent crimes. The media also use violence as a staple in telling fictional stories to entertain us. Thus, the media amplify and reconfigure the violence in real life and continuously pump these messages into our culture.

The culture is responding with a range of negative effects. Each year about 25,000 people are murdered, and more than 2 million are injured in assaults. On the highways, aggressive behavior such as tailgating, weaving through busy lanes, honking or screaming at other drivers, exchanging insults, and even engaging in gunfire is a factor in nearly 28,000 traffic deaths annually, and the problem is getting worse at a rate of 7% per year. Gun-related deaths increased more than 60% from 1968 to 1994, to about 40,000 annually, and this problem is now considered a public health epidemic by 87% of surgeons and 94% of internists across the United States. Meanwhile, the number of pistols manufactured in the United States continues to increase—up 92% from 1985 to 1992.

Teenagers are living in fear. A Harris poll of 2,000 U.S. teenagers found that most of them fear violence and crime and that this fear is affecting their everyday behavior. About 46% of respondents said they have changed their daily behavior because of a fear of crime and violence; 12% said they carry a weapon to school for protection; 12% have altered their route to school; 20% said they have avoided particular parks or playgrounds; 20% said they have changed their circle of friends; and 33% have stayed away from school at times because of fear of violence. In addition, 25% said they did not feel safe in their own neighborhood, and 33% said they fear being a victim of a drive-by shooting. Nearly twice as many teenagers reported gangs in their school in 1995 compared to 1989, and this increase is seen in all types of neighborhoods; violent crime in schools increased 23.5% during the same period.

This problem has far-reaching economic implications. The U.S. Department of Justice estimates the total cost of crime and violence (such as child abuse and domestic violence, in addition to crimes such as murder, rape,

and robbery) to be $500 billion per year, or about twice the annual bu
of the Defense Department. The cost includes real expenses (such as leg
fees, the cost of lost time from work, the cost of police work, and the cost o1
running the nation's prisons and parole systems) and intangibles (such as
loss of affection from murdered family members). Violent crime is responsible for 14% of injury-related medical spending and up to 20% of mental
health care expenditures.

The problem of violence in our culture has many apparent causes,
including poverty, breakdown of the nuclear family, shift away from traditional morality to a situational pluralism, and the mass media. The media are
especially interesting as a source of the problem. Because they are so visible,
the media are an easy target for blame. In addition, they keep reminding us of
the problem in their news stories. But there is also a more subtle and likely
more powerful reason why the media should be regarded as a major cause of
this public health problem: They manufacture a steady stream of fictional
messages that convey to all of us in this culture what life is about. Media stories tell us how we should deal with conflict, how we should treat other people, what is risky, and what it means to be powerful. The media need to share
the blame for this serious public health problem.

How do we address the problem? The path to remedies begins with a
solid knowledge base. It is the task of social scientists to generate much of this
knowledge. For the past five decades, social scientists and other scholars have
been studying the topic of media violence. This topic has attracted researchers
from many different disciplines, especially psychology, sociology, mental
health science, cultural studies, law, and public policy. This research addresses
questions such as these: How much media violence is there? What are the
meanings conveyed in the way violence is portrayed? and What effect does
violence have on viewers as individuals, as members of particular groups, and
as members of society? Estimates of the number of studies conducted to
answer these questions range as high as 3,000 and even 3,500... .

Effects of Exposure to Media Violence

Does exposure to violence in the media lead to effects? With each passing
year, the answer is a stronger yes. The general finding from a great deal of
research is that exposure to violent portrayals in the media increases the probability of an effect. The most often tested effect is referred to as *learning to
behave aggressively*. This effect is also referred to as direct imitation of violence, instigation or triggering of aggressive impulses, and disinhibition of
socialization against aggressive behavior. Two other negative effects—desensitization and fear—are also becoming prevalent in the literature.

Exposure to certain violent portrayals can lead to positive or prosocial
effects. Intervention studies, especially with children, have shown that when a
media-literate person talks through the action and asks questions of the
viewer during the exposure, the viewer will be able to develop a counterread-
ing of the violence; that is, the viewer may learn that violent actions are wrong
even though those actions are shown as successful in the media portrayal.

ave been documented to occur immediately or over the ate effects happen during exposure or shortly after the ...in about an hour). They might last only several minutes, or ...ight last weeks. Long-term effects do not occur after one or several exposures; they begin to show up only after an accumulation of exposures over weeks or years. Once a long-term effect eventually occurs, it usually lasts a very long period of time.

This [selection] focuses on the issues of both immediate effects and long-term effects of exposure to media violence....

From the large body of effects research, I have assembled 10 major findings. These are the findings that consistently appear in quantitative metaanalyses and narrative reviews of this literature. Because these findings are so widespread in the literature and because they are so rarely disputed by scholars, they can be regarded as empirically established laws.

Immediate Effects of Violent Content

The first six laws illuminate the major findings of research into the immediate effects of exposure to media violence. Immediate effects occur during exposure or within several hours afterward.

1. Exposure to violent portrayals in the media can lead to subsequent viewer aggression through disinhibition.

This conclusion is found in most of the early reviews. For example, Stein and Friedrich closely analyzed 49 studies of the effects of antisocial and prosocial television content on people 3 to 18 years of age in the United States. They concluded that the correlational studies showed generally significant relationships (r = .10 to .32) and that the experiments generally showed an increase in aggression resulting from exposure to television violence across all age groups.

This conclusion gained major visibility in the 1972 Surgeon General's Report which stated that there was an influence, but this conclusion was softened by the industry members on the panel....

Some of the early reviewers disagreed with this conclusion....

In the two decades since this early disagreement, a great deal more empirical research has helped overcome these shortcomings, so most (but not all) of these critics have been convinced of the general finding that exposure to media violence can lead to an immediate disinhibition effect. All narrative reviews since 1980 have concluded that viewing of violence is consistently related to subsequent aggressiveness. This finding holds in surveys, laboratory experiments, and naturalistic experiments. For example, Roberts and Maccoby concluded that "the overwhelming proportion of results point to a causal relationship between exposure to mass communication portrayals of violence and an increased probability that viewers will behave violently at some subsequent time." Also, Friedrich-Cofer and Huston concluded that "the weight of the evidence from different methods of investigation supports the hypothesis that television violence affects aggression."

Meta-analytical studies that have reexamined the data quantitatively across sets of studies have also consistently concluded that viewing of aggression is likely to lead to antisocial behavior. For example, Paik and Comstock conducted a meta-analysis of 217 studies of the effects of television violence on antisocial behavior and reported finding a positive and significant correlation. They concluded that "regardless of age—whether nursery school, elementary school, college, or adult—results remain positive at a high significance level." Andison looked at 67 studies involving 30,000 participants (including 31 laboratory experiments) and found a relationship between viewing and subsequent aggression, with more than half of the studies showing a correlation (r) between .31 and .70. Hearold looked at 230 studies involving 100,000 participants to determine the effect of viewing violence on a wide range of antisocial behaviors in addition to aggression (including rule breaking, materialism, and perceiving oneself as powerless in society). Hearold concluded that for all ages and all measures, the majority of studies reported an association between exposure to violence and antisocial behavior....

On balance, it is prudent to conclude that media portrayals of violence can lead to the immediate effect of aggressive behavior, that this can happen in response to as little as a single exposure, and that this effect can last up to several weeks. Furthermore, the effect is causal, with exposure leading to aggression. However, this causal link is part of a reciprocal process; that is, people with aggressive tendencies seek out violent portrayals in the media.

2. The immediate disinhibition effect is influenced by viewer demographics, viewer traits, viewer states, characteristics in the portrayals, and situational cues.

Each human is a complex being who brings to each exposure situation a unique set of motivations, traits, predispositions, exposure history, and personality factors. These characteristics work together incrementally to increase or decrease the probability of the person's being affected.

2.1 Viewer Demographics
The key characteristics of the viewer that have been found to be related to a disinhibition effect are age and gender, but social class and ethnic background have also been found to play a part.

Demographics of age and gender. Boys and younger children are more affected. Part of the reason is that boys pay more attention to violence. Moreover, younger children have more trouble following story plots, so they are more likely to be drawn into high-action episodes without considering motives or consequences. Age by itself is not as good an explanation as is ability for cognitive processing.

Socioeconomic status. Lower-class youth watch more television and therefore more violence.

Ethnicity. Children from minority and immigrant groups are vulnerable because they are heavy viewers of television.

2.2 Viewer Traits

The key characteristics of viewer traits are socialization against aggression, ... cognitive processing, and personality type.

Socialization against aggression.   Family life is an important contributing factor. Children in households with strong norms against violence are not likely to experience enough disinhibition to exhibit aggressive behavior. The disinhibition effect is stronger in children living in households in which ... children are abused by parents, watch more violence, and identify more with violent heroes; and in families that have high-stress environments.

Peer and adult role models have a strong effect in this socialization process. Male peers have the most immediate influence in shaping children's aggressive behaviors in the short term; adult males have the most lasting effect 6 months later....

Cognitive processing.   Viewers' reactions depend on their individual interpretations of the aggression. Rule and Ferguson (1986) said that viewers first must form a representation or cognitive structure consisting of general social knowledge about the positive value that can be attached to aggression. The process of developing such a structure requires that viewers attend to the material (depending on the salience and complexity of the program). Then viewers make attributions and form moral evaluations in the comprehension stage. Then they store their comprehension in memory.

Cognitive processing is related to age. Developmental psychologists have shown that children's minds mature cognitively and that in some early stages they are unable to process certain types of television content well.... [U]ntil age 5, they are especially attracted to and influenced by vivid production features, such as rapid movement of characters, rapid changes of scenes, and unexpected sights and sounds. Children seek out and pay attention to cartoon violence, not because of the violence, but because of the vivid production features. By ages 6 to 11, children have developed the ability to lengthen their attention spans and make sense of continuous plots....

Personality type.   The more aggressive the person is, the more influence viewing of violence will have on that person's subsequent aggressive behavior (Comstock et al., 1978; Stein & Friedrich, 1972). And children who are emotionally disturbed are more susceptible to a disinhibition effect (Sprafkin et al., 1992)....

2.3 Viewer States

The degrees of physiological arousal, anger, and frustration have all been found to increase the probability of a negative effect.

Aroused state.   Portrayals (even if they are not violent) that leave viewers in an aroused state are more likely to lead to aggressive behavior (Berkowitz & Geen, 1966; Donnerstein & Berkowitz, 1981; Tannenbaum, 1972; Zillman, 1971).

Emotional reaction.   Viewers who are upset by the media exposure (negative hedonic value stimuli) are more likely to aggress (Rule & Ferguson, 1986; Zillmann et al., 1981). Such aggression is especially likely when people are left in a state of unresolved excitement (Comstock, 1985).... In his meta-analysis of 1,043 effects of television on social behavior, Hearold (1986) concluded that frustration... is not a necessary condition, but rather a contributory condition....

Degree of identity.   It has been well established that the more a person, especially a child, identifies with a character, the more likely the person will be influenced by that character's behavior.

Identity seems to be a multifaceted construct composed of similarity, attractiveness, and hero status. If the perpetrator of violence is perceived as *similar* to the viewer, the likelihood of learning to behave aggressively increases (Lieberman Research, 1975; Rosekrans & Hartup, 1967). When violence is performed by an *attractive* character, the probability of aggression increases (Comstock et al., 1978; Hearold, 1986). Attractiveness of a villain is also an important consideration (Health et al., 1989)....

2.4 Characteristics in the Portrayals
Reviews of the literature are clear on the point that people interpret the meaning of violent portrayals and use contextual information to construct that meaning.

In the media effects literature, there appear to be five notable contextual variables: rewards and punishments, consequences, justification, realism, and production techniques....

Rewards and punishments.   Rewards and punishments to perpetrators of violence provide important information to viewers about which actions are acceptable. However, there is reason to believe that the effect does not work with children younger than 10, who usually have difficulty linking violence presented early in a program with its punishment rendered later (Collins, 1973).

In repeated experiments, viewers who watch a model rewarded for performing violently in the media are more likely to experience a disinhibition effect and behave in a similar manner. But when violence is punished in the media portrayal, the aggressiveness of viewers is likely to be inhibited (Comstock et al., 1978). In addition, when nonaggressive characters are rewarded, viewers' levels of aggression can be reduced.

The absence of punishment also leads to disinhibition. That is, the perpetrators need not be rewarded in order for the disinhibition effect to occur....

Consequences.   The way in which the consequences of violence are portrayed influences the disinhibition effect... . For example, Goranson showed people a film of a prize fight in which either there were no consequences or the loser of the fight received a bad beating and later died. The participants who did not see the negative consequences were more likely to behave aggressively after the viewing.

A key element in the consequences is whether the victim shows pain, because pain cues inhibit subsequent aggression. Moreover, Swart and Berkowitz (1976) showed that viewers could generalize pain cues to characters other than the victims.

Justification.   Reviews of the effects research conclude that justification of violent acts leads to higher aggression. For example, Bryan and Schwartz observed that "aggressive behavior in the service of morally commendable ends appears condoned. Apparently, the assumption is made that moral goals temper immoral actions.... Thus, both the imitation and interpersonal attraction of the transgressing model may be determined more by outcomes than by moral principles."

Several experiments offer support for these arguments. First, Berkowitz and Rawlings (1963) found that justification of filmed aggression lowers viewers' inhibitions to aggress in real life.

Justification is keyed to motives. Brown and Tedeschi (1976) found that offensive violence was regarded as more violent even when the actions themselves were not as violent. For example, a verbal threat that is made offensively is perceived as more violent than a punch that is delivered defensively.

The one motive that has been found to lead to the strongest disinhibition is vengeance. For example, Berkowitz and Alioto introduced a film of a sporting event (boxing and football) by saying that the participants were acting either as professionals wanting to win or as motivated by vengeance and wanting to hurt the other. They found that the vengeance film led to more shocks and longer duration of shocks in a subsequent test of participants. When violence was portrayed as vengeance, disinhibition was stronger than when violence was portrayed as self-defense or as a means of achieving altruistic goals.

Young children have difficulty understanding motives. For example, Collins (1973) ran an experiment on children aged 8 to 15 to see if a time lag from portrayal of motivation to portrayal of aggression changed participants' behaviors or interpretations. Participants were shown either a 30-minute film in which federal agents confronted some criminals or a control film of a travelogue. In the treatment film, the criminals hit and shot the federal agents, displaying negative motivation (desire to escape justice) and negative consequences (a criminal fell to his death while trying to escape). Some participants saw the sequence uninterrupted; others saw the motivation, followed by a 4-minute interruption of commercials, then the aggression. Both 18 days before the experiment and then again right after the viewing, participants were asked their responses to a wide range of hypothetical interpersonal conflict situations. There was a difference by age. Third graders displayed more aggressive choices on the postviewing measure when they had experienced the separation condition; sixth and 10th graders did not exhibit this effect. The author concluded that among younger children, temporal separation of story elements obscures the message that aggression was negatively motivated and punished....

Realism.   When viewers believe that the aggression is portrayed in a realistic manner, they are more likely to try it in real life.

Production techniques.   Certain production techniques can capture and hold attention, potentially leading to differences in the way the action is perceived. Attention is increased when graphic and explicit acts are used to increase the dramatic nature of the narrative, to increase positive dispositions toward the characters using violence, and to increase levels of arousal, which is more likely to result in aggressive behavior....

   3. Exposure to violence in the media can lead to fear effects.

The best available review is by Cantor (1994), who defines fear effect as an immediate physiological effect of arousal, along with an emotional reaction of anxiety and distress.

   4. An immediate fear effect is influenced by a set of key factors about viewers and the portrayals.

4.1 Viewer Factors

Identification with the target.   The degree of identification with the target is associated with a fear effect. For example, characters who are attractive, who are heroic, or who are perceived as similar to the viewer evoke viewer empathy. When a character with whom viewers empathize is then the target of violence, viewers experience an increased feeling of fear.

   The identification with characters can lead to an enjoyment effect. For example, Tannenbaum and Gaer (1965) found that participants who identified more with the hero felt more stress and benefited more from a happy ending in which their stress was reduced. However, a sad or indeterminate ending increased participants' stress.

Prior real-life experience.   Prior experience with fearful events in real life leads viewers, especially children, to identify more strongly with the characters and events and thereby to involve them more emotionally.

Belief that the depicted violent action could happen to the viewer.   When viewers think there is a good chance that the violence they see could happen to them in real life, they are more likely to experience an immediate fear effect.

Motivations for exposure.   People expose themselves to media violence for many different reasons. Certain reasons for exposure can reduce a fear effect. If people's motivation to view violence is entertainment, they can employ a discounting procedure to lessen the effects of fear.

Level of arousal.   Higher levels of arousal lead to higher feelings of fear.

Ability to use coping strategies.   When people are able to remind themselves that the violence in the media cannot hurt them, they are less likely to experience a fear effect.

Developmental differences.   Children at lower levels of cognitive development are unable to follow plot lines well, so they are more influenced by individual violent episodes, which seem to appear randomly and without motivation.

Ability to perceive the reality of the portrayals.   Children are less able than older viewers to understand the fantasy nature of certain violent portrayals.

4.2 Portrayal Factors

Type of stimulus.   Cantor (1994) says that the fright effect is triggered by three categories of stimuli that usually are found in combination with many portrayals of violence in the media. First is the category of dangers and injuries, stimuli that depict events that threaten great harm. Included in this category are natural disasters, attacks by vicious animals, large-scale accidents, and violent encounters at levels ranging from interpersonal to intergalactic. Second is the category of distortions of natural forms. This category includes familiar organisms that are shown as deformed or unnatural through mutilation, accidents of birth, or conditioning. And third is the category of experience of endangerment and fear by others. This type of stimulus evokes empathy for particular characters, and the viewer then feels the fear that the characters in the narrative are portraying.

Unjustified violence.   When violence is portrayed as unjustified, viewers become more fearful.

Graphicness.   Higher levels of explicitness and graphicness increase viewer fear.

Rewards.   When violence goes unpunished, viewers become more fearful.

Realism.   Live-action violence provokes more intense fear than cartoon violence does. For example, Lazarus et al. found that showing gory accidents to adults aroused them physiologically less when the participants were told that the accidents were fake. This effect has also been found with children. In addition, fear is enhanced when elements in a portrayal resemble characteristics in a person's own life.

5. Exposure to violence in the media can lead to desensitization.

In the short term, viewers of repeated violence can show a lack of arousal and emotional response through habituation to the stimuli.

6. An immediate desensitization effect is influenced by a set of key factors about viewers and the portrayals.

Children and adults can become desensitized to violence upon multiple exposures through temporary habituation. But the habituation appears to be relatively short term.

6.1 Viewer Factors
People who are exposed to larger amounts of television violence are usually found to be more susceptible to immediate desensitization.

6.2 Portrayal Factors
There appear to be two contextual variables that increase the likelihood of a desensitization effect: graphicness and humor.

Graphicness.   Graphicness of violence can lead to immediate desensitization. In experiments in which participants are exposed to graphic violence, initially they have strong physiological responses, but these responses steadily decline during the exposure. This effect has also been shown with children, especially among the heaviest viewers of TV violence.

Humor.   Humor contributes to the desensitization effect.

Long-Term Effects of Violent Content

Long-term effects of exposure to media violence are more difficult to measure than are immediate effects. The primary reason is that long-term effects occur so gradually that by the time an effect is clearly indicated, it is very difficult to trace that effect back to media exposures. It is not possible to argue that any single exposure triggers the effect. Instead, we must argue that the long-term pattern of exposure leads to the effect. A good analogy is the way in which an orthodontist straightens teeth. Orthodontists do not produce an immediate effect by yanking teeth into line in one appointment. Instead, they apply braces that exert very little pressure, but that weak pressure is constant. A person who begins wearing braces might experience sore gums initially, but even then there is no observable change to the alignment of the teeth. This change in alignment cannot be observed even after a week or a month. Only after many months is the change observable.

It is exceedingly difficult for social scientists to make a strong case that the media are responsible for long-term effects. The public, policymakers, and especially critics of social science research want to be persuaded that there is a causal connection. But with a matter of this complexity that requires the long term evolution of often conflicting influences in the naturalistic environment of viewers' everyday lives, the case for causation cannot be made in any manner stronger than a tentative probabilistic one. Even then, a critic could point to a "third variable" as a potential alternative explanation.

7. Long-term exposure to media violence is related to aggression in a person's life.

Evidence suggests that this effect is causative and cumulative (Eron, 1982). This effect is also reciprocal: Exposure to violence leads to increased aggression, and people with higher levels of aggression usually seek out higher levels of exposure to aggression.

Huesmann, Eron, Guerra, and Crawshaw (1994) conclude from their longitudinal research that viewing violence as a child has a causal effect on patterns of higher aggressive behavior in adults. This finding has appeared in studies in the United States, Australia, Finland, Israel, Poland, the Netherlands, and South Africa. While recognizing that exposure to violence on TV is not the only cause of aggression in viewers, Huesmann et al. conclude that the research suggests that the effect of viewing television violence on aggression "is relatively independent of other likely influences and of a magnitude great enough to account for socially important differences."

The long-term disinhibition effect is influenced by "a variety of environmental, cultural, familial, and cognitive" factors. A major influence on this effect is the degree to which viewers identify with characters who behave violently. For example, Eron found that the learning effect is enhanced when children identify closely with aggressive TV characters. He argued that aggression is a learned behavior, that the continued viewing of television violence is a very likely cause of aggressive behavior, and that this is a long-lasting effect on children.

Once children reach adolescence, their behavioral dispositions and inhibitory controls have become crystallized to the extent that their aggressive habits are very difficult to change, and achievement have been found to be related to this effect. Huesmann et al. concluded that low IQ makes the learning of aggressive responses more likely at an early age, and this aggressive behavior makes continued intellectual development more difficult into adulthood.

Evidence also suggests that the effect is contingent on the type of family life. In Japan, for example, Kashiwagi and Munakata (1985) found no correlation between exposure to TV violence and aggressiveness of viewers in real life for children in general. But an effect was observed among young children living in families in which the parents did not get along well.

8. Media violence is related to subsequent violence in society.

When television is introduced into a country, the violence and crime rates in that country, especially crimes of theft, increase. Within a country, the amount of exposure to violence that a demographic group typically experiences in the media is related to the crime rate in neighborhoods where those demographic groups are concentrated. Finally, some evidence suggests that when a high-profile violent act is depicted in the news or in fictional programming, the incidents of criminal aggression increase subsequent to that coverage.

All these findings are subject to the criticism that the researchers have only demonstrated co-occurrence of media violence and real-life aggression. Researchers are asked to identify possible "third variables" that might be alternative explanations for the apparent relationship, and then to show that the relationship exists even after the effects of these third variables are controlled. Although researchers have been testing control variables, critics are still concerned that one or more important variables that have yet to be controlled may account for a possible alternative explanation of the effect.

> *9. People exposed to many violent portrayals over a long time will come to exaggerate their chances of being victimized.*

This generalized fear effect has a great deal of empirical support in the survey literature. But this relationship is generally weak in magnitude, and it is sensitive to third variables in the form of controls and contingencies. The magnitude of the correlation coefficients (r) is usually low, typically in the range of .10 to .30, which means that exposure is able to explain only less than 10% of the variation in the responses of cultivation indicators....

The magnitude of the cultivation effect is relatively weak even by social science standards. Cultivation theorists have defended their findings by saying that even though the effect is small, it is persistent....

This cultivation effect is also remarkably robust. In the relatively large literature on cultivation, almost all the coefficients fall within a consistently narrow band. Not only is this effect remarkable in its consistency, but this consistency becomes truly startling when one realizes the wide variety of measures (of both television exposure and cultivation indicators) that are used in the computations of these coefficients.

> *10. People exposed to many violent portrayals over a long time will come to be more accepting of violence.*

This effect is the gradual desensitizing of viewers to the plight of victims, as well as to violence in general. After repeated exposure to media violence over a long period of time, viewers lose a sense of sympathy with the victims of violence. Viewers also learn that violence is a "normal" part of society, that violence can be used successfully, and that violence is frequently rewarded.

The probability of this long-term effect is increased when people are continually exposed to graphic portrayals of violence. For example, Linz, Donnerstein, and Penrod (1988a) exposed male participants to five slasher movies during a 2-week period. After each film, the male participants exhibited decreasing perceptions that the films were violent or that they were degrading to women.

Conclusion

After more than five decades of research on the effects of exposure to media violence, we can be certain that there are both immediate and long-term effects. The strongest supported immediate effect is the following: Exposure to violent portrayals in the media increases subsequent viewer aggression. We also know that there are other positive and negative immediate effects, such as fear and desensitization. As for long-term effects, we can conclude that exposure to violence in the media is linked with long-term negative effects of trait aggression, fearful worldview, and desensitization to violence. The effects process is highly complex and is influenced by many factors about the viewers, situational cues, and contextual characteristics of the violent portrayals.

Violence Viewing and Science

Examining the Research

For the moment, it is prudent not to question the forces that gave rise to the violence effects literature and have sustained it for five decades nor to tease out the unarticulated assumptions enmeshed in it. Let us begin by taking this extensive literature entirely on its own terms. What will become clear is that although the majority of the published studies on the topic do report antisocial findings, the average extent of the findings is slight—often so much so that the findings are open to several interpretations....

Those who pore over the violence effects literature agree that the case against televised fantasy viciousness is most broadly and clearly made in the large number of laboratory studies, such as those done by Bandura. Overall, these studies offer support for the imitative hypothesis—that younger viewers will exhibit a tendency to act out the aggression seen on the screen. In this group of studies, many find the issue reduced to a pristine clarity, parsed of all needless complexity and obscurity, and answered with sufficient experimental evidence. What is found in this literature can be rightfully generalized to the real world, some believe, to spark a host of inferences and even policies. However, the laboratory is not the real world, and may be so unreal as to discredit the results.

The unnaturalness of laboratory studies is frequently commented on by those who have reservations regarding this research (Buckingham, 1993, p. 11; Gunter & McAteer, 1990, p. 13; Noble, 1975, p. 125), but the extent of the artificiality is rarely defined, leaving those who are unfamiliar with these settings or the nature of these experiments with little sense of what is meant by "unnatural."...

[In a behavioral laboratory setting] in a room with other unmet children, the child may be unexpectedly frustrated or angered by the experimenters—shown toys but not allowed to touch them, perhaps, or spoken to brusquely. The child is then instructed to look at a video monitor. It would be highly unlikely for the young subject to sense that this experience in any way resembled television viewing as done at home.... Most signally, at home television viewing is an entirely voluntary activity: The child is in front of the set because the child has elected to do so and in most instances has elected the content, and he or she will elect other content if the current material does not satisfy. In the behavioral laboratory, the child is compelled to watch and, worse, compelled to watch material not of the child's choosing and probably not of the child's liking. The essential element of the domestic television-viewing experience, that of pleasure, has been methodically stripped away.

Furthermore, what the child views in a typical laboratory experiment will bear little resemblance to what the child views at home. The footage will comprise only a segment of a program and will feature only aggressive actions. The intermittent relief of commercials or changed channels is missing, as are television stories' routine endings bringing dramatic closure in which everything is set right, with the correct values ascendant.

The child then may be led to another room that resembles the one in the video segment and encouraged to play while being observed. This is the room that, in Bandura et al.'s (1963) famous experiment, contained the Bobo doll identical to the one shown on the screen. Is it any wonder that uneasy children, jockeying for notice and position in a newly convened peer group, having seen a videotaped adult strike the doll without repercussions, and being tacitly encouraged by hovering experimenters who do not seem to disapprove of such action, would also hit the doll? As Noble (1975) wryly asked, "What else can one do to a self-righting bobo doll except hit it?" (p. 133). There are typically only a limited number of options, all behavioral, for the young subjects. Certainly, no researcher is asking them about the meanings they may have taken from the screened violence.

In summary, laboratory experiments on violence viewing are concocted schemes that violate all the essential stipulations of actual viewing in the real world (Cook, Kendzierski, & Thomas, 1983, p. 180) and in doing so have nothing to teach about the television experience (although they may say much about the experimenters). Viewing in the laboratory setting is involuntary, public, choiceless, intense, uncomfortable, and single-minded, whereas actual viewing is voluntary, private, selective, nonchalant, comfortable, and in the context of competing activities. Laboratory research has taken the viewing experience and turned it inside out so that the viewer is no longer in charge. In this manner, experimenters have made a mockery out of the everyday act of television viewing. Distorted to this extent, laboratory viewing can be said to simulate household viewing only if one is determined to believe so....

The inadequacies of laboratory research on television violence effects are apparent in the small body of research on the matter of desensitization or, as Slaby (1994) called it, "the bystander effect." The few attempts to replicate the finding of the four Drabman and Thomas experiments (Drabman & Thomas 1974a, 1974b, 1976; Thomas & Drabman, 1975)—that children exposed to violent footage would take longer to call for the intercession of an adult supervisor—have produced inconsistent results. Horton and Santogrossi (1978) failed to replicate in that the scores for the control group did not differ from the scores for the experimental groups. In addition, Woodfield (1988) did not find statistically significant differences between children exposed to violent content and children exposed to nonviolent content....

A third attempt to replicate by Molitor and Hirsch (1994) did duplicate the original findings, apparently showing that children are more likely to tolerate aggression in others if they are first shown violent footage. An examination of their results, however, does give rise to questions about the rigor of the research. This experiment was set up with the active collaboration of the original researchers and may be less of an attempt to relicate (or not) than an attempt to vindicate. Forty-two Catholic school fourth- and fifth-grade children were assigned to two treatment groups (there was no control group). As for all laboratory experiments, the viewing conditions were so thoroughly alien that results may have been induced by subtle clues from the adult laboratory personnel, especially for obedient children from a parochial school setting. Children shown violent content (a segment from *Karate Kid*) waited longer on average before requesting adult intervention than did children shown nonviolent content (footage from the 1984 Olympic games). Again, this finding could be interpreted as evidence of catharsis: The violent content might have lowered levels of arousal and induced a momentary lassitude. The findings could also have resulted from a sense of ennui: Postexperiment interviews revealed that all the children shown *Karate Kid* had seen the movie before, some as many as 10 times (p. 201). By comparison, the Olympic contests might have seemed more exciting and stimulated swifter reactions to the videotaped misbehavior. The first author was one of the laboratory experimenters; therefore, the specter of expectancy bias cannot be dismissed.

Even if desensitization were to exist as a replicable laboratory finding, the pressing question is whether or not the effect generalizes to the real world. Are there any data in support of the notion that exposure to television violence makes people callous to hostility in everyday life? The evidence on this is scarce and in the negative. Studying many British youngsters, Belson (1978) could find no correlation between levels of television violence viewing and callousness to real violence or inconsiderateness to others (pp. 471–475, 511–516). Research by Hagell and Newburn (1994) can answer the question of whether some youngsters who view heightened hours of television become "desensitized" to violence and embark on criminal lives; unexpectedly, teenage criminals view on average less television, and less violent content, than their law-abiding peers.

Reviewers of the small desensitization literature conclude there is no empirical evidence that anything like the bystander effect actually exists in real life (Gauntlett, 1995, p. 39; Van der Voort, 1986, p. 327; Zillmann, 1991, p. 124). Even George Comstock (1989), normally sympathetic to the violence effects literature, concedes about desensitization studies that "what the research does not demonstrate is any likelihood that media portrayals would affect the response to injury, suffering, or violent death experienced first-hand" (p. 275).

I now turn from the contrivances of laboratory research to the more promising methodology of field experiments, in which typically children in circumstances familiar to them are rated on aggressiveness through the observation of their behavior, exposed to either violent or nonviolent footage, and then unobtrusively rated again. Although this literature holds out the hope of conclusive findings in natural settings, the actual results display a disquiet-ingly wide range of outcomes. Some of the data gathered indicate, instead of an elevation in aggressive behaviors, a diminishment in aggressive behaviors following several weeks of high-violence viewing. Feshbach and Singer (1971) were able to control the viewing diets of approximately 400 boys in three pri-vate boarding schools and four homes for wayward boys. For 6 weeks, half the boys were randomly assigned to a viewing menu high in violent content, whereas the other half made their selections from nonaggressive shows. Aggression levels were determined by trained observers in the weeks before and after the controlled viewing period. No behavioral differences were reported for the adolescents in the private schools, but among the poorer, semidelinquent youths, those who had been watching the more violent shows were calmer than their peers on the blander viewing diet. The authors con-cluded that "exposure to aggressive content on television seems to reduce or control the expression of aggression in aggressive boys from relatively low socioeconomic backgrounds" (p. 145).

Although Wood et al. (1991) report that the eight field experiments they reviewed did, overall, demonstrate an imitative effect from watching televised violence, other reviewers of this literature do not concur (Cumberbatch & How-itt, 1989, p. 41; Freedman, 1988, p. 151). McGuire (1986) comments dismissively on "effects that range from the statistically trivial to practically insubstantial" (p. 213). Most decisively, Gadow and Sprafkin (1989), themselves contributors to the field experiment research, concluded their thorough review of the 20 studies they located by stating that "the findings from the field experiments offer little support for the media aggression hypothesis" (p. 404).

In the aftermath of the thoroughgoing artificiality of the laboratory studies, and the equivocation of the field experiment results, the burden of proof must fall on the third methodology, that of correlational studies. In the search for statistical correlations (or not) between violence viewing and aggressive or criminal behavior, this literature contains several studies impres-sive for their naturalness and their size. Not all these studies uncover a parallel between, on the one hand, increased levels of violence viewing and, on the other hand, increased rates of misbehavior, by whatever measure. For example, for a sample of 2,000 11- to 16-year-olds, Lynn, Hampson, and Agahi (1989) found no correlation between levels of violence viewing and levels of aggres-sion. Nevertheless, many studies do report a positive correlation. It should be noted that the magnitude of this co-occurrence is usually quite small, typi-cally producing a low correlation coefficient of 10 to 20 (Freedman, 1988, p. 153). Using these correlations (small as they are), the question becomes one of the direction(s) of possible causality. Does violence viewing lead to subse-quent aggression as is commonly assumed? Could more aggressive children prefer violent content, perhaps as a vicarious outlet for their hostility?... Could any of a host of other factors give rise to both elevated variables?

Following his substantial correlational study of 1,500 London adolescents, Belson (1978) highlighted one of his findings—that boys with high levels of exposure to television violence commit 49% more acts of serious violence than do those who view less—and on this basis issued a call for a reduction in video carnage (p. 526). Closer examination of his data (pp. 380–382), however, reveals that the relationship between the two variables is far more irregular than he suggests in his text. Low viewers of television violence are more aggressive than moderate viewers, whereas very high violence viewers are less aggressive than those in the moderate to high range. Moreover, "acts of serious violence" constituted only one of Belson's four measures of real-life aggression; the other three were "total number of acts of violence," "total number of acts of violence weighted by degree of severity of the act," and "total number of violent acts excluding minor ones." Findings for these three variables cannot be said to substantiate Belson's conclusion. That is, for these measures, the linking of violence viewing to subsequent aggression was negated by reverse correlations—that aggressive youngsters sought out violent content (pp. 389–392). Three of his measures refuted his argument, but Belson chose to emphasize a fourth, itself a demonstrably inconsistent measure....

For the total television effects literature, whatever the methodology, the reviews...by Andison (1977), Hearold (1986), and Paik and Comstock (1994) are not the only ones that have been compiled. Other overviews reach very different summary judgments about this body of studies in its entirety. A review published contemporaneously with that of Andison considered the same research projects and derived a different conclusion (Kaplan & Singer, 1976). Kaplan and Singer examined whether the extant literature could support an activation view (that watching televised fantasy violence leads to aggression), a catharsis view (that such viewing leads to a decrease in aggression), or a null view, and they determined that the null position was the most judicious. They wrote, "Our review of the literature strongly suggests that the activating effects of television fantasy violence are marginal at best. The scientific data do not consistently link violent television fantasy programming to violent behavior" (p. 62).

In the same volume in which Susan Hearold's (1986) meta-analysis of violence studies appeared, there was also published a literature review by William McGuire (1986). In contrast to Hearold, it was McGuire's judgment that the evidence of untoward effects from violence viewing was not compelling. Throughout the 1980s, an assured critique of the violence effects literature [was] issued from Jonathan Freedman (1984, 1986, 1988). Freedman cautiously examined the major studies within each of the methodological categories.... Regarding correlational studies, he noted that "not one study produced strong consistent results, and most produced a substantial number of negative findings" (1988, p. 158). Freedman's general conclusion is that "considering all of the research—laboratory, field experiments, and correlational studies—the evidence does not support the idea that viewing television violence causes aggression" (1988, p. 158).

Freedman's dismissal of the violence effects literature is echoed in other literature reviews from British scholars, who may enjoy an objective distance on this largely American research agenda. Cumberbatch and Howitt (1989) discussed the shortcomings of most of the major studies and stated that the research data "are insufficiently robust to allow a firm conclusion about television violence as studied" (p. 51). David Gauntlett (1995)...analyzed at length most of the consequential studies. He believes that "the work of effects researchers is done" (p. 1). "The search for direct 'effects' of television on behavior is over: Every effort has been made, and they simply cannot be found" (p. 120). Ian Vine (1997) concurs: "Turning now to the systemic evidence from hundreds of published studies of the relationship between viewing violence and subsequent problematic behaviors, the most certain conclusion is that there is no genuine consensus of findings" (p. 138)....

Discourse Within Discourse

Opened up for inspection, the sizable violence effects literature turns out to be an uneven discourse—inconsistent, flawed, pocked. This literature proves nothing conclusively, or equivalently, this literature proves everything in that support for any position can be drawn from its corpus. The upshot is that, no matter what some reformers affirm, the campaign against television violence is bereft of any strong, consensual scientific core. Flaws extend through to the very premises of the literature—flaws so total that they may crowd out alternative viewpoints and produce in some amind-numbed acquiescence. Specifically, the literature's two main subjects—television and the viewer—are assumed to be what they are not.

Viewers are conceived of as feckless and vacuous, like jellyfish in video tides. Viewers have no intentions, no discretion, and no powers of interpretation. Into their minds can be stuffed all matter of content. Most often, the viewer postulated in the effects literature is young, epitomizing immaturity and malleability. This literature, wrote Carmen Luke (1990), "had constructed a set of scientifically validated truths about the child viewer as a behavioral response mechanism, as passive and devoid of cognitive abilities. The possibility that viewers bring anything other than demographic variables to the screen was conceptually excluded" (p. 281). Although there is ample evidence that the young are highly active, selective, and discriminating viewers (Buckingham, 1993; Clifford, Gunter, & McAleer, 1995; Durkin, 1985; Gunter & McAteer, 1990; Hawkins & Pingree, 1986; Hodge & Tripp, 1986; Noble, 1975), this is never the version in the violence effects literature.

Television, on the other hand, is seen as powerful, coercive, and sinister. The medium is not a servant but a tyrant. It rules rather than pleases. It is omnipotent; it cannot be regulated, switched, modulated, interpreted, belittled, welcomed, or ignored. All the things that television is in the real world it is not within the violence effects literature.

The relationship between television content and viewers, as implied in this research, is one way only, as television pounds its insidious message into a hapless audience; there is no conception of a return flow of information by which viewers via ratings indicate preferences for certain content rather than other content. The only result allowable from the viewing experience is that of direct and noxious effects. Other possibilities—of pleasures, relaxation, reinterpretations, therapy, and so on—are not to be considered. The television viewing experience, twisted beyond recognition, is conceived of in pathological terms; in fact, a large amount of the research throughout the past decades has been funded by national mental health budgets.

All these preconceptions apply before a bit of research is actually conducted. The surprising result is not that there have been worrisome findings reported but that, given these presuppositions, the negative findings were not much grander still....

The war on television violence, the larger discourse, has united many allies with otherwise weak ties—prominent authorities and grassroots organizations, liberals and conservatives, and the religious and the secular. We must ask why they put aside their differences, lift their voices together, and join in this particular cause. This implausible alliance constitutes a force field that waxes and wanes throughout the decades, losing strength at one point and gaining it at another; it would seem to have a rhythm all its own. What can account for the regular reoccurrence of this public discourse denouncing television violence?

POSTSCRIPT

Is Television Harmful for Children?

Much of what we know about the effects of television comes from the study of children enjoying traditional television, but this knowledge is being challenged by the impact of emerging telecommunications technology. The Internet, cable television programming, video games, and VCRs have changed the face of television within the home. Indeed, VCRs have greatly increased the control that parents have over the material to which children are exposed at young ages and have greatly increased the diversity of content that children can be exposed to as they get older. The Internet, a 500-channel world, increasing international programming ventures, and regulatory changes will alter the way children interact with electronic media. What influence that will have is very hard to predict.

One conclusion is inescapable. There is now much more diversity of media content available, and there are many more choices for parents and children. One of the clearest findings of research on the impact of violence on child aggression is that parents, through their behavior and their positive and negative comments, can have a major influence on whether or not children behave aggressively subsequent to exposure. With choices come hard decisions for parents. The promise of television and other media can now be better fulfilled, with more choices than ever before. Alternatively, a diet of violence and mindlessness is easily found.

Although this issue concerns children, there are important developmental and social differences due to age. Young children, particularly preschoolers, are most likely to be controlled by their parents, are most likely to have difficulty understanding some of the narratives and conventions of media fare, and are arguably the most vulnerable to learning from the messages of the media to which they are exposed. The "tween" years are a transition to more adult programs and themes and are a time of great transition socially. Poised between the worlds of adulthood and childhood, the tween partakes of both, sometimes with difficult consequences. Tweens are not even considered by the media to be part of the "child" audience. Their viewing patterns are much more like those of adults, and like adults they are presumed to be cognitively able to protect themselves from the effects of violence or even advertising. So they proudly proclaim that the media have no effect on them.

The National Television Violence Study, 3 vols. (Sage Publications, 1996–1998), conducted by a consortium of professors from several universities, offers a commentary on the state of violence on American television for viewers, policymakers, industry leaders, and scholars. Robert Liebert and Joyce Sprafkin's *The Early Window: Effects of Television on Children and Youth*, 3rd ed. (Pergamon Press, 1988) is an excellent introduction to the history and issues of media effects. Judith Van Evra offers a view of existing research in *Television and Child Development,* 2d ed. (Lawrence Erlbaum, 1998). School violence has revived the debate on media violence and children, according to Paige Albiniak in "Media: Littleton's Latest Suspect," *Broadcasting & Cable* (May 3, 1999). Not only television but video games come under attack. Lieutenant Colonel Dave Grossman, a former Army ranger and paratrooper, writes about video games that teach children to kill by using the same warfare tactics used to train the military, in the *Saturday Evening Post* (July/ August and September/October 1999). Many articles were written after the Columbine tragedy that implicated violent video games in the violence of U.S. society.

ISSUE 3

Is Emphasis on Body Image in the Media Harmful to Females Only?

YES: Mary C. Martin and James W. Gentry, from "Stuck in the Model Trap: The Effects of Beautiful Models in Ads on Female Pre-Adolescents and Adolescents," *Journal of Advertising* (Summer 1997)

NO: Michelle Cottle, from "Turning Boys Into Girls," *The Washington Monthly* (May 1998)

ISSUE SUMMARY

YES: Marketing professors Mary C. Martin and James W. Gentry address the literature dealing with advertising images and the formation of body identity for preadolescent and adolescent females. They report a study to explore how social comparison theory influences young women.

NO: *Washington Monthly* editor Michelle Cottle takes the perspective that females are not the only ones influenced by media image. She cites polls and magazine advertising that indicate that males are exposed to images of idealized body type as well, and she argues that these images also have an impact on the male psyche.

There is plenty of evidence to support the idea that young girls are influenced by the body images of models and actresses they see in the media. In her book *The Beauty Myth* (Anchor Books, 1992), Naomi Wolf writes that the typical model or actress is significantly below what the medical establishment considers a "healthy" body weight. The desire to look like a model or actress has contributed to what could be termed an outbreak in eating disorders among females. Wolf warns that 1 out of 10 college women develop an eating disorder while in college, but the desire to be thin often starts as early as age eight for many girls.

Little attention has been given to the self-images of boys, while the unhealthy aspects of eating disorders and idealized body image has been primarily attributed to girls. In the following selections the authors help us to understand this phenomenon on an even broader scale.

Mary C. Martin and James W. Gentry take the position that idealized body image is a female problem, and they attempt to study whether or not social comparison theory (the idea that females compare their own physical attractiveness with models) influences self-esteem. Their studies of fourth- and sixth-graders help to illuminate differential cognitive levels and the way images influence self-perceptions.

Michelle Cottle adds an interesting dimension to the problem of images and idealized body type. She asserts that men's magazines have also taken the approach to making males feel inadequate through images and stories that work against male vanity. The images and stories she describes raise questions about the content of magazines and the way pictures and stories affect us psychologically.

These issues will undoubtedly spark lively discussions about whether or not images and stories actually do shape the way we think about ourselves in relation to idealized images. The psychological effects of media are difficult to assess, even though the presence of images is pervasive, but it is hard to ignore their potential power. The history of media effects research has much to offer in the way we think about the following selections.

Mary C. Martin
and James W. Gentry

 **YES**

Stuck in the Model Trap

A growing concern in our society is the plight of female pre-adolescents and adolescents as they grow up facing many obstacles, including receiving less attention than boys in the classroom, unrealistic expectations of what they can and cannot do, decreasing self-esteem, and being judged by their physical appearance. In particular, girls are generally preoccupied with attempting to become beautiful. As Perry suggests, "Today's specifications call for blonde and thin—no easy task, since most girls get bigger during adolescence. Many become anorexics or bulimics; a few rich ones get liposuction. We make their focus pleasing other people and physical beauty." Further, studies show that self-esteem drops to a much greater extent for female than male pre-adolescents and adolescents, with self-perceptions of physical attractiveness contributing to the drop.

Another growing concern in our society is the role of advertising in contributing to those obstacles. For example, advertising has been accused of unintentionally imposing a "sense of inadequacy" on women's self-concepts. Studies suggest that advertising and the mass media may play a part in creating and reinforcing a preoccupation with physical attractiveness and influence consumer perceptions of what constitutes an acceptable level of physical attractiveness. Further, studies have found that female college students, adolescents, and preadolescents compare their physical attractiveness with that of models in ads and that female pre-adolescents and adolescents have desires to be models. An aspiring young model, for example, describes "the model trap":

> Deep down inside, I still want to be a supermodel.... As long as they're there, screaming at me from the television, glaring at me from magazines, I'm stuck in the model trap. Hate them first. Then grow to like them. Love them. Emulate them. Die to be them. All the while praying this cycle will come to an end.

Clearly, such findings raise concern about advertising ethics. Jean Kilbourne, for example, addresses how female bodies are depicted in advertising imagery and the potential effects on women's physical and mental health in her videos *Still Killing Us Softly* and *Slim Hopes*. The use of highly attractive models in ads as an "ethical issue" received little or no attention in published research from 1987 to 1993, but the ethics of that practice have begun to be

From Mary C. Martin and James W. Gentry, "Stuck in the Model Trap: The Effects of Beautiful Models in Ads on Female Pre-Adolescents and Adolescents," *Journal of Advertising* (Summer 1997). Copyright © 1997 by The American Academy of Advertising. Reprinted by permission. References omitted.

questioned by consumers and advertisers. For example, a consumer movement against advertising has arisen in the United States. The organization Boycott Anorexic Marketing (BAM) is attempting to get consumers to boycott
products sold by companies that use extremely thin models in their ads. Such
criticisms of advertising are "much too serious to dismiss cavalierly."

Using social comparison theory as a framework, we propose that female
pre-adolescents and adolescents compare their physical attractiveness with
that of advertising models. As a result, their self-perceptions and self-esteem
may be affected. In response to the criticisms, we conducted a study to assess
those unintended consequences of advertising. However, unlike previous
empirical studies of those effects, ours incorporated the role of a motive for
comparison—self-evaluation, self-improvement, or self-enhancement—which
may help to explain the inconsistent findings in the advertising/marketing
and psychology literature. Specifically, our premise was that changes in self-
perceptions and/or self-esteem may be influenced by the type of motive operating at the time of comparison.

Physical Attractiveness and Self-Esteem in Children and Adolescents

Cultural norms in the United States dictate the importance of being physically
attractive, especially of being thin. The emphasis on being physically attractive begins in infancy and continues throughout childhood and adolescence.
How physically attractive a child or adolescent perceives him/herself to be
heavily influences his/her self-esteem, particularly beginning in fifth grade.
However, the effect of self-perceptions of physical attractiveness on self-
esteem differs between girls and boys. For example, Harter, in a cross-sec-
tional study of third through eleventh graders, found that self-perceptions of
physical attractiveness and levels of global self-esteem appeared to decline systematically over time in girls but not for boys. Other researchers have documented such decreases throughout adolescence for girls. Boys' self-esteem, in
contrast, tends to increase from early through late adolescence.

The nature of physical attractiveness differs for male and female children and adolescents as well. Girls tend to view their bodies as "objects," and
their physical beauty determines how they and others judge their overall
value. Boys tend to view their bodies as "process," and power and function are
more important criteria for evaluating their physical self. For example, Lerner,
Orlos, and Knapp found that female adolescents' self-concepts derived primarily from body attractiveness whereas male adolescents' self-concepts were
related more strongly to perceptions of physical instrumental effectiveness.
The difference in body orientation results in girls paying attention to individual body parts and boys having a holistic body perspective. Because the ideal
of attractiveness for girls is more culturally salient, girls have a greater likelihood of being negatively affected by the feminine ideal than boys have of
being negatively affected by the masculine ideal.

Advertising and Social Comparison

Television commercials and magazine advertisements that contribute to the "body-as-object" focus for female pre-adolescents and adolescents, using difficult-to-attain standards of physical attractiveness to market products, are pervasive. For example, in an analysis of *Seventeen*, a magazine with "the potential to influence a substantial proportion of the adolescent female population," Guillen and Barr found that models' body shapes were less curvaceous than those in magazines for adult women and that the hip/waist ratio decreased from 1970 to 1990, meaning that models' bodies had become thinner over time. In addition, nearly half of the space of the most popular magazines for adolescent girls is devoted to advertisements.

Social comparison theory holds that people have a drive to evaluate their opinions and abilities, which can be satisfied by "social" comparisons with other people. With that theory as a framework, recent studies have found that female college students and female pre-adolescents and adolescents do compare their physical attractiveness with that of models in ads. In turn, those comparisons may result in changes in self-perceptions of physical attractiveness or self-perceptions of body image. Given the importance of self-perceptions of physical attractiveness in influencing female self-esteem, the comparisons may result in changes in self-esteem as well....

Using social comparison theory as a basis, Richins found no support for the hypothesis that exposure to advertising with highly attractive models would temporarily lower female college students' self-perceptions of physical attractiveness. "By late adolescence, however, the sight of extremely attractive models is 'old news' and unlikely to provide new information that might influence self-perception." Martin and Kennedy assessed the effects of highly attractive models in ads on female pre-adolescents and adolescents but found no support for a lowering of self-perceptions. Relying on Festinger's original conception of the theory, those researchers did not account for motive, and appear to have assumed that the motive for comparison was self-evaluation (i.e., girls compare themselves with models in ads to evaluate their own level of physical attractiveness). However, more recent research has shown that social comparisons may occur for other reasons, suggesting that female preadolescents and adolescents may compare themselves to models in ads for any one (or a combination) of three motives: self-evaluation, self-improvement, or self-enhancement. For example, Martin and Kennedy found that self-evaluation and self-improvement are common motives when female pre-adolescents and adolescents compare themselves with models in ads. Self-enhancement, in contrast, is not common and does not seem to occur naturally. Similarly, in a series of pretests reported by Martin, self-evaluation and self-improvement were found to be common motives in college students, but self-enhancement was not. Gentry, Martin, and Kennedy, however, found stronger support for self-enhancement in a study using in-depth interviews of first and fifth graders. As girls mature, their motives for comparison apparently vary.

The incorporation of motive may help to clarify the inconsistent findings in the literature. Our subsequent discussion explores possible differential effects of comparisons with advertising models on female pre-adolescents' and adolescents' self-perceptions and self-esteem, depending on whether self-evaluation, self-enhancement, or self-improvement is the primary motive at the time of comparison. We do not examine what motives are occurring naturally, but rather how advertising affects girls when they have a particular motive. Our overriding research question is whether motives make a difference in terms of self-perceptions and self-esteem. Finding differences between motives would clearly encourage consumer educators to stress one motive for social comparison over another. Our hypotheses specify the direction of change for each motive, thus implying response differences between subjects who have a particular comparison motive and subjects in a control group. Finding differences between motives would answer our research question even though differences between a motive group and the control group may not be significant.

Self-Evaluation as a Motive for Comparison

As the motive for comparison, Festinger originally proposed self-evaluation, the judgment of value, worth, or appropriateness of one's abilities, opinions, and personal traits. Information obtained from social comparison is not used for self-evaluation until the age of seven or eight, even though social comparison has been found to occur in children of preschool age. In the context of advertising, given that advertising models represent an ideal image of beauty, we expect comparison to be generally upward. That is, female pre-adolescents and adolescents will generally consider advertising models to be superior in terms of physical attractiveness. Therefore, if self-evaluation is the primary motive at the time of comparison (a girl is attempting to judge the value or worth of her own physical attractiveness or body image against that of advertising models), comparisons are likely to result in lowered self-perceptions and lowered self-esteem....

Method...

Subjects

Female pre-adolescents and adolescents in grades four (n = 82; mean age = 9.8 years), six (n = 103; mean age = 11.9 years), and eight (n = 83; mean age = 13.8 years) from a public school system in the Midwest participated in the study (total sample size 268). The public school system is in a county where 98% of the population is white and the median family income is $31,144. Although the sample is not representative of all pre-adolescent and adolescent girls in the United States, it does represent a segment of girls most susceptible to problems linked to physical attractiveness such as eating disorders. As an incentive to participate, the subjects took part in a drawing for two prizes of $50 each. In addition, a $500 donation was made to the public school system.

Fourth, sixth, and eighth graders were chosen for the study because research suggests that the period between the fourth and eighth grades is important in girls' development of positive perceptions of the self. It is a period when female bodies are changing drastically and adult definitions of "beauty" are becoming relevant social norms. We suggest that a girl's transition in this time period is more of a discontinuity than a linear transformation because of the conflicting biological and social processes. For example, Martin and Kennedy found, in an experiment with fourth, eighth, and twelfth grade girls, that self perceptions of physical attractiveness decreased as the subjects got older. Fourth graders' self-perceptions were significantly higher than those of eighth graders, but eighth graders' self-perceptions were not significantly different from those of twelfth graders. Other evidence suggests that self-perceptions of physical attractiveness start to become particularly important during fifth grade. For example, Krantz, Friedberg, and Andrews found a very high correlation between self-perceived attractiveness and self-esteem in fifth graders.... The strength of the relationship in fifth graders more than tripled the variance accounted for at the third-grade level.

Classroom teachers administered the questionnaires to the subjects at the schools during an hour of class time. To separate the measurement of covariates from the manipulation, two separate booklets were used. The first booklet contained the covariate measures. After subjects completed that booklet, they handed it in and were given a second booklet with a set of ads and dependent variable measures. The assignment to treatments was randomized by giving each classroom a random assortment of the five types of questionnaires with ads. Teachers administered the questionnaires to minimize any source effects caused by having an unfamiliar authority figure collect the data. To facilitate understanding, the teachers administered the questionnaires orally by reading each question aloud and allowing appropriate time for the subjects to mark their responses.

Advertising Stimuli

Full-color ads were created by cutting and pasting stimuli from magazine ads in *Seventeen, Sassy, Teen*, and *YM*. Those magazines were chosen because they are the top four teen magazines in the United States and because they maintain consistency with respect to type of beauty. The stimuli were cut from original ads in a way that eliminated information about the sources. The ads created were for commonly advertised but fictional brand name adornment products: Satin Colors lipstick, Generation Gap jeans, and Hair in Harmony hair care products. The ads appeared to be professionally prepared, were kept very simple, and were realistic as they included partial- and full-body photos of models extracted from actual hair care, jeans, and lipstick ads.

To ensure that the subjects perceived the models in the ads as highly attractive, means of two items that measured the models' perceived attractiveness were calculated for each of the three ads. On 7-point semantic differential scales, subjects were asked to rate the model in the ad from "very overweight and out of shape, fat" to "very fit and in shape, thin" and "very unattractive, ugly" to "very attractive, beautiful" prior to measurement of the dependent variables. The range of mean responses to those items was 5.1 to

6.4, far above the midpoint value of four. Hence, the subjects perceived the models as highly attractive.

Manipulation of Motives

Motives were manipulated through instructions given prior to exposure to a set of ads, advertising headlines and copy, and a listing exercise. The manipulations were based on the following operational definitions of each motive.

1. Self-evaluation—a girl's explicit comparison of her physical attractiveness with that of models in ads to determine whether she is as pretty as or prettier than the models on specific dimensions such as hair, eyes, and body.
2. Self-improvement—a girl's explicit comparison of her physical attractiveness with that of models in ads to seek ways of improving her own attractiveness on specific dimensions such as hairstyle and makeup.
3. Self-enhancement 1—a girl's explicit comparison of her physical attractiveness with that of models in ads in an attempt to enhance her self-esteem by finding ways in which she is prettier than the model on specific dimensions (inducement of a downward comparison).
4. Self-enhancement 2—a girl's discounting of the beauty of models in ads and, in turn, the avoidance of an explicit comparison of her own physical attractiveness with that of the models in an attempt to protect/maintain her self-esteem.

Prior to exposure to a set of ads, the subjects were given instructions in which they were shown a drawing of "Amy looking at an advertisement in a magazine" and were told a story about Amy comparing herself with a model in an ad for a particular motive. Then the subjects were asked to look at the ads on the following pages and view the ads as Amy had viewed them.

As consistency in ad design across experimental groups was essential, the headline and copy were the only components manipulated in the four sets of ads designed to induce particular motives. Minor deviations from the ad design were necessary for the control group because their ads did not include a model. The instructions, headlines, and copy were developed from "stories" written by female adolescents in projective tests in previous studies....

The subjects also completed a listing exercise after viewing each ad. They looked at each ad and listed specific ways in which the manipulated motive may have occurred. For example, in the self-improvement condition, subjects were asked to look at the model and "list ideas you get on how to improve your looks." The intent of the study was not to measure naturally occurring motives for social comparison, but rather to investigate how the use of various motives changes cognitive and affective reactions to stimuli showing physically attractive models.

If a subject successfully completed the listing exercises, the manipulation was considered successful. One author analyzed the responses to each listing exercise, coding for the subject's success or failure in completing it.

Criteria for a successful response were specific references to aspects of physical attractiveness that were compared in the ad and no indication that another motive was present. For example, for a successful manipulation of self-improvement, one respondent listed the following ideas she got from looking at the model in the ad: "Use the product. Get a perm. Wear lots of make-up and have as pretty of a face as she does."

A response failed if it indicated that no motive or another motive was present. The failed responses were discarded, resulting in seven subjects being dropped (three subjects from the self-evaluation condition, one subject from the self-improvement condition, and three subjects from the self-enhancement 2 condition). For example, one subject in the self-evaluation condition was dropped because, when asked to list "ways in which your hair, face, and body look compared to the model's hair, face, and body," she wrote, "She looks different because I am a different person. I don't really compare to her." One subject in the self-improvement condition was dropped because, when asked to "list the ideas you get from the model on how you could improve the way you look," she wrote, "I could never look like her and will not try. I know that she has to be willing to work to look like she does. I don't worry about the way I look, it's just not at all that important to me."...

Discussion

In general, our results suggest that motives do play an important role in the study context as we found differential effects for changes in self-perceptions of physical attractiveness, self-perceptions of body image, and self-esteem. Consistent with predictions of social comparison theory, female pre-adolescents' and adolescents' self-perceptions and self-esteem can be detrimentally affected, particularly when self-evaluation occurs: self-perceptions of physical attractiveness were lowered in all subjects.... In sixth graders, self-perceptions of body image were lowered (i.e., body was perceived as larger) in subjects who self-evaluated....

On a positive note, the inclusion of motives shows that detrimental effects do not always occur. That is, positive temporary effects occur when either self-improvement or self-enhancement is the motive for comparison: self-perceptions of physical attractiveness were raised in subjects who self-improved or self-enhanced through downward comparisons.... Self-perceptions and self-esteem were unaffected in most cases in subjects who self-enhanced by discounting the beauty of models.... The only exception occurred when sixth graders' self-perceptions of body image were raised (i.e., body was perceived as skinnier)....

Social comparison theory, as it currently stands, cannot explain all of our results. In particular, how the processes may change over the course of one's lifetime is not articulated theoretically or empirically. A closer examination of the results and some speculation may help to explain the inconsistent and contradictory support for the hypotheses. Though no statistically significant differences were detected, the findings for the fourth graders are interesting and offer some food for thought. Their self-evaluations produced the lowest self-perceptions of physical attractiveness and the highest (i.e., most skinny) self-perceptions of body image in comparison with the other motives. Perhaps in childhood girls (like boys) desire to grow up and "get bigger." Hence, if the fourth graders in our study desired to "get bigger," a skinnier body image would actually represent a "lowering" of self-perceptions. In that case, low self-perceptions of physical attractiveness and skinny self-perceptions of body image after self-evaluation would be consistent, supporting the notion that self-evaluation through comparisons with models in ads has detrimental effects on female pre-adolescents and adolescents.

In comparison with the fourth graders, the sixth graders produced somewhat different results. Sixth graders' self-evaluations produced the lowest self-perceptions of physical attractiveness and the lowest (i.e., the least skinny) self-perceptions of body image in comparison with the other motives. For sixth graders, unlike fourth graders, the direction of changes in self-perceptions of physical attractiveness and body image were consistent. Perhaps a transition occurs between the fourth and sixth grade, from "bigger is better" to "skinnier is better."

In self-esteem, only fourth graders were affected after self-enhancement. Self-esteem was raised in fourth graders who self-enhanced through downward comparisons.... However, self-esteem was lowered in fourth graders who self-enhanced by discounting the beauty of the models.... Martin and Kennedy found that fourth graders aspire to be models more than older adolescents, and perhaps fourth graders are discounting their own future when they discount the beauty of models. Further, fourth graders may be young enough not to realize that not all will grow up to be as beautiful as advertising models. The lack of effects of self-enhancement on sixth and eighth graders' self-esteem may be due to their reluctance to accept that they can look better than advertising models...or that they can discount the beauty of models....

Implications and Directions for Future Research

Our results have implications for advertisers and educators. Educators can use the framework of social comparison theory to instruct children and adolescents about how (i.e., which motives to use) and when (i.e., in what circumstances and with whom) to use others for comparison. With respect to advertising models, children and adolescents may be able to use the processes of self-improvement and self-enhancement to their advantage, as both led to temporary increases in self-perceptions (in comparison with the control group or girls in another manipulated condition). As Martin and Kennedy found, however, self-enhancement is not a naturally occurring motive when female pre-adolescents and adolescents compare themselves with models in ads. Hence, the involvement of educators would be crucial. Not only would emphasis on self-enhancement be advantageous in terms of self-perceptions, but advertisers could benefit as well, as research suggests that making consumers feel physically attractive encourages sales of cosmetic and other adornment products. That possibility is encouraging, but must be viewed with caution until further research has been conducted. Our results suggest that the relationships between motives and self-perceptions and self-esteem are not straightforward and that there are particular times in childhood and adolescence when efforts to instruct young people in how to view ads may be most appropriate. Simply beginning education at a very early age is not the answer. For example, self-enhancement by discounting the beauty of models essentially did not work for fourth graders, as it caused their self-esteem to decrease. Discounting the beauty of models appears to have led fourth graders to discount their own futures in terms of physical attractiveness. In addition, if fourth graders believe "bigger is better," they may not have enough intellectual maturity to realize that "bigger is better" conflicts with the beauty and slenderness of advertising models.

Sixth and eighth graders, in contrast, may be reluctant to accept the notion of discounting models' beauty, hence the lack of effect on their self-esteem. That reluctance might be due partly to their having developed a more sophisticated level of advertising skepticism, as "adolescents have the confidence to rely on their own judgment and the discernment necessary to separate advertising truth from advertising hype." Boush and his coauthors found that self-esteem is related directly to mistrust of advertiser motives and disbelief of advertising claims. Hence, education before sixth grade may be critical to get female preadolescents and adolescents to accept the notion of discounting the beauty of advertising models.

The period between the fourth and eighth grades appears to be a critical one on which future research would be beneficial to assess further what role each of the motives has and for what ages. Other issues also warrant attention. For example, in our study, the models in the ads were in their late teens or early adulthood. Future research might address the effects of younger models, as well as more ordinary-looking models, in ads. Another need is to assess whether the type of physical attractiveness is important.... Further, future research should incorporate the role of "esteem relevance" and "perceived control" to determine whether and to what extent those variables account for natural tendencies to have one motive rather than another. In addition, differential levels of esteem relevance and perceived control may lead to different types and levels of responses. For example, cognitive responses (e.g., self-perceptions) may differ from affective responses (e.g., self-esteem) after comparisons with models in ads, which may help to explain the inconsistent results found here and in similar studies.

Finally, some researchers have acknowledged that the minimal effects or lack of effects found in studies assessing temporary changes in self-perceptions or self-esteem may differ from what may be found in the long term. Thornton and Moore concluded that "with long-term comparisons such as this, particularly with the pervasive presence of idealized media images in our culture and the continued, and perhaps increasing, emphasis placed on physical appearance, there exists the potential for bringing about more significant and lasting changes in the self-concept." The motive of self-improvement, however, represents a unique situation in that temporary changes may differ from the long-term changes. When one commonly compares oneself to advertising models for self-improvement, one may eventually realize that the ideal is not as attainable as originally believed....

Given the criticisms of advertising based on its cultural and social consequences, a better understanding of the role of comparison motives and the other issues mentioned here is needed. Such understanding may lead to a unified effort by educators to help prevent detrimental effects on female preadolescents and adolescents. However, a unified effort by educators may not be enough, and a call for legislation to control the use of models in advertising may arise in response to consumer movements such as Boycott Anorexic Marketing (BAM). Advertising researchers must respond with studies to determine more clearly the unintended consequences of advertising.

NO

Michelle Cottle

Turning Boys Into Girls

I love *Men's Health* Magazine. There. I'm out of the closet, and I'm not ashamed. Sure, I know what some of you are thinking: What self-respecting '90s woman could embrace a publication that runs such enlightened articles as "Turn Your Good Girl Bad" and "How to Wake Up Next to a One-Night Stand"? Or maybe you'll smile and wink knowingly: What red-blooded hetero chick *wouldn't* love all those glossy photo spreads of buff young beefcake in various states of undress, rippled abs and glutes flexed so tightly you could bounce a check on them? Either way you've got the wrong idea. My affection for *Men's Health* is driven by pure gender politics—by the realization that this magazine, and a handful of others like it, are leveling the playing field in a way that *Ms.* can only dream of. With page after page of bulging biceps and Gillette jaws, robust hairlines and silken skin, *Men's Health* is peddling a standard of male beauty as unforgiving and unrealistic as the female version sold by those dewy eyed pre-teen waifs draped across the covers of *Glamour* and *Elle*. And with a variety of helpful features on "Foods That Fight Fat," "Banish Your Potbelly," and "Save Your Hair (Before it's Too Late)," *Men's Health* is well on its way to making the male species as insane, insecure, and irrational about physical appearance as any *Cosmo* girl.

Don't you see, ladies? We've been going about this equality business all wrong. Instead of battling to get society fixated on something besides our breast size, we should have been fighting spandex with spandex. Bra burning was a nice gesture, but the greater justice is in convincing our male counterparts that the key to their happiness lies in a pair of made-for-him Super Shaper Briefs with the optional "fly front endowment pad" (as advertised in *Men's Journal*, $29.95 plus shipping and handling). Make the men as neurotic about the circumference of their waists and the whiteness of their smiles as the women, and at least the burden of vanity and self-loathing will be shared by all.

This is precisely what lads' mags like *Men's Health* are accomplishing. The rugged John-Wayne days when men scrubbed their faces with deodorant soap and viewed gray hair and wrinkles as a badge of honor are fading. Last year, international market analyst Euromonitor placed the U.S. men's toiletries market—hair color, skin moisturizer, tooth whiteners, etc.—at $3.5 billion. According to a survey conducted by DYG researchers for *Men's Health* in

November 1996, approximately 20 percent of American men get manicures or pedicures, 18 percent use skin treatments such as masks or mud packs, and 10 percent enjoy professional facials. That same month, *Psychology Today* reported that a poll by Roper Starch Worldwide showed that "6 percent of men nationwide actually use such traditionally female products as bronzers and foundation to create the illusion of a youthful appearance."

What men are putting *on* their bodies, however, is nothing compared to what they're doing to their bodies: While in the 1980s only an estimated one in 10 plastic surgery patients were men, as of 1996, that ratio had shrunk to one in five. The American Academy of Cosmetic Surgery estimates that nationwide more than 690,000 men had cosmetic procedures performed in '96, the most recent year for which figures are available. And we're not just talking "hair restoration" here, though such procedures do command the lion's share of the male market. We're also seeing an increasing number of men shelling out mucho dinero for face peels, liposuction, collagen injections, eyelid lifts, chin tucks, and, of course, the real man's answer to breast implants: penile enlargements (now available to increase both length and diameter).

Granted, *Men's Health* and its journalistic cousins (*Men's Journal, Details, GQ,* etc.) cannot take all the credit for this breakthrough in gender parity. The fashion and glamour industries have perfected the art of creating consumer "needs," and with the women's market pretty much saturated, men have become the obvious target for the purveyors of everything from lip balm to lycra. Meanwhile, advances in medical science have made cosmetic surgery a quicker, cleaner option for busy executives (just as the tight fiscal leash of managed care is driving more and more doctors toward this cash-based specialty). Don't have several weeks to recover from a full-blown facelift? No problem. For a few hundred bucks you can get a micro-dermabrasion face peel on your lunch hour.

Then there are the underlying social factors. With women growing ever more financially independent, aspiring suitors are discovering that they must bring more to the table than a well-endowed wallet if they expect to win (and keep) the fair maiden. Nor should we overlook the increased market power of the gay population—in general a more image-conscious lot than straight guys. But perhaps most significant is the ongoing, ungraceful descent into middle age by legions of narcissistic baby boomers. Gone are the days when the elder statesmen of this demographic bulge could see themselves in the relatively youthful faces of those insipid yuppies on "Thirtysomething." Increasingly, boomers are finding they have more in common with the *parents* of today's TV, movie, and sports stars. Everywhere they turn some upstart Gen Xer is flaunting his youthful vitality, threatening boomer dominance on both the social and professional fronts. (Don't think even Hollywood didn't shudder when the Oscar for best original screenplay this year went to a couple of guys barely old enough to shave.) With whippersnappers looking to steal everything from their jobs to their women, post-pubescent men have at long last discovered the terror of losing their springtime radiance.

Whatever combo of factors is feeding the frenzy of male vanity, magazines such as *Men's Health* provide the ideal meeting place for men's insecurities and marketers' greed. Like its more established female counterparts, *Men's Health* is an affordable, efficient delivery vehicle for the message that physical imperfection, age, and an underdeveloped fashion sense are potentially crippling disabilities. And as with women's mags, this cycle of insanity is self-perpetuating: The more men obsess about growing old or unattractive, the more marketers will exploit and expand that fear; the more marketers bombard men with messages about the need to be beautiful, the more they will obsess. Younger and younger men will be sucked into the vortex of self-doubt. Since 1990, *Men's Health* has seen its paid circulation rise from 250,000 to more than 1.5 million; the magazine estimates that half of its 5.3 million readers are under age 35 and 46 percent are married. And while most major magazines have suffered sluggish growth or even a decline in circulation in recent years, during the first half of 1997, *Men's Health* saw its paid circulation increase 14 percent over its '96 figures. (Likewise, its smaller, more outdoorsy relative, Wenner Media's *Men's Journal*, enjoyed an even bigger jump of 26.5 percent.) At this rate, one day soon, that farcical TV commercial featuring men hanging out in bars, whining about having inherited their mothers' thighs will be a reality. Now *that's* progress.

Vanity, Thy Name Is Man

Everyone wants to be considered attractive and desirable. And most of us are aware that, no matter how guilty and shallow we feel about it, there are certain broad cultural norms that define attractive. Not surprisingly, both men's and women's magazines have argued that, far from playing on human insecurities, they are merely helping readers be all that they can be—a kind of training camp for the image impaired. In recent years, such publications have embraced the tenets of "evolutionary biology," which argue that, no matter how often we're told that beauty is only skin deep, men and women are hardwired to prefer the Jack Kennedys and Sharon Stones to the Rodney Dangerfields and Janet Renos. Continuation of the species demands that specimens with shiny coats, bright eyes, even features, and other visible signs of ruddy good health and fertility automatically kick-start our most basic instinct. Of course, the glamour mags' editors have yet to explain why, in evolutionary terms, we would ever desire adult women to stand 5'10" and weigh 100 pounds. Stories abound of women starving themselves to the point that their bodies shut down and they stop menstruating—hardly conducive to reproduction—yet Kate Moss remains the dish du jour and millions of Moss wannabes still struggle to subsist on a diet of Dexatrim and Perrier.

Similarly, despite its title, *Men's Health* is hawking far more than general fitness or a healthful lifestyle. For every half page of advice on how to cut your stress level, there are a dozen pages on how to build your biceps. For every update on the dangers of cholesterol, there are multiple warnings on the horrors of flabby abs. Now, without question, gorging on Cheetos and Budweiser while your rump takes root on the sofa is no way to treat your body if you plan on living past 50. But chugging protein drinks, agonizing over fat grams, and counting the minutes until your next Stairmaster session is equally unbalanced. The line between taking pride in one's physical appearance and being obsessed by it is a fine one—and one that disappeared for many women long ago.

Now with lads' mags taking men in that direction as well, in many cases it's almost impossible to tell whether you're reading a copy of *Men's Health* or of *Mademoiselle*: "April 8. To commemorate Buddha's birthday, hit a Japanese restaurant. Stick to low-fat selections. Choose foods described as *yakimono*, which means 'grilled'," advised the monthly "to do list" in the April *Men's Health*. (Why readers should go Japanese in honor of the most famous religious leader in India's history remains unclear.) The January/February list was equally thought provoking: "January 28. It's Chinese New Year, so make a resolution to custom-order your next takeout. Ask that they substitute wonton soup broth for oil. Try the soba noodles instead of plain noodles. They're richer in nutrients and contain much less fat." The issue also featured a "Total Body Workout Poster" and one of those handy little "substitution" charts (loathed by women everywhere), showing men how to slash their calorie intake by making a few minor dietary substitutions: mustard for mayo, popcorn for peanuts, seltzer water for soda, pretzels for potato chips....

As in women's magazines, fast results with minimum inconvenience is a central theme. Among *Men's Health's* March highlights were a guide to "Bigger Biceps in 2 Weeks," and "20 Fast Fixes" for a bad diet; April offered "A Better Body in Half the Time," along with a colorful four-page spread on "50 Snacks That Won't Make You Fat." And you can forget carrot sticks—this think-thin eating guide celebrated the wonders of Reduced Fat Cheez-its, Munch 'Ems, Fiddle Faddle, Oreos, Teddy Grahams, Milky Ways, Bugles, Starburst Fruit Twists, and Klondike's Fat Free Big Bear Ice Cream Sandwiches. Better nutrition is not the primary issue. A better butt is. To this end, also found in the pages of *Men's Health* is the occasional, tasteful ad for liposuction—just in case nature doesn't cooperate.

But a blueprint to rock-hard buns is only part of what makes *Men's Health* the preeminent "men's lifestyle" magazine. Nice teeth, nice skin, nice hair, and a red-hot wardrobe are now required to round out the ultimate alpha male package, and *Men's Health* is there to help on all fronts. In recent months it has run articles on how to select, among other items, the perfect necktie and belt, the hippest wallet, the chicest running gear, the best "hair-thickening" shampoo, and the cutest golfing apparel. It has also offered advice on how to retard baldness, how to keep your footwear looking sharp, how to achieve different "looks" with a patterned blazer, even how to keep your lips from chapping at the dentist's office: "[B]efore you start all that 'rinse and spit' business, apply some moisturizer to your face and some lip balm to your lips. Your face and lips won't have that stretched-out dry feeling.... Plus, you'll look positively radiant!"

While a desire to look good for their hygienists may be enough to spur some men to heed the magazine's advice (and keep 'em coming back for more), fear and insecurity about the alternatives are generally more effective motivators. For those who don't get with the *Men's Health* program, there must be the threat of ridicule. By far the least subtle example of this is the free subscriptions for "guys who need our help" periodically announced in the front section of the magazine. April's dubious honoree was actor Christopher Walken:

Chris, we love the way you've perfected that psycho persona. But now you're taking your role in "Things to Do in Denver When You're Dead" way too seriously with that ghostly pale face, the "where's the funeral?" black clothes, and a haircut that looks like the work of a hasty undertaker.... Dab on a little Murad Murasun Self-Tanner ($21).... For those creases in your face, try Ortho Dermatologicals' Renova, a prescription anti-wrinkle cream that contains tretinoin, a form of vitamin A. Then, find a barber.

Or how about the March "winner," basketball coach Bobby Knight: "Bob, your trademark red sweater is just a billboard for your potbelly. A darker solid color would make you look slimmer. Also, see 'The Tale of Two Bellies' in our February 1998 issue, and try to drop a few pounds. Then the next time you throw a sideline tantrum, at least people won't say, 'look at the crazy *fat* man.'"

Just as intense as the obsession with appearance that men's (and women's) magazines breed are the sexual neuroses they feed. And if one of the ostensible goals of women's mags is to help women drive men wild, what is the obvious corollary objective for men's magazines? To get guys laid—well and often. As if men needed any encouragement to fixate on the subject, *Men's Health* is chock full of helpful "how-tos" such as, "Have Great Sex Every Day Until You Die" and "What I Learned From My Sex Coach," as well as more cursory explorations of why men with larger testicles have more sex ("Why Big Boys Don't Cry"), how to maintain orgasm intensity as you age ("Be one of the geysers"), and how to achieve stronger erections by eating certain foods ("Bean counters make better lovers"). And for those having trouble even getting to the starting line, last month's issue offered readers a chance to "Win free love lessons."

The High Price of Perfection

Having elevated men's physical and sexual insecurities to the level of grand paranoia, lads' mags can then get down to what really matters: moving merchandise. On the cover of *Men's Health* each month, in small type just above the magazine's title, appears the phrase "Tons of useful stuff." Thumbing through an issue or two, however, one quickly realizes that a more accurate description would read: "Tons of expensive stuff." They're all there: Ralph Lauren, Tommy Hilfiger, Paul Mitchell, Calvin Klein, Clinique, Armani, Versace, Burberrys, Nautica, Nike, Omega, Rogaine, The Better Sex Video Series.... The magazine even has those annoying little perfume strips guaranteed to make your nose run and to alienate everyone within a five-mile radius of you.

Masters of psychology, marketers wheel out their sexiest pitches and hottest male models to tempt/intimidate the readership of *Men's Health*. Not since the last casting call for "Baywatch" has a more impressive display of firm, tanned, young flesh appeared in one spot. And just like in women's magazines, the articles themselves are designed to sell stuff. All those helpful tips on choosing blazers, ties, and belts come complete with info on the who, where, and how much. The strategy is brilliant: Make men understand exactly how far short of the ideal they fall, and they too become vulnerable to the lure of high-priced underwear, cologne, running shoes, workout gear, hair dye, hair strengthener, skin softener, body-fat monitors, suits, boots, energy bars, and sex aids. As Mark Jannot, the grooming and health editor for *Men's Journal*, told "Today" show host Matt Lauer in January, "This is a huge, booming market. I mean, the marketers have found a group of people that are ripe for the picking. Men are finally learning that aging is a disease." Considering how effectively *Men's Health* fosters this belief, it's hardly surprising that the magazine has seen its ad pages grow 510 percent since 1991 and has made it onto *Adweek's* 10 Hottest Magazines list three of the last five years.

To make all this "girly" image obsession palatable to their audience, lads' mags employ all their creative energies to transform appearance issues into "a guy thing." *Men's Health* tries to cultivate a joking, macho tone throughout ("Eat Like Brando and Look Like Rambo" or "Is my tallywhacker shrinking?") and tosses in a handful of Y-chromosome teasers such as "How to Stay Out of Jail," "How to Clean Your Whole Apartment in One Hour or Less," and my personal favorite, "Let's Play Squash," an illustrated guide to identifying the bug-splat patterns on your windshield. Instead of a regular advice columnist, which would smack too much of chicks' magazines, *Men's Health* recently introduced "Jimmy the Bartender," a monthly column on "women, sex, and other stuff that screws up men's lives."

It appears that, no matter how much clarifying lotion and hair gel you're trying to sell them, men must never suspect that you think they share women's insecurities. If you want a man to buy wrinkle cream, marketers have learned, you better pitch it as part of a comfortingly macho shaving regimen. Aramis, for example, assures men that its popular Lift Off! Moisture Formula with alpha hydroxy will help cut their shave time by one-third. "The biggest challenge for products started for women is how to transfer them to men," explained George Schaeffer, the president of OPI cosmetics, in the November issue of *Soap-Cosmetics-Chemical Specialties*. Schaeffer's Los Angeles-based company is the maker of Matte Nail Envy, and unobtrusive nail polish that's proved a hit with men. And for the more adventuresome shopper, last year Hard Candy cosmetics introduced a line of men's nail enamel, called Candy Man, that targets guys with such studly colors as Gigolo (metallic black) and Testosterone (gunmetal silver).

On a larger scale, positioning a makeover or trip to the liposuction clinic as a smart career move seems to help men rationalize their image obsession. "Whatever a man's cosmetic shortcoming, it's apt to be a career liability," noted Alan Farnham in a September 1996 issue of *Fortune*. "The business world is prejudiced against the ugly." Or how about *Forbes'* sad attempt to differentiate between male and female vanity in its Dec. 1 piece on cosmetic surgery: "Plastic surgery is more of a cosmetic thing for women. They have a thing about aging. For men it's an investment that pays a pretty good dividend." Whatever you say, guys.

The irony is rich and bittersweet. Gender equity is at last headed our way—not in the form of women being less obsessed with looking like Calvin Klein models, but of men becoming hysterical over the first signs of crows feet. Gradually, guys are no longer pumping up and primping simply to get babes, but because they feel it's something everyone expects them to do. Women, after all, do not spend $400 on Dolce & Gabbana sandals to impress their boyfriends, most of whom don't know Dolce & Gabbana from Beavis & Butthead (yet). They buy them to impress other women—and because that's what society says they should want to do. Most guys haven't yet achieved this level of insanity, but with grown men catcalling the skin tone and wardrobe of other grown men (Christopher Walken, Bobby Knight) for a readership of still more grown men, can the gender's complete surrender to the vanity industry be far behind?

The ad for *Men's Health* web site says it all: "Don't click here unless you want to look a decade younger...lose that beer belly...be a better lover...and more! Men's Health Online: The Internet site For Regular Guys." Of course, between the magazine's covers there's not a "regular guy" to be found, save for the occasional snapshot of one of the publication's writers or editors-usually taken from a respectable distance. The moist young bucks in the Gap jeans ads and the electric-eyed Armani models have exactly as much in common with the average American man as Tyra Banks does with the average American woman. Which would be fine, if everyone seemed to understand this distinction. Until they do, however, I guess my consolation will have to be the image of thousands of once-proud men, having long scorned women's insecurities, lining up for their laser peels and trying to squeeze their middle-aged asses into a snug set of Super Shaper Briefs—with the optional fly front endowment pad, naturally.

POSTSCRIPT

Is Emphasis on Body Image in the Media Harmful to Females Only?

The selections by Martin and Gentry and by Cottle contain negative criticism about advertising, but they also suggest that age affects how susceptible people are to different aspects of advertising images. While one selection focuses on girls at a time in their lives when their bodies are changing, the second selection indicates that adult males, too, can be highly influenced by the images they see and by what seems to be a preoccupation with youth.

These selections also raise questions about the magazine industry and the hypersegmentation by market. If people's tastes and choices of media are being met by a wider variety of specialized publications (or even lifestyle TV channels, such as ESPN or Lifetime), perhaps there is a shift in the idea of a "mass audience." This concept has traditionally meant that the audience was characterized by homogeneity. Perhaps now the audience is less characterized by a sameness, but the content of the media may suggest a "homogenized" ideal for the different groups that make up the audience.

Standards of beauty and success are culturally defined. It is often interesting to pick up magazines or newspapers from other countries or ethnic groups and examine the images in ads to see if specific cultural differences are apparent.

There are many excellent references on the topics raised by this issue. John Tebbel and Mary Ellen Zuckerman have produced a history of magazines entitled *The Magazine in America, 1741–1990* (Oxford University Press, 1991). Books like Naomi Wolf's *The Beauty Myth* (Anchor Books, 1992) and Julia T. Wood's *Gendered Lives: Communication, Gender, and Culture* (Wadsworth, 1994) are particularly insightful regarding the images of women and minorities.

Some videotapes are also available for extended discussion, such as Jeanne Kilbourne's *Still Killing Us Softly and Slim Hopes* (Media Education Foundation).

ISSUE 4

Do African American Stereotypes Still Dominate Entertainment Television?

YES: Donald Bogle, from *Primetime Blues: African Americans on Network Television* (Farrar, Straus and Giroux, 2001)

NO: John McWhorter, from "Gimme a Break!" *The New Republic* (March 5, 2001)

ISSUE SUMMARY

YES: Professor and author Donald Bogle offers a comprehensive analysis of African Americans on network series. He traces their role on prime time from the negative stereotypes of the 1950s to the current more subtle stereotypes of the 1990s. Bogle tackles the shows of the 1990s, particularly the popular and controversial *Martin*.

NO: Professor and author John McWhorter counters that stereotypes are diminishing in America. In his review of Bogle's book, McWhorter asserts that Bogle has donned an ideological straitjacket, which blinds him to the strides that African Americans have made in prime time. He concludes that the continued search for stereotypes prevents us from seeing the very real changes that have taken place in the media.

Intense controversy exists about how racial and ethnic groups are portrayed in the media. Many scholars argue that racial representations in popular culture help to mold public opinion and set the agenda for public discourse on race issues in the media and in society as a whole. Do members of an audience identify with the characters portrayed? Do expressions of and images in the media communicate effectively about specific cultures? How much can we learn about other cultures through media portrayals?

Despite such shows as the infamous *Amos 'n' Andy*, portrayals of African Americans were for the most part absent from early television programming. By the 1970s, a number of shows focused on black families, including *Sanford and Son, Good Times,* and *The Jeffersons*. Few shows in the history of television have been as popular as *The Cosby Show*, which debuted in 1984 and attracted white as well as black audiences. These financially successful shows paved the way for programming that highlighted black characters and families. In the

1990s there were many shows that focused on black families or friendship groups. Yet critics noted that the primary audience for these shows was African American viewers, and at the end of the 1990s, the National Association for the Advancement of Colored People (NAACP) challenged the major networks to better integrate the prime-time population.

Both Donald Bogle and John McWhorter discuss the general issues of how minorities are characterized on television. Both are concerned with the issue of equal access, and by implication both are concerned with the issue of the participation of minorities in media industries.

Bogle discusses how decades of television programs, most often sitcoms, have provided a distorted picture of the African American population. His book includes comprehensive analyses of hundreds of shows. In the following selection he examines one of the more popular shows of the 1990s—*Martin*—to demonstrate both the positive and negative aspects of the program. Although he presents the analysis of only one show, he gives a hint of the richness of description to be found in his book. According to Jannette Dates (*TV Quarterly*, Spring 2001) Bogle implies that "television, the medium said by many to show Americans' true values, systematically deterred whites from learning about African American realities and prevented blacks from full participation in the most important means of communication ever invented by mankind" (p. 78).

McWhorter decries the "Can You Find the Stereotype?" game. He accuses Bogle and many others of being blind to the many positive changes in the media environment. Keeping black viewers indignant over their "perceived victimhood" is, he argues, central to the stereotype game. Ultimately, McWhorter, a linguist, argues that it is "just television"—a perspective sure to anger both black and white mass communication scholars.

The issues of race presented in these selections should lead you to think broadly about the roles represented by African Americans within the media, behind the camera, and beyond media. In recent years more writing has begun to emerge that reflects the role of African Americans in the United States and that bespeaks of greater class differentiation and economic interests. An interesting question to ask might be whether or not viewing politically powerful African Americans challenges traditional media roles and representations. For example, have highly visible African American leaders such as Colin Powell challenged media stereotypes? How long might it take to reverse harmful stereotypes that may have been portrayed in media for generations?

 **YES**

The 1990s: Free-for-Alls

The restless, politically contentious 1990s closed a century *and* a millennium. The decade was a heady mix of pessimistic low expectations and surprisingly, by decade's end, high hopes for the future. In the early years, as the Bush era came to a close, Americans were faced with a war in the Persian Gulf, unprecedented unemployment statistics, and vast company layoffs as corporations talked of downsizing. The national mood changed, however, once William Jefferson Clinton assumed the presidency with ambitious plans to boost the economy and reform health care. As Clinton appointed more African Americans and women to his cabinet than any American President before him, he looked as if he really might be able to overhaul history and lead (as he would say in his reelection campaign) to a bridge to the next century. The good news was that the economy soared, unemployment was at record lows, and Wall Street profits were at record highs. But along with the boom years came a series of White House scandals that ultimately led to the historic impeachment hearings of William Jefferson Clinton, the President of the United States. Though Clinton remained in office, and high in the opinion polls, the pundits cried that permanent damage had been done to the presidency—and the country.

In the early 1990s, the nation seemed to have mixed feelings about race, racial problems, and racial/cultural identities. Some preferred to believe, as they had in the 1980s, that America had outgrown its racial divisions and conflicts. Affirmative action and quotas, they contended, were unfair and unnecessary. But an entirely different mood arose at colleges and universities, where a traditional Eurocentric view of history and culture was challenged. The rise of multicultural studies marked the new view of the American experience as a mosaic of cultural contributions and insights, its very fabric woven together by the input of Native Americans, Africans, Asians, and Europeans. A new generation of African Americans was more conscious of its cultural roots in this Afrocentric era. Young rap/hip-hop artists celebrated Black life and culture and also examined—with hard-hitting lyrics—long-held American social/ political injustices and inequities.

Throughout the era, the nation was stunned by a series of events—many televised—in which race reared its ugly head. Television viewers could daily turn on the tube and witness the Clarence Thomas/Anita Hill hearings, in which

Thomas referred to the Senate investigation of him on charges of sexual harassment as a "high-tech lynching," while Hill emerged as a solitary figure being judged not by her peers buy by a panel of senators that was all male and all white. In March 1991, the nightly news shows broadcast a videotape of four white Los Angeles police officers brutally beating African American motorist Rodney King. Little more than a year later, in April 1992, after those same police officers were acquitted in a state trial on charges of having used excessive force on King, civil disorders erupted in Los Angeles's African American community. Fifty-three Americans ended up dead while property damaged totaled some $1 billion. Riots also broke out in other parts of the country. At the end of the 1990s, the nation would learn of a shockingly vicious hate crime in Texas. A Black man was chained to a pickup truck by three white men who then dragged him to his death. Mainstream America was forced to acknowledge that the nation's racial attitudes had not changed as much as many might have hoped.

In one way or another, all these events would affect television's prime-time African American images.

But in this new decade, television programming was also affected by further changes in the medium itself as the networks continued to see an erosion of their viewership. By 1990, the number of households wired for cable rose from 20 percent to 37. In turn, the networks' 67 percent share of American homes slipped to 57 percent. Viewers in more than half of those cable-wired households could choose from some fifty channels. The once seemingly undifferentiated TV audience that the three networks had always catered to could now tune in to cable's Black Entertainment Television or the Food Channel or the Sci-Fi Channel or the History Channel, all of which successfully tapped the tastes of specific viewers. Many established cable networks like Lifetime also offered original productions. In the summer of 1998, cable would triumph when it "captured more TV households than ABC, NBC, CBS and Fox combined *for the entire month of August.*" By the end of the decade, the future for the networks looked even bleaker. Of the nation's 100 million households with television, some 70 million would have cable.

With all the changes in viewer tastes and habits as the twentieth century drew to a close, network television often appeared frantic in both its search for and its avoidance of shows centered on African Americans. TV power brokers like Cosby and Oprah still found the networks receptive to just about anything they wanted to do. A newcomer like Will Smith looked as if he were his network's darling. For a brief spell, the network Black-cast series was also fashionable. But as the decade progressed, the three major networks, unable to come up with hit Black shows, reverted to form and played it safe, airing fewer and fewer Black-cast series. In their place the new "alternative" networks like Fox and later UPN and WB became known for taking a chance on weekly Black material. These networks solidified their power bases by courting the African American audience, but often with controversial images that might have made Kingfish and Sapphire [characters from the controversial *Amos 'n' Andy* radio show that was produced for television starting in 1951] blush....

Martin Mania: The Rise of Martin Lawrence

...Fox hit pay dirt—and heated controversy—with the sitcom *Martin*. The series chronicled the adventures of Insane Martin Payne (Martin Lawrence), the host of a talk show at the Detroit radio station WZUP. Away from work, Martin pursues, beds, and eventually weds the girl of his dreams, Gina (Tisha Campbell), a marketing executive. Also around are Martin's friends Tommy (Thomas Mikal Ford) and Cole (Carl Anthony Payne Jr.) as well as Gina's secretary and close friend, Pam (Tichina Arnold). There were also such characters as Sheneneh Jenkins, Jerome, security guard Otis, and Martin's mother, Mrs. Payne, all of whom were played by Martin Lawrence.

Martin Lawrence was already known for his stand-up comedy. Lawrence had been born Martin Fitzgerald Lawrence (named, so he said, after Martin Luther King Jr. and John Fitzgerald Kennedy) in 1965 in Frankfurt, Germany, where his father, John, was stationed in the air force. By the time Martin was seven, his parents divorced. While his mother, Chlora, took her other children to live in Landover, Maryland, a suburb of Washington, D.C., Martin was left with his father but joined his siblings when he was in the third grade. To keep the family afloat, Chlora Lawrence worked various jobs as a cashier and in department stores.

As a heavy, hyperactive kid nicknamed Chubby, Martin was so disruptive at school that his teachers sometimes permitted him to tell the class jokes if he promised to be quiet afterward. At home, Lawrence watched Jimmie Walker on *Good Times* (maybe that was his biggest mistake), Redd Foxx, and Richard Pryor, all of whom, along with Eddie Murphy, would be influences. "Richard taught me that honest emotions about sex could be really funny on stage," said Lawrence. Slimming down to some ninety pounds at age fifteen, he became a Golden Gloves boxer. Upon graduation from high school in 1984, he performed at local clubs while working as a janitor at a five-and-dime.

The big break came with a 1987 appearance on television's *Star Search*. Not long afterward, he won a supporting role in the syndicated series *What's Happening Now!!* Spike Lee cast him in *Do the Right Thing*. Then came roles in the movies *House Party* and *Boomerang*.

Lawrence continued performing stand-up comedy routines in which he created energetic minidramas, often centered on relationships. He acted all the parts. Discussing a variety of subjects from racism to the use of condoms, he could be both macho and sensitive. When addressing the subject of male sexual boasts, he seemed surprisingly candid. "Brothers, quit braggin' [about your equipment]," he once said. Then he confessed to being minimally endowed. "But I *work* with what I've got," he said. Audiences loved the honesty. "He is so large. He's like the first in a new wave of comics behind Robin Harris," said producer Russell Simmons. "He's part of a whole new generation that is a little freer. The energy is different. It's not shock humor. The language is so natural." Still, Lawrence was criticized for his "woman-hating" material. Often Lawrence could revel in graphic discussions about feminine hygiene, odors, and yeast infections.

His stand-up performances reached a wider audience when he became the host of HBO's sexually explicit *Def Comedy Jam*. In many respects, that series served as a launching pad for *Martin*. *Def Comedy Jam*'s executive producer, Stan Lathan, called him "a mirror of the current hip-hop generation. The kids are all trying to maintain this macho exterior even though they have a lot of inner sensitivity and insecurities."

Much as Lawrence had done in concerts, his sitcom *Martin* was intended as a new take on contemporary relationships and friendships, done with a hip-hop beat and rhythm. It also set out to comically dramatize the rather traditional sexual/gender attitudes of a young African American male. On its premiere episode, radio host Martin, who specializes in talk about romance and relationships, discussed male sensitivity on the air. When a male listener admits to crying, Martin gets his dander up. What is the world coming to? "You shave your face or your bikini line?" he asks. "Stand up, pull your pants down, man, and look at the front of your drawers. You're missing a flap, girlfriend." Throughout the series, the openly sexist Martin battled his girlfriend Gina for the upper hand. Though she fought him, and though Martin was sometimes made to look foolish, the series glorified rather than challenged his attitudes, not only with Gina but with the world at large.

From the start, the reviewers—to put it mildly—*hated* the series. "Clearly, 'Martin' intends to mine the same misogynistic mucho-macho vein that is a hallmark of 'Def Comedy,'" wrote the *New York Post*'s Michele Greppi. "It deserves a deaf ear."

In the *Los Angeles Times*, television critic Howard Rosenberg wrote of the racism of a "world-class crude" episode in which an oversexed Martin struggles to forgo having sex—for two weeks—with his girlfriend, Gina. "Bumping, grinding and pawing, he was all over her in public—his body pumping like a piston, his tongue thrusting lewdly—acting generally like an animal. 'I'm telling you, baby, I gots to have it!'" At one point, as a desperate Martin tries to calm himself down, Gina discovers he is wearing an ice pack on his penis. "That the half hour was endorsed by Fox's standards and practices department for airing at all was bad enough," wrote Rosenberg. "That it was on at 8 p.m.— and thus potentially available to young kids galore—made it an even greater abomination." He added that perhaps "the bottom line here *is* the bottom line, that anything goes on Fox when it comes to making a buck."

Everything about the show seemed caricatured. In the first year, the primary set—Martin's living room—with its bold colors (purples, yellows, greens) looked like something out of a cartoon. The acting too was fast-paced and frenetic, with most cast members playing to the manic rhythm established by Lawrence. There never seemed to be a quiet moment when a character could relax and—heaven forbid—reflect about what he/she was saying. Worse, the scripts presented the characters with too broad a stroke. Martin's friend Cole, with his oversized clothes and his large hats, seemed so dim-witted that one wondered how he survived in the world. Certainly, he didn't look as if he could function in any workplace; one more sign that Black males had nothing to contribute to establishment culture. (Watching actor Payne, viewers must have asked how an actor who was so appealing and refreshing on *The Cosby Show* could have sunk so low. His saving grace was his vulnerability: he almost looked helpless. Somehow he never lost his fundamental charm.) On the other hand, Tommy appeared as if he *might* be on the ball; certainly he wasn't childlike like Cole and certainly he had more common sense than Martin. But no one was sure where Tommy worked. Or if he worked at all. It was as bad as the situation with Kingfish.

Then there was Gina's friend Pam, decked out in her tighter than skin-tight dresses while the camera gave viewers a lingering, leering look at her. She became the butt of Martin's repeated jokes. The two regularly traded insults. Of course, bickering Black couples were a staple of Black sitcoms; Kingfish and Sapphire; Fred Sanford and Aunt Esther; George Jefferson and Florence. But Sapphire was usually on Kingfish's back because of something stupid he had done. George Jefferson's criticism of Florence—for not being able to cook, for being lazy, or for being late—grew out of his belief that she failed to meet her responsibilities as an employee in his home. In turn, she criticized him for being cheap and pretentious.

But Martin's criticism of Pam were usually tied to her looks. Or her attributes (or lack of) as a woman. He talked about her bad breath, her nappy hair, her figure—and compared her to a horse and a camel. "Why can't I find at least a half decent man?" Pam once asked Gina. "Don't you have any mirrors at home?" said Martin. Pam could match him in the insult department. She made fun of his size and other male inadequacies. For Martin, Gina was always the ideal woman; Pam, the unpleasant leftover, a disgrace to the other sex. Because of the casting, the subtext of the Martin/Pam spats seemed to comment on color. Once again, a lighter African American woman, Gina, played by the lighter actress Tisha Campbell, was the dreamgirl; Pam, played by the browner Tichina Arnold, became a Black woman who cannot meet certain physical standards. As much as Martin yelled and screamed at Pam, he could never directly refer to her color as a sign of her lack of beauty. Never could he call her a *dark* heifer or a *Black* witch. That would have alienated the African American viewer. But for many, color preference was tied in to those battles. In this respect, *Martin* could be pernicious and poisonous.

The characters played by Lawrence himself were the most blatant caricatures. The jivey Jerome, who looked like a reject from *Superfly*, was as sexist as Martin. One afternoon when he eyed Gina walking off with Pam, he felt compelled to *compliment* her by saying, "Girl, you sure is *swollen*." Unlike Richard Pryor, who could uncover the pathos or pain inside his winos and junkies, Lawrence could never invest a character like Jerome with any insights. At the same time, as his character Mother Emma Payne badgered and blasted Gina (whom she felt was totally inappropriate for her baby Martin), she was one more old-style mammy, a direct descendant of Sapphire's Mama.

Much the same might be said of Sheneneh, one of Lawrence's best-known creations. Living across the hall from Martin, Sheneneh sashayed about wearing opulent extensions in her hair, tight short skirts to emphasize her bulging hips and bodacious backside, tight blouses to showcase her ample breasts. Like Martin's mother, she despised Gina.

Part of the cruel fun was watching Sheneneh dump on Gina and other women. On one episode, the conniving Sheneneh took advantage of Gina and forced her to work in Sheneneh's Sho'Nuf Hair Salon. All sorts of comic horrors transpire here. First Gina was told she must have a professional look. The next thing we know, we see Gina *coiffed* in out-sized curly braids. A customer, Mira, said she needed a pedicure because her corns were fixing to pop. "Why don't you take your shoes off, so we can get started," she was told. "They are off," the woman answered. Sheneneh then used an electric power tool to work on the woman's feet.

Shortly afterward, Mira told Gina, "Look, I got to get my perm. I can't sit here all day. I got *mens* waiting to see me." Gina gave her a perm but without a neutralizer. Mira ended up practically bald, except for patches of hair above her ears and long hair in the back. Sheneneh, however, persuaded Mira that she looked stylish. But Sheneneh let Gina know that Mira "was tore up from the floor up. I damn near threw up."

Throughout, *Martin*'s misogyny was apparent (and, sadly, part of the appeal for some misguided males). The series delighted in turning Sheneneh and other women (with the notable exception of Gina and perhaps Pam) into grotesque figures; objects of tawdry jokes and scorn. With her extensions, her eye pops, her competitive attitude toward Gina and other women, Sheneneh was a ribald parody of a pushy, know-it-all, forever attitudinizing, desperately trying-to-be-hip, always-in-your-face young urban Black woman.

Yet *Martin* quickly emerged as a very popular hit. Perhaps young viewers were drawn in by the simple fact that *Martin* was far franker about sex (and the fact that the hero had to have it) than previous Black sitcoms. At times, Martin, like other Black male characters on sitcoms, seemed a tad obsessed with sex. But for viewers, what distinguished Martin was indeed the relationship with Gina. The story line of three of the most popular earlier episodes centered on Martin and Gina as they fought, broke up, and then got back together. Before the final episode, viewers were invited to vote, via a 900 number, on which of the two should apologize. The verdict: Martin should get on his knees. Viewers were always willing to forgive him his trespasses. Hip, loose, free, and very up-front about his desires, he may have struck the young as being an assault (much like Kingfish) on traditional, polite bourgeois society.

Another aspect of his appeal—though his critics would be loath to admit it—was that Martin had a joie de vivre that was infectious; he was something of the indomitable optimist (the opposite of the beleaguered, sometimes cornered Kingfish) with catchphrases that encapsulated his energy and perspective on life. "You go, girl!" "You so crazy!" "Wass Up!" and "Don't go there" caught on and entered the popular lexicon of people who didn't even know of the series.

Martin Lawrence's looks no doubt led viewers not only to feel sorry for him but also to patronize him. Thin and short with large eyes and protruding ears, he was never anyone's idea of a hunk (which, of course, made his slams against Pam seem all the more absurd). All mouth, he was a fiercely unthreatening hero. In this respect, he was obviously similar to Sherman Hemsley's George Jefferson but without the charm or wily intelligence and without the wicked way of turning a line inside out. Martin Lawrence usually bopped and hopped his way through a performance, using his energy rather than any act-ing talent to create his character. Nonetheless, had the character Martin been tall, muscular, deep-voiced, less hyper, he might have been scary and totally unacceptable. No one would sit by and listen to a buck figure express some of the sexist sentiments of a Martin.

For the same reason, Lawrence no doubt succeeded with his characters Sheneneh, Jerome, and Mama Payne. Despite the fact that they're cruel paro-dies, they're such outlandish clowns that it's hard not to laugh at them, even though you do so at your own peril. In the minds of viewers, these characters were all the same person: It's Martin—the perpetual runty adolescent—dressed up in the clothes and makeup of Mommy and her friends. You almost feel sorry for this overcaffeinated adolescent's desperate need to get attention—by any means necessary. Yet viewers were always drawn to him. Later in movies like *Life*, Lawrence also extended his talents as an actor.

The demographics indicated that *Martin* was popular with those 18- to 49-year-old viewers that pleased advertisers. To appeal to them even more, the series featured such guest stars as rappers Snoop Doggy Dogg and Biggie Smalls as well as football star Randall Cunningham. But the series also found favor with even younger viewers. *Martin* ranked in the top five among viewers age 12 to 17 and in the top ten with ages 2 to 11. "I'm huge with the under-5 crowd," said star Martin Lawrence. One only wonders about the ideas those poor kids came away with.

As *Martin* continued its run, it was toned down. Later episodes were bet-ter, yet more traditional television fare, at times as much influenced by *I Love Lucy* as episodes of *227* and *Amen*. A memorable episode featured Marla Gibbs as an exacting drill sergeant of a housekeeper determined to make Martin and Gina stick to a schedule. The episode played on our knowledge of Gibbs's TV career from the days of *The Jeffersons* to *227*. In some episodes, Judyann Elder and J. A. Preston had funny bits as the parents of Gina. Here the series touched on class friction within the African American community. Some characters on *Martin* almost started to look like actual human beings.

In time, viewers became as familiar with the off-screen Martin Lawrence as with the character he played. The success of the series and the new fame that grew out of it appeared to take a toll on him. He became a favorite of the gossips and the tabloids. In 1993, the press reported that he dumped his man-ager and co-creator of *Martin*, Topper Carew. The next year, a story broke that Lawrence had failed to perform concert dates in Cleveland, Atlanta, and Buf-falo. Lawrence, along with his agent and tour promoter, was sued for fraud and breach of contract for the cancellation of the concerts. Later came news that Lawrence had been arrested after he stood at a busy Los Angeles intersec-tion, screaming and ranting incoherently at passersby. Police discovered that he was carrying a concealed weapon. Another arrest came in August 1996 at California's Burbank airport. There he was charged with carrying a loaded handgun in his luggage. Most damaging to his professional image was a sexual harassment suit filed by his TV co-star Tisha Campbell. Campbell left the show but later returned just before its last episodes were filmed.

By the fifth season, the overall ratings for *Martin* plunged. It ranked number 106 out of approximately 130 shows. Yet Lawrence's Black constituency stuck with the program. It was the third most watched show by African Americans. Still, that couldn't save it. Fox dropped the sit-com in August 1997. Afterward its reruns scored well in syndication.

NO

John McWhorter

Gimme a Break!

I.

Like Donald Bogle, I grew up in Philadelphia watching the increasing presence of black Americans on television. Bogle has some years on me, having been in attendance since the 1960s. My own memories of television begin in the early 1970s, when my mother demanded that I sit by her side to watch the new flood of black shows such as *Good Times, Sanford and Son*, and *The Jeffersons*, as well as mainstream shows attending to race such as *All in the Family* and *Maude*. And, of course, watching the entire run of *Roots* was a required rite of passage, even though it meant staying up past my bedtime for many nights in a row.

A part of this regimen was surely due to black Americans' cultural affection for television. As Bogle notes in his new book, *Primetime Blues: African Americans on Network Television*, a Nielsen survey in 1990 showed that blacks watched an average of seventy hours of television a week, and non-blacks watched an average of forty-seven hours; and it is certainly true that television was a more central ritual in my household than in the homes of my white friends. Yet my mother, a professor of social work, also considered black television a part of my early education in racial consciousness. She regarded the shows as a way to inculcate me with the basics of black history, and with the message that the whole world was not white, and that black America included many people not as fortunate as we were.

As we passed into the 1980s and 1990s, the black presence on television grew so steadily that had I been born later, it would have been impractical to try to find everything that blacks did on the tube. In the 1950s, white racists could be satisfied to find blacks on television only in the very occasional series, a few supporting roles, scattered variety show appearances, and one-shot dramatic productions from which they could easily avert their gaze. Today blacks are so numerous on television in all of its genres, represented in such a wide sociological and psychological range, that the same bigot would feel inundated by the objects of his scorn every time he turned on his set, and incensed at how sympathetically they are portrayed and how intimately they interact with whites.

I have always considered the history of blacks on television to be a clear sign that the color line is ever dissolving in America. But Bogle arrives at the opposite conclusion. His book concedes that progress has been made in a sheerly numerical sense, but it argues that overall the black presence on television has been an endless recycling of a passel of injuriously stereotypical images. It is a "Do the Right Thing" affair, exposing the eternal racism that always lurks behind allegedly positive developments that give the appearance of black progress. But Bogle's pessimistic argument is ultimately owed primarily to the ideological fashions of our moment. It cannot withstand a fair and thorough empirical look at the subject. It is a perfect product of the distortions, some of them benevolently meant, that have dominated the thinking of black intellectuals since the late 1960s.

❧

But Bogle's early chapters, on the 1950s and 1960s, are masterful, and they put one in mind of his accomplishments in his earlier writings. With *Brown Sugar*, which appeared in 1980, Bogle did the history of black popular entertainment a signature service with a smart survey of black "divas" from Ma Rainey to Donna Summer, bringing to the light of day the work of many figures who had faded from consciousness. His biography of Dorothy Dandridge was published in 1987, and it was a long overdue chronicle of the life and the work of this world-class beauty and gifted actress who was denied the career that she deserved by the naked racism of her era, and died in despair at the age of forty-two.

With the crisp prose and the masterful eye for detail that were evident in those books, Bogle now takes us through black television of the 1940s, 1950s, and 1960s, bringing to light performances barely recorded in accessible sources. Thus we learn that the very first experimental television broadcast by NBC in 1939 was not, say, a half-hour with Jack Benny, but a variety show starring none other than Ethel Waters. Bogle traces Waters's little-known but fascinating television career, which most famously included a stint playing the maid Beulah. *Beulah* was more representative of the black presence on stone-age television than its more frequently discussed contemporary *Amos 'n' Andy*, which even by the early 1950s was a tatty, recidivist affair rooted in an obsolete minstrel humor and thriving more on familiarity than on pertinence.

Beulah is remembered for depicting a black woman who has nothing better to do than center her life around the white family that employs her, other than waiting for her ne'er-do-well boyfriend, Bill, to propose. This was not an exclusively black convention, of course: Shirley Booth's Hazel on *Hazel* and Ann B. Davis's Alice on *The Brady Bunch* occupied similar spaces. What makes *Beulah* so excruciating to watch today is that Beulah is, in addition, none too bright. It is only with the thickest fortification of historical perspective that one can today endure the opening tags, in which Beulah looks us dead in the eye and offers such aperçus as the fact that she is "the maid who's always in the kitchen—but never knows what's cookin'…! HYEH HYEH HYEH HYEH…!"

Bogle is correct in noting that the miraculous Waters managed to draw some kind of character out of the wan scripts. Waters's episodes are the only ones that can be even approximately tolerated today, as she conveys a kind of warmth and sexual affection between her and Bill, and manages to evoke an impression of will and intelligence despite what her lines have her utter. Throughout her life Waters could not help filling empty space with her charisma. Bogle movingly describes an episode of the usually frothy *Person to Person* in 1954, in which Waters diverted the interview into sincere psychological self-revelation. Waters was intense....

II.

The sun began breaking through the clouds in the 1960s, as the civil rights era brought race relations and "the Negro question" to the forefront of American consciousness. Perhaps the most immediately memorable black figure of this era on television is Bill Cosby's erudite Scotty on *I Spy*, portrayed as every bit the equal of his white partner in undercover operations. From the vantage point of our identity politics, however, we instantly note the absence of any racial identity in Scotty, and this is largely true of other blacks in series of this decade, such as Greg Morris on *Mission Impossible*, Lloyd Haines on *Room 222*, and Nichelle Nichols's Uhura on *Star Trek*. For Bogle, as for many analysts, this reflected white America's desire to "tame" the Negro, who was beginning to be seen as a threat.

Certainly this was a part of the story—but it was not until the end of the decade that the salad bowl would triumph over the melting pot as the dominant metaphor for immigration in the minds of most Americans. In an era in which the central objective of civil rights leaders was still integration, many white producers and writers sincerely considered themselves to be doing good by portraying blacks without any particular "cultural" traits. Today, of course, the seams show, and the space to which blacks were assigned on television requires major historical adjustment....

❧❦❧

Drama shows were somewhat more concerned with addressing the tensions that would soon transform the integrationist imperative into a separatist one, though usually more in the name of economic and racial justice than in the name of what we call "diversity."...

This is all a far cry from Beulah in the Hendersons' kitchen. Still, throughout most of the 1960s there was not a single "black show" proper. This changed in 1968 with *Julia*, starring Diahann Carroll; and the response to this show by black commentators signaled that a new era in black American ideology had arrived. *Julia* portrayed a middle-class widow raising a young son while working as a nurse. With the "assimilated" Carroll's chiseled features and crisp standard English, *Julia* wore the race issue lightly. There was only an occasional episode that depicted Julia encountering and defeating prejudice, which was portrayed as an occasional excrescence rather than the manifestation of a profound moral and social malaise.

Basically, *Julia* was a more sober version of its contemporary *That Girl*. And so black writers, actors, and critics fiercely condemned this little show for neglecting the tragedies of blacks in the inner cities. The Black Power movement was just then forging a new sense of a "black identity" opposed to the mainstream one, which promoted the suffering poor blacks—the blacks most unlike middle-class whites—as the "real" blacks. For this radical (but increasingly pervasive) view, middle-class blacks had some explaining to do. They had deserted their "roots."

The black response to *Julia* was predicated upon this new idea—it is now so deeply ensconced in mainstream black thought that it no longer feels like a "position" at all—that the essence of blackness is suffering. A middle-class nurse living in a nice apartment and interacting easily with whites was obviously "inauthentic." Objections to *Amos 'n' Andy* in the early 1950s were based in part on the fact that even if the show was undeniably amusing, this parody of black reality was one of the only depictions of blacks on television. By the time *Julia* aired, however, black misery and the new "black identity" were not exactly absent from American television. The problem now was not that *Julia* was the only view of blacks on television; the problem was that this side of black life did not deserve to be shown at all.

III.

Fifteen years or so earlier, the critics would have eaten up *Julia* with a spoon. A comparison with *Amos 'n' Andy* is again useful. Bogle presents a list of objections to that show by the NAACP—and in a full page of complaints, the fact that the show did not address black poverty is not even mentioned. Most black thinkers of the earlier period would have had no more interest in seeing black misfortune dutifully "explored" on television than white viewers had in seeing depictions of Appalachia or the poor rural South; and they would have applauded a portrait of members of their race doing well as a genuine advance from the "mammy" days. And yet the NAACP of the period was certainly interested in the problem of black poverty.

The difference hinged on the contrast between an ideology focused on achievement despite acknowledged obstacles and an ideology predicated upon the treacherous notion that achievement is an extraordinary affair of luck until all the obstacles are removed. This latter view—fatalistic, doctrinaire—instantly casts those people blessed with only ordinary capabilities and not with luck—that is, poor people—as the "real" black people. This ideology remains with us today, pervading the thought of most black American pundits and professors. Bogle is one of their company. In its discussion of *Julia*, his book suddenly begins a disappointing decline into a narrow and numbingly circular litany of complaint. Bogle frames the thirty remaining years of black work on television as an almost unbroken procession of veiled injustice and exploitation.

Bogle at this point falls into the same trap that mars his *Toms, Coons, Mulattoes, Mammies, and Bucks*—or, rather, its revised edition. That book first appeared in 1973, and it was my first primer on blacks in film. It aptly identified five eponymous stereotypes running throughout black roles in American movies, making the useful point that the "blaxploitation" genre, whatever its visceral thrill and the work that it gave black actors, was in essence a recapitulation of the types on view as far back as *The Birth of a Nation*. But in 1989 Bogle updated his book and revealed himself as a man with a hammer to whom everything is a nail. What was a valid and penetrating thesis applied to blacks in film up to the early 1970s came to be reflexively applied to the next fifteen years of American popular culture, with no significant acknowledgment made of the stunning maturation of the black role on the silver screen that occurred during those years.

Is Eddie Murphy an exciting phenomenon, playing lead roles in film after film, and often producing films as well? Not at all, because he is sexually appetitive, and therefore he is merely a recapitulation of the oversexed black "buck" who chases the Camerons' young daughter off a cliff in D.W. Griffith's racist film. Was Lonette McKee's performance in *Sparkle* a signature piece of acting? Not quite, because she is light-skinned, and therefore her sad fate in the plot renders her a "tragic mulatto," despite her character's not being of mixed race. And so on. Richard Pryor, speaking for the ghetto, gets one of Bogle's rare stamps of approval—but with the ominous qualification that he may exemplify a new type aborning, the "Crazy Nigger."

◆

Bogle pigeonholes almost every black contribution to American television from 1970 to 2000 into one of several dogmatic categories. As a result, his inquiry degenerates into a game that one might call "Can You Find the Stereotype?" As the years wear on, the relation of Bogle's analysis to the reality that it is describing grows more and more slender. All large, nurturing black women are "mammies," mere recapitulations of Hattie McDaniel and Beulah. This type includes even Oprah Winfrey, whose inspiring success is thereby rendered suspect. Any feisty black woman who speaks her mind to men is a "Sapphire," the idea being that the Kingfish's shrewish wife on *Amos 'n' Andy* established a "stereotype" about the black female that is now best avoided. And so our pleasure in watching LaWanda Page's immortal Aunt Esther on *Sanford and Son* or Nell Carter's lead character on *Gimme a Break!* must be a guilty one....

In Bogle's doctrinaire framework, it is all but impossible for any black performance to pass as kosher. Instead the analysis of every black character is a "damned if they do, damned if they don't" exercise designed more to feed the flames of indictment of the white man than to illuminate any actual truths. *Benson* was indeed a little dicey in depicting an intelligent, middle-aged black man as a butler in a governor's mansion as late as 1979. Within two years, however, the show's writers had Benson elected state budget director; eventually he became lieutenant governor; and finally he ran against the governor himself.

The series ended with Benson and the governor awaiting the election results together. One would think this series aggressively negated the Beulah stereotype, even at the expense of some plausibility. What counts for Bogle, however, is that the show ends with Benson "by his good white friend's side." Physically, yes—but he was watching the progress of an election in which he had attempted to unseat the man from his livelihood! How would Bogle have contrived his analysis if the series had ended with Benson watching the returns by himself?

It gets worse. If a show addresses racism in history (*Homefront, I'll Fly Away*), then Bogle takes it to mean that racism is safely confined to the past. But then if producers had refrained from depicting slavery and segregation on television, surely Bogle would have decried this as "whites denying the wrongs of the past." Meanwhile Bogle repeatedly dismisses as "self-congratulatory" shows in which whites denounce racism—though a black character who wears racial indignation on his sleeve merely restores us to the Angry Black Man. In Gary Coleman's savvy comments about racism in *Diff'rent Strokes*, Bogle detects the message that such comments are acceptable "*only* out of the mouths of babes," when in fact black adults had been sounding off about racism for a decade on other shows. This is not serious engagement with a cultural development. It is the promulgation of professional underdog-ism in black America, and as with most such work, it is accomplished only at the expense of empirical seriousness.

IV.

...One of the saddest results of the ideological straitjacket that Bogle imposes upon black television is that it blinds him to some remarkable and historically important performances. In *Gimme a Break!* in the early 1980s, Nell Carter played a live-in housekeeper to a widowed white police officer (Dolph Sweet), and became essentially a surrogate mother to his children. In Bogle's account, "For African American viewers, *Gimme a Break!* was little more than a remake of *Beulah*." But this is only what Bogle and assorted black commentators chose to make of it. The show was quite popular in the black American community, and it owed its popularity not least to the fact that its resemblance to *Beulah* was only superficial.

Beulah was meekly deferent to her employers, but Nell brooked no nonsense from the Chief. Bogle may read this as a revival of "Sapphire" (despite Nell's decidedly unsexual rapport with Sweet), but most of us simply enjoyed seeing a black woman holding her own against a white man. Beulah never knew what was cookin', but Nell ran the house to such an extent that the show barely skipped a beat when Sweet died during the run. Beulah's life outside the house was a cipher, but Nell was depicted as dreaming of a singing career, and Carter could really sing. (I can hear the party-faithful Bogle asking why black people always have to sing and dance; but if Carter hadn't been allowed to use her amazing voice, he would certainly have complained of the suppression of her talent.)

...Few vintage performances are immune from Bogle's straitened standpoint. Sherman Hemsley's loudmouthed George Jefferson is a retread of the "coon," regardless of the joy that black audiences regularly felt at the sight of

Hemsley's strutting bantam entrance into the lobby of his and Louise's new "dee-luxe apartment in the sky" in the opening credits, which seemed to encapsulate the prospect of advancement without a surrender of pride. Hemsley's cocky yet contoured reading of what could have been a shallow, shrill character was most of what kept this silly show going for eleven seasons....

V.

It is his separatist ideology that ruins Bogle's pleasure. It is also what keeps him from ever addressing the paradoxical nature of his expectations, such as his implication that there should be a moratorium on black participation in certain entertainment clichés long beloved by audiences of any extraction, including black Americans. One comes away from Bogle's book with the impression that he considers black television to have a special therapeutic mission from which the rest of television is exempt. In *Toms, Coons, Mulattoes, Mammies, and Bucks*, he proposed that "black films can liberate audiences from illusions, black and white, and in so freeing can give all of us vision and truth. It is a tremendous responsibility, much greater than that placed on ordinary white moviemakers"; and at the end of *Primetime Blues* he considers television to have "a long way to go in honestly and sensitively recording African American life."

And so Bogle reserves his highest praise for *The Cosby Show*, and for the brooding, quirky, and still-missed 1980s "dramedy" *Frank's Place*, and for the *succès d'estime* drama *I'll Fly Away*, which depicted a black maid working for an integrationist white lawyer in the segregated South of the 1950s. Ever vigilant against the mammy stereotype, and imbued with his evangelical conception of black television, Bogle also appears to have a particular predilection for low-key, dreamy black women, heaping special praise on Louise Beavers of *Beulah*, Gloria Reuben of *ER*, Regina Taylor of *I'll Fly Away*, and Lisa Bonet of *The Cosby Show.*

Working with this, we can construct a future that would presumably meet with Bogle's approval. All black television series would portray financially stable people infused with a combination of intellectual curiosity and good old-fashioned mother wit. All characters would regularly display passionate commitment to uplifting the blacks left behind, while at the same time participating in mainstream society—but with a healthy dose of "authentic" anti-assimilationist resistance as well. All characters would be romantically fulfilled, but within the bounds of carefully considered serial monogamy. Humor would be low-key, avoiding any hint of "raucousness," yet always with one foot in African American folk traditions. Mothers and wives would be portrayed by small, light-skinned women, preferably of dreamy affect, who would never engage their husbands in anything but the most civil conduct. Black characters in mainstream programs would at all times refrain from "nurturing" whites and would display a primary rootedness in black culture, while at the same time refraining from going as far as being perceived as "angry" or as "the Other." In sum: all black shows would essentially be recapitulations of *The Cosby Show*.

❧❦❧

I cherished *The Cosby Show* in its early years for gracefully depicting a black family whose lives were not defined by impecuniousness or tragedy: here was where black America was headed, rather than where it had been. Yet the common consensus among black commentators, as Bogle notes, was that the show carried an implication that the black underclass was a marginal issue. Maybe it did. But the real problem was that the show became downright dull. "That's just Ozzie and Harriet," my father groused during its first season. The show's "statement" was eloquent, but after a while it became a weekly sermon, and hard to recognize as entertainment.

Sanford and Son, by contrast, was entertainment. But under Bogle's rule, this show would have had Lamont working his way out of Watts by attending college, while Fred took continuing education classes alongside, all the while giving his white teachers hell as he resisted "assimilation." Instead of giving work to his old chitlin' circuit friend LaWanda Page, and thereby surrendering to the "Sapphire stereotype," Redd Foxx should have let her languish in obscurity while casting a petite, reserved, light-skinned woman—probably given to spells of wide-eyed reverie—as Aunt Esther, with her and Sanford getting along warmly. The show should have been an hour-long drama, so that it might more fully "explore" the "personas" and "issues." In later seasons, Lamont should have entered the corporate world.

But who would have watched this show, or another like it? It is fine for entertainment to be edifying, but it must also be entertaining. Moreover, Bogle's requirements for entertainment would make it even less true to life than he now thinks it is. For there is no room for natural human exuberance in Bogle's ideal. Surely an essential aspect of African American experience—its amazing vitality—would go missing if all black shows were of the gentle and genteel tone of *The Cosby Show, Frank's Place,* and *I'll Fly Away.* Consider Bogle's ideal of "dreamy" women: really, Louise Beavers was never much of an actress; and even Bogle notes Gloria Reuben's "flat voice"; and most viewers considered *A Different World* to have hit its stride only when the similarly flat-voiced Lisa Bonet left the show. I confess that I prefer LaWanda Page to Lisa Bonet any day of the week. And I doubt that I am alone.

This is, after all, commercial television. In the eternal tug-of-war between art and commerce in popular entertainment, commerce has always come out on top, even if art occasionally slips through. More to the point, popular entertainment has always been founded upon character types, from Pierrot and Harlequin to Sapphire and the Kingfish. To assail all such black personages as "stereotypes" is intellectually irresponsible—unless one is prepared to accuse, say, West African villagers of trucking in "stereotypes" in keeping alive the stock characters in their culturally central folk tales. Why is Anansi, the wily spider at the heart of tales passed down the generations in Africa and the Caribbean, any less a stereotype than George Jefferson? This point is all the more significant given that black writers are as complicit as white writers in promulgating these "stereotypes," as Bogle surely agrees.

Bogle is too familiar with popular entertainment and its history not to understand this. But this means that his proposition that black television must shoulder a unique and "tremendous responsibility" cannot be taken seriously, except as another cry of victimhood. That "tremendous responsibility" is just another way to keep black readers eternally indignant at perceived racism in America. Bogle's chronicle of fifty-plus years of black television is more a reflection of the centrality of victimhood to modern black identity than an accurate history of race in this medium and this time. If you put an African American of the 1950s before a television set in 2001, he would surely be stunned and elated by the evidence of progress that would pass before his eyes.

⋅⊙⋅

Bogle is hardly alone in his approach to black television. There now exists a whole literature of books and articles by black writers playing endless rounds of the "Can You Find the Stereotype?" game. This impulse to uncover rot behind all black success runs so deep in so many black writers that many might find it difficult to imagine just what else a survey of black television could be about. Yet there are many, many things that Bogle and the others neglect, because they do not fit the arc of a victimologist's argument.

Thus Bogle zips perfunctorily by the welter of black sitcoms on the new UPN and WB networks. True, the shows put a new low in lowest common denominator, operating at a ding-dong *Laverne & Shirley* level that has been foreign to most white sitcoms since about 1980. And yet these shows are extremely popular with black viewers. The people who recently made a boisterous cartoon such as *The Parkers* the top-rated show among blacks do not share Bogle and his comrades' idea of an evening's entertainment. While Bogle waits for "honesty" and "sensitivity," millions of other African Americans are happily sitting down to *Homeboys in Outer Space, The Wayans Bros., Malcolm & Eddie*, and their ilk.

These sitcoms have been very popular with black audiences, while richer fare, such as the heavily black and highly regarded *Homicide*, has not fared so well; and this is a fact that is worth exploring. Bogle is correct that there has always been a sad dearth of black dramas as opposed to black comedies—but surely this is in part because black audiences have repeatedly been less likely to take them to heart. There are rich issues of culture, class, tradition, and psychology to be mined that could engage even the most essentialist-minded of writers. But Bogle falls short here, preferring to malign the nerdy character of Urkel in *Family Matters* as "deracialized" for not infusing his persona with any identifiable "blackness."

Empirical studies have suggested, contrary to the common wisdom, that blacks are not depicted as criminals on television today out of proportion to their representation in the population. I would have liked to see Bogle ponder this question, charting the evolution of the black criminal on television (in the 1950s, the criminal was usually a working-class white) and possibly refuting the studies in some way. And perhaps because they do not lend themselves to the "Can You Find the Stereotype?" game, Bogle largely neglects black variety shows after Flip Wilson, when these shows, especially in the 1970s, contributed some definitive moments for black viewers. Who could forget little Janet Jackson's imitation of Mae West on *The Jacksons* in the mid-1970s? I also fondly remember Telma Hopkins and Joyce Vincent Wilson's savory skits as working-class Lou-Effie and Maureen on *Tony Orlando and Dawn*.

I do not wish to suggest that there is no basis for an anxiety about stereotypes. I cannot find a positive word to say about Jimmie "J.J." Walker's sad takeover of *Good Times*, even though I was one of the kids in the schoolyards shouting "Dy-no-MITE!!!" And too often black cast members are the ones with the least defined personas, a notable current example being Victoria Dillard's Janelle on *Spin City*, a character whose facelessness after six seasons would be unimaginable in any white character on any program. And yet we are a long, long way from Andy and the Kingfish—a long way even from Scotty.

And why, we must ask in the end, is the issue so urgent at all? To be sure, popular entertainment has an influence upon the formation of identity in America; but the stereotype obsession presumes something more. It presumes that anything short of a "sensitive" and "honest" depiction of black experience constitutes an obstacle to black advancement. This, I think, is a very brittle claim. Granted, it was hardly a picnic when practically the only image of blacks on television was *Amos 'n' Andy*. But given the profoundly richer and more positive situation today, it is difficult to argue that only Bogle's ideal would discourage a black youth from using drugs, or lead a young black woman to work harder in school, or raise the rate of blacks opening small businesses. Quite the contrary. A great many individuals and groups have worked their way up in American history despite the ugly stereotypes in popular entertainment.

In other words, it's just television. Real life happens outside the little box. Yes, there is evidence that television can affect behavior. But if, between 1970 and 2000, blacks had been depicted only "sensitively" and "honestly" on television, their history during the period would certainly have unfolded exactly as it did, with the same ratio of triumphs to setbacks. The assumption that television must carefully reflect reality, and even airbrush reality, but never exaggerate or parody reality—and that it must do so only in the case of blacks—is unwarranted by history or psychology or politics; and it represents a gross misunderstanding of popular entertainment. No form of entertainment has ever achieved such representational justice, and the implication that black Americans are helpless without it renders us passive victims rather than masters of our own fates.

Yet Bogle's book will surely stand as the authoritative source on the subject. It will be endlessly borrowed from university libraries by black undergraduates in classes on "Race and the Media," dutifully writing papers illuminating the "stereotypes" underlying almost anything anyone black has ever done on television. Black thinkers—many of whom, like most busy intellectuals and journalists, do not actually watch much television—will continue to decry "the scarcity of positive portrayals of blacks in the media." And the NAACP will continue to harangue the big networks—which are watched by fewer people each year—as racist for not happening to have included black characters in a particular season's lineup. Never mind that blacks are all over the myriad shows on the dozens of other stations now available on cable, as well as in shows from past seasons on the big networks themselves. (The networks, of course, will eagerly accept their guilt and quickly cast black actors in roles written as race-neutral—with the result that their shows will include various black-white "friendships" devoid of any natural chemistry, as on *The Weber Show*, where the seasoned stage and film actor Wendell Pierce cavorts perfunctorily with white actors looking as if he walked in from some other show, or worse, like a "Negro" token circa 1966. The show's white writers, hip to the "deracialization" gospel, have made certain to include the occasional exchange acknowledging the character's color, which in such a lightweight show only makes the falsity of the whole business stand out even more.)

But, as I say, it's just television. Regardless of the essentialism of thinkers such as Donald Bogle, the African American community is well on its way past its old radical platitudes to a truly integrated—dare I say "deracialized"?—future, which is the only future possible. And for the fortunate people in that future, *Primetime Blues* will serve as a poignant document of a time when black thought in America was unwittingly dominated by an appetite for self-defeat.

POSTSCRIPT

Do African American Stereotypes Still Dominate Entertainment Television?

In this issue, as in a related issue of how the media portrays gender, an important question arises: What are the consequences of long-term exposure to media messages? This question leads naturally to another essential question: What are the unintended consequences of television viewing? Although these selections focus on African Americans, the same concerns apply to other racial and ethnic groups.

Whether race portrayals are changing or not, a number of studies over the years have demonstrated the impact of negative or limited portrayals of blacks and other minorities. Clint C. Wilson and Felix Gutierrez, in *Minorities and the Media: Diversity and the End of Mass Communication* (Sage Publications, 1985), examine portrayals of blacks, Native Americans, Latinos, and Asians. Carolyn Martindale, in *The White Press and Black America* (Greenwood Press, 1986), explores newspaper coverage of race-related news and analyses its deficiencies. Sut Jhally and Justin Lewis write of the impact of *The Cosby Show* on perceptions of African Americans in *Enlightened Racism* (Westview, 1992).

Scholars struggle with how to talk about representation. In Horace Newcomb's *Television: The Critical View*, 6th ed. (Oxford, 2000), Herman Gray has written an important essay about the issue of what he calls representational politics. See also Gray's book *Watching Race: Television and the Struggle for the Sign of Blackness* (University of Minnesota Press, 1997). The two selections represent exactly the problem that scholars have as they try to uncover hidden patterns that undermine equality, acknowledge real strides forward, and demonstrate why certain choices are more positive than others. A number of books over the years have examined the issues of race and representation in media. They include Sasha Torres, ed., *Living Color: Race and Television in the United States* (Duke University Press, 1998) and Janette Dates and William Barlow, eds., *Split Image: African Americans in the Mass Media* (Howard University Press, 1993).

Other attempts to understand race in U.S. society are found in Cornel West's *Keeping Faith: Philosophy and Race in America* (Routledge, 1993) and bell hooks's *Black Looks: Race and Representation* (South End Press, 1992). For a personal look at the lived experience of one author, see *Colored People: A Memoir* by Henry Louis Gates, Jr. (Vintage Books, 1995).

On the Internet . . .

Cultural and Media Studies

Cultural and Media Studies (CMS) is located at the University of Natal-Durban in South Africa. CMS was established to develop strategies of cultural resistance through media and culture after the Soweto uprising of 1976. With the advent of democratic political processes in South Africa, CMS now works in policy research and to develop support for communication projects.

http://www.nu.ac.za/cms/

Freedom Forum

The Freedom Forum is a nonpartisan, international foundation dedicated to free press, free speech, and free spirit for all people. Its mission is to help the public and the news media understand one another better. The newseum area of this site is very intriguing.

http://www.freedomforum.org

Fairness and Accuracy in Reporting

Fairness and Accuracy in Reporting (FAIR) is a national media watch group that offers well-documented criticism of media bias and censorship. FAIR advocates for greater diversity in the press and scrutinizes media practices that marginalize public interest, minority, and dissenting viewpoints.

http://www.fair.org

Television News Archive, Vanderbilt University

Since August 5, 1968, the Television News Archive has systematically recorded, abstracted, and indexed national television newscasts. This database is the guide to the Vanderbilt University collection of network television news programs.

http://tvnews.vanderbilt.edu

Advertising Age

The Web site of *Advertising Age* magazine provides access to articles and features about media advertising, such as history of television advertising.

http://adage.com

PART 2

Media Ethics

*M*edia ethics concerns the delicate balance between society's interests and the interests of individuals, groups, and institutions such as the press and the government. Questions of ethics are, by definition, issues of right and wrong. But they are among the most difficult issues we face because they require decisions of us, even in the face of articulate and intelligent opposition. What is the appropriate balance between responsibility and liberty? Who should decide where the lines between right and wrong are to be drawn, and on what values should these decisions be made? Are all decisions relative to the individual case, or are there larger, overriding principles to which we should all pledge our allegiance? Most important, to whom should we entrust the power to make and implement ethical choices? In this section, the reader must grapple with the questions ethics ask of us and critically examine the purposes and actions of some of the most fundamental institutions we know.

- Should the Names of Rape Victims Be Reported?
- Should Tobacco Advertising Be Restricted?
- Is Advertising Ethical?

ISSUE 5

Should the Names of Rape Victims Be Reported?

YES: Michael Gartner, from "Naming the Victim," *Columbia Journalism Review* (July/August 1991)

NO: Katha Pollitt, from "Naming and Blaming: Media Goes Wilding in Palm Beach," *The Nation* (June 24, 1991)

ISSUE SUMMARY

YES: President of NBC News Michael Gartner justifies his decision to name the accuser in the William Kennedy Smith rape case, stating that names add credibility to a story. He further argues that a policy of identifying accusers in rape cases will destroy many of society's wrongly held impressions and stereotypes about the crime of rape.

NO: Using examples from the William Kennedy Smith case, journalist and social critic Katha Pollitt identifies six reasons commonly cited by proponents of naming alleged rape victims and argues that not one of them justifies the decision to reveal victims' identities without their consent.

In 1991 a woman stated that she was raped at the Kennedy compound in Palm Beach, Florida, one night during the Easter weekend. After an investigation by the local police, William Kennedy Smith, nephew of Senator Edward M. Kennedy (D-Massachusetts), was charged with the assault. The subsequent trial later that same year resulted in an acquittal for Smith. The case received widespread media coverage, in part because it involved a Kennedy, and in part because the circumstances of the case tapped into the ongoing national debate over so-called acquaintance rape, or date rape. On the night of the incident, Smith and the woman met at an exclusive club, they spent some time drinking and partying, and the woman later drove Smith home and accepted his invitation to take a walk on the beach. According to the woman, the police, and the local prosecutor, what eventually took place that night was rape. Smith, his supporters, and the jury, however, saw it as consensual sex. In addition to raising the question of date rape, the case also provoked controversy because of how various news organizations handled the issue of whether or not to reveal the woman's identity.

Shielding the names and identities of victims of rape has long been a press tradition. But when theWilliam Kennedy Smith story first broke, both the NBC television network and *The New York Times* reported the woman's name; furthermore, *The New York Times* ran a story that gave details on her personal background. These actions sparked controversy among the public and among journalists and media critics.

Who should control the decision to use the names of victims when the media reports rape cases? Should it be only the victims? Considering that the names of other crime victims are generally not withheld, does concealing identities in news coverage of rape perpetuate stereotypes about rape? What rights does the alleged rapist have? What, in short, are the legitimate privacy interests of those involved? How can those interests be balanced with the public interest and the press's responsibility to fully report a story?

These are difficult ethical questions for journalists. In making a decision, how does a journalist balance competing demands, such as the common good versus the rights of an individual, or absolute freedom of the press versus the right to privacy? Does one value predominate over another?

Michael Gartner, president of NBC News, decided to break with journalistic tradition and broadcast the name of the alleged victim of the incident at the Kennedy compound without her consent. In the following memo to his staff dated April 24, 1991, Gartner outlines his reasons for making the controversial decision. Some NBC affiliates complained, and even among his own staff the decision was not unanimously supported, but Gartner maintains that it is usually journalistically responsible to reveal the names of rape victims. Katha Pollitt, in opposition, argues that society's attitudes toward rape justify privacy for rape victims. Naming names is media exploitation, she asserts, and it does not serve a good purpose.

Michael Gartner  **YES**

Naming the Victim

This past April [1991]—following a woman's allegations that she had been raped by Senator Edward Kennedy's nephew William Kennedy Smith— NBC News broke ranks with a tradition honored by other mainstream news organizations by reporting the name of the alleged victim without her consent. The following day *The New York Times* published the woman's name, asserting that the NBC disclosure had already made her name public knowledge. These decisions set off a great deal of internal discussion at both organizations and in the press at large. In this memo to his staff, Michael Gartner, president of NBC News, justifies his decision.

To the staff:

Why did NBC News name the woman who says she was raped at the Kennedy compound in Florida over the Easter weekend? How was that decision made?

For years, the issue has been debated by journalists and feminists: should the names of rape victims or alleged rape victims be made public? Among journalists, there is no agreement; among feminists, there is no agreement.

At NBC, we debated the journalistic arguments.

Some background: I have been deeply interested in this subject for years, discussing it and debating it. Years ago, I concluded that journalistically it is usually right to name rape victims. Usually, but not always.

Here is my reasoning:

First, we are in the business of disseminating news, not suppressing it. Names and facts are news. They add credibility, they round out the story, they give the viewer or reader information he or she needs to understand issues, to make up his or her own mind about what's going on. So my prejudice is always toward telling the viewer all the germane facts that we know.

Second, producers and editors and news directors should make editorial decisions; editorial decisions should not be made in courtrooms, or legislatures, or briefing rooms—or by persons involved in the news. That is why I oppose military censorship, legislative mandate, and the general belief that we should only print the names of rape victims who volunteer their names. In no other category of news do we give the newsmaker the option of being named. Those are decisions that should be made in newsrooms—one way or another.

Third, by not naming rape victims we are part of a conspiracy of silence, and that silence is bad for viewers and readers. It reinforces the idea that somehow there is something shameful about being raped. Rape is a crime of violence, a horrible crime of violence. Rapists are horrible people; rape victims are not. One role of the press is to inform, and one way of informing is to destroy incorrect impressions and stereotypes.

Fourth, and finally, there is an issue of fairness. I heard no debate in our newsroom and heard of no debate in other newsrooms on whether we should name the suspect, William Smith. He has not been charged with anything. Yet we dragged his name and his reputation into this without thought, without regard to what might happen to him should he not be guilty—indeed, should he not even be charged. Rapists are vile human beings; but a suspect isn't necessarily a rapist. Were we fair? Probably, yes, because he was thrust into the news, rightly or wrongly. But so was Patricia Bowman, and we should treat her the same way journalistically. We are reporters; we don't take sides, we don't pass judgment.

Those are the points made in our internal debates. At NBC News, I first raised the issue when the woman was raped in Central Park. We had one story on Nightly News, and after that I told some colleagues that if that were to become a continuing national story we should debate the question of naming the woman. As it turned out, it did not become a continuing national story, and we did not have the debate at that time.

Two weeks ago, I began debating in my own mind the issue of the Florida case. I joined in the debate with some colleagues from outside NBC News last week. On Monday of this week, I raised the issue with three colleagues within NBC News. We discussed it at some length. Should we do this, and if we did it how should we frame it?

On Tuesday, the discussions continued. They were passionate and spirited, but not mean-spirited. By the end of the day, the debate probably encompassed 30 persons, men and women of all views. There was no unanimity; if a vote had been taken, it probably would have been not to print the name. But I decided, for the reasons listed here, to air the name. The fact that her identity was known to many in her community was another factor—but not a controlling one—in my decision.

There were those—including some involved in the preparation, production and presentation of the piece—who disagreed intellectually. But no one asked to be removed from the story, and everyone did a thorough job. The story was clear and fair and accurate; it was not sensational, and—for those who think it was done for the ratings or the like—it was not hyped or promoted. It was presented as just another very interesting story in a Nightly News broadcast that, that night, was full of especially compelling stories.

At 5:00 P.M., we did send an advisory to affiliates that we were naming the woman, for our Florida affiliates, especially, needed to be told in advance. In the time since, six of our 209 affiliates have complained to us about the decision; at least one, WBZ in Boston, bleeped out the woman's name and covered her picture. Several affiliates said we ran counter to their own policies, but just as we respect their views they respected ours and ran the story.

Several other affiliates called to say they agreed with our decision. Most said nothing.

I am particularly proud of the process we went through in reaching our conclusion; in fact, the process was more important than the conclusion. There was vigorous and free debate about an issue of journalism; all sides were discussed. The story was shaped and reshaped as a result of that debate. When we ultimately decided to air the name, everyone involved at least understood the reasons, and everyone then did the usual first-rate work.

Our decision engendered a national debate. Much of the debate has been focused on the wrong issues, but much of it has been focused on the right issue: the crime of rape. The debate itself has raised the awareness of the horribleness of the crime, the innocence of victims, the vileness of rapists. That has been a beneficial side-effect.

Rape is rarely a national story. If another rape becomes a big story, we will have the same debate again. The position at NBC News is this: we will consider the naming of rape victims or alleged rape victims on a case-by-case basis.

Katha Pollitt

Media Goes Wilding in Palm Beach

$\mathbf{I}$ drink, I swear, I flirt, I tell dirty jokes. I have also, at various times, watched pornographic videos, had premarital sex, hitchhiked, and sunbathed topless in violation of local ordinances. True, I don't have any speeding tickets, but I don't have a driver's license either. Perhaps I'm subconsciously afraid of my "drives"? There are other things, too, and if I should ever bring rape charges against a rich, famous, powerful politician's relative, *The New York Times* will probably tell you all about them—along with, perhaps, my name. Suitably adorned with anonymous quotes, these revelations will enable you, the public, to form your own opinion: Was I asking for trouble, or did I just make the whole thing up?

In April the media free-for-all surrounding the alleged rape of a Palm Beach woman by William Smith, Senator Ted Kennedy's nephew, took a vicious turn as the *Times*—following NBC, following the *Globe* (supermarket, not Boston, edition), following a British scandal sheet, following *another* British scandal sheet—went public with the woman's name, and a lot more: her traffic violations, her mediocre high school grades, her "little wild streak," her single motherhood, her mother's divorce and upwardly mobile remarriage. Pretty small potatoes, really; she sounds like half my high school classmates. But it did make a picture: bad girl, loose woman, floozy.

Or did it? In a meeting with more than 300 outraged staff members, national editor Soma Golden said that the *Times* could not be held responsible for "every weird mind that reads [the paper]." NBC News chief Michael Gartner was more direct: "Who she is, is material in this.... You try to give viewers as many facts as you can and let them make up their minds." Forget that almost none of these "facts" will be admissible in court, where a jury will nonetheless be expected to render a verdict.

In the ensuing furor, just about every advocate for rape victims has spoken out in favor of preserving the longstanding media custom of anonymity, and in large part the public seems to agree. But the media,[1] acting in its capacity as the guardian of public interest, has decided that naming the victim is an issue up for grabs. And so we are having one of these endless, muddled, two-sides-to-every-question debates that, by ignoring as many facts as possible and by weighing all arguments equally, gives us that warm American feeling that truth must lie somewhere in the middle. Anna Quindlen, meet Alan Dershowitz. Thank you very much, but our time is just about up.

Sometimes, of course, the truth does lie somewhere in the middle. But not this time. There is no good reason to publish the names of rape complainants without their consent, and many compelling reasons not to. The arguments advanced in favor of publicity reveal fundamental misconceptions about both the nature of the media and the nature of rape.

Let's take a look at what proponents of naming are saying.

The media has a duty to report what it knows   Where have you been? The media keeps information secret all the time. Sometimes it does so on the ground of "taste," a waffle-word that means whatever an editorial board wants it to mean. Thus, we hear about (some of) the sexual high jinks of heterosexual celebrities but not about those of socially equivalent closet-dwellers, whose opposite-sex escorts are portrayed, with knowing untruthfulness, as genuine romantic interests. We are spared—or deprived of, depending on your point of view—the gruesome and salacious details of many murders. (Of all the New York dailies, only *Newsday* reported that notorious Wall Street wife-killer Joseph Pikul was wearing women's underwear when arrested. Not fit to print? I was *riveted*.) Sometimes it fudges the truth to protect third parties from embarrassment, which is why the obituaries would have us believe that eminent young bachelors are dying in large numbers only from pneumonia.

And of course sometimes it censors itself in "the national interest." The claim that the media constitutes a fourth estate, a permanent watchdog, if not outright adversary, of the government, has always been a self-serving myth. Watergate occurred almost twenty years ago and has functioned ever since as a kind of sentimental talisman. Like Charles Foster Kane's Rosebud sled. As we saw during the gulf war, the media can live, when it chooses, quite comfortably with government-imposed restrictions. Neither NBC nor *The New York Times*, so quick to supply their audiences with the inside scoop on the Palm Beach woman, felt any such urgency about Operation Desert Storm.

Anonymous charges are contrary to the American way   Anonymous charges are contrary to American *jurisprudence*. The Palm Beach woman has not made an anonymous accusation. Her name is known to the accused and his attorney, and if the case comes to trial, she will have to appear publicly in court, confront the defendant, give testimony and be cross-examined. But the media is not a court, as the many lawyers who have made this argument—most prominently Alan Dershowitz and Isabelle Pinzler of the American Civil Liberties Union's Women's Rights Project—ought to know.

The media itself argues in favor of anonymity when that serves its own purposes. Reporters go to jail rather than reveal their sources, even when secrecy means protecting a dangerous criminal, impeding the process of justice or denying a public figure the ability to confront his or her accusers. People wouldn't talk to reporters, the press claims, if their privacy couldn't be guaranteed —the same greater-social-good argument it finds unpersuasive when made about rape victims and their reluctance to talk, unprotected, to the police. The media's selective interest in concealment, moreover, undermines its vaunted mission on behalf of the public's right to know. Might not the identity of an anonymous informant (one of those "sources close to the White House" or "highly placed observers," for instance) help the public "make up its mind" about the reliability of the statements? I don't want to digress here into the complex issue of protecting sources, but there can be little question that the practice allows powerful people, in and out of government, to manipulate information for their own ends. Interestingly, the *Times* story on the Palm Beach woman concealed (thirteen times!) the names of those spreading malicious gossip about her, despite the *Times*'s own custom of not using anonymous pejoratives. That custom was resuscitated in time for the paper's circumspect profile of William Smith, which did not detail the accusations against him of prior acquaintance rapes that have been published by *The National Enquirer* and the gossip columnist Taki, and which referred only vaguely to "rumors" of "a pattern of aggressiveness toward women in private." (These, the *Times* said, it could not confirm—unlike the accuser's "little wild streak.")

How *did* the *Times* manage to amass such a wealth of dirt about the Palm Beach woman so quickly? It's hard to picture the reporter, distinguished China hand Fox Butterfield, peeking into the window of her house to see what books were on the toddler's shelf. Could some of his information or some of his leads have come, directly or circuitously, from the detectives hired by the Kennedy family to investigate the woman and her friends—detectives who, let's not forget, have been the subject of complaints of witness intimidation? The *Times* denies it, but rumors persist. One could argue that, in this particular case, *how* the *Times* got the story was indeed part of the story—perhaps the most important part.

That anonymity is held to be essential to the public good in a wide variety of cases but is damned as a form of censorship in the Palm Beach case shows that what the media is concerned with is not the free flow of information *or* the public good. What is at stake is the media's status, power and ability to define and control information in accordance with the views of those who run the media.

Consider, for example, the case of men convicted of soliciting prostitutes. Except for the occasional athlete, such men receive virtual anonymity in the press. Remember the flap in 1979 when Manhattan D.A. Robert Morgenthau released a list of recently convicted johns and the *Daily News* and two local radio stations went public with it? Universal outrage! Never mind that solicitation is a crime, that convictions are a matter of public record, that the wives and girlfriends of these men might find knowledge of such arrests extremely useful or that society has a declared interest in deterring prostitution. Alan Dershowitz, who in his syndicated column has defended both the content of the *Times* profile and its use of the woman's name, vigorously supported privacy for johns, and in fact made some of the same arguments that he now dismisses. Reporting, he said, was vindictive, subjected ordinary people to the glaring light of publicity for a peccadillo, could destroy the johns' marriages and reputations, and stigmatized otherwise decent people. Dershowitz did not, however, think privacy for johns meant privacy for prostitutes: They, he argued, have no reputation to lose. Although solicitation is a two-person crime, Dershowitz thinks the participants have unequal rights to privacy. With rape, he treats the rapist and his victim as *equally* placed with regard to privacy, even though rape is a one-person crime.

But here the woman's identity was already widely known   Well, I didn't know it. I did, however, know the name of the Central Park jogger—like virtually every other journalist in the country, the entire readership of *The Amsterdam News* (50,000) and the listening audience of WLIB-radio (45,000). Anna Quindlen, in her courageous column dissenting from the *Times*'s profile naming the Palm Beach woman, speculated that roughly equivalent large numbers of people knew the identity of the jogger as knew that of William Smith's alleged victim before NBC and the *Times* got into the act. Yet the media went to extraordinary lengths to protect the remaining shreds of the jogger's privacy—film clips were blipped, quotes censored.

What separates the jogger from the Palm Beach woman? You don't have to be the Rev. Al Sharpton to suspect that protecting the jogger's identity was more than a chivalrous gesture. Remember that she too was originally blamed for her assault: What was she doing in the park so late? Who did she think she was? It's all feminism's fault for deluding women into thinking that their safety could, or should, be everywhere guaranteed. But partly as a result of the severity of her injuries, the jogger quickly became the epitome of the innocent victim, the symbol, as Joan Didion pointed out in *The New York Review of Books*, for New York City itself (white, prosperous, plucky) endangered by the black underclass. A white Wellesley graduate with a Wall Street job attacked out of nowhere by a band of violent black strangers and, because of her comatose state, unable even to bring a rape complaint—this, to the media, is "real rape." The Palm Beach woman, on the other hand, is of working-class origins, a single mother, a frequenter of bars, who went voluntarily to her alleged attacker's house (as who, in our star-struck society, would not?). The jogger could have been the daughter of the men who kept her name out of the news. But William Smith could have been their son.

Rape is like other crimes and should be treated like other crimes. Isn't that what you feminists are always saying?   As the coverage of the Palm Beach case proves, rape isn't treated like other crimes. There is no other crime in which the character, behavior and past of the complainant are seen as central elements in determining whether a crime has occurred. There are lots of crimes that could not take place without carelessness, naïveté, ignorance or bad judgment on the part of the victims: mail fraud ("Make $100,000 at home in your spare time!"), confidence games and many violent crimes as well. But when my father was burglarized after forgetting to lock the cellar door, the police did not tell him he had been asking for it. And when an elderly lady (to cite Amy Pagnozzi's example in the *New York Post*) is defrauded of her life savings by a con artist, the con artist is just as much a thief as if he'd broken into his victim's safe deposit box. "The complainant showed incredibly bad judgment, Your Honor," is not a legal defense.

Why is rape different? Because lots of people, too often including the ones in the jury box, think women really do want to be forced into sex, or by acting or dressing or drinking in a certain way, give up the right to say no, or are the sort of people (i.e., not nuns) who gave up the right to say no to one man by saying yes to another, or are by nature scheming, irrational and crazy. They also think men cannot be expected to control themselves, are entitled to take by force what they cannot get by persuasion and are led on by women who, because they are scheming, irrational and crazy, change their minds in mid-sex. My files bulge with stories that show how widespread these beliefs are: The Wisconsin judge who put a child molester on probation because he felt the 3-year-old female victim had acted provocatively; the Florida jury that exonerated a rapist because his victim was wearing disco attire; and so on.

In a bizarre column defending Ted Kennedy's role on the night in question, William Safire took aim at the Palm Beach woman, who was "apparently" not "taught that drinking all night and going to a man's house at 3:30 A.M. places one in what used to be called an occasion of sin." (All her mother's fault, as usual.) The other woman present in the Kennedy mansion that night, a waitress named Michelle Cassone, has made herself a mini-celebrity by telling any reporter who will pay for her time that she too believes that women who drink and date, including herself, are "fair game."

By shifting the debate to the question of merely naming victims, the media pre-empts a discussion of the way it reports all crimes with a real or imaginary sexual component. But as the *Times* profile shows, naming cannot be divorced from blaming. When the victim is young and attractive (and in the tabloids *all* female victims are attractive), the sexual element in the crime is always made its central feature—even when, as in the case of Marla Hanson, the model who was slashed by hired thugs and whose character was savaged in *New York*, there is no sexual element. I mean no belittlement of rape to suggest it was one of the lesser outrages visited on the Central Park jogger. She was also beaten so furiously she lost 80 percent of her blood and suffered permanent physical, neurological and cognitive damage. Yet, paradoxically, it was the rape that seized the imagination of the media, and that became the focus of the crime both for her defenders and for those who defended her attackers.

Naming rape victims will remove the stigma against rape   Of all the arguments in favor of naming victims, this is the silliest, and the most insincere. Sure, NBC's Michael Gartner told *Newsweek*, the consequences will be "extraordinarily difficult for this generation, but it may perhaps help their daughters and granddaughters." How selfish of women to balk at offering themselves on the altar of little girls yet unborn! If Gartner wishes to make a better world for my descendants, he is amply well placed to get cracking. He could demand non-sensationalized reporting of sex crimes; he could hire more female reporters and producers; he could use NBC News to dispel false notions about rape—for example, the idea that "who the woman is, is material." Throughout the country there are dozens of speakouts against rape at which victims publicly tell of their experiences. Every year there are Take Back the Night marches in Manhattan. Where are the cameras and the reporters on these occasions? Adding misery to hundreds of thousands of women a year and—as just about every expert in the field believes—dramatically lowering the already abysmal incidence of rape reporting (one in ten) will not help my granddaughter; it will only make it more likely that her grandmother, her mother and she herself will be raped by men who have not been brought to justice.

This argument is, furthermore, based on a questionable assumption. Why would society blame rape victims less if it knew who they were? Perhaps its censure would simply be amplified. Instead of thinking, If ordinary, decent, conventional women get raped in large numbers it *can't* be their fault, people might well think, Goodness, there are a lot more women asking for it than we thought. After the invasion of Kuwait, in which scores of women were raped by Iraqi soldiers, there was no dispensation from the traditional harsh treatment of rape victims, some of whom, pregnant and in disgrace, had attempted suicide, gone into hiding or fled the country. One woman told *USA Today* that she wished she were dead. America is not Kuwait, but here, too, many believe that a woman can't be raped against her will and that damaged goods are damaged goods. (Curious how publicity is supposed to lessen the stigma against rape victims but only adds to the suffering of johns.)

One also has to wonder about the urgency with which Gartner and the other male proponents of the anti-stigma theory, with no history of public concern for women, declare themselves the best judge of women's interests and advocate a policy that they themselves will never have to bear the consequences of. Gartner cited, as did many others, the *Des Moines Register* profile of a named rape victim but neglected to mention that the victim, Nancy Ziegenmeyer, volunteered the use of her name, seven months after reporting the crime—in other words, after she had had a chance to come to terms with her experience and to inform her family and friends in a way she found suitable. (Ziegenmeyer, by the way, opposes involuntary naming.) Why is it that, where women are concerned, the difference between choice and coercion eludes so many? Rapists, too, persuade themselves that they know what women really want and need.

William Smith's name has been dragged through the mud. Why should his accuser be protected? Actually, William Smith has been portrayed rather favorably in the media. No anonymous pejoratives for him: He is "one of the least spoiled and least arrogant of the young Kennedys" (*Time*); an "unlikely villain" (*Newsweek*); "a man of gentleness and humor," "the un-Kennedy," "a good listener" (*The New York Times*); from a "wounded," "tragic" family (*passim*). Certainly he has been subjected to a great deal of unpleasant media attention, and even if he is eventually found innocent, some people will always suspect that he is guilty. But no one forced the media to sensationalize the story; that was a conscious editorial decision, not an act of God. Instead of heaping slurs on the Palm Beach woman in order to even things up, the media should be asking itself why it did not adopt a more circumspect attitude toward the case from the outset.

The tit-for-tat view of rape reporting appeals to many people because of its apparent impartiality. Feminists of the pure equal-treatment school like it because it looks gender neutral (as if rape were a gender-neutral crime). And nonfeminist men like it because, while looking gender neutral, it would, in practice, advantage men. "Should the press be in the business of protecting certain groups but not others—," wrote *Washington Post* columnist Richard Cohen, "alleged victims (females), but not the accused (males)? My answer is no." Cohen, like Michael Gartner, presents himself as having women's best interests at heart: "If rape's indelible stigma is ever to fade, the press has to stop being complicitous in perpetuating the sexist aura that surrounds it." Thus, by some mysterious alchemy, the media, which is perhaps the single biggest promoter of the sexist aura surrounding crimes of violence against women, can redeem itself by jettisoning the only policy it has that eases, rather than augments, the victim's anguish.

Behind the tit-for-tat argument lies a particular vision of rape in which the odds are even that the alleged victim is really the victimizer—a seductress, blackmailer, hysteric, who is bringing a false charge. That was the early word on the Palm Beach woman, and it's hard not to conclude that publicizing her identity was punitive: She's caused all this trouble, is visiting yet more "tragedy" on America's royal family, and had better be telling the truth. In fact, the appeal of naming the victim seems to rest not in the hope that it "may perhaps" someday make rape reporting less painful but in the certainty that right now it makes such reporting *more* painful, thereby inhibiting false accusations. Although studies have repeatedly shown that fabricated rape charges are extremely rare, recent years have seen a number of cases: Tawana Brawley, for example, and Cathleen Crowell Webb, who recanted her testimony after finding Jesus and then hugged her newly freed, no-longer-alleged-assailant on the *Donahue* show. A year ago a Nebraska woman who admitted filing a false charge was ordered by a judge to purchase newspaper ads and radio spots apologizing to the man she had accused. (She was also sentenced to six months in jail.) It is not unknown for other criminal charges to be fabricated, but has anyone ever been forced into a public apology in those cases? The tenor of the equal-publicity argument is captured perfectly by the (female) letter writer to *Time* who suggested that newspapers publish both names and both photos too. Why not bring back trial by ordeal and make the two of them grasp bars of red-hot iron?

✦

Fundamentally, the arguments about naming rape victims center around two contested areas: acquaintance rape and privacy. While the women's movement has had some success in expanding the definition of rape to include sexual violation by persons known to the victim—as I write, *The New York Times* is running an excellent series on such rape, containing interviews with women named or anonymous by their choice (atonement?)—there is also a lot of backlash.

The all-male editorial board of the *New York Post*, which rather ostentatiously refused to print the Palm Beach woman's name, has actually proposed a change in the law to distinguish between "real rape" (what the jogger suffered) and acquaintance rape, confusedly described as a "sexual encounter, forced or not," that "has been preceded by a series of consensual activities." *Forced or not?*

At the other end of the literary social scale, there's Camille (No Means Yes) Paglia, academia's answer to Phyllis Schlafly, repackaging hoary myths about rape as a bold dissent from feminist orthodoxy and "political correctness." Indeed, an attack on the concept of acquaintance rape figures prominently in the many diatribes against current intellectual trends on campus. It's as though the notion of consensual sex were some incomprehensible French literary theory that threatened the very foundations of Western Civ. And, come to think of it, maybe it does.

Finally, there is the issue of privacy. Supporters of naming like to say that anonymity implies that rape is something to be ashamed of. But must this be its meaning? It says a great deal about the impoverishment of privacy as a value in our time that many intelligent people can find no justification for it but shame, guilt, cowardice and prudishness. As the tabloidization of the media proceeds apace, as the boundaries between the public and the personal waver and fade away, good citizenship has come to require of more and more people that they put themselves forward, regardless of the cost, as exhibit A in a national civics lesson. In this sense, rape victims are in the same position as homosexuals threatened with "outing" for the good of other gays, or witnesses forced to give painful and embarrassing testimony in televised courtrooms so that the couch potatoes at home can appreciate the beauty of the legal process.

But there are lots of reasons a rape victim might not want her name in the paper that have nothing to do with shame. She might not want her mother to know, or her children, or her children's evil little classmates, or obscene phone callers, or other rapists. Every person reading this article probably has his or her secrets, things that aren't necessarily shameful (or things that are) but are liable to misconstructions, false sympathy and stupid questions from the tactless and ignorant. Things that are just plain nobody's business unless you want them to be.

Instead of denying privacy to rape victims, we should take a good hard look at our national passion for thrusting unwanted publicity on people who are not accused of wrong-doing but find themselves willy-nilly in the news. ("How did it *feel* to watch your child being torn to pieces by wild animals?" "It felt terrible, Maury, terrible.") I've argued here that society's attitudes toward rape justify privacy for rape complainants, and that indeed those attitudes lurk behind the arguments for publicity. But something else lurks there as well: a desensitization to the lurid and prurient way in which the media exploits the sufferings of any ordinary person touched by a noteworthy crime or tragedy. Most of the people who have spoken out against anonymity are journalists, celebrity lawyers, media executives and politicos—people who put themselves forward in the press and on television as a matter of course and who are used to taking their knocks as the price of national attention. It must be hard for such people to sympathize with someone who doesn't want to play the media game—especially if it's in a "good cause."

I'm not at all sure there is a good cause here. Titillation, not education, seems the likely reason for the glare on the Palm Beach case. But even if I'm unduly cynical and the media sincerely wishes to conduct a teach-in on rape, the interests of the public can be served without humiliating the complainant. Doctors educate one another with case histories in which patients are identified only by initials and in which other nonrelevant identifying details are changed. Lawyers file cases on behalf of Jane Doe and John Roe and expect the Supreme Court to "make up its mind" nonetheless.

If the media wants to educate the public about rape, it can do so without names. What the coverage of the Palm Beach case shows is that it needs to educate itself first.

Note

1. I use "media" in the singular (rather than the strictly grammatical plural) because I am talking about the communications industry as a social institution that, while hardly monolithic (as the debate over naming shows), transcends the different means—"media" plural—by which the news is conveyed.

POSTSCRIPT

Should the Names of Rape Victims Be Reported?

During the extensive televised coverage of the William Kennedy Smith trial, a dot was used to cover the woman's face. After the trial's conclusion, the woman herself went public and gave a handful of print and broadcast interviews.

With regard to rape and other sex crimes, the media must answer questions beyond whether or not to name the victims. Do common news practices, for example, yield biases that perpetuate myths and injustice? Helen Benedict, in *Virgin or Vamp: How the Press Covers Sex Crimes* (Oxford University Press, 1992), harshly critiques the manner in which newspapers have handled sex crimes.

Ethical guidelines require journalists to make specific choices as they balance freedom and responsibility in their day-to-day reporting. In making decisions, journalists are most often guided by the practices of the profession, their education, their on-the-job socialization, and the written codes of the organizations for which they work. Debates such as the one presented here are inevitable when traditional practices come under scrutiny.

The history of journalism has borne witness to many styles of approaching a story. In his book *Goodbye Gutenberg: The Newspaper Revolution of the 1980s* (Oxford University Press, 1980), Anthony Smith says, "Investigation has become the most highly praised and highly prized form of journalism, taking the place of opinion leadership, the historic purpose of the press." He suggests that the investigative reporter typically finds him- or herself in the position of both judge and jury—the authority to whom the public turns to get the whole story.

Ethical issues are not easily resolved: We should always struggle to discuss them, think about them, and let them guide our consciences. Only when we cease thinking about them is it too late to do anything about them.

There are many books on different styles of journalism, and the biographies of such people as Horace Greeley, William Randolph Hearst, Joseph Pulitzer, and even Rupert Murdoch show how each individual shaped a special time in journalism history. Other sources that describe journalistic themes and public reaction include Ben H. Bagdikian's *The Information Machines: Their Impact on Men and the Media* (Harper & Row, 1971); the Roper Organization's *Trends in Public Attitudes Toward Television and Other Media, 1969–1974* (Television Information Office, 1975); and John P. Robinson's *Daily News Habits of the American Public*, ANPA New Research Center Study No. 15 (September 22, 1978). Also, among the periodicals that cover journalistic styles and practices are *Columbia Journalism Review, Editor and Publisher, and American Society of Newspaper Editors (ASNE) Newsletter.*

Further readings on ethics and the media include Everette Dennis, Donald Gillmore, and Theodore Glasser, eds., *Media Freedom and Accountability* (Greenwood Press, 1989) and Bruce Swain, *Reporters' Ethics* (Iowa State University Press, 1978), which examine a number of issues that reporters must face. More recent books include *Ethical Issues in Journalism and the Media* edited by Andres Beasly and Ruth Chadwick (Routledge, Chapman & Hall, 1992) and *Good News: Social Ethics and the Press* by Clifford G. Christians, John P. Ferre, and Mark Fackler (Oxford University Press, 1993).

ISSUE 6

Should Tobacco Advertising Be Restricted?

YES: Joseph R. DiFranza et al., from "RJR Nabisco's Cartoon Camel Promotes Camel Cigarettes to Children," *Journal of the American Medical Association* (December 11, 1991)

NO: George J. Annas, from "Cowboys, Camels, and the First Amendment—The FDA's Restrictions on Tobacco Advertising," *The New England Journal of Medicine* (December 5, 1996)

ISSUE SUMMARY

YES: Doctor Joseph R. DiFranza and his colleagues report a national study that examines the possibility of children being tempted to smoke because of the tobacco industry's use of images that appeal to and are remembered by children. Because of the profound health risks, DiFranza et al. call for restrictions on tobacco ads.

NO: Attorney George J. Annas agrees that the tobacco industry has marketed products to children, but he maintains that efforts to restrict advertising are inappropriate, perhaps even illegal. He argues that some of the restrictions that have been placed on tobacco advertisements violate the First Amendment.

T he marketing of tobacco products has been controversial for some time, but discussions have become more heated in recent years as the extent of the tobacco industry's knowledge of nicotine as an addictive drug and the long-term effects of smoking on a person's health has come into question. Court cases and public scrutiny of the tobacco industry have led to legal sanctions and restrictions on the marketing of tobacco products, most specifically with regard to tobacco ads that appeal to children. Although tobacco industry officials state that they do not try to induce children to smoke, evidence indicates that advertising strategies do, indeed, target a potential audience of young people. Research shows that most long-term smokers begin smoking at the age of 12 or 13 and become hooked for life.

In the following selections, Joseph R. DiFranza and his colleagues raise ethical concerns about the effects of the tobacco industry's using appeals that may tempt children to start smoking, and they explain how advertising effectively reaches consumers. Arguing from a legal position, George J. Annas examines the Federal Drug Administration's current efforts to restrict advertising, particularly to the youth market. Citing several precedents regarding the restriction of advertising, he draws the conclusion that current governmental efforts to curb ads will remain ineffective and may violate the advertisers' First Amendment right to free speech.

This issue brings up several topics for discussion. One important question is whether or not children should be protected from activities and behaviors that may have long-term negative effects. Also, should advertisers exercise standards regarding the products they promote? Should the tobacco industry divulge all of their research regarding the hazards of smoking? Do ethical standards change when appeals are made to children as potential consumers?

Annas raises another important ethical dimension: How far can the First Amendment be used in defending free speech? Since the Bill of Rights was written—over 200 years ago—the type of "speech" that Americans engage in has changed dramatically. Does the right of free speech extend to advertising?

Advertising has traditionally been classified as "commercial" speech, which gives greater license to its use. Should commercial speech also be subject to a more stringent interpretation when the rights of children are involved? If so, should other products be given special consideration? At what point does censorship enter into the picture? Also, if tobacco advertising can be restricted, what about advertising for other potentially harmful products?

Issues involving tobacco advertising are timely and important. Many states have enacted laws to encourage counteradvertising to promote the health benefits of not smoking. The figures of Joe Camel and the Marlboro Man have been banned from all advertising. A range of data suggests that antismoking campaigns have different levels of effects. In many ways, antismoking campaigns use many of the same tools and techniques to get the public's attention as do the advertisers of tobacco products. What can be learned from these campaigns about strategies for instituting long-term behavior change?

Joseph R. DiFranza et al.  **YES**

RJR Nabisco's Cartoon Camel Promotes Camel Cigarettes to Children

With the number of US smokers declining by about 1 million each year, the tobacco industry's viability is critically dependent on its ability to recruit replacement smokers. Since children and teenagers constitute 90% of all new smokers, their importance to the industry is obvious. Many experts are convinced that the industry is actively promoting nicotine addiction among youth.

Spokespersons for the tobacco industry assert that they do not advertise to people under 21 years of age, the sole purpose of their advertising being to promote brand switching and brand loyalty among adult smokers. However, industry advertising expenditures cannot be economically justified on this basis alone. This study was therefore undertaken to determine the relative impact of tobacco advertising on children and adults.

There is abundant evidence that tobacco advertising influences children's images of smoking. In Britain, the proportion of children who gave "looks tough" as a reason for smoking declined after tough images were banned from cigarette advertisements. Children as young as the age of 6 years can reliably recall tobacco advertisements and match personality sketches with the brands using that imagery. In fact, cigarette advertising establishes such imagery among children who are cognitively too immature to understand the purpose of advertising. Subsequently, children who are most attuned to cigarette advertising have the most positive attitudes toward smoking, whether or not they already smoke. Children who are more aware of, or who approve of, cigarette advertisements are more likely to smoke, and those who do smoke buy the most heavily advertised brands.

Historically, one brand that children have not bought is Camel. In seven surveys, involving 3400 smokers in the seventh through 12th grades, conducted between 1976 and 1988 in Georgia, Louisiana, and Minnesota, Camel was given as the preferred brand by less than 0.5%. In 1986, Camels were most popular with smokers over the age of 65 years, of whom 4.4% chose Camels, and least popular among those 17 to 24 years of age, of whom only 2.7% preferred Camels.

In 1988, RJR Nabisco launched the "smooth character" advertising campaign, featuring Old Joe, a cartoon camel modeled after James Bond and Don

From Joseph R. DiFranza, John W. Richards, Jr., Paul M. Paulman, Nancy Wolf-Gillespie, Christopher Fletcher, Robert D. Jaffe, and David Murray, "RJR Nabisco's Cartoon Camel Promotes Camel Cigarettes to Children," *Journal of the American Medical Association*, vol. 266, no. 22 (December 11, 1991), pp. 3149–3152. Copyright © 1991 by The American Medical Association. Reprinted by permission. References omitted.

Johnson of "Miami Vice." Many industry analysts believe that the goal of this campaign is to reposition Camel to compete with Philip Morris' Marlboro brand for the illegal children's market segment. To determine the relative impact of Camel's Old Joe cartoon advertising on children and adults, we used four standard marketing measures.

1. Recognition. We compared the proportions of teenagers and adults aged 21 years and over who recognize Camel's Old Joe cartoon character.
2. Recall. We compared the ability of teenagers and adults to recall from a masked Old Joe advertisement the type of product being advertised and the brand name.
3. Appeal. We compared how interesting and appealing a series of Old Joe cartoon character advertisements were to teenagers and adults.
4. Brand preference. We compared brand preferences of teenaged smokers prior to the Old Joe cartoon character campaign with those 3 years into the campaign to determine if the campaign had been more effective with children or with adults, and to determine if Camel had been repositioned as a children's brand.

Methods

Subjects

Since adolescent brand preferences may vary from one geographic location to another, we selected children from Georgia, Massachusetts, Nebraska, New Mexico, and Washington, representing five regions. One school in each state was selected based on its administration's willingness to participate. Schools with a smoking prevention program focused on tobacco advertising were excluded.

A target of 60 students in each grade, 9 through 12, from each school was set. In large schools, classes were selected to obtain a sample representative of all levels of academic ability. Students were told that the study concerned advertising and were invited to participate anonymously.

Since adult brand preferences are available from national surveys, adult subjects were recruited only at the Massachusetts site. All drivers, regardless of age, who were renewing their licenses at the Registry of Motor Vehicles on the days of the study during the 1990–1991 school year were asked to participate. Since licenses must be renewed in person, this is a heterogeneous population.

Materials

Seven Camel Old Joe cartoon character advertisements were obtained from popular magazines during the 3 years prior to the study. One ad was masked to hide all clues (except Old Joe) as to the product and brand being advertised.

The survey instrument collected demographic information and information on past and present use of tobacco, including brand preference. Children were considered to be smokers if they had smoked one or more cigarettes during the previous week. Previously validated questions were used to determine children's intentions regarding smoking in the next month and year and their attitudes toward the advertised social benefits of smoking.

Subjects rated the ads as "cool or stupid" and "interesting or boring." Subjects were asked if they thought Old Joe was "cool" and if they would like to be friends with him. Each positive response to these four questions was scored as a one, a negative response as a zero. The "appeal score" was the arithmetic sum of the responses to these four questions, with the lowest possible score per respondent being a zero and the highest a four.

Procedure

Subjects were first shown the masked ad and asked if they had seen the Old Joe character before. They were then asked to identify the product being advertised and the brand name of the product. Subjects who could not answer these questions were required to respond "Don't know" so they would not be able to write in the correct answer when the unmasked advertisements were shown. The subjects were then shown, one at a time, the six unmasked advertisements and asked to rate how the advertisements and the Old Joe cartoon character appealed to them. Subjects then completed the remainder of the survey instrument.

Adolescent brand preference data from this study were compared with the data obtained by seven surveys completed prior to the kickoff of Camel's Old Joe cartoon character campaign early in 1988.

Tests of significance were made using the Two-tailed Student's t Test for continuous data and the X^2 and Fisher's Exact Test for discrete data. A P value of less than .05 was used to define statistical significance.

The study was conducted during the 1990–1991 school year.

Results

A total of 1060 students and 491 subjects from the Registry of Motor Vehicles were asked to participate. Usable surveys were obtained from 1055 students (99%) and 415 license renewal applicants (84.5%). Seventy drivers were under 21 years of age, leaving 345 adults aged 21 years or older. Students ranged in age from 12 to 19 years (mean, 15.99 years) and adults from 21 to 87 years (mean, 40.47 years). Females represented 51.0% of the students and 54.8% of the adults.

Children were much more likely than adults to recognize Camel's Old Joe cartoon character (97.7% vs 72.2%). It is not plausible that the children were simply saying they had seen Old Joe when they had not, since they also demonstrated a greater familiarity with the advertisement on the two objective measures.

When shown the masked advertisement, the children were much more successful than the adults in identifying the product being advertised (97.5% vs 67.0%) and the Camel brand name (93.6% vs 57.7%). Even when the analysis was limited to those subjects who were familiar with the Old Joe cartoon character, children were still more likely than adults to remember the product (98.6% vs 89.6%) and the Camel brand name (95.0% vs 79.1%). This confirms that Old Joe cartoon advertisements are more effective at communicating product and brand name information to children than to adults.

Because Massachusetts adults may not be representative of adults in the other four states where children were surveyed, the above analyses were repeated comparing only Massachusetts children and adults. In all cases the differences between adults and children were significant and of even greater magnitude, excluding the possibility that the above findings were due to a lighter level of advertising exposure in the Massachusetts area.

On all four measures, the children found the Camel cartoon advertisements more appealing than did the adults. Children were more likely to think the advertisements looked "cool" (58.0% vs 39.9%) or "interesting" (73.6% vs 55.1%). More of the children thought Old Joe was "cool" (43.0% vs 25.7%) and wanted to be friends with him (35.0% vs 14.4%).

The brand preference data revealed a dramatic reversal in the market segment pattern that existed prior to Camel's Old Joe cartoon character campaign. Camel was given as the preferred brand by 32.8% of children up to the age of 18 years who smoked, 23.1% of Massachusetts adult smokers aged 19 and 20 years, and 8.7% of those 21 years of age and over. The figures for the Massachusetts adults were significantly higher than the national market share for Camel, 4.4%, suggesting that Massachusetts adults may be more familiar with the Old Joe Camel campaign than adults in general. Camel cigarettes are now most popular with children and progressively less popular with older smokers.

About equal proportions of adults (28.2%) and children (29.0%) reported some current cigarette use, making it unlikely that this factor influenced any of the above findings. Although there were some statistically significant differences in the responses of children from different regions, these were not the focus of this study.

When compared with nonsmokers, children who were currently smoking gave higher approval ratings to the advertisements. Approving attitudes toward cigarette advertisements seem to precede actual smoking. Among the nonsmoking children, those who either were ambivalent about their future smoking intentions or expressed a definite intention to smoke were more approving of the advertisements than those children who intended not to smoke.

Children were more likely to smoke if they believed that smoking is pleasurable and that it makes a person more popular, all common themes in cigarette advertising. Among nonsmoking children, those who believed that smoking would make them more attractive were eight times more likely to express an intention to smoke in the next year.

Comment

Our data demonstrate that in just 3 years Camel's Old Joe cartoon character had an astounding influence on children's smoking behavior. The proportion of smokers under 18 years of age who choose Camels has risen from 0.5% to 32.8%. Given that children under 18 years account for 3.3% of all cigarette sales, and given a national market share of 4.4% for Camel, we compute that Camel's adult market share is actually 3.4%. Given a current average price of

153.3 cents per pack, the illegal sale of Camel cigarettes to children under 18 years of age is estimated to have risen from $6 million per year prior to the cartoon advertisements to $476 million per year now, accounting for one quarter of all Camel sales.

From both a legal and moral perspective, it is important to determine if the tobacco industry is actively promoting nicotine addiction among youngsters. However, from a public health perspective it is irrelevant whether the effects of tobacco advertising on children are intentional. If tobacco advertising is a proximate cause of disease, it must be addressed accordingly. In the following discussion we will examine the evidence produced by this study, the marketing practices of the tobacco industry as a whole as revealed in industry documents, and the marketing practices used by RJR Nabisco, in particular, to promote Camel cigarettes. The quotations cited below are from tobacco industry personnel and from documents obtained during litigation over Canada's ban of tobacco advertising.

Our data show that children are much more familiar with Camel's Old Joe cartoon character than are adults. This may be because children have more exposure to these advertisements, or because the advertisements are inherently more appealing to youngsters. The tobacco industry has long followed a policy of preferentially placing selected advertisements where children are most likely to see them. For example, print advertisements are placed in magazines "specifically designed to reach young people." Paid cigarette brand promotions appear in dozens of teen movies. Camels are featured in the Walt Disney movies *Who Framed Roger Rabbit?* and *Honey I Shrunk the Kids.*

The industry targets poster advertisements for "key youth locations/ meeting places in the proximity of theaters, records [sic] stores, video arcades, etc." It is common to see Old Joe poster advertisements in malls, an obvious gathering spot for young teens. Billboards, T-shirts, baseball caps, posters, candy cigarettes, and the sponsorship of televised sporting events and entertainment events such as the Camel "Mud and Monster" series are all used to promote Camels. All are effective marketing techniques for reaching children.

The fact that children are much more attracted to the themes used in the Old Joe cartoon character advertisements may also explain why they are more familiar with them. The themes used in tobacco advertising that is targeted at children are the result of extensive research on children conducted by the tobacco industry to "learn everything there was to learn about how smoking begins." Their research identifies the major psychological vulnerabilities of children, which can then be exploited by advertising to foster and maintain nicotine addiction.

The marketing plan for "Export A" cigarettes describes their "psychological benefits"; "Export smokers will be perceived as...characterized by their self-confidence, strength of character and individuality which makes them popular and admired by their peers."

Consider a child's vulnerability to peer pressure. According to one industry study, "The goading and taunting that exists at the age of 11 or 12 to get nonsmokers to start smoking is virtually gone from the peer group circles by 16 or 17." If peer influence is virtually gone by the age of 16 years, who is the intended target group for RJR-MacDonald's Tempo brand, described as individuals who are "[e]xtremely influenced by their peer group"? (RJR-Mac-Donald is a wholly owned subsidiary of RJR Nabisco.) The recommended strategy for promoting this brand is the "[m]ajor usage of imagery which portrays the positive social appeal of peer group acceptance." In one Camel advertisement, a cowboy (a Marlboro smoker?) is being denied admission to a party because "only smooth characters [ie, Camel smokers] need apply." It appears that Camel advertisements are also targeted at individuals who are influenced by their peer group.

Children use tobacco, quite simply, because they believe the benefits outweigh the risks. To the insecure child, the benefits are the "psychological benefits" promised in tobacco advertisements: confidence, an improved image, and popularity. Children who believe that smoking will make them more popular or more attractive are up to 4.7 times more likely to smoke.

Previous research makes it clear that children derive some of their positive images of smoking from advertising. Children who are aware of tobacco advertising, and those who approve of it, are also more likely to be smokers. Children's favorable attitudes toward smoking and advertising precede actual tobacco use and correlate with the child's intention to smoke, suggesting that the images children derive from advertising encourage them to smoke. Our data confirm these earlier findings. Among nonsmoking children, those who were more approving of the Old Joe advertisements were more likely either to be ambivalent about their smoking intentions or to express a definite intention to smoke. Nonsmoking children who believed that smoking would make them more popular were eight times more likely to express an intention to smoke in the future.

Since a child's intention to smoke is considered to be a good predictor of future smoking behavior, it seems reasonable to conclude that a belief in the psychological benefits of smoking, derived from advertising, precedes, and contributes to, the adoption of smoking.

There are other lines of evidence indicating that tobacco advertising increases the number of children who use tobacco. In countries where advertising has been totally banned or severely restricted, the percentage of young people who smoke has decreased more rapidly than in countries where tobacco promotion has been less restricted. After a 24-year decline in smokeless tobacco sales, an aggressive youth-oriented marketing campaign has been followed by what has been termed "an epidemic" of smokeless tobacco use among children, with the *average* age for new users being 10 years.

Many of the tobacco industry documents cited above provide abundant evidence that one purpose of tobacco advertising is to addict children to tobacco. In the words of one advertising consultant, "Where I worked we were trying very hard to influence kids who were 14 to start to smoke." Two marketing strategy documents for Export A also reveal that it is the youngest children they are after. "Whose behavior are we trying to affect?: new users." The goal is "[o]ptimizing product and user imagery of Export 'A' against young starter smokers." The average age for starter smokers is 13 years.

The industry also researches the best ways of keeping children from quitting once they are "hooked on smoking." The purpose of one tobacco industry study was to assess the feasibility of marketing low-tar brands to teens as an alternative to quitting. The study found that for boys, "[t]he single most commonly voiced reason for quitting among those who had done so... was sports." The tobacco industry's sponsorship of sporting events, such as the Camel Supercross motorcycle race, should be seen in relation to its need to discourage teenage boys from quitting. Similarly, its emphasis on slimness serves as a constant reinforcement of teenage girls' fears of gaining weight as a result of quitting.

Our study provides further evidence that tobacco advertising promotes and maintains nicotine addiction among children and adolescents. A total ban of tobacco advertising and promotions, as part of an effort to protect children from the dangers of tobacco, can be based on sound scientific reasoning.

NO

George J. Annas

Cowboys, Camels, and the First Amendment

The Marlboro Man and Joe Camel have become public health enemies number one and two, and removing their familiar faces from the gaze of young people has become a goal of President Bill Clinton and his health care officials.[1] The strategy of limiting the exposure of children to tobacco advertisements is based on the fact that almost all regular smokers begin smoking in their teens. This approach is politically possible because most Americans believe that tobacco companies should be prohibited from targeting children in their advertising.

Shortly before the 1996 Democratic National Convention, the President announced that he had approved regulations drafted by the Food and Drug Administration (FDA) to restrict the advertising of tobacco products to children. At the convention, Vice-President Al Gore told the delegates, "Until I draw my last breath, I will pour my heart and soul into the cause of protecting our children from the dangers of smoking."[2] In a press conference at the White House immediately following the announcement, Health and Human Services Secretary Donna Shalala said, "This is the most important public health initiative in a generation. It ranks with everything from polio to penicillin. I mean, this is huge in terms of its impact."[3]

No one doubts that a substantial reduction in the number of teenage smokers would mean a substantial reduction in the number of adult smokers when these teenagers grow up, and this reduction would have a major effect on health and longevity. Since almost 50 million Americans smoke, the result of reducing the number of young smokers substantially would indeed be "huge in terms of its impact." The real question is not whether the goal is appropriate but whether the means proposed to reach it are likely to be effective. In this regard, the FDA regulations may be unsuccessful for either of two related reasons: the implementation of the regulations may not reduce the number of teenagers who start smoking, or some of the regulations may be found to violate the First Amendment.

From George J. Annas, "Cowboys, Camels, and the First Amendment—The FDA's Restrictions on Tobacco Advertising," *The New England Journal of Medicine*, vol. 335, no. 23 (December 5, 1996), pp. 1779–1783. Copyright © 1996 by The Massachusetts Medical Society. Reprinted by permission.

The Regulations

The FDA's new regulations are designed to reduce the demand for tobacco products among teenagers, which is consistent with the goal of the Healthy People 2000 program to reduce by half (to 15 percent) the proportion of children who use tobacco products.[1,4] The FDA has somewhat modified the time line: the goal of its regulations is to cut underage smoking by half in seven years. Although the FDA has never before asserted jurisdiction over cigarettes or smokeless tobacco, the agency bases its claim to jurisdiction over these two types of products on its authority to regulate medical devices, defining cigarettes as a "drug-delivery device." Of course, this means that the FDA also defines nicotine as a drug. The regulations apply to sellers, distributors, and manufacturers of tobacco products. Sellers may not sell cigarettes or smokeless tobacco to anyone under the age of 18 years and must verify the age of purchasers under 26 by checking a form of identification bearing a photograph, in a "direct, face-to-face exchange." Exceptions are sales through mail orders and vending machines located in facilities that persons under the age of 18 years are not permitted to enter at any time. The distribution of free samples is also outlawed, as is the sale of cigarettes in packs of fewer than 20 (so-called kiddie packs). All cigarettes and smokeless tobacco products must bear the following statement: "Nicotine delivery devices for persons 18 or older."[1]

The most controversial portions of the regulations deal with advertising. One section outlaws all outdoor advertising within 1000 feet of public playgrounds and elementary and secondary schools. Advertising is restricted to "black text on a white background."[1] This restriction applies to all billboards but not to "adult publications." Such publications are defined by the regulations as "any newspaper, magazine, periodical or other publication...whose readers younger than 18 years of age constitute 15 percent or less of the total readership as measured by competent and reliable survey evidence; and that is read by fewer than 2 million persons younger than 18 years of age."[1] Tobacco manufacturers and distributors are prohibited from marketing any item (other than cigarettes or smokeless tobacco) that bears a brand name used for cigarettes or smokeless tobacco and are prohibited from offering any gift to a person purchasing cigarettes or smokeless tobacco products.[1] Finally, "no manufacturer, distributor, or retailer may sponsor or cause to be sponsored any athletic, musical, artistic, or other social or cultural event, or any entry or team in any event, [under] the brand name [of a tobacco product] (alone or in conjunction with any other words)."[1] Such events, may, however, be sponsored under the name of the corporation that manufactures the tobacco product, provided that the corporate name existed before 1995 and does not include a brand name.

The Legal Challenge

Tobacco companies have already filed suit to enjoin enforcement of the regulations. According to FDA Commissioner David Kessler, the FDA decided to assert its jurisdiction over cigarettes when the scientific community determined that the nicotine in tobacco products is addictive, and when the FDA concluded that the tobacco companies were probably manipulating the levels of nicotine to maintain their market of addicted users.[5] Under the legislation that gives the FDA its authority, a drug is any product "intended to affect the structure or any function of the body." The FDA contends that cigarettes and smokeless tobacco can be properly viewed as devices for delivering the drug nicotine, because they meet all three independent criteria for determining whether a product is a drug-delivery device: "a reasonable manufacturer would foresee that the product will be used for pharmacologic purposes [or] that consumers actually use it for such purposes [or] the manufacturer experts or designs the product to be used in such a manner."[5]

The primary argument of the tobacco companies is that Congress has consistently refused to give the FDA jurisdiction over tobacco products, and until now, the FDA itself has consistently said that it has no jurisdiction over such products. Moreover, the companies assert that if the FDA had jurisdiction over cigarettes as a drug or drug-delivery device, the FDA would have to ban them as not being "safe," which Congress has repeatedly refused to do or permit.

The second argument used by the tobacco companies, which is the focus of this article, is that the regulations violate the First Amendment of the U.S. Constitution by restricting the right to free speech in advertising. Congress could vote to give the FDA authority over tobacco but could not, of course, change the First Amendment.

The First Amendment and Advertising

The basic test used to determine whether the government can ban advertising is set out in the Supreme Court's 1980 opinion in *Central Hudson Gas & Electric Corporation v. Public Service Commission of New York.*[6] This case involved a regulation that prohibited electric utilities from advertising to promote the use of electricity. The court adopted a four-part test to determine whether this regulation was constitutional: (1) to be protected by the First Amendment, the advertising must concern a lawful activity and not be misleading, (2) for the ban to be valid, the state's interest in banning the advertising must be "substantial," (3) the ban must "directly advance" the state's interest, and (4) it must be no more extensive than necessary to further the state's interest.[6] In *Central Hudson*, the Supreme Court concluded that although the state had a substantial interest in energy conservation that was advanced by the ban on advertising, the ban nonetheless failed the fourth part of the test. The ban failed that part because it was overly broad, prohibiting the promotion of potentially energy saving electric services, and there was no proof that a more limited restriction of advertising could not have achieved the same goal. The court suggested, as an example, that a narrower regulation could have required "that the advertisements include information about the relative efficiency and expense of the offered services."

In 1986, in *Posadas de Puerto Rico Associates v. Tourism Company of Puerto Rico*, the Supreme Court upheld a ban on advertisements for casino gambling in Puerto Rico.[7] The court held that this ban met the four parts of the test in

Central Hudson. Adding that the government could ban advertising for any activity that it could outlaw, the court said it would be "a strange constitutional doctrine which would concede to the legislature the authority to totally ban a product or activity, but deny to the legislature the authority to forbid the stimulation of demand for the product or activity through advertising."[7] The court gave a number of other examples of "vice" products or activities, including cigarettes, alcohol beverages, and prostitution, which struck many in the public health community as warranting restricted advertising. Of course, fashions change, and many states now promote and advertise gambling, in the form of lotteries and casinos, as good for the financial health of the government. Nonetheless, in the wake of the May 1996 decision in *44 Liquormart v. Rhode Island*,[8] the most recent and comprehensive case involving free speech in advertising, it is unlikely that *Posadas* will continue to be invoked. Moreover, the four-part test in *Central Hudson* will be more strictly applied in the future.

The *44 Liquormart* Case

In *44 Liquormart v. Rhode Island*, a liquor retailer challenged the Rhode Island laws that banned all advertisements of retail liquor prices, except at the place of sale, and prohibited the media from publishing any such advertisements, even in other states. 44 Liquormart had published an advertisement identifying various brands of liquor that included the word "wow" in large letters next to pictures of vodka and rum bottles. An enforcement action against the company resulted in a $400 fine. After paying the fine, 44 Liquormart appealed, seeking a declaratory judgment that the two statutes and the implementing regulations promulgated under them violated the First Amendment.

The U.S. District Court declared the ban on price advertising unconstitutional because it did not "directly advance" the state's interest in reducing alcohol consumption and was "more extensive than necessary to serve that interest."[9] The Court of Appeals reversed the decision, finding "inherent merit" in the state's argument that competitive price advertising would lower prices and that lower prices would induce more sales.[10] In reviewing these decisions, the Supreme Court unanimously found that the state laws violated the First Amendment, but no rationale for this opinion gained more than four votes. Justice John Paul Stevens (who wrote the principal opinion) began his discussion by quoting from an earlier case involving advertisements of prices for prescription drugs:

> Advertising, however tasteless and excessive it sometimes may seem, is nonetheless dissemination of information as to who is producing and selling what product, for what reason, and at what price. So long as we preserve a predominantly free enterprise economy, the allocation of our resources in large measure will be made through numerous private economic decisions. It is a matter of public interest that those decisions, in the aggregate, be intelligent and well informed. To this end, the free flow of commercial information is indispensable.[8]

Justice Stevens went on to note that "complete speech bans, unlike content-neutral restrictions on the time, place, or manner of expression...are particularly dangerous because they all but foreclose alternative means of disseminating certain information."[8] Bans unrelated to consumer protection, Stevens noted further, should be treated with special skepticism when they "seek to keep people in the dark for what the government perceives to be their own good." Stevens moved on to apply *Central Hudson's* four-point test. He concluded that "there is no question that Rhode Island's price advertising ban constitutes a blanket prohibition against truthful, nonmisleading speech about a lawful product." Stevens also agreed that the state has a substantial interest in "promoting temperance."

But can the state meet part three of the test, by showing that the ban is effective in advancing this interest? Four justices defined the third part of the test as requiring the state to "bear the burden of showing not merely that its regulation will advance its interest but also that it will do so 'to a material degree.' "[8] This requirement is necessary because of the "drastic nature" of the state's ban: "the wholesale suppression of truthful, nonmisleading information." Justice Stevens concluded that Rhode Island did not meet this requirement and could not do so without "any findings of fact" or other evidence. The common-sense notion that prohibitions against price advertising will lead to higher prices and thus lower consumption (an assumption made in *Central Hudson*) was found insufficient to support a finding that the restriction of advertising would "significantly reduce market-wide consumption."[8] "Speculation or conjecture" does not suffice.[9]

As for the fourth part of the test, Justice Stevens concluded that the ban also failed because Rhode Island did not show that alternative forms of regulation that do not limit speech, such as limiting per capita purchases or using educational campaigns that address the problem of excessive drinking, could not be equally or more effective in reducing consumption. All nine members of the Supreme Court agreed with this conclusion. Finally, Justice Stevens (again on behalf of four justices) argued that in *Posadas* the court had wrongly concluded that since the state could ban a product or activity, it could ban advertising about it. He argued that the First Amendment was much stronger than that decision implied, noting "We think it quite clear that banning speech may sometimes prove far more intrusive than banning conduct," and thus it is not true that "the power to prohibit an activity is necessarily 'greater' than the power to suppress speech about it.... The text of the First Amendment makes clear that the Constitution presumes that attempts to regulate speech are more dangerous than attempts to regulate conduct."[8] Stevens also rejected the idea that "vice" activities have less protection from the First Amendment than other commercial activities, noting that the distinction would be "difficult, if not impossible, to define."

Free Speech and the FDA Regulations

Selling cigarettes and smokeless tobacco to persons under the age of 18 is illegal is all states, so advertising to this age group is not protected by the First

Amendment. Nor does outlawing vending machines that children have access to pose a problem with respect to the First Amendment. Because the FDA regulations are intended to apply only to children and do not foreclose alternative sources of information, it is impossible to predict with certainty how the Supreme Court will respond to a First Amendment challenge (assuming the court finds that the FDA has authority in this area). Nonetheless, the areas of primary concern can be identified.

Bans will be subject to a higher standard of review than restrictions. Forms of advertising that are banned include the distribution of products (other than cigarettes and smokeless tobacco) with the tobacco brand name or insignia on them, the placement of billboards within 1000 feet of playgrounds and elementary and secondary schools, and the use of brand names for sporting and cultural events. If the court adopts the strict version of the third part of the test in *Central Hudson,* the FDA will have to present evidence that these bans will reduce underage smoking to a material degree. Moreover, to meet the fourth part of the test, which the court unanimously found was not met in *44 Liquormart,* the FDA must also show that no other, less restrictive method, such as antismoking advertising or better enforcement of existing laws, would work as well. This will be difficult, especially since the FDA commissioner has already said he believes that antismoking advertising is effective in helping young people understand the risks of smoking and that, after the publication of its rules, the agency plans "to notify the major cigarette and smokeless-tobacco companies that it will begin discussing a requirement that they fund an education program in the mass media."[5] The court could decide that a nonspeech ban should have been tried first.

Restrictions on advertising may be easier to uphold, but even they are not obviously permissible. The tobacco companies spend $6 billion a year in advertising and promotion, about $700 million of which is spent on magazine advertisements.[11] The core antiadvertising regulation requires that advertisements on all billboards and in publications that do not qualify as adult publications be limited to black text on a white background.[1] This is a restriction (not a ban) and does not prohibit the inclusion of factual information (such as the price of liquor, which was at issue in 44 *Liquormart*). The rationale for these rules is that images in bright colors, of which Joe Camel is the primary example, entice children to start smoking or continue to smoke. Since no objective information is being banned or restricted, the court may find that such a restriction need meet only a common-sense test.[12] If, however, the court takes a more sophisticated view of advertising—which is largely focused on image rather than text—it may well hold that the same rules apply and that therefore the burden of proof is on the FDA to demonstrate that such a restriction would reduce underage smoking to a material degree. No study has yet been able to show evidence of this effect. Consistent with the view that "pop art" should be protected at least as much as text is the view that advertising images are forms designed to elicit certain responses and as such are entitled to at least as much protection from the First Amendment as objective information.

Drastic restrictions on advertising may also be ineffective or even counterproductive. In Britain, for example, where both Joe Camel and the Marlboro Man are outlawed and tobacco advertisers are prohibited from using anything that suggests health, fresh air, or beauty, creative advertisers have found other ways to promote tobacco products. Advertisements for Silk Cut cigarettes feature various images of silk being cut (e.g., scissors dancing a can-can in purple silk skirts and a rhinoceroses whose horn pierces a purple silk cap), and Marlboro advertisements portray bleak and forbidding western U.S. landscapes with the words, "Welcome to Marlboro Country." It has been suggested that by using such surreal images, tobacco advertisers may be appealing to fantasies of death and sexual violence that have a powerful (if unconscious) appeal to consumers.[13] Such imagery may actually have greater appeal for teenagers than Joe Camel. U.S. advertising agencies have already experimented with black-and-white, text-only advertisements. One agency proposed that the required phrase, "a nicotine-delivery device," can be used in conjunction with the phrase ".cyber cigarettes" on one line, under the phrase (in larger type) "pleasure.com" and a sideways smiling face, formed by a colon, a hyphen, and a closed parenthesis[:-)], to suggest that nicotine is a pleasure of the cyberspace age.[14]

The FDA knows it has a First Amendment problem here. In its comments accompanying the regulations, the agency argues that it is not required to "conclusively prove by rigorous empirical studies that advertising causes initial consumption of cigarettes and smokeless tobacco."[1] In fact, the FDA says it is impossible to prove this. Instead, the agency argues it need only demonstrate that there is "more than adequate evidence" that "tobacco advertising has an effect on young people's tobacco use behavior if it affects initiation, maintenance, or attempts at quitting."1 The FDA's position follows from the conclusion of the Institute of Medicine:

> Portraying a deadly addiction as a healthful and sensual experience tugs against the nation's efforts to promote a tobacco-free norm and to discourage tobacco use by children and youths. This warrants legislation restricting the features of advertising and promotion that make tobacco use attractive to youths. The question is not, "Are advertising and promotion the causes of youth initiation?" but rather, "Does the preponderance of evidence suggest that features of advertising and promotion tend to encourage youths to smoke?" The answer is yes and this is a sufficient basis for action, even in the absence of a precise and definitive causal chain.[11]

The Surgeon General has reached a similar conclusion:

> Cigarette advertising uses images rather than information to portray the attractiveness and function of smoking. Human models and cartoon characters in cigarette advertising convey independence, healthfulness, adventureseeking, and youthful activities—themes correlated with psychosocial factors that appeal to young people.[15]

The Supreme Court may make an exception for tobacco advertisements because of the clear health hazards and the use of restrictions instead of bans, but the extent of the restrictions will have to be justified. In this regard, the 15 percent young-readership rule for publications is difficult to justify as either not arbitrary or not more restrictive than necessary. The FDA admits, for example, that its rule would require the following magazines to use black-and-white, text-only advertisements: *Sports Illustrated* (18 percent of its readers are under the age of 18), *Car and Driver* (18 percent), *Motor Trend* (22 percent), *Road and Track* (21 percent), *Rolling Stone* (18 percent), *Vogue* (18 percent), *Mademoiselle* (20 percent), and *Glamour* (17 percent).[1] The FDA seems particularly offended by "a cardboard Joe Camel pop-out" holding concert tickets in the center of *Rolling Stone*.[5] (Some Americans might wish to censor the photograph of a naked Brooke Shields on the cover of the October 1996 issue as well, although that image is clearly protected by the First Amendment.) A 25 percent rule, for example, would exempt all these magazines.

The FDA justifies the 15 percent rule by arguing that young people between the ages of 5 and 17 years constitute approximately 15 percent of the U.S. population and that "if the percentage of young readers of a publication is greater than the percentage of young people in the general population, the publication can be viewed as having particular appeal to young readers."[1] A similar argument can, of course, be made with regard to sporting and cultural events—some of which may have very few young people in attendance.[15] On the other hand, the billboard restrictions seem to have a more solid justification.

Tobacco companies profit handsomely by selling products that cause serious health problems and contribute to the deaths of millions of Americans. There is also little doubt that nicotine is physically addictive and that it is in the interest of tobacco companies to get children addicted early, since very few people take up smoking after the age of 18 years. The FDA admits, however, that it cannot prove that cigarette advertising causes children to begin to smoke, and the agency has not tried alternative measures, such as strictly enforcing current laws that prohibit sales to minors and engaging in a broad-based educational campaign against smoking, to reduce the number of children who smoke. Until the FDA either proves that cigarette advertising causes children to start smoking or uses methods of discouraging smoking that stay clear of the First Amendment, bans and restrictions on advertising will raise enough problems with the First Amendment to ensure that they will be tied up in court for years. This does not mean, however, that no immediate legal actions can be taken against tobacco companies. In a future article, I will discuss current trends in litigation against these companies and assess the likely impact of antismoking lawsuits on the tobacco companies.

References

1. Food and Drug Administration, Department of Health and Human Services. Regulations restricting the sale and distribution of cigarettes and smokeless tobacco to protect children and adolescents. Fed Regist 1996;61 (168):44, 396-618.

2. Gore speech: "America is strong. Bill Clinton's leadership paying off." New York Times, August 29, 1996: B12.

3. Press Briefing by Secretary of HHS Donna Shalala, FDA Commissioner David Kessler, and Assistant Secretary Phil Lee. White House, Office of Press Secretary, August 23, 1996.

4. Trends in smoking initiation among adolescents and young adults—United States, 1980–1989. MMWR Morb Mortal Wkly Rep 1995;44:521–5.

5. Kessler DA, Witt AM, Barnett PS, et al. The Food and Drug Administration's regulation of tobacco products. N Engl J Med 1996; 335:988–94.

6. Central Hudson Gas & Electric Corp. v. Public Service Commission of New York, 447 U.S. 557 (1980).

7. Posadas du Puerto Rico Associates v. Tourism Company of Puerto Rico, 478 U.S. 328 (1986).

8. 44 Liquormart, Inc. v. Rhode Island, 116 S. Ct. 1495 (1996).

9. 44 Liquor Mart, Inc. v. Racine, 829 F. Supp. 543 (R.I. 1993).

10. 44 Liquor Mart, Inc. v. Rhode Island, 39 F. 3d 5 (1st Cir. 1994).

11. Committee on Preventing Nicotine Addiction in Children and Youths. Institute of Medicine. Growing up tobacco free: preventing nicotine addiction in children and youths. Washington, D.C.: National Academy Press, 1994:131.

12. Glantz L. Regulating tobacco advertising: the FDA regulations and the First Amendment. Am J Public Health (in press).

13. Parker-Pope T. Tough tobacco-ad rules light creative fires. Wall Street Journal. October 9, 1996:B1.

14. Brownlee L. How agency teams might cope with U.S. ad restraints. Wall Street Journal. October 9, 1996:B1.

15. Department of Health and Human Services. Preventing tobacco use among young people: a report of the Surgeon General. Washington, D.C.: Government Printing Office, 1994:195.

POSTSCRIPT

Should Tobacco Advertising Be Restricted?

While advertising has always had many critics, one of the most consistent arguments against advertising is that it teaches children that consumer culture is a natural way of life. It becomes increasingly more difficult to defend the practice of advertising when products that are deemed harmful to the public become the subject of the debate.

Over the years, liquor and tobacco have been the most problematic products. After liquor advertising was banned and tobacco companies were sued by consumers for causing health problems, the debate quickly focused on whether children were being introduced to smoking at an early age. One argument against tobacco advertising was that the companies doing it were in search of new consumers because their products caused earlier consumers to become ill and die.

The techniques used by tobacco advertisers were not in themselves unusual, but it did seem that coupons for sporting gear, CDs, and other premiums that appealed to the young really did focus on trying to get young people (8-13) to start smoking. In the first round of court battles on this topic, many tobacco advertisers promised to stop using promotional materials that could be interpreted as targeting young people.

There are several resources available with which to further examine this issue. The government report on the Hearing Before the Committee on Labor and Human Resources of the United States Senate, 101st Congress, Second Session, on the Tobacco Product Education and Health Protection Act of 1990 (Senate Hearing 101-707, available in most government repository libraries on microfiche) is one of the first fully documented sources on the tobacco industry's disclosure of addictive agents in cigarettes.

Simon Chapman has written a book on the techniques and marketing tools used for cigarette advertising entitled *Great Expectorations: Advertising and the Tobacco Industry* (Comedia Publishing Group, 1986). Bruce Maxwell and Michael Jacobson have examined appeals to certain target audiences in their book *Marketing Disease to Hispanics: The Selling of Alcohol, Tobacco, and Junk Foods* (Center for Science in the Public Interest, 1989).

There are a number of good, general references on advertising, including Roland Marchand's *Advertising the American Dream* (University of California Press, 1985) and Robert Goldman's *Reading Ads Socially* (Routledge, 1992).

Among books that are critical of the advertising industry in general, a recent text lends itself to the discussion of the potential for the regulation of the advertising industry: Matthew P. McAllister's *The Commercialization of American Culture: New Advertising, Control and Democracy* (Sage Publications, 1995).

Is Advertising Ethical?

YES: John E. Calfee, from "How Advertising Informs to Our Benefit," *Consumers' Research* (April 1998)

NO: Russ Baker, from "The Squeeze," *Columbia Journalism Review* (September/October 1997)

ISSUE SUMMARY

YES: John E. Calfee, a former U.S. Trade Commission economist, takes the position that advertising is very useful to people and that the information that advertising imparts helps consumers make better decisions. He maintains that the benefits of advertising far outweigh the negative criticisms.

NO: Author Russ Baker focuses on the way in which advertisers seek to control magazine content and, thus, go beyond persuasion and information into the realm of influencing the content of other media.

Professor Dallas Smythe first described commercial media as a system for delivering audiences to advertisers. This perception of the viewing public as a "market" for products as well as an audience for advertising—a main source of media revenue—reflects the economic orientation of the current media system in America. The unplanned side effects of advertising, however, concern many critics. For example, socialization into consumption, consumerism, materialism, and high expectations are one set of concerns. Many of these questions have often been asked: Is advertising deceptive? Does it create or perpetuate stereotypes? Does it create conformity? Does it create insecurity in order to sell goods? Does it cause people to buy things that they do not really need?

John E. Calfee addresses some of these questions in the following selection, but he focuses on how the information in ads benefits consumers. He takes the position that advertising is in the public interest and that even controversies about ads may be beneficial because they can result in competitive pricing for consumers. Citing some specific cases, he states that individuals can learn about important issues (such as health) through ads. He even considers what he calls "less bad" ads, which give consumers important negative information that can be useful to their well-being.

In the second selection, Russ Baker provides many different examples to show that the advertising industry has become too large and too powerful. He maintains that by giving corporations too much say in magazine and newspaper copy, advertisers may ultimately distort free press and free inquiry. When publishers bow to corporate control over material that is not advertising, they may lose focus and become mere extensions of advertisers.

These two selections raise concerns about the ethical nature of ads. Calfee focuses only on the good that advertising does, while Baker addresses the ethical nature of the control that corporations and advertising have in influencing media content. Both authors examine important concepts of fairness, honesty, and integrity in the world of advertising.

John E. Calfee  # YES

How Advertising Informs to Our Benefit

A great truth about advertising is that it is a tool for communicating information and shaping markets. It is one of the forces that compel sellers to cater to the desires of consumers. Almost everyone knows this because consumers use advertising every day, and they miss advertising when they cannot get it. This fact does not keep politicians and opinion leaders from routinely dismissing the value of advertising. But the truth is that people find advertising very useful indeed.

Of course, advertising primarily seeks to persuade and everyone knows this, too. The typical ad tries to induce a consumer to do one particular thing—usually, buy a product—instead of a thousand other things. There is nothing obscure about this purpose or what it means for buyers. Decades of data and centuries of intuition reveal that all consumers everywhere are deeply suspicious of what advertisers say and why they say it. This skepticism is in fact the driving force that makes advertising so effective. The persuasive purpose of advertising and the skepticism with which it is met are two sides of a single process. Persuasion and skepticism work in tandem so advertising can do its job in competitive markets. Hence, ads represent the seller's self interest, consumers know this, and sellers know that consumers know it.

By understanding this process more fully, we can sort out much of the popular confusion surrounding advertising and how it benefits consumers.

How useful is advertising? Just how useful is the connection between advertising and information? At first blush, the process sounds rather limited. Volvo ads tell consumers that Volvos have side-impact air bags, people learn a little about the importance of air bags, and Volvo sells a few more cars. This seems to help hardly anyone except Volvo and its customers.

But advertising does much more. It routinely provides immense amounts of information that benefits primarily parties other than the advertiser. This may sound odd, but it is a logical result of market forces and the nature of information itself.

The ability to use information to sell products is an incentive to create new information through research. Whether the topic is nutrition, safety, or more mundane matters like how to measure amplifier power, the necessity of achieving credibility with consumers and critics requires much of this research to be placed in the public domain, and that it rest upon some academic credentials. That kind of research typically produces results that apply to more than just the brands sold by the firm sponsoring the research. The lack of property rights to such "pure" information ensures that this extra information is available at no charge. Both consumers and competitors may borrow the new information for their own purposes.

Advertising also elicits additional information from other sources. Claims that are striking, original, forceful or even merely obnoxious will generate news stories about the claims, the controversies they cause, the reactions of competitors (A price war? A splurge of comparison ads?), the reactions of consumers and the remarks of governments and independent authorities.

Probably the most concrete, pervasive, and persistent example of competitive advertising that works for the public good is price advertising. Its effect is invariably to heighten competition and reduce prices, even the prices of firms that assiduously avoid mentioning prices in their own advertising.

There is another area where the public benefits of advertising are less obvious but equally important. The unremitting nature of consumer interest in health, and the eagerness of sellers to cater to consumer desires, guarantee that advertising related to health will provide a storehouse of telling observations on the ways in which the benefits of advertising extend beyond the interests of advertisers to include the interests of the public at large.

A cascade of information   Here is probably the best documented example of why advertising is necessary for consumer welfare. In the 1970s, public health experts described compelling evidence that people who eat more fiber are less likely to get cancer, especially cancer of the colon, which happens to be the second leading cause of deaths from cancer in the United States. By 1979, the U.S. Surgeon General was recommending that people eat more fiber in order to prevent cancer.

Consumers appeared to take little notice of these recommendations, however. The National Cancer Institute decided that more action was needed. NCI's cancer prevention division undertook to communicate the new information about fiber and cancer to the general public. Their goal was to change consumer diets and reduce the risk of cancer, but they had little hope of success given the tiny advertising budgets of federal agencies like NCI.

Their prospects unexpectedly brightened in 1984. NCI received a call from the Kellogg Corporation, whose All-Bran cereal held a commanding market share of the high-fiber segment. Kellogg proposed to use All-Bran advertising as a vehicle for NCI's public service messages. NCI thought that was an excellent idea. Soon, an agreement was reached in which NCI would review Kellogg's ads and labels for accuracy and value before Kellogg began running their fiber-cancer ads.

The new Kellogg All-Bran campaign opened in October 1984. A typical ad began with the headline, "At last some news about cancer you can live with." The ad continued: "The National Cancer Institute believes a high fiber, low fat diet may reduce your risk of some kinds of cancer. The National Cancer Institute reports some very good health news. There is growing evidence that may link a high fiber, low fat diet to lower incidence of some kinds of cancer. That's why one of their strongest recommendations is to eat high-fiber foods. If you compare, you'll find Kellogg's All-Bran has nine grams of fiber per serving. No other cereal has more. So start your day with a bowl of Kellogg's All-Bran or mix it with your regular cereal."

The campaign quickly achieved two things. One was to create a regulatory crisis between two agencies. The Food and Drug Administration thought that if a food was advertised as a way to prevent cancer, it was being marketed as a drug. Then the FDA's regulations for drug labeling would kick in. The food would be reclassified as a drug and would be removed from the market until the seller either stopped making the health claims or put the product through the clinical testing necessary to obtain formal approval as a drug.

But food advertising is regulated by the Federal Trade Commission, not the FDA. The FTC thought Kellogg's ads were non-deceptive and were therefore perfectly legal. In fact, it thought the ads should be encouraged. The Director of the FTC's Bureau of Consumer Protection declared that "the [Kellogg] ad has presented important public health recommendations in an accurate, useful, and substantiated way. It informs the members of the public that there is a body of data suggesting certain relationships between cancer and diet that they may find important." The FTC won this political battle, and the ads continued.

The second instant effect of the All-Bran campaign was to unleash a flood of health claims. Vegetable oil manufacturers advertised that cholesterol was associated with coronary heart disease, and that vegetable oil does not contain cholesterol. Margarine ads did the same, and added that vitamin A is essential for good vision. Ads for calcium products (such as certain antacids) provided vivid demonstrations of the effects of osteoporosis (which weakens bones in old age), and recounted the advice of experts to increase dietary calcium as a way to prevent osteoporosis. Kellogg's competitors joined in citing the National Cancer Institute dietary recommendations.

Nor did things stop there. In the face of consumer demand for better and fuller information, health claims quickly evolved from a blunt tool to a surprisingly refined mechanism. Cereals were advertised as high in fiber and low in sugar or fat or sodium. Ads for an upscale brand of bread noted: "Well, most high-fiber bran cereals may be high in fiber, but often only one kind: insoluble. It's this kind of fiber that helps promote regularity. But there's also a kind of fiber known as soluble, which most high-fiber bran cereals have in very small amounts, if at all. Yet diets high in this kind of fiber may actually lower your serum cholesterol, a risk factor for some heart diseases." Cereal boxes became convenient sources for a summary of what made for a good diet.

Increased independent information   The ads also brought powerful secondary effects. These may have been even more useful than the information that actually appeared in the ads themselves.

One effect was an increase in media coverage of diet and health. *Consumer Reports*, a venerable and hugely influential magazine that carries no advertising, revamped its reports on cereals to emphasize fiber and other ingredients (rather than testing the foods to see how well they did at providing a complete diet for laboratory rats). The health-claims phenomenon generated its own press coverage, with articles like "What Has All-Bran Wrought?" and "The Fiber Furor." These stories recounted the ads and scientific information that prompted the ads; and articles on food and health proliferated. Anyone who lived through these years in the United States can probably remember the unending media attention to health claims and to diet and health generally.

Much of the information on diet and health was new. This was no coincidence. Firms were sponsoring research on their products in the hope of finding results that could provide a basis for persuasive advertising claims. Oat bran manufacturers, for example, funded research on the impact of soluble fiber on blood cholesterol. When the results came out "wrong," as they did in a 1990 study published with great fanfare in *The New England Journal of Medicine*, the headline in *Advertising Age* was "Oat Bran Popularity Hitting the Skids," and it did indeed tumble. The manufacturers kept at the research, however, and eventually the best research supported the efficacy of oat bran in reducing cholesterol (even to the satisfaction of the FDA). Thus did pure advertising claims spill over to benefit the information environment at large.

The shift to higher fiber cereals encompassed brands that had never undertaken the effort necessary to construct believable ads about fiber and disease. Two consumer researchers at the FDA reviewed these data and concluded they were "consistent with the successful educational impact of the Kellogg diet and health campaign: consumers seemed to be making an apparently thoughtful discrimination between high- and low-fiber cereals," and that the increased market shares for high-fiber non-advertised products represented "the clearest evidence of a successful consumer education campaign."

Perhaps most dramatic were the changes in consumer awareness of diet and health. An FTC analysis of government surveys showed that when consumers were asked about how they could prevent cancer through their diet, the percentage who mentioned fiber increased from 4% before the 1979 Surgeon General's report to 8.5% in 1984 (after the report but before the All-Bran campaign) to 32% in 1986 after a year and a half or so of health claims (the figure in 1988 was 28%). By far the greatest increases in awareness were among women (who do most of the grocery shopping) and the less educated: up from 0% for women without a high school education in 1984 to 31% for the same group in 1986. For women with incomes of less than $15,000, the increase was from 6% to 28%.

The health-claims advertising phenomenon achieved what years of effort by government agencies had failed to achieve. With its mastery of the art of brevity, its ability to command attention, and its use of television, brand advertising touched precisely the people the public health community was most desperate to reach. The health claims expanded consumer information along a broad front. The benefits clearly extended far beyond the interests of the relatively few manufacturers who made vigorous use of health claims in advertising.

A pervasive phenomenon   Health claims for foods are only one example, however, of a pervasive phenomenon—the use of advertising to provide essential health information with benefits extending beyond the interests of the advertisers themselves.

Advertising for soap and detergents, for example, once improved private hygiene and therefore, public health (hygiene being one of the under-appreciated triumphs in twentieth century public health). Toothpaste advertising helped to do the same for teeth. When mass advertising for toothpaste and tooth powder began early in this century, tooth brushing was rare. It was common by the 1930s, after which toothpaste sales leveled off even though the advertising, of course, continued. When fluoride toothpastes became available, advertising generated interest in better teeth and professional dental care. Later, a "plaque reduction war" (which first involved mouthwashes, and later toothpastes) brought a new awareness of gum disease and how to prevent it. The financial gains to the toothpaste industry were surely dwarfed by the benefits to consumers in the form of fewer cavities and fewer lost teeth.

Health claims induced changes in foods, in non-foods such as toothpaste, in publications ranging from university health letters to mainstream newspapers and magazines, and of course, consumer knowledge of diet and health.

These rippling effects from health claims in ads demonstrated the most basic propositions in the economics of information. Useful information initially failed to reach people who needed it because information producers could not charge a price to cover the costs of creating and disseminating pure information. And this problem was alleviated by advertising, sometimes in a most vivid manner.

Other examples of spillover benefits from advertising are far more common than most people realize. Even the much-maligned promotion of expensive new drugs can bring profound health benefits to patients and families, far exceeding what is actually charged for the products themselves.

The market processes that produce these benefits bear all the classic features of competitive advertising. We are not analyzing public service announcements here, but old-fashioned profit-seeking brand advertising. Sellers focused on the information that favored their own products. They advertised it in ways that provided a close link with their own brand. It was a purely competitive enterprise, and the benefits to consumers arose from the imperatives of the competitive process.

One might see all this as simply an extended example of the economics of information and greed. And indeed it is, if by greed one means the effort to earn a profit by providing what people are willing to pay for, even if what they want most is information rather than a tangible product. The point is that there is overwhelming evidence that unregulated economic forces dictate that much useful information will be provided by brand advertising, and *only* by brand advertising.

Of course, there is much more to the story. There is the question of how competition does the good I have described without doing even more harm elsewhere. After all, firms want to tell people only what is good about their brands, and people often want to know what is wrong with the brands. It turns out that competition takes care of this problem, too.

Advertising and context   It is often said that most advertising does not contain very much information. In a way, this is true. Research on the contents of advertising typically finds just a few pieces of concrete information per ad. That's an average, of course. Some ads obviously contain a great deal of information. Still, a lot of ads are mainly images and pleasant talk, with little in the way of what most people would consider hard information. On the whole, information in advertising comes in tiny bits and pieces.

Cost is only one reason. To be sure, cramming more information into ads is expensive. But more to the point is the fact that advertising plays off the information available from outside sources. Hardly anything about advertising is more important than the interplay between what the ad contains and what surrounds it. Sometimes this interplay is a burden for the advertiser because it is beyond his control. But the interchange between advertising and environment is also an invaluable tool for sellers. Ads that work in collaboration with outside information can communicate far more than they ever could on their own.

The upshot is advertising's astonishing ability to communicate a great deal of information in a few words. Economy and vividness of expression almost always rely upon what is in the information environment. The famously concise "Think Small" and "Lemon" ads for the VW "Beetle" in the 1960s and 1970s were highly effective with buyers concerned about fuel economy, repair costs, and extravagant styling in American cars. This was a case where the less said, the better. The ads were more powerful when consumers were free to bring their own ideas about the issues to bear.

The same process is repeated over again for all sorts of products. Ads for computer modems once explained what they could be used for. Now a simple reference to the Internet is sufficient to conjure an elaborate mix of equipment and applications. These matters are better left vague so each potential customer can bring to the ad his own idea of what the Internet is really for.

Leaning on information from other sources is also a way to enhance credibility, without which advertising must fail. Much of the most important information in advertising—think of cholesterol and heart disease, antilock brakes and automobile safety—acquires its force from highly credible sources *other* than the advertiser. To build up this kind of credibility through material actually contained in ads would be cumbersome and inefficient. Far more effective, and far more economical, is the technique of making challenges, raising questions and otherwise making it perfectly clear to the audience that the seller invites comparisons and welcomes the tough questions. Hence the classic slogan, "If you can find a better whisky, buy it."

Finally, there is the most important point of all. Informational sparseness facilitates competition. It is easier to challenge a competitor through pungent slogans—"Where's the beef?", "Where's the big saving?"—than through a step-by-step recapitulation of what has gone on before. The bits-and-pieces approach makes for quick, unerring attacks and equally quick responses, all under the watchful eye of the consumer over whom the battle is being fought. This is an ideal recipe for competition.

It also brings the competitive market's fabled self-correcting forces into play. Sellers are less likely to stretch the truth, whether it involves prices or subtleties about safety and performance, when they know they may arouse a merciless response from injured competitors. That is one reason the FTC once worked to get comparative ads on television, and has sought for decades to dismantle government or voluntary bans on comparative ads.

'Less-bad' advertising   There is a troubling possibility, however. Is it not possible that in their selective and carefully calculated use of outside information, advertisers have the power to focus consumer attention exclusively on the positive, i.e., on what is good about the brand or even the entire product class? Won't automobile ads talk up style, comfort, and extra safety, while food ads do taste and convenience, cigarette ads do flavor and lifestyle, and airlines do comfort and frequency of departure, all the while leaving consumers to search through other sources to find all the things that are wrong with products?

In fact, this is not at all what happens. Here is why: Everything for sale has something wrong with it, if only the fact that you have to pay for it. Some products, of course, are notable for their faults. The most obvious examples involve tobacco and health, but there are also food and heart disease, drugs and side effects, vacations and bad weather, automobiles and accidents, airlines and delay, among others.

Products and their problems bring into play one of the most important ways in which the competitive market induces sellers to serve the interests of buyers. No matter what the product, there are usually a few brands that are "less bad" than the others. The natural impulse is to advertise that advantage— "less cholesterol," "less fat," "less dangerous," and so on. Such provocative claims tend to have an immediate impact. The targets often retaliate; maybe their brands are less bad in a different respect (less salt?). The ensuing struggle brings better information, more informed choices, and improved products.

Perhaps the most riveting episode of "less-bad" advertising ever seen occurred, amazingly enough, in the industry that most people assume is the master of avoiding saying anything bad about its product.

Less-bad cigarette ads   Cigarette advertising was once very different from what it is today. Cigarettes first became popular around the time of World War I, and they came to dominate the tobacco market in the 1920s. Steady and often dramatic sales increases continued into the 1950s, always with vigorous support from advertising. Tobacco advertising was duly celebrated as an outstanding example of the power and creativity of advertising. Yet amazingly, much of the advertising focused on what was wrong with smoking, rather than what people liked about smoking.

The very first ad for the very first mass-marketed American cigarette brand (Camel, the same brand recently under attack for its use of a cartoon character) said, "Camel Cigarettes will not sting the tongue and will not parch the throat." When Old Gold broke into the market in the mid-1920s, it did so with an ad campaign about coughs and throats and harsh cigarette smoke. It settled on the slogan, "Not a cough in a carload."

Competitors responded in kind. Soon, advertising left no doubt about what was wrong with smoking. Lucky Strike ads said, "No Throat Irritation—No Cough...we...removed...harmful corrosive acids," and later on, "Do you inhale? What's there to be afraid of?...famous purifying process removes certain impurities." Camel's famous tag line, "more doctors smoke Camels than any other brand," carried a punch precisely because many authorities thought smoking was unhealthy (cigarettes were called "coffin nails" back then), and smokers were eager for reassurance in the form of smoking by doctors themselves. This particular ad, which was based on surveys of physicians, ran in one form or another from 1933 to 1955. It achieved prominence partly because physicians practically never endorsed non-therapeutic products.

Things really got interesting in the early 1950s, when the first persuasive medical reports on smoking and lung cancer reached the public. These reports created a phenomenal stir among smokers and the public generally. People who do not understand how advertising works would probably assume that cigarette manufacturers used advertising to divert attention away from the cancer reports. In fact, they did the opposite.

Small brands could not resist the temptation to use advertising to scare smokers into switching brands. They inaugurated several spectacular years of "fear advertising" that sought to gain competitive advantage by exploiting smokers' new fear of cancer. Lorillard, the beleaguered seller of Old Gold, introduced Kent, a new filter brand supported by ad claims like these: "Sensitive smokers get real health protection with new Kent," "Do you love a good smoke but not what the smoke does to you?" and "Takes out more nicotine and tars than any other leading cigarette—*the difference in protection is priceless*," illustrated by television ads showing the black tar trapped by Kent's filters.

Other manufacturers came out with their own filter brands, and raised the stakes with claims like, "Nose, throat, and accessory organs not adversely affected by smoking Chesterfields. First such report ever published about any cigarette," "Takes the fear out of smoking," and "Stop worrying...Philip Morris and only Philip Morris is entirely free of irritation used [sic] in all other leading cigarettes."

These ads threatened to demolish the industry. Cigarette sales plummeted by 3% in 1953 and a remarkable 6% in 1954. Never again, not even in the face of the most impassioned anti-smoking publicity by the Surgeon General or the FDA, would cigarette consumption decline as rapidly as it did during these years of entirely market-driven anti-smoking ad claims by the cigarette industry itself.

Thus advertising traveled full circle. Devised to bolster brands, it denigrated the product so much that overall market demand actually declined. Everyone understood what was happening, but the fear ads continued because they helped the brands that used them. The new filter brands (all from smaller manufacturers) gained a foothold even as their ads amplified the medical reports on the dangers of smoking. It was only after the FTC stopped the fear ads in 1955 (on the grounds that the implied health claims had no proof) that sales resumed their customary annual increases.

Fear advertising has never quite left the tobacco market despite the regulatory straight jacket that governs cigarette advertising. In 1957, when leading cancer experts advised smokers to ingest less tar, the industry responded by cutting tar and citing tar content figures compiled by independent sources. A stunning "tar derby" reduced the tar and nicotine content of cigarettes by 40% in four years, a far more rapid decline than would be achieved by years of government urging in later decades. This episode, too, was halted by the FTC. In February 1960 the FTC engineered a "voluntary" ban on tar and nicotine claims.

Further episodes continue to this day. In 1993, for example, Liggett planned an advertising campaign to emphasize that its Chesterfield brand did not use the stems and less desirable parts of the tobacco plant. This continuing saga, extending through eight decades, is perhaps the best documented case of how "less-bad" advertising completely offsets any desires by sellers to accentuate the positive while ignoring the negative. *Consumer Reports* magazine's 1955 assessment of the new fear of smoking still rings true:

> "...companies themselves are largely to blame. Long before the current medical attacks, the companies were building up suspicion in the consumer by the discredited 'health claims' in their ads.... Such medicine-show claims may have given the smoker temporary confidence in one brand, but they also implied that cigarettes in general were distasteful, probably harmful, and certainly a 'problem.' When the scientists came along with their charges against cigarettes, the smoker was ready to accept them."

And that is how information works in competitive advertising.

Less-bad can be found wherever competitive advertising is allowed. I already described the health-claims-for-foods saga, which featured fat and cholesterol and the dangers of cancer and heart disease. Price advertising is another example. Prices are the most stubbornly negative product feature of all, because they represent the simple fact that the buyer must give up something else. There is no riper target for comparative advertising. When sellers advertise lower prices, competitors reduce their prices and advertise that, and soon a price war is in the works. This process so strongly favors consumers over the industry that one of the first things competitors do when they form a trade group is to propose an agreement to restrict or ban price advertising (if not ban all advertising). When that fails, they try to get advertising regulators to stop price ads, an attempt that unfortunately often succeeds.

Someone is always trying to scare customers into switching brands out of fear of the product itself. The usual effect is to impress upon consumers what they do not like about the product. In 1991, when Americans were worried about insurance companies going broke, a few insurance firms advertised that they were more solvent than their competitors. In May 1997, United Airlines began a new ad campaign that started out by reminding fliers of all the inconveniences that seem to crop up during air travel.

Health information is a fixture in "less-bad" advertising. Ads for sleeping aids sometimes focus on the issue of whether they are habit-forming. In March 1996, a medical journal reported that the pain reliever acetaminophen, the active ingredient in Tylenol, can cause liver damage in heavy drinkers. This fact immediately became the focus of ads for Advil, a competing product. A public debate ensued, conducted through advertising, talk shows, news reports and pronouncements from medical authorities. The result: consumers learned a lot more than they had known before about the fact that all drugs have side effects. The press noted that this dispute may have helped consumers, but it hurt the pain reliever industry. Similar examples abound.

We have, then, a general rule: sellers will use comparative advertising when permitted to do so, even if it means spreading bad information about a product instead of favorable information. The mechanism usually takes the form of less-bad claims. One can hardly imagine a strategy more likely to give consumers the upper hand in the give and take of the marketplace. Less-bad claims are a primary means by which advertising serves markets and consumers rather than sellers. They completely refute the naive idea that competitive advertising will emphasize only the sellers' virtues while obscuring their problems.

NO

The Squeeze

> In an effort to avoid potential conflicts, it is required that Chrysler Corpo-
> ration be alerted in advance of any and all editorial content that encom-
> passes sexual, political, social issues or any editorial that might be
> construed as provocative or offensive. Each and every issue that carries
> Chrysler advertising requires a written summary outlining major theme/
> articles appearing in upcoming issues. These summaries are to be for-
> warded to PentaCom prior to closing in order to give Chrysler ample time
> to review and reschedule if desired.... As acknowledgment of this letter we
> ask that you or a representative from the publication sign below and
> return to us no later than February 15.
>
> —from a letter sent by Chrysler's ad agency, PentaCom, a division of
> BBDO North America, to at least fifty magazines

Is there any doubt that advertisers mumble and sometimes roar about reporting that can hurt them? That the auto giants don't like pieces that, say, point
to auto safety problems? Or that Big Tobacco hates to see its glamorous, cheer-
ful ads juxtaposed with articles mentioning their best customers' grim way of
death? When advertisers disapprove of an editorial climate, they can—and
sometimes do—take a hike.

But for Chrysler to push beyond its parochial economic interests—by
demanding summaries of upcoming articles while implicitly asking editors to
think twice about running "sexual, political, social issues"—crosses a sharply
defined line. "This is new," says Milton Glaser, the *New York* magazine
cofounder and celebrated designer. "It will have a devastating effect on the
idea of a free press and of free inquiry."

Glaser is among those in the press who are vocally urging editors and
publishers to resist. "If Chrysler achieves this," he says, "there is no reason to
hope that other advertisers won't ask for the same privilege. You will have
thirty or forty advertisers checking through the pages. They will send notes to
publishers. I don't see how any good citizen doesn't rise to this occasion and
say this development is un-American and a threat to freedom."

Hyperbole? Maybe not. Just about any editor will tell you: the ad/edit
chemistry is changing for the worse. Corporations and their ad agencies have
clearly turned up the heat on editors and publishers, and some magazines are

From Russ Baker, "The Squeeze," *Columbia Journalism Review* (September/October 1997). Copyright © 1997 by Russ Baker. Reprinted by permission of *Columbia Journalism Review*.

capitulating, unwilling to risk even a single ad. This makes it tougher for those who do fight to maintain the ad-edit wall and put the interests of their readers first. Consider:

- A major advertiser recently approached all three newsweeklies—*Time, Newsweek*, and *U.S. News*—and told them it would be closely monitoring editorial content. So says a high newsweekly executive who was given the warning (but who would not name the advertiser). For the next quarter, the advertiser warned the magazines' publishing sides it would keep track of how the company's industry was portrayed in news columns. At the end of that period, the advertiser would select one—and only one—of the magazines and award all of its newsweekly advertising to it.
- An auto manufacturer—not Chrysler—decided recently to play art director at a major glossy, and the magazine played along. After the magazine scheduled a photo spread that would feature more bare skin than usual, it engaged in a back-and-forth negotiation with that advertiser over exactly how much skin would be shown. CJR's source says the feature had nothing to do with the advertiser's product.
- Kimberly-Clark makes Huggies diapers and advertises them in a number of magazines, including *Child, American Baby, Parenting, Parents, Baby Talk*, and *Sesame Street Parents*. Kimberly-Clark demands—in writing in its ad insertion orders—that these ads be placed only "adjacent to black and white happy baby editorial," which would definitely not include stories about, say Sudden Infant Death Syndrome or Down's syndrome. "Sometimes we have to create editorial that is satisfactory to them," a top editor says. That, of course, means something else is likely lost, and the mix of the magazine is altered.
- Former Cosmo Girl Helen Gurley Brown disclosed to *Newsday* that a Detroit auto company representative (the paper didn't say which company) asked for—and received—an advance copy of the table of contents for her bon voyage issue, then threatened to pull a whole series of ads unless the representative was permitted to see an article titled "How to Be Very Good in Bed." Result? "A senior editor and the client's ad agency pulled a few things from the piece," a dispirited Brown recalled, "but enough was left" to salvage the article.

Cosmo is hardly the only magazine that has bowed to the new winds. Kurt Andersen, the former *New York* magazine editor—whose 1996 firing by parent company, K-III was widely perceived to be a result of stories that angered associates of K-III's founder, Henry R. Kravis—nonetheless says that he always kept advertisers' sensibilities in mind when editing the magazine. "Because I worked closely and happily with the publisher at *New York*, I was aware who the big advertisers were," he says. "My antennae were turned on, and I read copy thinking, 'Is this going to cause Calvin Klein or Bergdorf big problems?' "

National Review put a reverse spin on the early-warning-for-advertisers discussion recently, as *The Washington Post* revealed, when its advertising director sent an advance copy of a piece about utilities deregulation to an energy supplier mentioned in the story, as a way of luring it into buying space.

And Chrysler is hardly the only company that is aggressive about its editorial environment. Manufacturers of packaged goods, from toothpaste to toilet paper, aggressively declare their love for plain-vanilla. Colgate-Palmolive, for example, won't allow ads in a "media context" containing "offensive" sexual content or material it deems "antisocial or in bad taste"—which it leaves undefined in its policy statement sent to magazines. In the statement, the company says that it "charges its advertising agencies and their media buying services with the responsibility of pre-screening any questionable media content or context."

Procter & Gamble, the second-largest advertising spender last year ($1.5 billion), has a reputation as being very touchy. Two publishing executives told Gloria Steinem, for her book *Moving Beyond Words*, that the company doesn't want its ads near anything about "gun control, abortion, the occult, cults, or the disparagement of religion." Even nonsensational and sober pieces dealing with sex and drugs are no-go.

Kmart and Revlon are among those that editors list as the most demanding. "IBM is a stickler—they don't like any kind of controversial articles," says Robyn Mathews, formerly of *Entertainment Weekly* and now *Time's* chief of makeup. She negotiates with advertisers about placement, making sure that their products are not put near material that is directly critical. AT&T, Mathews says, is another company that prefers a soft climate. She says she often has to tell advertisers, "We're a *news* magazine. I try to get them to be realistic."

Still, the auto companies apparently lead the pack in complaining about content. And the automakers are so powerful—the Big Three pumped $3.6 billion into U.S. advertising last year—that most major magazines have sales offices in Detroit.

After *The New Yorker*, in its issue of June 12, 1995, ran a Talk of the Town piece that quoted some violent, misogynist rap and rock lyrics—along with illustrative four-letter words—opposite a Mercury ad, Ford Motor Company withdrew from the magazine, reportedly for six months. The author, Ken Auletta, learned about it only this year. "I actually admire *The New Yorker* for not telling me about it," he says. Yet afterwards, according to *The Wall Street Journal*, the magazine quietly adopted a system of warning about fifty companies on a "sensitive advertiser list" whenever potentially offensive articles are scheduled.

◦◉◦

It is the Chrysler case, though, that has made the drums beat, partly because of Chrysler's heft and partly because the revelation about the automaker's practice came neatly packaged with a crystalline example of just what that practice can do to a magazine.

In the advertising jungle Chrysler is an 800-pound gorilla—the nation's fourth-largest advertiser and fifth-largest magazine advertiser (it spent some

$270 million at more than 100 magazines last year, behind General Motors, Philip Morris, Procter & Gamble, and Ford). Where it leads, other advertisers may be tempted to follow.

The automaker's letter was mailed to magazines in January 1996, but did not come to light until G. Bruce Knecht of *The Wall Street Journal* unearthed it this April in the aftermath of an incident at *Esquire*. The *Journal* reported that *Esquire* had planned a sixteen-page layout for a 20,000-word fiction piece by accomplished author David Leavitt. Already in page proofs and scheduled for the April '97 issue, it was to be one of the longest short stories *Esquire* had ever run, and it had a gay theme and some raw language. But publisher Valerie Salembier, the *Journal* reported, met with then editor-in-chief Edward Kosner and other editors and voiced her concerns: she would have to notify Chrysler about the story, and she expected that when she did so Chrysler would pull its ads. The automaker had bought four pages, the *Journal* noted—just enough to enable the troubled magazine to show its first year-to-year ad-page improvement since the previous September.

⌘

Kosner then killed the piece, maintaining he had editorial reasons for doing so. Will Blythe, the magazine's literary editor, promptly quit. "I simply can't stomach the David Leavitt story being pulled," he said in his letter of resignation. "That act signals a terrible narrowing of the field available to strong, adventuresome, risk-taking work, fiction and nonfiction alike. I know that editorial and advertising staffs have battled—sometimes affably, other times savagely—for years to define and protect their respective turfs. But events of the last few weeks signal that the balance is out of whack now—that, in effect, we're taking marching orders (albeit, indirectly) from advertisers."

The Chrysler letter's public exposure is a rough reminder that sometimes the biggest problems are the most clichéd: as financial concerns become increasingly paramount it gets harder to assert editorial independence.

After the article about *Esquire* in the *Journal*, the American Society of Magazine Editors—the top cops of magazine standards, with 867 members from 370 magazines—issued a statement expressing "deep concern" over the trend to give "advertisers advance notice about upcoming stories." Some advertisers, ASME said, "may mistake an early warning as an open invitation to pressure the publisher to alter, or even kill, the article in question. We believe publishers should—and will—refuse to bow to such pressure. Furthermore, we believe editors should—and will—follow ASME's explicit principle of editorial independence, which at its core states: 'The chief editor of any magazine must have final authority over the editorial content, words, and pictures that appear in the publication.' "

On July 24, after meeting with the ASME board, the marketing committee of the Magazine Publishers of America—which has 200 member companies that print more than 800 magazines—gathered to discuss this issue, and agreed to work against prior review of story lists or summaries by advertisers. "The magazine industry is united in this," says ASME's president, Frank Lalli, managing editor of *Money*. "There is no debate within the industry."

How many magazines will reject Chrysler's new road map? Unclear. Lalli says he has not found any publisher or editor who signed and returned the Chrysler letter as demanded. "I've talked to a lot of publishers," he says, "and I don't know of any who will bow to it. The great weight of opinion among publishers and editors is that this is a road we can't go down."

Yet Mike Aberlich, Chrysler's manager of consumer media relations, claims that "Every single one has been signed." Aberlich says that in some cases, individual magazines agreed; in others a parent company signed for all its publications.

CJR did turn up several magazines, mostly in jam-packed demographic niches, whose executives concede they have no problem with the Chrysler letter. One is *Maxim*, a new book aimed at the young-men-with-bucks market put out by the British-based Dennis Publishing. "We're going to play ball," says *Maxim*'s sales manager, Jamie Hooper. The startup, which launched earlier this year, signed and returned the Chrysler letter. "We're complying. We definitely have to."

At *P.O.V.*, a two-and-a-half-year-old magazine backed largely by Freedom Communications, Inc. (owners of *The Orange County Register*) and aimed at a similar audience, publisher Drew Massey says he remembers a Chrysler letter, can't remember signing it, but would have no problem providing advance notice. "We do provide PentaCom with a courtesy call, but we absolutely never change an article." Chrysler, alerted to *P.O.V.*'s August "Vice" issue, decided to stay in. Massey argues that the real issue is not about edgy magazines like *P.O.V.*, but about larger and tamer magazines that feel constrained by advertisers from being adventurous.

Hachette Filipacchi, French-owned publisher of twenty-nine U.S. titles, from *Elle* to *George*, offered Chrysler's plan for a safe editorial environment partial support. Says John Fennell, chief operating officer: "We did respond to the letter, saying we were aware of their concern about controversial material and that we would continue—as we have in the past—to monitor it very closely and to make sure that their advertising did not appear near controversial things. However, we refused to turn over or show or discuss the editorial direction of articles with them."

⌥

It has long been a widely accepted practice in the magazine industry to provide "heads-up"—warnings to advertisers about copy that might embarrass them—say, to the friendly skies folks about a scheduled article on an Everglades plane crash, or to Johnnie Walker about a feature on the death of a hard-drinking rock star. In some instances, advertisers are simply moved as far as possible from the potentially disconcerting material. In others, they are offered a chance to opt out of the issue altogether, ideally to be rescheduled for a later edition.

In the 1980s, Japanese car makers got bent out of shape about news articles they saw as Japan-bashing, says *Business Week*'s editor-in-chief, Stephen B. Shepard, a past ASME president. Anything about closed markets or the trade imbalance might be seen as requiring a polite switch to the next issue.

Chrysler, some magazine people argue, is simply formalizing this long-standing advertiser policy of getting magazine executives to consider their special sensitivities while assembling each issue. But Chrysler's letter clearly went beyond that. PentaCom's president and c.e.o., David Martin, was surprisingly blunt when he explained to *The Wall Street Journal* the automaker's rationale: "Our whole contention is that when you are looking at a product that costs $22,000, you want the product to be surrounded by positive things. There's nothing positive about an article about child pornography."

Chrysler spokesman Aberlich insists the brouhaha is no big deal: "Of the thousands of magazine ads we've placed in a year, we've moved an ad out of one issue into the next issue about ten times a year. We haven't stopped dealing with any magazine." He compares placing an ad to buying a house: "You decide the neighborhood you want to be in." That interesting metaphor, owning valuable real estate, leads to other metaphors—advertisers as editorial NIMBYs (Not In My Back Yard) trying to keep out anybody or anything they don't want around.

As for the current contretemps, Aberlich says it's nothing new, that Chrysler has been requesting advance notice since 1993. "We sent an initial letter to magazines asking them to notify us of upcoming controversial stuff—graphic sex, graphic violence, glorification of drug use." But what about the updated and especially chilling language in the 1996 letter, the one asking to look over editors' shoulders at future articles, particularly *political, social* material and *editorial that might be construed as provocative?* Aberlich declines to discuss it, bristling, "We didn't give you that letter."

⋅◈⋅

How did we get to the point where a sophisticated advertiser dared send such a letter? In these corporate-friendly times, the sweep and powers of advertisers are frenetically expanded everywhere. Formerly pure public television and public radio now run almost-ads. Schools bombard children with cereal commercials in return for the monitors on which the ads appear. Parks blossom with yogurt and sneaker-sponsored events.

Meanwhile, a growing number of publications compete for ad dollars—not just against each other but against the rest of the media, including news media. Those ads are bought by ever-larger companies and placed by a shrinking number of merger-minded ad agencies.

Are magazines in a position where they cannot afford to alienate any advertiser? No, as a group, magazines have done very well lately, thank you. With only minor dips, ad pages and total advertising dollars have grown impressively for a number of years. General-interest magazines sold $5.3 billion worth of advertising in 1987. By 1996 that figure had more than doubled, to $11.2 billion.

Prosperity can enhance independence. The magazines least susceptible to advertiser pressures are often the most ad-laden books. Under its new editor-in-chief, David Granger, the anemic *Esquire* seems to be getting a lift, but GQ had supplanted it in circulation and in the serious-article business, earning many National Magazine Awards. This is in part because it first used advertiser-safe service pieces and celebrity profiles to build ad pages, then had more space to experiment and take risks.

Catherine Viscardi Johnston, senior vice president for group sales and marketing at *GQ*'s parent company, the financially flush Condé Nast, says that in her career as a publisher she rarely was asked to reschedule an ad—perhaps once a year. Meddling has not been a problem, she says: "Never was a page lost, or an account lost. Never, never did an advertiser try to have a story changed or eliminated."

At the other extreme, *Maxim*, which signed the Chrysler letter, does face grueling ad-buck competition. The number of new magazine startups in 1997 may well exceed 1,000, says Samir Husni, the University of Mississippi journalism professor who tracks launches. And *Maxim*'s demographic—21- to 24-year-old males—is jam-packed with titles.

This is not to say that prosperity and virtue go hand in hand. Witness Condé Nast's ad-fat *Architectural Digest*, where editor-in-chief Paige Rense freely admits that only advertisers are mentioned in picture captions. The range of standards among magazines is wide.

And that range can be confusing. "Some advertisers don't understand on a fundamental level the difference between magazines that have a serious set of rules and codes and serious ambitions, and those that don't," says Kurt Andersen. "The same guy at Chrysler is buying ads in *YM* and *The New Yorker.*"

If it is up to editors to draw the line, they will have to buck the industry's impulse to draw them even deeper into their magazines' business issues. Hachette Filipacchi's U.S. president and c.e.o., David Pecker, is one who would lower the traditional ad-edit wall. "I actually know editors who met with advertisers and lived to tell about it," he said in a recent speech. Some editors at Hachette—and other news organizations—share in increased profits at their magazines. Thus, to offend an advertiser, it might be argued, would be like volunteering for a pay cut. So be it; intrepid editors must be prepared to take that.

◦❀◦

Ironically, in fretting over public sensibilities, advertisers may not be catering to their consumers at all. In a recent study of public opinion regarding television—which is even more dogged by content controversies than magazines—87 percent of respondents said it is appropriate for network programs to deal with sensitive issues and social problems. (The poll was done for ABC, NBC, and CBS by the Roper Starch Worldwide market research firm.) Asked who should "have the most to say about what people see and hear on television," 82 percent replied that it ought to be "individual viewers themselves, by deciding what they will and will not watch." Almost no one—just 9 percent—thought advertisers should be able to shape content by granting or withholding sponsorship. Even

PentaCom admitted to the *Journal* that its own focus groups show that Chrysler owners are not bothered by Chrysler ads near controversial articles.

So what's eating these folks? Partially, it may be a cultural phenomenon. Ever since magazines began to attract mass audiences and subsidize subscription rates with advertising, many magazines have chased readers—just as networks chase viewers now—with evermore salacious fare. But corporate executives have often remained among the most conservative of Americans. Nowhere is this truer than in heartland locations like Chrysler's Detroit or Procter & Gamble's Cincinnati.

Ad executives say one factor in the mix is sponsors' fear of activist groups, which campaign against graphic or gay or other kinds of editorial material perceived as "anti-family." Boycotts like the current Southern Baptist campaign against Disney for "anti-family values" may be on the rise, precisely because advertisers do take them seriously. This, despite a lack of evidence that such boycotts do much damage. "Boycotts have no discernible impact on sales. Usually, the public's awareness is so quickly dissipated that it has no impact at all," says Elliot Mincberg, vice-president and general counsel of People For the American Way, a liberal organization that tracks the impact of pressure groups. Why, then, would advertisers bother setting guidelines that satisfy these groups at all? "They're trying to minimize their risk to *zero*," says an incredulous Will Blythe, *Esquire*'s former literary editor.

Yet not every advertiser pines for the bland old days. The hotter the product, it seems, the cooler the heads. The "vice" peddlers (booze & cigarettes), along with some apparel and consumer electronics products, actually like being surrounded by edgy editorial copy—unless their own product is zapped. Party *on*!

Even Chrysler's sensitivities appear to be selective. *Maxim*'s premier issue featured six women chatting provocatively about their sex lives, plus several photos of women in scanty come-hither attire, but Chrysler had no grievances.

⋅◦⊙◦⋅

The real danger here is not censorship by advertisers. It is self-censorship by editors. On one level, self-censorship results in omissions, small and large, that delight big advertisers.

Cigarettes are a clear and familiar example. The tobacco companies' hefty advertising in many a magazine seems in inverse proportion to the publication's willingness to criticize it. Over at the American Cancer Society, media director Susan Islam says that women's magazines tend to cover some concerns adequately, but not lung cancer: "Many more women die of lung cancer, yet there have hardly been any articles on it."

To her credit, *Glamour*'s editor-in-chief, Ruth Whitney, is one who has run tobacco stories. She says that her magazine, which carries a lot of tobacco advertising, publishes the results of every major smoking study. But Whitney concedes they are mostly short pieces. "Part of the problem with cigarettes was—we did do features, but there's nobody in this country who doesn't know cigarettes kill." Still, everybody also knows that getting slimmer requires exercise and eating right, which has not prevented women's magazines from running that story in endless permutations. Tobacco is in the news, and magazines have the unique job of deepening and humanizing such stories.

Specific editorial omissions are easier to measure than how a magazine's world view is altered when advertisers' preferences and sensitivities seep into the editing. When editors act like publishers, and vice versa, the reader is out the door.

Can ASME, appreciated among editors for its intentions, fire up the troops? The organization has been effective on another front—against abuses of special advertising sections, when advertisements try to adapt the look and feel of editorial matter. ASME has distributed a set of guidelines about just what constitutes such abuse.

To enforce those guidelines, ASME executive director Marlene Kahan says the organization sends a couple of letters each month to violators. "Most magazines say they will comply," she reports. "If anybody is really egregiously violating the guidelines on a consistent basis, we'd probably sit down and have a meeting with them." ASME can ban a magazine from participating in the National Magazine Awards, but Kahan says the organization has not yet had to do that. In addition, ASME occasionally asks the organization that officially counts magazine ad pages, the Publishers Information Bureau, not to count advertising sections that break the rules as ad pages—a tactic that ASME president Lalli says tends to get publishers' attention.

Not everyone in the industry thinks ASME throws much of a shadow. "ASME can't bite the hand that feeds them," says John Masterton of *Media Industry Newsletter*, which covers the magazine business. During Robert Sam Anson's brief tenure as editor of *Los Angeles* magazine, the business side committed to a fifteen-page supplement, to be written by the editorial side and called "The Mercedes Golf Special." Mercedes didn't promise to take any ads, but it was hoped that the carmaker would think kindly of the magazine for future issues. The section would appear as editorial, listed as such in the table of contents. Anson warned the business side that, in his opinion, the section would contravene ASME guidelines, since it was in effect an ad masquerading as edit. A senior executive told him not to worry—that at the most they'd get a "slap on the wrist." The section did not run in the end, Anson says, because of "deadline production problems."

⋴⦿⋼

The Chrysler model, however—with its demand for early warnings, and its insistence on playing editor—is tougher for ASME to police. Special advertising sections are visible. Killed or altered articles are not. And unless it surfaces, as in the *Esquire* case, self-censorhip is invisible.

One well-known editor, who asks not to be identified, thinks the problem will eventually go away. "It's a self-regulating thing," he says. "At some point, the negative publicity to the advertisers will cause them to back off."

Of course, there is nothing particularly automatic about that. It takes an outspoken journalistic community to generate heat. And such attention could backfire. The *Journal's* Knecht told the audience of public radio's *On the Media* that his reporting might actually have aggravated the problem: "One of the negative effects is that more advertisers who weren't aware of this system have gone to their advertising agencies and said, 'Hey, why not me too! This sounds like a pretty good deal!' "

Except, of course, that it really isn't. In the long run everybody involved is diminished when editors feel advertisers' breath on their necks. Hovering there, advertisers help create content that eventually bores the customers they seek. Then the editors of those magazines tend to join the ranks of the unemployed. That's just one of the many reasons that editors simply cannot bend to the new pressure. They have to draw the line—subtly or overtly, quietly or loudly, in meetings and in private, and in their own minds.

POSTSCRIPT

Is Advertising Ethical?

Since a number of media technologies have become vehicles for advertising (such as the Internet and even broadcast/cable infomercials), questions about the ethics of advertising have taken yet another turn. In some ways, the current presence of advertising raises questions that are very basic to the phenomenon of advertising. Do the ads we see register on our conscious or subconscious minds? Do ads really make us buy things or think of things in a certain way? Do we perceptually "screen" unwanted information?

In recent years some of the basic questions about ads have shifted because our "use patterns" of media have changed. Today a prime-time network television program has more ad time than ever before. Remote controls allow viewers to "zap" through commercials on tape or change channels when commercials appear. Ads in the form of company logos are displayed on clothing and other personal items, which have, in turn, emphasized brand affiliation and status.

Because of the new technologies that facilitate perceptual screening of ads, the advertising agencies themselves have looked toward new ways of attracting audiences and reinforcing a positive feeling with the products. In the future we can expect to see more sponsorship of programs, just as we see sporting stadiums and concert halls named for the corporation that funded them. We can also expect to see new techniques that use product placement and product identification inserted in TV programs and films. Already, the Internet is loaded with multiple ads, to the point that the Federal Trade Commission (FTC) has started asking whether some regulation of Internet advertising should be considered.

There are no easy answers when it comes to ethical questions. No matter what you may think about advertising, the industry has become entrenched in our society. It may be easier to ask whether advertising is ethical in certain circumstances, such as in our earlier issue, but without creating a system of censorship, and while still honoring the First Amendment and freedom of speech, we find it difficult to answer the broader questions.

Since the development of the advertising industry, the question of advertising ethics has periodically resurfaced. *The Journal of Advertising Ethics* is a good source to begin investigating what leaders in the industry themselves say about ethical practices, but articles are often tied to specific products or issues. There have been some defenses of the ad industry, such as Yale Brozen's *Advertising and Society* (New York University Press, 1974) and Theodore Levitt's article "The Morality(?) of Advertising," *Harvard Business Review* (July/August 1970).

Stuart Ewen and Elizabeth Ewen's *Channels of Desire: Mass Images and the Shaping of American Consciousness* (McGraw-Hill, 1982) offers the idea that advertising in Western society has had a major influence on public consciousness. Stuart Ewen's more recent book *PR! A Social History of Spin* (Basic Books, 1996) also investigates the origin, effect, and impact of the public relations industry in America.

On the Internet . . .

Center for Media and Public Affairs

The site for the Center for Media and Public Affairs (CMPA) offers information about ongoing debates concerning media fairness and impact, with particular attention to political campaigns and political journalism.

http://www.cmpa.com

Poynter Online: Research Center

The Poynter Institute for Media Studies provides extensive links to information and resources on all aspects of media, including political journalism. This is a good general resource with an extensive list of references.

http://www.poynter.org/research/index.htm

Pew Research Center for People and the Press

The purpose of the Pew Research Center for People and the Press Web site is to serve as a forum for ideas on the media and public policy through public opinion research. This site serves as an important information resource for political leaders, journalists, scholars, and public interest organizations.

http://people-press.org

Society of Professional Journalists

The Web site for *The Electronic Journalist,* the online service for the Society of Professional Journalists (SPJ), will lead you to a number of articles on media ethics, accuracy, media leaders, and other topics.

http://www.spj.org

NewsLink

The *American Journalism Review*'s NewsLink Web site provides links to newspapers around the country. You may access regional and national coverage, as well as smaller publications in specific regions. Links to organizations that are concerned with the ethics and quality of media coverage may be found on this site, as well.

http://www.ajr.org

NewspaperLinks

The Newspaper Association of America's NewspaperLinks Web site provides a state-by-state search for newspaper links. International newspaper links as well as college newspaper links can also be found on this site.

http://newspaperlinks.com/home.cfm

PART 3

Media and Politics

*T*he presence of media has changed the relationship between government, politics, and the press. Media have changed democratic practices such as campaigns, voting, and debating. How can we evaluate the performance of the press in these all-important events? What are the principles and practices of campaigns and of the operation of the press? What part do media play in the creation of negativity concerning politics? Are media biased?

- Does Electronic Media Enhance Political Knowledge?
- Is Negative Campaigning Bad for the American Political Process?
- Do the Media Have a Liberal Bias?

ISSUE 8

Does Electronic Media Enhance Political Knowledge?

YES: Erik P. Bucy and Kimberly S. Gregson, from "Media Participation: A Legitimizing Mechanism of Mass Democracy," *New Media & Society*, (2001)

NO: Diane Owen, "Effects of Electronic Media on Democratic Attitudes," www.civiced.org/papers_oct99_owens.html.

ISSUE SUMMARY

YES: Erik Bucy and Kimberly Gregson examine the conditions under which individuals feel psychologically engaged with a political system through participating in direct interaction with candidates for an office. They examine political radio, tv, electronic town forums, and the use of the Internet as ways of increasing a special type of *space* for participation.

NO: Diane Owen is far more critical of what really happens in the different media contexts; she agrees that political radio has been the most successful forum for like-minded citizens to agree with political views, but she takes a far more pessimistic view of how different media formats have actually contributed to quality interactions, or better understanding of political issues.

One long-standing problem in American political life has to do with figuring out how we can encourage citizens to participate in the political process. Another equally vexing problem is whether media coverage of political issues encourages citizens to think about civic problems and participate in seeking solutions, or whether media coverage actually contributes to more passive citizens, who view politics as "just another story" for which they experience no consequences.

Understanding how individuals become interested in political issues, and why they vote the way they do (if they vote at all) has been a topic that has interested communications researchers for decades. One of the first major studies conducted by Paul F. Lazarsfeld, Bernard Berelson, and Hazel Gaudet, was titled, *The People's Choice: How the Voter Makes Up His Mind in a*

Presidential Campaign; published in 1948 (Columbia University Press), it examined the possible role of media in a political campaign. Since then, many attempts have been made to explore newer technologies, particularly the Internet, as a site for information about candidates and campaigns, or possibly as a means of linking like-minded people for political action.

The two selections in this issue examine the problem from two perspectives. Bucy and Gregson provide a context for understanding the issue of citizen participation in governmental processes, and examine how interactive media have provided a conduit for spontaneous interaction between citizens, political figures, and journalists. While they remain guarded about the effectiveness of various media forms, they do feel that the newer media formats provide "a public space for citizens to debate politics and express their support for, or discontent with, policies or a particular office holder without requiring any material response from the political system."

Diane Owen agrees that we have a plethora of media outlets for political information today, but she feels that the forms of media do not give the public quality information that either encourages participation or accommodates meaningful discussion. She criticizes news sources and claims that the American public now distrusts news and information that comes from companies controlled by big business, and states that call-in programs often become uncivil. As a result, many venues for political talk have become places where people "vent" frustrations rather than engage in constructive dialogue.

Owen also looks at the possible future of citizen involvement by discussing "The Next Generations' Attitudes" toward political orientations. Her conclusions in this area indicate a greater belief that young people today had more negative opinions of President Clinton and the Monica Lewinsky issue than their parents, and that fewer children today have political aspirations; far fewer than earlier generations. If this skepticism toward government continues, from where will our next government leaders appear?

Erik P. Bucy and
Kimberly S. Gregson

 **YES**

Media Participation: A Legitimizing Mechanism of Mass Democracy

After his career in public life was over, Thomas Jefferson lamented in a series of letters that the American Constitution he was instrumental in shaping 'had given all power to the citizens without giving them the opportunity of *being* republicans and of *acting* as citizens.'

Modern democracy suffers a similar fate. In the wake of the 1988 presidential election a Markle Commission study found that voters were increasingly resigned to occupying a spectator position and perceived campaigns to be more the property of candidates, insiders and establishment media than citizens for whom the election drama was staged. Since the 1990s, however, the infusion of new media formats into politics has altered the participatory landscape in important ways; with the possible exception of voting, most forms of active political involvement can now take place through new media.

New media formats rich in civic potential include the obvious, and much discussed, participatory venues—the internet/world wide web, talk radio, call-in television and electronic townhall forums—as well as entertainment programs that feature spontaneous, informal discussions about politics with both political and nonpolitical guests. Yet the civic richness and growing accessibility of these new media formats (sometimes called the *new news*) do not mean that a vibrant, electronic republic will necessarily replace the existing world of traditional politics. Indeed, given the tendency of the traditional party system to normalize political activity, hopes for a radical transformation of politics, even in cyberspace, are likely to go unrealized. Instead, the new media's main contribution to political life may be to make accessible a system that had become highly orchestrated, professionalized and exclusionary and to produce positive citizen evaluations of the public sphere.

A previous investigation found that political audiences regarded certain new media formats, especially call-in shows and the internet, as useful and valuable to civic life. This article builds on the 'new media use as political participation' argument by specifying that this emergent form of electronic democracy (a type of political participation *through* media) involves not just net activism, as recent works have addressed, but also the broader range of citizen actions that can take place online, over the airwaves and through expo-

From *New Media and Society*, vol. 3, 2001, pp. 357-376. Copyright © 2001 by Sage Publications, Inc. Reprinted by permission.

sure to political messages—actions which invite involvement. These actions include, but are not limited to, direct leader/legislator contact, public opinion formation, participating in civic discussions and agenda building, mediated interactions with candidates and other political actors, donating to political causes, and joining mobilizing efforts—each of which may contribute to the psychological feeling of being engaged with the political system. Collectively, we refer to this class of activity as *media participation*. Second, we argue that active and passive modes of participation (generally corresponding to new and old media) may be distinguished by the types of empowerment and rewards—both symbolic and material—that civic activity affords. We conclude by making the case that civic engagement through media, even if only symbolically empowering for the citizen, contributes substantially to legitimizing the political systems of mass democracies.

Before addressing the specific nature of media participation, traditional conceptions of political participation are examined to provide a context for the changing nature of civic involvement.

Political Participation and Democratic Theory

Political participation is typically defined as direct citizen involvement in, or influence over, governmental processes. Thus, Verba and Nie describe participation as 'activities by private citizens that are more or less directly aimed at influencing the selection of governmental personnel and/or the actions they take'. Conway more specifically defines participation as 'activities of citizens that attempt to influence the structure of government, the selection of government officials, or the policies of government'. She notes that these activities may either be supportive of the existing politics, authorities or structure, or they may seek to change current arrangements. Conway distinguishes between active and passive forms of involvement, as well as conventional and unconventional participation. Active participation, which is goal-oriented and motivated by the desire for a specific, personally rewarding outcome, includes such activities as voting, seeking office, writing letters to public officials, or working for a candidate, party or interest group. Passive forms of involvement, which are more ritualized and suggest a certain amount of detachment, include attending ceremonies or other meetings supportive of the government, being aware of government actions and decisions, or merely paying attention to the political environment; for instance, following campaigns and elections through the mass media.

Regardless of their exact form, participatory mechanisms are considered vital to the effective functioning of a strong democracy, in part because they are viewed as maintaining open access to the political system....

Evidence of scant political interest, knowledge and participation among citizens has presented political science with the problem of reconciling democratic theory with reality. Under theories of elite or stratified pluralism, the dominant response to this theory–reality disconnect, low levels of interest and participation–are accepted as normal and interpreted as a sign of general system satisfaction. Voting is still considered important because it helps insure responsiveness of elected officials. But much participation beyond this is regarded as detrimental because it may result in too many demands being placed on the system, interfere with the government's ability to act swiftly when events demand a quick response, and over-politicize social relationships. As Whiteman noted 'limited participation and apathy have a positive sanction for the whole system by cushioning the shock of disagreement, adjustment, and change' when groups that may not share the same values and norms as the majority press for recognition and accommodation. Low public interest also provides political elites with the maneuvering room necessary for policy shifts that may contradict previously stated positions. Popular participation, in this view, should thus be limited to elections; voters can control their leaders by voting them in or out of office but direct citizen influence on policy making between elections should be minimal.

Elite pluralism stems from the political writings of Walter Lippmann, who felt that ordinary citizens were not competent to deal effectively with the complexities of political affairs. Lippmann would rather see society governed by a technocratic elite of experts who relied on scientific methods to rationally administer government than depend on the sentiments of a disengaged 'phantom' public. Instead of prescribing that individuals actively participate in politics, elite pluralism thus places the onus of civic vitality on diverse and competing elites who should remain circulating and accessible to the masses. In theory, the ability of political 'spectators' in a pluralist system to enter the civic arena and become 'gladiators' in competition for resources or political influence provides a check on power holders and compels them to act responsively. Politicians and other elites may anticipate and proactively respond to potential demands not because, on balance, citizens make many demands but because political action helps to keep spectators from becoming active in the arena....

Interactivity and the New Media

New media formats that came to national prominence during the 1992 election, and which have been a staple of campaigns since, popularized the concept of interactivity in politics and have given audience researchers and political communication scholars a new perspective from which to work. A principal component of the new media is the notion of political interactivity, or mediated real-time feedback between political actors and citizens. A primary feature setting interactive media apart from traditional campaign news coverage or political advertising is the potential for spontaneous interaction between political figures, journalists and citizens. Rather than being proscribed a passive role in the political process, the electorate is symbolically or materially empowered (as discussed later) through the two-way communication architecture to interact directly with candidates. Although constrained by such structural factors as available airtime, social conventions that inhibit extended conversations between people of high and low social status, and the sheer number of audience members (both in studio and at home) relative to political guests, interactive formats provide the appearance at least of an unscripted, unrehearsed civic discussion. If nothing else, new media formats may cultivate the perception of system responsiveness, offering citizens the opportunity to engage in corrective communication with power holders. This form of mediated talk has the capacity to adjust elite impressions of mass opinion to better reflect actual public sentiment.

Given the time and role constraints on audiences, not to mention status and political knowledge differentials, full interactivity between public figures and private citizens is clearly not achievable even through new media formats. However, a semblance or subjective sense of it might be. Some election research has found, for instance, that political television audiences may perceive new media formats to allow for feedback, even if true interactivity is only partially realized, via the mechanism of *perceived interactivity*. From this perspective, whether a communication event is regarded as interactive by an outside observer may be irrelevant if the experience of participation leads to a heightened sense of self-efficacy and system responsiveness in the individual....

Civic Relevance of New Media Formats

- *Political entertainment television:* Set in the casual atmosphere of an informal conversation or comedy skit, political entertainment television relies on interpersonal humor, insider gossip and banter with celebrities and other high-status guests—frequently politicians—to foster a sense of parasocial involvement or illusion of intimacy with media *personae*. Through the host's interaction with the show's guests and staff, or through the cast's acting in a bit, members of the audience are invited to feel that this sense of fellowship and social intimacy extends to them, fostering the perception of a face-to-face exchange about a political topic. Shows that feature political entertainment, such as *Politically Incorrect, Saturday Night Live*, and *The Late Show* with David Letterman, benefit from their parasocial character and accessibility but their interactivity is limited by the lack of a real-time feedback mechanism (other than applause from the studio audience). Recent surveys by the Pew Research Center have documented the information value of political entertainment shows, especially for young viewers, and during the 2000 campaign CBS broadcast a weekly round-up of political humor from the late-night television talk shows. Since the 1988 presidential election the Center for Media and Public Affairs in Washington, DC has also tracked political jokes told on late-night television (the vast majority of which have been leveled at presidents or presidential contenders).
- *Political talk radio:* Perhaps more than any of the other new media formats, political talk radio gives voice to the average citizen through its 'open mike' character. Talk radio provides verbal proximity to media and political elites, as well as access to a mass audience of fellow listeners, via the direct feedback of listener calls. By extending the voice, radio facilitates a sort of amplified conversation that may shape public sentiments and crystallize opinion on certain issues. Moreover, talk radio programs often deliberately attempt to mobilize the public to participate in civic affairs or contact officials, serving as a vehicle for

political socialization. For reception to be meaningful, talk radio listening requires dedicated attention with the intent of comprehending the discussion. Listening, in turn, may teach the important civic skill of needing and tolerating opposing arguments. Indeed, Tankel asserts that a major attraction of talk radio is the multiplicity of voices heard on the air. Research on the talk radio audience has shown listeners to be significantly more civic-minded and participatory than nonlisteners. Callers, in particular, are more likely to participate in other political activities. Talk radio can be best understood, Tankel suggests, 'as a behavior in which the listener is an active participant rather than as a process that constructs a passive recipient.'

- *Political call-in television:* Combining the strengths of talk radio with the power of visuals, political call-in television places the viewer in the front row, if not of the political *action*, at least of the political *discussion*. Because of television's visual nature, this format invites close scrutiny of the political guest's physical appearance and nonverbal demeanor, perhaps at the expense of what's said. Importantly, call-in television endows the audience member with more sensory modalities—sight as well as sound—than the guest, who can only hear the audio of the caller. The disembodied voice of the caller is awkward for the elite guest and host but in some way empowers the caller because the transparency, though at a distance, is unidirectional. The guest is visually impaired, the caller visually enabled. Call-in formats thus provide visual *and* verbal proximity to elites, as well as open-mike access to a wide audience (although small by television standards). Public affairs cable channels such as C-SPAN and CNN, which feature daily call-in segments, 'may well stimulate increased levels of political involvement or create new vehicles for political participation.' Such participation has the potential for changing the climate of opinion and influencing the behavior of decision makers, while enhancing the political efficacy of citizens.
- *Electronic townhall forums:* Electronic townhall forums that feature a participatory studio audience, and sometimes an interactive viewing audience, offer a form of vicarious participation unrivaled by other media. For the home audience, the surrogate experience of viewing a townhall forum is intensified by the ability to witness the active involvement of fellow citizens, whose presence reminds viewers of their own democratic role and civic identity. In response to a citizen question during the second presidential debate of 1996 (which was conducted as a townhall forum) about opening the political process to more grassroots involvement, President Clinton referred to surrogate participation and commented on the need to make elections more accessible through campaign finance reform and by opening the airwaves to citizen control: 'You see, it's not just you that are participating here. For every one of you who stood up here and asked a question tonight, I promise you, there's 100,000 Americans that said, "I wish I could have asked that question."' Through the airing of issues and questions that represent citizen interests rather than journalistic fixations—the two diverge considerably—the public debate is recast so voters come to know their own minds, as it were, before facing a critical choice and thereby have the opportunity to build 'a more conscious

democracy.' The visibility of citizen stand-ins who vocalize collective sentiment and concerns creates a sense of civic relevance that consultant-controlled campaigning all but obliterates.

- *Internet/world wide web:* Through convergence and remediation—the repurposing or refashioning of old media with new media, not just in turns of content but by incorporating old media forms into new media venues—the internet/world wide web introduces myriad ways to engage voters and facilitate participation in politics. As a civic medium, the internet fulfills at least four political functions. First, it provides access to news and political information, frequently faster and more in-depth than traditional media. Second, the internet links candidates and office holders with citizens through political web sites and email. Third, the internet provides a space for political discussion, especially through usenet groups organized around various topics. And, fourth, the internet can serve as a barometer of public opinion with the capacity of offering reaction to events and decisions in real-time—although, as Wu and Weaver caution, the validity of online polling is dubious. Quite possibly, the internet/world wide web presents more political information and opportunities for civic engagement than has ever existed. The web is a complex symbolic environment, however, and users spend a considerable amount of time just orienting to the medium. Before it becomes a true medium of the masses, questions of *social access*—the mix of technical knowledge, psychological skills, and economic resources required for effectual use of information and communication technologies—will have to be addressed.

A question inevitably arises as to whether new media formats allow citizens to influence the actual substance and outcome of politics. According to net activists and some early confirmatory research, interactive political experiences that occur in cyberspace, via cable channels and over the airwaves are deemed every bit as 'real', useful and important as their nonmediated corollaries—such traditional measures of political activity as attending meetings and rallies, volunteering, writing to legislators, and contacting community leaders. In addition, citizen action through new media formats has already had direct political influence in certain instances, as the talk radio furor over congressional pay raises and Zoe Baird's 1993 ill-fated nomination to US Attorney General demonstrated. Yet an over-emphasis on the traditional, political value of media participation risks losing sight of the more important *individual* consequence of daily citizen involvement with new media—the psychological rewards and personal empowerment derived from civic media use....

Discussion

Elite theories of democracy stress that optimal civic conditions depend on a certain amount of citizen involvement but not too much so as to cause instability. In direct contradiction to this limited view of public life is the democratic ethos, well entrenched in American society, that all citizens have the *option* to participate, regardless of whether their participation is healthy for the system. Fortunately for government, not everyone chooses to exercise these political rights. To the contrary, conventional public participation in civic life has been on a downward spiral for the past three or four decades. During the same period, media use (notably television and more recently the internet) has been on the rise, prompting some political thinkers to sound the alarm bell of social and political erosion. Conceptualizing new media use as a form of political participation that provides symbolic empowerment resolves the dilemma of civic decline; suddenly, there is a form of participation in which a growing segment of the public regularly engages. Importantly, media participation entails *active* civic involvement, not just passive surveillance of the political environment. Recognizing the value of mediated citizenship reconciles the desire of realists to keep public involvement in (actual) political affairs minimal with the admonitions of classical democracy's proponents for full citizen participation.

In contrast to passive spectatorship under a one-way communication system, media participation in an interactive environment presents the citizen with a civic role and ready avenue of involvement across a variety of communication modalities. Indeed, rather than being slighted by a form of 'pseudo participation', as traditionalists might characterize new media use, the citizen benefits from the awareness that media participation provides proximity to political elites, makes politics continuously available and entertaining (i.e. accessible), offers open-mike access to a wide audience, socializes citizens to participate in public affairs, and allows voters to cultivate a civic identity and know their own minds. For the electorate, regular involvement with media, particularly new media formats, may well be taking the place of direct, sporadic participation in politics. Even if only symbolically empowering for the individual, the experience of media participation is pivotal to maintaining the perception of system responsiveness and thereby serves as an important legitimizing mechanism for mass democracy. Through the generalized occurrence of media participation throughout society, the political world has achieved a previously unknown openness. This should be viewed as a positive development: no other system of civic involvement and public communication seems to shoulder the needs of participatory democracy so effectively.

Except under unusual circumstances when the mass public becomes highly attentive to and mobilized over an issue, as with a controversial high-level nomination, new media formats probably have little or no direct impact on political decisions. There is no guarantee, for example, that policy makers will pay attention to, let alone heed the advice from, an online discussion or instant survey. Often skewed and typically produced from unscientific samples, these 'public opinion' indicators can be highly inaccurate (although the results of a growing number of legitimate surveys are now posted online). The vast majority of media participation, then, may have no direct political impact except to encourage others to register their opinion. Nevertheless, new media formats provide a public space for citizens to debate politics and express their support for, or discontent with, policies or a particular office holder without requiring any material response from the political system. This arrangement is advantageous for both the individual and the system. For the individual, the psychological rewards and peer activation that new media formats provide may spur previously inactive spectators to initiate some limited form of civic engagement and motivate already active citizens to further their involvement, despite the wishes of those already active in the arena. For the system, media participation may enhance the perception of governmental accessibility and openness by, first and foremost, giving citizens the opportunity to act *as* citizens. Democracy thus benefits from opportunities for civic activity through media, even though citizen involvement by traditional standards is indirect.

Critics of media participation who view it as a watered-down or thin form of democracy should bear in mind that even conventional political participation seldom brings immediate results from government. Continuous involvement in civic affairs through media, however, may produce immediate and ongoing psychological benefits for the citizen. Although it has been presented as a theoretical proposition here, media participation has already been empirically associated with increased feelings of efficacy and conventional participation in studies of the new media audience (Hollander, 1995–6; Newhagen, 1994). From the skeptic's vantage point, new media formats sacrifice certain forms of interpersonal deliberation for mediated versions and increase the potential for manipulation by political professionals. But the capabilities of the new technology can also be used to 'tie individuals and institutions into networks that will make real participatory discussion and debate possible across great distances.' Even if elections were conducted purely by way of new media, they would still be participatory in nature. At the very least, new media formats expose elites to views and opinions they might not otherwise have heard and, in the case of electronic townhall forums, provide citizens with the sense of front-row participation that political correspondents routinely enjoy at press conferences. Rather than relying on journalistic stand-ins, citizens can question authority without media interference.

To the extent that media participation contributes to the agenda-building process of public issue formation, it may be *more* important to long-term stability than voting and other sporadic forms of conventional political activity. Campaigns and elections may fortify the short-term stability of a system, especially if they generate high voter turn-out, but their infrequent occurrence does not provide the ongoing, interstitial involvement that participatory democracy demands. Indeed, when the republic was young, Jefferson expressed concern over the danger inherent in allowing the people 'a share in public power without providing them at the same time with more public space than the ballot box and with more opportunity to make their voices heard in public than election day.' New media formats satisfy this need for popular involvement by delivering a continuous stream of opportunities for civic engagement without overextending the government's ability to respond. The new media thereby increase the number of access points in the political pressure system, improving though not guaranteeing the likelihood that citizen concerns will be heard. By making allowances for continuing mass involvement, new media formats serve the socially valuable purpose of bringing closer to reality the classical goal of full participation without overextending already burdened political institutions.

NO

Diane Owen

Effects of Electronic Media on Democratic Attitudes

The past decade has witnessed fundamental changes in the American mass media environment. Contemporary media technologies and format innovations have created new ways of communicating and reaching audiences. New actors, such as talk show hosts and tabloid reporters, have entered the political communications environment, altering the rules by which journalists, leaders, and citizens negotiate the public sphere. The nature of the political media product has changed, becoming almost inextricably infused with entertainment content. In sum, the United States has entered a "new media" age.

Electronic media dominate in the "new media" era even more than in the recent past. Technologies, such as the Internet, have rendered print communication electronic, as traditional news organizations establish online counterparts to their newspapers and magazines. Further, the substance, form, and style of electronic communication has been altered radically. New-style electronic formats, such as Internet discussion groups and chat rooms, create new public spaces and provide unprecedented opportunities for political discourse. It is clear that the transformation of the American media system has important implications for democratic citizenship, especially as audiences' relationships to mass communication have been influenced significantly. However, perspectives on the prospects for democratic political systems in the "new media" era vary widely....

The "New Media" World and Citizenship Orientations

Some observers have heralded coming of the "new media" age as the catalyst that has instigated a populist political movement where citizens have greater access to the political world than ever before. The most optimistic articulation of this view posits that mass media serve to stimulate political interest and activism among the mass public. Ordinary citizens are able to establish meaningful and effective roles for themselves in the political arena that has

From a paper delivered to the Democracy and the Globalization of Politics and the Economy International Conference, October 1999. Copyright © 1999 by Diana Owen. Reprinted by permission of the author.

been primarily the domain of elites. Talk radio, for example, can provide an unstructured outlet for public expression.

There is some evidence that this kind of populism is not an impossibility in the current media environment. There is more political information disseminated today through a vast diversity of sources than at any time in history. Political news is available for general audiences through network evening newscasts, real time news broadcasts, including CNN and MSNBC, morning news/entertainment programs, like the *Today* show, and televised news magazines, such as *Dateline* and *20/20*. The wide range of available formats also permits information to be targeted at specific audience segments, including those who traditionally have been under-represented in the political world. Cable television, call-in radio forums, and Internet platforms, in particular, allow citizens to receive information that is relevant to them personally, and to make contact with others who have similar social and political orientations. As opposed to the "sound-bite" journalism that characterizes much mainstream political media, newer forums have more time and space for the presentation of contextual and historical material as well as extended discussions of issues, actors, and events....

More realistic assessments contend that the infrastructure for mass media to foster greater civic involvement is in place, but the communications environment has been allowed to develop haphazardly. Citizens and leaders need to carefully consider the opportunities offered by electronic media to foster democratic ideals, and take steps, including legislative efforts, to assure that these goals are met. As it stands, the "new media" environment has failed to provide the public with quality political information, to accommodate meaningful discourse, or to encourage political engagement.

The imperative behind political communication in the current era is profit, and not a sense of public service which was at least in the back of reporters' minds in the pre-"new media" period. As such, the content of political news and information has become increasingly entertainment-oriented. Traditional news sources, including the network newscasts, have adopted reporting strategies that sometimes resemble those of supermarket tabloids. The overall tenor of political news is negative, if not downright uncivil and vitriolic. Journalists operate under the credo that only bad news is worth reporting where politics is concerned. Citizens are rarely treated to stories about how political institutions are functional or how government officials are admirable public servants, although in reality this is a large part of the story. Instead, news media highlight political discord, malfeasance, and scandal. Further, heavily reported scandals involving public officials today, in keeping with the dominant entertainment news frame, are more likely to involve personal issues than policy problems, as was the case during a prior era of "watchdog journalism."

The public is clearly dissatisfied with the current political media offerings. While many Americans consider themselves to be "news junkies" and express a strong need to keep informed, they don't trust many news sources. A majority of citizens believe that the news is unduly influenced by powerful business and political interests who play into the media's own desire to make profits. Further, they consider the news to be too sensational and scandal-ridden. The public feels that the press is intrusive, and goes too far in invading people's personal lives in the interest of getting a story. Audience members are concerned about the accuracy of reporting, especially as media organizations compete to be the first with a breaking story. In fact, journalist norms of sourcing and fact-checking largely have become a thing of the past, as the pace of news reporting has accelerated. The credibility of political news is challenged further as questionable sources emerge from the depths of cyberspace to drive the media agenda, as was the case with Matt Drudge during the Clinton/Lewinsky affair.

In addition, the tone and content of political discourse in the forums that promote citizen participation, such as call-in programs and Internet chat rooms, are hardly civil or constructive. Encouraged by hosts driven by audience ratings, political talk has become, in large part, an opportunity for venting rather than an effective discussion forum. Some scholars, including political theorist Benjamin Barber, go so far as to contend that the electronic "public square" breeds faction, disaffection, and discontent.

It is often difficult in the "new media" age for citizens to sort through the profusion of political material and decide what is useful and what is not. Faced with "data glut," the public tunes out. Frequently, there is much news, but few stories, as multifarious press organizations dwell upon a single theme. In addition, the traditional hierarchy of media organizations, where it was possible to establish the quality of information by the brand name associated with it, is eroding. Political scandals that break in the tabloid press go on to grace the front page of *The New York Times*.

The "new media" environment is still the bastion of society's more privileged members, and has done little to encourage participation among the traditionally unengaged. The newer communication formats, such as talk radio and the Internet, attract audiences from higher socio-economic and educational groups who tend to be politically active in other ways. Even as the Internet user base increases and becomes more "ordinary," it still is not available to millions of citizens without the resources and skills to take part. In some ways, the Internet has widened the political information and participation gap between societal 'have's' and 'have-not's'.

While some observers view the enhanced ability to target particular audiences for political media in the current environment to be an advantage, others consider the increased segmentation of the media market to be problematic. Audience segmentation creates discrete communities of special interests who may lose sight of the greater societal good. Discussion remains confined to separate media spheres of like-minded participants, lessening the ability for a multitude of voices to be heard.

For the most part, political and media elites still control the agenda of media forums, and will only go so far to stimulate public discussion and feedback. Call-in radio and television programs frequently use citizen callers as props designed to spark commentary by hosts and guest elites. Political leaders and candidates regularly establish Web sites to publicize their activities and campaigns. These sites contain lots of information, but far fewer opportunities for citizen interaction. Campaign sites, in particular, routinely include mechanisms for recruiting volunteers online and providing updates to interested parties. Few campaign sites contain email or discussion forums, as candidates do not want to address controversial issues that online users might raise.

In sum, the "new media" environment offers novel opportunities for democratic politics. "New media" forums have the ability to spark citizen interest, increase awareness and knowledge of public affairs, and prompt political participation. There are signs that this is occurring, as a significant number of people seek out political information online and take part in discussions in electronic space. Still, the democratizing potential of the current mass media system is largely unrealized. Rather than encourage the public to become politically attentive and engaged, the media environment may actually deter involvement. The content and presentational style of much news turns the public off to politics, as the political world appears trivial, scandalous, and nasty.

It may be the case that media politics even may be a deterrent to actual political participation. Communications scholar Roderick Hart argues that watching governance has become a substitute for engaging in politics for many people. Electronic communications today leave citizens with the false impression that they are close to politicians, and that taking real steps to gain the attention of elites is unnecessary. Similarly, political scientist Robert Putnam contends that attending to media, political or otherwise, takes time away from engaging in other activities, especially community affairs.

Electronic Media and Citizen Attitudes

...It has been widely observed that American citizens are traditionally poorly informed about political affairs. The apparent abundance of political information has not translated generally into greater civic knowledge. Nor has the increase in educational attainment over the past three decades corresponded to a commensurate gain in knowledge. A variety of reasons have been offered as explanations for this phenomenon. People are too busy to monitor politics. They do not consider politics a priority, as they fail to see the connection to their daily lives. Government and Washington appear remote and are run by political insiders.

Media-related explanations also have been suggested. The news product may be unsuitable to fostering political learning. Even when people are exposed to political news, they process a minuscule amount of information and forget the little that registers within a very short period of time. Political information frequently is presented in a fragmented style which includes little substantive information or context. The negative character and entertainment focus of political news undercuts its significance. Further, sources of political information that present more detailed and substantive perspectives on politics frequently are pitched at more educated and elite audiences, and have an insider orientation.

There is, however, an indication that some citizens may be exhibiting increased levels of political interest and knowledge as a result of their use of newer communication formats. Regular talk radio listeners and callers as well as users of online media resources are significantly more politically informed than the general public. While it may be the case that talk radio and online media audience members are naturally more inclined to seek information, their use of these media enhances the depth and breadth of their knowledge. Talk radio and online media users are more likely to hold more sophisticated and detailed opinions on public policy issues than other citizens. Talk radio listeners, in particular, acknowledge that they gain information from their use of the medium. The talk radio audience also tends to hold more extreme and conservative political views than nonlisteners....

While not the sole culprit, media have been blamed for exacerbating public distrust of government and politicians, and for diminishing faith in the democratic process. As we have discussed in the previous section, news media give an inordinate amount of attention to political scandal, infighting, and corruption to the exclusion of positive information or issue content. Communications scholars Joseph Cappella and Kathleen Hall Jamieson provide empirical validation of these conjectures. They demonstrate that the press frames political news in terms of political strategies, conflict, and politicians' motives, which are rarely portrayed as legitimate. These standard news frames encourage citizens to question politicians' values and actions, and lead to increased political cynicism.

It is reasonable to speculate that the audiences for particular forms of electronic media, especially television and radio call-in programs and online political discussion groups, might be more cynical about government than the general public. The content of these media forums is especially dense with negative messages about government and scathing personal attacks on public officials. President Clinton, in the wake of the bombing of the federal building in Oklahoma City, publically denounced talk radio for promoting a culture of intolerance. However, users of these media are no more likely to distrust government and political leaders than others in society.

The final political attitude we examine is political efficacy, which refers to an individual's belief that she or he can influence the political process and successfully reach political leaders. The concept of efficacy is frequently considered in terms of two distinct dimensions. Internal efficacy indicates people's perceptions that they personally have the skills necessary to navigate the political realm successfully. External efficacy deals with whether people believe that the government is responsive to attempts by ordinary citizens like themselves to affect government. Efficacy is closely linked to political trust, as those who are most supportive of government are more likely to believe they can influence the political world. Citizens who have a strong sense of political efficacy also are more inclined to participate in public affairs and to take part in community service activities.

As is the case with trust in government, Americans' collective sense of political efficacy, both internal and external, has been on the decline since the Watergate era. Individuals do not believe that they can make a difference in politics. They perceive that politics is too complicated for them to understand. They do not feel that their vote counts. Further, the public senses that the government doesn't care what the people think, and that average citizens have no say in political affairs.

Considering whether citizens' sense of political efficacy is in any way influenced by the "new media" environment is an interesting proposition, especially in light of the populist potential of particular media formats. Several scenarios are possible. It may be the case that citizens who already are strongly efficacious will be attracted to interactive media and use them to enhance their political presence. Alternatively, these formats may appeal to people who do not feel that they can influence government or political leaders via conventional channels, such as voting, letter writing, or circulating petitions. They may turn to mass media forums out of a sense of frustration. They may perceive that the interactive forums will be receptive to political outsiders like themselves. It is also possible that the "new media" environment may have little to do with fostering or undermining citizens' sense of efficacy.

There is some support for the contention that interactive communication formats may heighten political efficacy. People who regularly go online and participate in political discussions have a more positive view of their ability to play a meaningful role in politics than the general public. However, participants in online political discussions may begin with a strong sense of efficacy, and their participation serves to reinforce this predisposition. Studies of the talk radio audience permit a more direct test of electronic media's ability to enhance efficacy. Research conducted in 1993 indicated that talk radio callers and listeners had a strong sense of civic duty and commitment, but lower levels of political efficacy than other citizens. By 1996, the talk radio audience's feelings of internal efficacy far exceeded those of nonlisteners. Talk radio devotees also evidenced an increase in their sense of external efficacy. Over time, regular talk radio listeners acquired a more favorable view of their own political power through their experience with the medium. Talk radio hosts do much to instill this perception in their listeners. Audience members' appreciation for the power of political talk is further reinforced by the fact that political leaders will appear as guests on talk radio programs and publically acknowledge their significance.

The Next Generations' Attitudes

...What influence does electronic media have on young people's political orientations? In the current media environment, the proliferation of communication sources coupled with the conflation of political and entertainment content renders it more likely that children and adolescents will be exposed to political information, either deliberately or inadvertently. Further, the nature of this content paints an unflattering picture of government and political leaders. Is this media-defined negativity reflected in young people's attitudes?

An analysis of the effects of the Clinton/Lewinsky affair on young people's attitudes provides some insights into the media's role in socializing citizens to politics. Early studies of children's relationship to the political world indicated that their impressions about the President played a central role in constructing their images of government, and formed the basis of general support for the democratic polity. However, children are able to make distinctions between the presidential personality and the presidential role. This distinction became clear during Watergate, as children maintained respect for government, while registering their disappointment in President Nixon.

Young people's attitudes toward the President and the political system are substantially more negative in the wake of the events surrounding the Clinton impeachment than they have been at any time during this century. In fact, children evaluated President Clinton far more harshly than did their parents, as only 43% of the youth sample of a Gallup poll held a favorable view compared to 55% of their parents. Further, young people strongly believed that President Clinton's conduct was wrong, and that the Senate should have voted to remove him from office. This perception again diverged from that of adults, as 47% of young people felt that Clinton should not remain as President as opposed to 36% of adults.

Young people received most of their information about Watergate from personal sources—parents, teachers, and sometimes peers. In contrast, parents reported overwhelmingly that their children received most of their information about the Clinton/Lewinsky matter from television. The media set the agenda for interpersonal discussion, as children's exposure to press reports prompted them to raise the issue with parents and teachers. The media's pervasive, sensational, tabloid-style coverage of the Clinton affair made it difficult to shelter children from the scandal. Some children were attentive to the news coverage because of its similarity to entertainment television programs and films. Children's interest in the event was amplified by the personal nature of the scandal. Further, the Clinton impeachment was framed by the media as a matter of the President lying, an issue to which young people could relate.

While young people had highly negative opinions of President Clinton, their evaluations of government were somewhat more generous. However, young people's views of government and politics today are markedly more negative than during Watergate. These findings are not encouraging, as support for political institutions and processes tends to dissipate with age. Young people have come to accept that scandalous behavior is the norm for political leaders. In addition, few children and adolescents dream of becoming President. Only 26% of young people polled by Gallup had presidential aspirations, which is far lower than the figure for prior generations.

Conclusion

In weighing the benefits and detriments of the effects of electronic media on democratic attitudes, it would appear that the bad transcends the good. There appears to be some gains in political knowledge and efficacy among segments of the public, particularly those who have regular experiences with the most populist and interactive forms of media. However, the audience profile for talk radio and online media users, especially, indicates that these are people from the higher economic and educational echelons who already are politically engaged in other ways. The "new media" environment does little to reach those whose political voice is muffled.

More troubling is the evidence that the current media environment appears to undermine citizens' faith in government officials and political institutions, as well as, in the democratic political process. This trend is suggested for both young people and adults. While it is important, indeed essential, for citizens to maintain a healthy skepticism about government to assure that officials do not abuse power, unbridled cynicism is detrimental to democracy. That this cynicism is couched in terms of the politics of scandal as presented by mass media is cause for concern.

POSTSCRIPT

Does Electronic Media Enhance Political Knowledge?

There was a time in which all of our media was "mass" media. That is, it was created by large organizations to be disseminated to a large, heterogeneous audience. When the flow of messages traveled from one large producing organization to the masses, it seemed as though politics were played out on a level playing field. Theoretically, everyone who had access to the same forms of media could ostensibly react to the same messages in their own ways. The results were more measurable, since the variables were more controlled.

But when the sources of political information began to grow, the dynamics of understanding how, what, and when different individuals used the messages became more complex. When people could actually search for information they wanted, the level of interest and the techniques used to persuade individuals to take action or change their beliefs became more aggressive, and more personal.

While each of these selections takes a different viewpoint on how citizens can participate in civic life by attending to different media content, in different media forms, the uniting concept is whether the media form itself enhances political knowledge. When we frame the question this way, it may be true according to Bucy and Gregson's argument that individuals may feel more empowered if they participate in the media interactions, but whether they increase their knowledge or not may depend on how invested they become in examining the quality of the interactions. Diane Owen, however, feels that the media are poorly organized and ineffective in informing the public. As a result, no matter how many venues are available, the structure of the media as we now know it leads to less involvement, and less knowledge.

From the earliest days of communication research, the relationship among government, citizens, and the media has yielded many theories and perspectives. At first, it was assumed media would have immediate and direct effects on peoples' beliefs and actions (see Lazarsfeld, Berelson, and Gaudet, *The Peoples' Choice*, 1948). Later, the second stage of research examined how the media helped individuals reinforce their preconceived attitudes and behaviors (see Eugene Burdick and Arthur J. Brodbeck (Eds.) *American Voting Behavior* (Free Press, 1959)). The third stage of research began to look at the way in which images of candidates were shaped by media, and accepted or rejected by the public (see Roderick P. Hart, *Seducing America: How Television Charms the Modern Voter*, Oxford University Press, 1994).

These two selections are indicative of the new era of political/media research. As these selections show, changes in media ownership and the resulting effects on political information have created new questions for how and why citizens might become politically involved. Some additional resources in this area include: Michael X. Delli Carpini and Scott Keeter, *What Americans Know About Politics and Why It Matters* (Yale University Press, 1996); Jeffrey F. Abramson, Christopher Arterton, and Gary R. Orren, *The Electronic Commonwealth: The Impact of New Media Technologies on Democratic Policies* (Basic Books, 1988); and Susan Herbst, "On Electronic Public Space: Talk Shows in Theoretical Perspective," *Political Communication 12* (2), pp. 263-274.

ISSUE 9

Is Negative Campaigning Bad for the American Political Process?

YES. Bruce E. Pinkleton, Nam-Hyun Um, Erica Weintraub Austin, "An Exploration of the Effects of Negative Political Advertising on Political Decision Making," *Journal of Advertising,* 341:1, Spring 2002, 13-25.

NO. Ruth Ann Lariscy and Spencer Tinkham, "Lessons from Negative Campaign Advertising,"*USA TODAY Magazine*, May 2004.

ISSUE SUMMARY

YES: Mass communication scholars examine the truth behind the assumption that negative campaigning has a negative impact on voters. Their experimental research study found that participants deemed negative ads fairly worthless and that such ads increased negativity about campaigns. Other potential consequences such as cynicism, efficacy, and apathy were not found.

NO: Political advertising scholars report on the lessons of their studies of negative campaign advertising. Negative ads, they argue, are more memorable. They help voters make distinctions between candidates; they influence voters. But not all negative ads are useful, and the authors help us make the distinction. Despite the revulsion that pervades public opinion toward negative ads, these authors argue that they are helpful to voters.

$\mathbf{N}$othing has transformed the American political process as much as the emergence of television as a force in elections. Today, many more people see candidates on television than hear them in person. Candidates appear in a variety of media formats—newspapers, television and radio interview shows, late-night talk shows, magazine covers, online, and even MTV. Never before have candidates used the power of media to such a comprehensive extent to reach potential voters.

But much of the public is fed up with political campaigns. Voters are disgusted with candidates and with politics in general. Viable candidates choose not to run rather than subject themselves and their families to the scrutiny of the press and the negativity of their opponent. Many in the public point the finger of blame at a relentless negativism governing the coverage and conduct of political campaigns that favors a horse-race mentality, leaps at opportunities to "go negative," and gleefully breaks stories of private failures.

Pinkleton, Um and Austin set out to prove what most already believe: that attack ads foster negative perceptions of politics, and ultimately voter apathy and cynicism. Their experimental study of college student reactions to a variety of campaign messages lends support to the fear that current campaign messages contribute to public disdain of politics and politicians. Extensive public discourse certainly lays the blame for these woes on the negativity of contemporary campaigning. *Peepshow: Media and Politics in an Age of Scandal* by Larry Sabato, Mark Stencel and Robert Lichter argues that scandal coverage has degraded politics, and blames journalists, politicians, and the public. In *The Nightly News Nightmare: Network Television's Coverage of U. S. Presidential Elections, 1988-2000*, Stephen Farnsworth and Robert Lichter (2002) look at campaign coverage over the past four presidential elections and track its changing nature in terms of objectivity, negativity, quantity, and overall quality.

Lariscy and Tinkham argue that negative campaigning persists because it works. The spin doctors have it right: negative campaigns can have a positive effect for their candidates. More importantly, from the perspective of Lariscy and Tinkham, it can be beneficial to voters. They find negative campaigning allows individuals to distinguish between candidates. They join with the others in decrying some forms of negative campaigning, but instead of calling for its abolition, they call for its appropriate use. Lariscy and Tinkham challenge the common perception that all negativity is bad. Rather than a bland campaign where each candidate speaks in favor of broad generalities, let record and behavior be revealed and debated. There must be a way for people to judge the character and record of those they select, otherwise the information needed to discriminate among candidates will never emerge

The careful reader will notice that a number of issues are implicated in this discussion. Beyond negative campaigning, issues such as attack journalism, dirty politics, and general incivility are referenced in public discourse. Politicians seeking votes and journalists seeking stories have created election politics that disappoint and alienate voters. Attempts at reform are many. In the 2004 Democratic primaries, John Edwards refused to "go negative." According to Lariscy and Tinkham, that may have cost him the nomination. The media are much better at policing false assertions. Journalists routinely engage in "ad watches" where the validity of claims made in ads is evaluated.

What should be the rules for politicians and journalists in an era of media preoccupation with private lives and political scandal? Despite the incivility of present campaigns, do we want to return to an era in which private lives are never considered appropriate for public discussion? Does it matter if candidates have experimented with drugs, joined subversive organizations as college students, made mediocre grades, evaded war service, or had affairs? What changes would make political campaigns and their coverage more substantive?

Bruce E. Pinkleton, Nam-Hyun Um,
and Erica Weintraub Austin

 **YES**

An Exploration of the Effects of Negative Political Advertising on Political Decision Making

A total of 236 students participated in an experiment testing the effects of positive, negative, and negative comparative political advertising on key variables in the political decision-making process. Participants exposed to negative advertising found it less useful for political decision making and were more negative toward political campaigns than were participants exposed to positive advertising. Negative political advertising had no effect on participants' cynicism, efficacy, or apathy. The findings suggest that, though negative advertising contributes to citizens' disgust with campaigns, this strategy does not automatically increase citizens' cynicism or apathy.

Negative campaign tactics and questionable media election coverage continue to attract the attention of citizens, journalists, and researchers. Citizens commonly complain about the negative tenor of campaigns, especially about negative political advertising. Researchers, political observers, and others, meanwhile, suggest that negative campaign tactics result in negativism toward the political process, ultimately producing cynicism and apathy among voters (Crotty and Jacobson 1980; Grove 1989; Taylor 1989). Scholars' concerns about negative political advertising seem particularly disconcerting when considered alongside complaints that media coverage of the political process lacks both depth and context. Political observers and others have singled out broadcast media in particular for providing "horserace"-oriented campaign coverage that focuses on who leads or trails in the polls rather than identifying and discussing candidates' issue stands and policy proposals relevant to voters.

Nevertheless, the impact of repeated citizen exposure to negative political advertising and poor public affairs media coverage is difficult to determine with specificity. Scholars express concern that the ultimate outcome may be citizens high in cynicism and apathy, unwilling to engage in the most basic forms of public affairs participation, such as voting (Ansolabehere and Iyengar 1995; Cappella and Jamieson 1997; Crotty and Jacobson 1980). Despite this plethora of arguments connecting exposure to negative political advertising and mediated campaign coverage to political disaffection and apathy, it is difficult to verify and measure the nature of these relationships on the basis of existing research.

Although general agreement exists that citizens' faith in government and related institutions has been declining along with voter turnout (e.g., Dennis and Webster 1975; Dionne 1991), less agreement exists regarding the reasons for this decline, and many questions remain unanswered pertaining to the links among media use, exposure to negative political advertising, and citizens' political malaise. Research makes it clear, for example, that voters dislike and distrust negative political advertisements (Garramone 1984). In fact, research results indicate that negative political advertising sometimes works against a sponsoring candidate by engendering more support for a targeted candidate (Faber, Tims, and Schmitt 1990; Garramone 1984; Roddy and Garramone 1988), typically referred to as a backlash effect. It is equally as clear, however, that candidates use negative political ads because they often contribute to campaign success (Doak 1995; Johnson-Cartee and Copeland 1991a; Nugent 1987; Pinkleton 1997, 1998). An examination of the role of negative political advertising in citizens' development of negativism, cynicism, and apathy provides the opportunity to reconcile these seemingly contradictory findings. Therefore, this study tests the effects of negative political advertising strategies on key aspects of voter decision making, including perceptions of the credibility and utility of advertising, negativism toward political campaigns, cynicism toward the political system, efficacy toward political participation, and voting apathy. This makes it possible to explore the potential for short-term, situationally based effects as well as longer term, more systemic-level effects.

Negative Political Advertising and Political Decision Making

Negative political advertising typically contains a one-sided attack on a targeted candidate designed to draw attention to the target's weaknesses, such as character flaws, voting record, public misstatements, broken promises, and the like (Johnson-Cartee and Copeland 1991a; Merritt 1984; Surlin and Gordon 1977). The contents of such advertising, sometimes called "mudslinging" or "attack advertising," impugn the character, record, or positions of the targeted candidate, creating doubt in voters' minds about the ability of the target to govern successfully. Negative campaign tactics are an often-used part of a candidate's campaign arsenal, despite the risk of creating sympathy for the target of the advertising, as already noted. Research results indicate that evaluations of both the sponsor and target of negative advertising worsen when campaigns use negative campaign tactics (Kaid and Boydston 1987; Merritt 1984; Pinkleton 1997), and study participants have rated the sponsor of negative advertising as more mean-spirited than the target (Pinkleton 1998). Nevertheless, when carefully constructed and used, negative campaign tactics reduce targeted candidate evaluations and voting intention to a much greater extent than they do sponsoring candidate evaluations (e.g., Johnson-Cartee and Copeland 1989, 1991a; Perloff and Kinsey 1992; Pinkleton 1997, 1998; Roddy and Garramone 1988), even among members of the targeted candidate's political party (Kaid and Boydston 1987).

Scholars generally attribute the reason for the greater effectiveness of negative advertising over positive advertising to the impact of negative information on information processing and judgmental decision making. Research regarding the role of negative information in individual impression formation, person perception, and various other information-processing tasks indicates that people tend to weight negative information more heavily than they do positive information when forming evaluations of social stimuli, including assessments of individual likability (Anderson 1965; Hamilton and Huffman 1971; Hamilton and Zanna 1972; Hodges 1974; Jordan 1965; Kellermann 1989). Research by Lau (1982, 1985) and Kernell (1977) has provided evidence supportive of negativity effects in political perception and behavior, including increased voter turnout due to negative candidate performance evaluations.

Not surprisingly, voters quickly tire of negative campaign tactics and commonly complain about the negative tenor of campaigns. Citizens consistently say negative advertising is unfair, uninformative, unethical, and deceptive (Garramone 1984; Merritt 1984; Steward 1975; Surlin and Gordon 1977). As a result, campaign consultants have increased the sophistication of campaigns by turning to a mix of strategies and tactics that includes the use of comparative advertising (Pfau et al. 1990; Salmore and Salmore 1989). Such advertising communicates negative information about a targeted candidate to voters while helping reduce the potential for backlash voting associated with the use of more obvious forms of attack advertising. The results of an analysis of the political advertising used in three national elections indicates that nearly half the advertising mentioned both candidates and almost a quarter contained direct candidate comparisons (Boiney and Paletz 1991).

Even though research results indicate that comparative advertising can be as effective as standard negative advertising in reducing targeted candidate evaluations and voting preferences, such advertising continues to suffer from perceptions of poor credibility (Johnson-Cartee and Copeland 1991a; Pinkleton 1997, 1998). Given voters' intense dislike of negative campaign tactics, study participants are likely to provide a low utility rating for negative political advertising.

> H1: Participants will rate negative advertisements lower in utility than positive advertisements.

Negativism

Voter disgust with negative campaign tactics also should result in greater negativism toward political campaigns more broadly. Scholars and journalists regularly express concerns about the detrimental impact of negative campaign tactics on citizens' attitudes toward politics. If negativism decreases citizens' interest in campaigns and attention to public affairs information, the result is potentially disastrous for democracies, because they rely on citizens to make informed decisions and vote accordingly. Research confirms that heightened citizen interest and involvement in public affairs is associated with increased use of information sources and greater public affairs knowledge (Chaffee and Schleuder 1986; McLeod and McDonald 1985; Pinkleton et al. 1997; Reagan 1996). If the public dislikes and distrusts negative campaign tactics, however, it seems more likely that its feelings of negativity will be directed toward the campaigns more than toward the media. Previous research shows that negativism toward the media is associated with decreased media use, but negativism toward campaigns is not (Pinkleton, Austin, and Fortman 1998). As a result, it is reasonable to expect that negativity increases resulting from exposure to negative political advertising will be directed toward political campaigns, as hypothesized.

> H2: Participants' negativism toward political campaigns will increase as advertisement negativity increases.

Cynicism

Cynicism, perhaps the most frequently explored aspect of political disaffection, commonly refers to a lack of confidence in and a feeling of distrust toward the political system (Dennis and Webster 1975; Dionne 1991; Lau and Erber 1985; Perloff and Kinsey 1992). This represents a more broadbased aspect of disaffection than negativism toward campaigns, which is likely more situation based. Crotty and Jacobson (1980) suggest that cynical citizens have essentially given up on the political process, viewing it as irrelevant to their lives. Scholars and others frequently express concern that increased cynicism—most commonly blamed on negative campaign tactics—contributes to low interest in public affairs and reduced voter turnout (Ansolabehere, Behr, and Iyengar 1993; Cappella and Jamieson 1997; Crotty and Jacobson 1980; Dennis and Webster 1975). Negative political advertising, these authors argue, turns off voters and contributes to an electorate that is ill informed and uninvolved (Cappella and Jamieson 1997; Diamond and Bates 1988; Salmore and Salmore 1989).

Some authors have argued that some negativism toward political messages may represent healthy skepticism rather than cynicism, which is characterized by an openness to additional information (e.g., Austin and Pinkleton 1995; Cappella and Jamieson 1997; Pinkleton, Austin, and Fortman 1998; Wilkins 2000). Skeptical citizens may seek information to confirm or disconfirm the veracity of previously received messages. Cynicism, however, represents a cognitive state essentially closed to new information (Cappella and Jamieson 1997). As a result, cynical persons may respond more to messages that further confirm their distrustful beliefs and less to positive messages.

Voters have expressed strong disengagement from gubernatorial and senatorial elections based on the negative tenor of the election campaigns and the lack of substantive discussion pertaining to issues of interest to voters (Ansolabehere and Iyengar 1995). Ultimately, previous studies suggest that negative election environments increase voter cynicism, particularly for voters who already feel alienated or disenfranchised. Some scholars have suggested that voters—especially young voters—get trapped in a downward cycle in which cynicism breeds low efficacy, which in turn increases cynicism and apathy (Chaffee and Becker 1975; Jennings and Niemi 1978; Lau and Erber 1985). Other experimental studies have found that negative political advertising tends to increase cynicism, whereas positive advertising tends to decrease cynicism (Ansolabehere and Iyengar 1995). According to this research evidence, candidates' negative messages may further clutter and reinforce a negative campaign environment, contributing to an increase in voters' cynicism, as hypothesized.

> H3: Participants' cynicism will increase as advertisement negativity increases.

Efficacy

Scholars frequently define self efficacy as a person's belief that, through his or her efforts, he or she can influence political and social events (Bandura 1986, 1997). Political decision-making studies often use the term "internal efficacy" to reflect people's beliefs about their own competence to understand and participate effectively in politics. According to Craig, Niemi, and Silver (1990), internal efficacy differs from distrust/cynicism, which refers to whether or not the government meets expectations and operates fairly. Internal efficacy also differs from external efficacy, which political scientists use to refer to beliefs about the responsiveness of governmental authorities and institutions. External efficacy parallels distrust/cynicism, which Craig, Niemi, and Silver (1990) have treated separately. Other studies have treated distrust/cynicism as a single construct on the basis of factor loadings (e.g., Austin and Pinkleton 1995; Pinkleton, Austin, and Fortman 1998). Scholars believe that cynical citizens' distrust of the government decreases their internal efficacy, the belief that they can exert any influence over systems of governance. This then leads them essentially to opt out of the political process.

Some researchers have found that voters may participate, despite their cynicism, if they are high in efficacy (Horn and Conway 1996). Others have found that negative advertising can both increase cynicism and decrease efficacy (Ansolabehere and Iyengar 1995). These scholars, however, have not separated measures of efficacy from measures of cynicism. Efficacy appears to have a direct, negative relationship with cynicism (Austin and Pinkleton 1995), and some scholars have combined measures of efficacy and cynicism as opposites of the same construct (Ansolabehere and Iyengar 1995). Others, however, have found them to be separate, if related, constructs (e.g., Austin and Pinkleton 1995; Bowen, Stamm, and Clark 2000; Chen 1992; Pinkleton et al. 1998). As a result, it is useful to test the effects of negative advertising on cynicism and efficacy separately. According to Bandura (1986, 1997), efficacy develops through successful experiences that cultivate confidence and expertise. Unsuccessful or frustrating experiences, however, can decrease efficacy. Thus, to the extent voters find negative advertising frustrating or lacking in usefulness, negative advertising should decrease individuals' efficacy, as hypothesized.

> H4: Participants' self efficacy will decrease as advertising negativity increases.

Apathy

In studies of the electorate, apathy reflects a failure to engage in even the most basic forms of public affairs participation, usually including voting. Research findings regarding self efficacy indicate that political disaffection may actually lead to greater action among citizens who posses higher levels of self efficacy (Bandura 1997). When typical methods of achieving social change appear ineffective, citizens with higher self efficacy may intensify their efforts rather than abandoning them. The likelihood of action is highest among those with high levels of self efficacy combined with cynicism toward the political system (Bandura 1986, 1997).

This reasoning, however, runs counter to the opinions of many other scholars, who suggest that the ultimate outcome of a political election process corrupted by negative political advertising is an apathetic citizenry (Ansolabehere, Behr, and Iyengar 1993; Cappella and Jamieson 1997; Crotty and Jacobson 1980; Dennis and Webster 1975). These scholars suggest that negative campaign tactics contribute to high levels of citizen cynicism and negativism and low levels of citizen efficacy. Ultimately, these authors argue, negative campaign tactics turn citizens off to such an extent that they simply refuse to participate in a political system they view as corrupt and largely unresponsive to their needs. Although scholars can make a reasonable argument connecting both cynicism and apathy to negative campaign tactics, researchers have not determined the basis for this relationship with empirical specificity. The problem may be that, whereas critics link cynicism with apathy, some scholars have found them to be separate and unrelated constructs (Austin and Pinkleton 1995; Chen 1992). Without scientific evidence, it is difficult to blame apathy on the existence of negative campaign messages in the media or even on the frequency of people's exposure to the media in general or public affairs information specifically (Pinkleton and Austin 1998). A research question regarding the effect of negative political advertising on apathy is in order, given the competing opinions about negative campaign tactics and voter apathy.

> RQ1: What is the effect of negative political advertising on participants' apathy?

In summary, existing research and criticisms suggest that negative political advertising can produce both deleterious and beneficial effects. To improve scholars' understanding of the effects of negative political advertising, this study tests hypotheses on variables that suggest the potential for short-term, situationally based effects as well as longer term, more systemic-level effects.

Method

Undergraduate students participated in a 1 x 4 pretest-posttest (between groups) experiment to test the hypotheses and answer the research question.... Female and male participants participated nearly equally. Participants' ages ranged from 18 to 37 years; just over 85% of participants were between the ages of 19 and 22 years. More than 60% of participants had voted in a previous election.

A total of 246 participants received one of three randomly assigned treatments or a control activity. A total of 236 usable cases remained after the elimination of 10 incomplete instruments... Participants in the treatment conditions received different messages about fictional candidates for a state senate seat in Georgia. The campaign ostensibly occurred far away from participants' home state to increase its realism and decrease the potential for students' knowledge of local election issues.

Procedures

The experiment employed a double-exposure design. Initially, participants read each candidate's biographic profile and completed a series of pretest scales. Following the completion of the pretest scales, participants read a stimulus advertisement or control essay. Participants listed the thoughts they had about each candidate following initial stimulus exposure. This free-recall protocol ensured that participants thought about the candidates and stimuli, with the results not analyzed for the purpose of this study. Following the thought-listing exercise, participants again read the advertising stimuli or control essay and filled out posttest scales. Debriefing followed the completion of the posttest scales.

Stimuli

The experiment employed three types of stimuli, including biographic candidate profiles, political advertisements, and a control group essay. Biographic profiles contained information about each candidates' education, employment background, political accomplishments, family, and related information. Pretesting of the stimuli, along with manipulation checks, confirmed that both of the profiles were approximately equal in communicating information about candidates' qualifications, intelligence, credibility, and related characteristics.

Three advertisements constituted the treatments and were based on real-world examples of direct mail political advertising. The stimuli contained two different candidate names for both the sponsoring and targeted candidates to avoid name-specific effects. To determine the specific issue positions used in the stimuli, pretest participants rated the importance of issues using seven-point, semantic differential scales. Instrument pretesting procedures served to identify five issues for inclusion in the stimuli. The issues pertained to the environment, crime and community safety, higher education funding, development of employment opportunities, and increased support for elementary and secondary education.

Each stimulus contained a similar execution of a different creative strategy. The most negative stimulus contained a direct attack on the targeted candidate. The headline encouraged readers to vote for the sponsoring candidate and contained biographic highlights of the ad's sponsor. The remaining copy in this stimulus directly attacked the targeted candidate on the key issue positions identified through pretesting. A comparative version of this ad received somewhat less negative ratings from participants in pretests. The headline and sponsoring candidate biographic information were the same. The candidates were directly compared in this ad; however, the sponsoring candidate was portrayed as supporting the desired position on the key pretest issues, and the targeted candidate was assailed as supporting the opposite position. The final stimulus received a positive evaluation from pretest participants. This ad contained the same headline and biographic information as the other ads but did not mention the target ed candidate. Only the desired positions of the sponsoring candidate were mentioned in this stimulus.

Control group participants read an essay. The essay contained geographic and historical information about Georgia and did not mention either the sponsoring or the targeted candidate....

Variable Measurement

[Items used to measure each variable are shown in Table 1.]...

As predicted by Hypothesis 1 and shown in Table 2, participants gave the negative ads a lower utility rating. There was no significant difference between the control group and the positive advertising strategy condition. There also were no significant differences between the comparative ad and the negative ad strategies, with both reported as less useful than the positive ad strategy, as shown in Figure 1.

As predicted by Hypothesis 2 and shown ... in Figure 2, the more negative the advertisement, the more negativism subjects reported toward political campaigns. There was no significant difference between the control group condition and the positive advertising condition....

Discussion

Despite widespread concern about the effects of negative campaign techniques, the effects of negative advertising strategies on voter decision making are poorly understood. Campaigns use them because they seem to work, and critics decry them because they appear to depress political participation. Therefore, this study tested the effects of negative political advertising on key variables in the political decision-making process to help explain how negative advertising affects political participation. Study results indicate that participants found negative advertising less useful than positive advertising. Whereas negative advertising produced greater contempt for campaigns, however, it had no effects on apathy.

As expected, the more negative the advertising, the less useful participants found it. This supports the findings of others who have suggested that negative ads provide little information that is helpful to voters (Ansolabehere and Iyengar 1995; Cappella and Jamieson 1997). Voters frequently say they dislike and distrust negative political advertising. These results appear to confirm that such feelings of dislike translate into more cognitively based assessments of information benefit. Nevertheless, political campaign consultants find negative political campaign advertising useful, because, when carefully

Table 1

Descriptive Statistics for Variables Used in the Analyses

Variable	m	alpha
Variables at Pretest		
Negativism toward campaigns	17.79	.76
Pol. campaigns too mean-spirited	4.38	
In general, pol. campaigns too negative	4.34	
Seems pol. ads are *against* something more often than they are *for* something	4.61	
Pol. advertising is too negative	4.46	
Cynicism	23.38	.84
Pol.s lose touch with people quickly	4.71	
Cand.s only interested in people's votes, not their opinions	4.51	
Too many pol.s only serve themselves or special interests	4.82	
Seems gov't run by a few big interests just out for themselves	4.50	
Pol.s lie to media & public	4.85	
Efficacy	11.82	.77
I have a real say in what the government does	3.11	
My vote makes a difference	3.82	
Voting an effective way to influence what government does	4.91	
Apathy (reverse coded)	15.44	.93
Voting in each election a high priority for me	3.68	
Voting in elections is important to me	4.10	
Would feel guilty if I didn't vote	3.41	
I like to vote	4.24	
Variables at Posttest		
Advertising utility	17.51	.81
Believable–unbelievable	4.40	
Unfair–fair	3.99	
Informative–uninformative	4.72	
Interesting–uninteresting	4.36	
Negativism re campaigns	18.68	.88
Pol. campaigns too mean-spirited	4.55	
In general, pol. campaigns too negative	4.66	
Seems like pol. ads *against* something more than they are *for* something	4.73	
Pol. advertising is too negative	4.73	
Cynicism	23.38	.88
Pol.s lose touch with people quickly	4.64	
Cand.s only interested in people's votes, not in their opinions	4.60	
Too many pol.s only serve themselves or special interests	4.68	
Seems our gov't run by a few big interests just out for themselves	4.63	
Pol.s lie to media & public	4.85	
Efficacy	11.46	.86
I have a real say in what the government does	3.47	
My vote makes a difference	3.81	
Voting is an effective way to influence what government does	4.19	
Apathy (reverse coded)	15.39	.94
Voting in each election a high priority for me	3.75	
Voting in elections important to me	4.03	
Would feel guilty if I didn't vote	3.50	
I like to vote	4.13	

Note: All items measured on seven-point scales. Except for semantic differential items, a high score indicates stronger agreement, and a low score indicates stronger disagreement. Reverse-coded items recoded for consistent directionality before inclusion in the appropriate index.

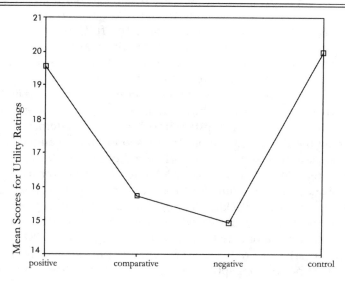

Figure 1
Effects of Experimental Manipulation on Advertising Utility Ratings

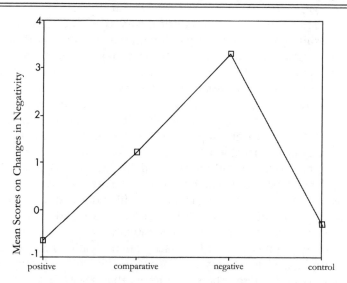

Figure 2
Effects of Experimental Manipulation on Participants' Negativity Toward Campaigns

created and executed, it successfully denigrates targeted candidate evaluations and voting intentions (Johnson-Cartee and Copeland 1991a; Kaid and Boydston 1987; Perloff and Kinsey 1992; Pinkleton 1997, 1998). This indicates that voter assessments of usefulness do not necessarily indicate effects or effectiveness.

Participants' assessments of usefulness were consistent with their perceptions of negativism toward political campaigns, indicating that the advertisements had some effects, despite their perceived uselessness among message recipients. Those exposed to the most negative stimuli reported the most negativity toward campaigns. In fact, the fully negative advertising condition produced perceptions nearly three times as negative (m=3.31) as the comparative advertising condition (m=1.23). The positive advertising condition (m=-.66) was no different than the control condition in terms of negativity. This finding is not surprising because of voters' stated disgust with negative political advertising. The bigger issue is whether increased negative advertising effects translate into long-term, systemic cynicism or whether they merely reflect a short-term response to the campaign at hand. Scholars suggest that some aspects of disaffection can be motivating to potential voters, in which case the heightened negativity ef fects could be viewed as a successful outcome for the promotion of political participation. When citizens engage in backlash voting, for example, this represents a form of political participation motivated by negativism (e.g., Faber, Tims, and Schmitt 1990; Garramone 1984; Roddy and Garramone 1988). One study found that negativism predicted a greater intention for voting through its effect on third-person perceptions, or the belief that others would be more gullible to the advertising (Austin and Pinkleton 1995). Others have noted that negative advertising tends to depress voting among less involved or less partisan citizens, tending to polarize more involved voters (e.g., Ansolabehere and Iyengar 1995).

The investigation of negative political advertising's effects on cynicism produced a result less consistent with common criticisms of political advertising, seeming to confirm that, at least in the short term, campaign-related negativism and cynicism, though related, have different causes and different outcomes. Campaign-related negativism appears to be a direct response to a specific, ongoing campaign or campaigns, representing a more transient state than cynicism. Cynicism, at least in this experimental manipulation, was not affected by negative political campaign techniques, in support of the position that it is more global and stable.

Scholars have only recently begun to delineate the differences between campaign-related negativism, which appears to be affected by negative political advertising, and more enduring cynicism, which does not change as easily. As a result, these findings suggest that what scholars and critics often say about cynicism may be true of negativism rather than cynicism. For example, though cynicism often is blamed for a lack of participation among citizens, it does not always associate directly with behavior (Pinkleton, Austin, and Fortman 1998). In contrast, researchers have found that negativism can be associated with public affairs behavior, in some cases motivating participation rather than discouraging it (Austin and Pinkleton 1995; Lau 1982). In addition, cynicism in some previous research has had sizable negative associations with efficacy, whereas negativism toward campaigns appears to affect efficacy less directly (Austin and Pinkleton 1995). Nevertheless, negativism—particularly toward the media rather than toward campaigns—and cynicism are clearly associated (Pinkleton, Austin, and Fortman 1998). As a result, critics' concerns that negativism may evolve into more global cynicism may be well placed, but short-term effects such as those demonstrated in this study should not be assumed to have long-term significance. More research would be helpful on this point.

Study results suggest that a drop in efficacy may occur as the negativity of political advertising increases, but our findings only bordered on statistical significance. This suggests that negative advertising may have the potential to damage political participation by virtue of its influences on efficacy, but it also suggests that efficacy may be somewhat resilient to short-term negative campaign cycles. Scholars have found that efficacy develops through continuing experiences (Bandura 1986, 1997), with some scholars suggesting that more novice participants tend to be more affected by negative events and news coverage (Chaffee and Becker 1975) and have less stable political orientations (Jennings and Niemi 1978; Lau and Erber 1985). It could be that a stronger manipulation in a more realistic campaign setting might produce significant changes in voter efficacy. As a result, concerns about the effects of negative campaign tactics cannot be dismissed on the basis of these results.

The findings regarding voting apathy, which associates with efficacy (Austin and Pinkleton 1995), were unambiguous, with the negative advertising executions having no effect on judgments of apathy. This could suggest that apathetic citizens are less affected by the negativism in advertising as a result of their lack of involvement in or attention to the political process. As a result, citizens who blame negative campaign tactics for their own lack of participation could be making excuses after the fact rather than reporting accurately on the roots of their own disinterest. It also could indicate that negative advertising's effects on apathy and efficacy, as well as on cynicism, are cumulative and difficult to detect in a short-term manipulation. It would be useful to replicate this study with more experienced voters and over a longer time period to determine whether the results would differ and to get a clearer understanding of the cause-and-effect relationship among variables. In particular, a study incorporating multiple messages and multiple exposures could provide more measurement opportunities and, thus, more powerful evidence of changes that may occur....

In summary, this study has demonstrated the complexities of political decision making, indicating that more studies need to address intermediary variables in political decision making. Despite scholars' concerns about the deleterious effects of negative campaign tactics on political participation, this study found little evidence of systemic-level damaging effects. Over the course of a campaign, however, people will likely see a barrage of both negative and comparative advertising. If this crush of advertising and media coverage has effects on negativity but none on efficacy, apathy, or cynicism, then the results of negative advertising may be what campaign strategists desire: A short-term increase in negativity that damages targeted candidate evaluations but leaves no long-term, damaging effects on the electorate. These results, however, do not rule out the possibility that, ultimately, negative advertising reduces public affairs participation. Although this study further confirms that negative advertising is perceived as negative and contributes to short-term disgust with campaigns, the findings suggest that this strategy does not automatically increase cynicism or citizen apathy.

References

Anderson, Norman H. (1965), "Averaging vs. Adding as a Stimulus-Combination Rule in Impression Formation," *Journal of Experimental Psychology*, 70 (4), 394–400.

Ansolabehere, Stephen, Roy Behr, and Shanto Iyengar (1993), *The Media Game*, New York: Macmillan.

—— and Shanto Iyengar (1995), Going Negative: *How Political Advertisements Shrink & Polarize the Electorate*, New York: The Free Press.

Austin, Erica W. and Bruce E. Pinkleton (1995), "Positive and Negative Effects of Political Disaffection on the Less Experienced Voter," *Journal of Broadcasting and Electronic Media*, 39 (2), 215–235.

Bandura, Albert (1986), *Social Foundations of Thought and Action: A Social Cognitive Theory*, Englewood Cliffs, NJ: Prentice-Hall

—— (1997), *Self Efficacy: The Exercise of Control*, New York: W. H. Freeman and Company.

Boiney, John and David L. Paletz (1991), "In Search of the Model Model: Political Science Versus Political Advertising Perspectives on Voter Decision Making," in *Television and Political Advertising, Volume 1: Psychological* Processes, Frank Biocca, ed., Hillsdale, NJ: Lawrence Eribaum Associates, 3–26.

Bowen, Lawrence, Keith Stamm, and Fiona Clark (2000), "Television Reliance and Political Malaise: A Contingency Analysis," *Journal of Broadcasting & Electronic Media*, 44 (1), 1–15.

Cappella, Joseph N. and Kathleen Hall Jamieson (1997), *Spiral of Cynicism: The Press and the Public Good*, New York: Oxford University Press.

Chaffee, Steven H. and Lee B. Becker (1975), "Young Voters' Reactions to Early Watergate Issues," American Politics Quarterly, 3 (4), 360–385.

—— and Joan Schleuder (1986), "Measurement and Effects of Attention to Media News," *Human Communication Research*, 13 (1), 76–107.

Chen, Kevin (1992), *Political Alienation and Voting Turnout in the United States 1960-1988*, San Francisco: Mellen Research University Press.

Craig, Stephen C., Richard G. Niemi, and Glenn E. Silver (1990), "Political Efficacy and Trust: A Report on the NES Pilot Study Items," *Political Behavior*, 12 (3), 289–313.

Crotty, William J. and Gary C. Jacobson (1980), *American Parties in Decline*, Boston: Little, Brown, and Company.

Dennis, Jack and Carol Webster (1975), "Childrens' Images of the President and of Government in 1962 and 1974," *American Politics Quarterly*, 3 (4), 386–405.

Diamond, Edwin and Stephen Bates (1988), *The Spot: The Rise of Political Advertising on Television*, Cambridge, MA: MIT Press.

Dionne, E.J., Jr. (1991), *Why Americans Hate Politics*, New York: Simon and Schuster.

Doak, David (1995), "Attack Ads: Rethinking the Rules," *Campaigns & Elections*, 16 (July), 20–21.

Faber, Ronald J., Albert R. Tims, and Kay G Schmitt (1990), "Accentuate the Negative?: The Impact of Negative Political Appeals on Voting Intent," in *Proceedings of the American Academy of Advertising,* Patricia Stout, ed., Austin, TX: American Academy of Advertising, 10–16.

Garramone, Gina M. (1984), "Voter Responses to Negative Political Ads," *Journalism Quarterly,* 61 (2), 25 0–259.

—— (1985), "Effects of Negative Political Advertising: The Roles of Sponsor and Rebuttal," *Journal of Broadcasting and Electronic Media,* 29 (2), 147–159.

—— and Sandra J. Smith (1984), "Reactions to Political Advertising: Clarifying Sponsor Effects," *Journalism Quarterly,* 61 (4), 771–775.

Grove, Lloyd (1989), "How Experts Fueled a Race with Vitriol," *The Washington Post,* (January 18), Al and A14.

Hamilton, David L. and Leroy J. Huffman (1971), "Generality of Impression-Formation Processes for Evaluative and Nonevaluative Judgments," *Journal of Personality and Social Psychology,* 20 (2), 200–207.

—— and Mark P. Zanna (1972), "Differential Weighting of Favorable and Unfavorable Attributes in Impression Formation," *Journal of Experimental Research in Personality,* 6(2–3), 204–212.

Hodges, Bert H. (1974), "Effect of Valence on Relative Weighting in Impression Formation," *Journal of Personality and Social Psychology,* 30 (3), 378–381.

Horn, Randolph C. and M. Margaret Conway (1996), "Public Judgment and Political Engagement in the 1992 Election," in *Broken Contract? Changing Relationships Between Americans and Their Government,* Stephen C. Craig, ed., Boulder, CO: Westview Press, 110–126.

Jennings, Kent M. and Richard G. Niemi (1978), "The Persistence of Political Orientations: An Over-Time Analysis of Two Generations," British Journal of Political Science, 8, 333–363.

Johnson-Cartee, Karen S. and Gary A. Copeland (1989), "Southern Voters' Reaction to Negative Political Ads in 1986," *Journalism Quarterly,* 66 (4), 888–893, 986.

—— and —— (199la), "Candidate-Sponsored Negative Political Advertising Effects Reconsidered," paper presented to Association for Education in Journalism and Mass Communication Convention, (August), Boston.

—— and —— (1991b), *Negative Political Advertising: Coming of Age,* Hillsdale, NJ: Lawrence Eribaum Associates.

Jordan, Nehemiah (1965), "The 'Asymmetry' of 'Liking' and 'Disliking': A Phenomenon Meriting Further Replication and Research," *Public Opinion Quarterly,* 29 (2), 315–322.

Kaid, Lynda L. and John Boydston (1987), "An Experimental Study of the Effectiveness of Negative Political Advertisements," *Communication Quarterly,* 35 (2), 193–201.

Kellermann, Kathy (1989), "The Negativity Effect in Interaction: It's All in Your Point of View," *Human Communication Research,* 16 (2), 147–183.

Kernell, S. (1977), "Presidential Popularity and Negative Voting: An Alternative Explanation of the Mid-Term Congressional Decline of the President's Party," *American Political Science Review,* 71, 44–66.

Lau, Richard R. (1982), "Negativity in Political Perception," *Political Behavior,* 4 (4), 353–377.

—— (1985), "Two Explanations for Negativity Effects in Political Behavior," *American Journal of Political Science,* 29 (1), 119–138.

—— and Ralph Erber (1985), "Political Sophistication: An Information-Processing Perspective," in *Mass Media & Political Thought*, Sidney Kraus and Richard M. Perloff, eds., Beverly Hills, CA: Sage Publications, 37–64.

McLeod, Jack M. and Daniel G. McDonald (1985), "Beyond Simple Exposure: Media Orientations and Their Impact on Political Processes," *Communication Research*, 12 (1), 3–33.

Merritt, Sharyne (1984), "Negative Political Advertising: Some Empirical Findings," *Journal of Advertising*, 13 (3), 27–38.

Nugent, John F. (1987), "Positively Negative," *Campaigns and Elections*, 7 (March/April), 47–49.

Perloff, Richard M. and Dennis Kinsey (1992), "Political Advertising as Seen by Consultants and Journalists," Journal of Advertising Research, 36 (May/June), 53–60.

Pfau, Michael, Henry C. Kenski, Michael Nitz, and John Sorenson (1990), "Efficacy of Inoculation Strategies in Promoting Resistance to Political Attack Messages: Application to Direct Mail," *Communication Monographs*, 57 (1), 25–43.

Pinkleton, Bruce E. (1997), "The Effects of Negative Comparative Political Advertising on Candidate Evaluations and Advertising Evaluations: An Exploration," *Journal of Advertising*, 26 (1), 19–29.

—— (1998), "Effects of Print Comparative Political Advertising on Political Decision-Making and Participation," *Journal of Communication,* 48 (4), 24–36.

—— and Erica W. Austin (1998), "Media and Participation: Breaking the Spiral of Disaffection," in *Engaging the Public: How Government and the Media Can Reinvigorate American Democracy*, Thomas J. Johnson, Carol E. Hays and Scott P. Hays, eds., Lanham, MD: Rowman & Littlefield Publishers, 75–86.

—— ,——, and Kristine K. J. Fortman (1998), "Relationships of Media Use and Political Disaffection to Political Efficacy and Voting Behavior," *Journal of Broadcasting & Electronic Media*, 42 (1), 34–49.

—— , Joey Reagan, Dustin Aaronson, and Chien-Fei Chen (1997), "The Role of Individual Motivations in Information Source Use and Knowledge Concerning Divergent Topics," *Communication Research Reports*, 14 (3), 291–301.

Reagan, Joey (1996), "The 'Repertoire' of Information Sources," *Journal of Broadcasting & Electronic Media*, 40 (1), 112–121.

Roddy, Brian L. and Gina M. Garramone (1988), "Appeals and Strategies of Negative Political Advertising," *Journal of Broadcasting & Electronic Media*, 32 (4), 415–427.

Salmore, Barbara G. and Stephen A. Salmore (1989), *Candidates, Parties, and Campaigns*, Washington, DC: Congressional Quarterly Press.

Steward, Charles J. (1975), "Voter Perception of Mudslinging in Political Communication," *Central States Speech Journal*, 26 (4), 279, 286.

Surlin, Stuart H. and Thomas F. Gordon (1977), "How Values Affect Attitudes Toward Direct Reference Political Advertising," *Journalism Quarterly*, 54 (1), 89–95.

Taylor, Paul (1989), "Consultants Rise Via the Low Road," *The Washington Post*, (January 17), A1, A14.

Wilkins, Karin Gwinn (2000), "The Role of Media in Public Disengagement from Public Life," *Journal of Broadcasting & Electronic Media*, 44 (4), 569–580.

NO

**Ruth Ann Weaver Lariscy
and Spencer F. Tinkham**

Accentuating the Negative

"...Studies demonstrate that, as time passes, the source of a negative [political advertisement] decays, but its content remains and becomes even more powerful."

BEWARE, Mr. and Ms. American Voter, highly skilled spinmeisters are coming after you—more precisely, your vote—with unprecedented negative attack advertising. Despite legislation designed to limit campaign mudslinging, negative advertising began earlier in this presidential race than any other in modern political history. To understand how the marketing consultants are working on you, keep in mind three important items: an ad does not have to be liked to be effective; negative ads help voters make distinctions among candidates; and not all negative ads are created equal.

Voters have a hard time with this first concept. Think for a few minutes about an ad slogan you find really annoying. If you are like most of us, you remember the ad, slogan, and product clearly, even if you disliked the ad intensely when it came on the radio or television. One reason why this type of negative ad works is because it is more complex than a positive one.

A positive ad ("Joe Smith is a war veteran, a patriot, and has true American values.") presents no overt conflict, elicits less rebuttal, and is absorbed easily. While "feel good" commercials can be enjoyable to viewers, they are not particularly informative, educational, or memorable. A positive message glides through the brain in much the same way that water from a garden hose washes easily over a smooth patio—nothing gets in its way, slows it down, or "sticks" very long.

A negative ad, however, sticks in the memory. ("Joe Smith never has served his country, used personal influence to avoid military service, and his commitment to true American values should be questioned.") Negative ads cause voters to think, make comparisons, sort through meanings, and assess the validity of claims. The brain expends more time and energy processing the negative message because of its complexity. A negative message is not smooth. It is like water from a garden hose running through a rocky ravine full of crags and cracks that make the journey more difficult. The water has to traverse slowly, navigating around obstacles, and sometimes getting stuck in little pools.

Negative information carries an inherent memory bias that the positive variety does not. Consider the following illustration: You walk into a room wearing a new suit and receive 15 compliments. It feels great. Then, one person says, "That is an okay look for last year's style." The good feelings stop. Regardless of the number of compliments received and how much you want to remember them, it is the one snide remark that sticks. Negative ads are more memorable than positive ones, even when you do not want them to be.

Not only does negative information stick, it sticks longer. In a series of experimental studies a couple of years ago with groups of registered voters from northeast Georgia, we produced professional quality political commercials for a fictitious candidate and his fictitious opponent in, of course, a fictitious congressional campaign. Using all the appropriate experimental protocol and controls, the participants were asked to evaluate a series of commercials, then answer the question, "If the election for Congress was held today between Candidate X and Candidate Y, who would you vote for?"

We were not surprised that the negative ad we created was especially effective immediately after it was shown, when there was no chance for response or rebuttal. In fact, a majority of those who saw only the attack ad voted for the attacker. When a specific rebuttal ad sponsored by the victim of the attack was viewed, the vote went to the victim. This, too, is not intuitively surprising.

The findings from the next stage of these studies were an eye-opener, however. In a period covering six weeks from the day of his or her vote for the fictitious candidate, each study participant was called back on the telephone. After reacquainting each with some basic information, we repeated the question we had asked the day of the study. The numbers shifted rather dramatically. The attacker overwhelmingly won the election. There even were a couple of instances when a participant would say, "You know, I'm not clear on the name, but I definitely would not vote for that one who lied." Of course, "being a liar" was at the heart of the attack ad.

In these experiments, we tested what psychologists call "the sleeper effect" and generated some intriguing results. The studies demonstrate that, as time passes, the source of a negative attack decays, but its content remains and becomes even more powerful. Simply put, you may forget where or when you learned something, but the negative information stays with you.

During the last two decades, political advertising has become (to the distress of many journalists and political observers) an increasingly important source of information for voters. Some scholars estimate that as many as half of the electorate make voting decisions based upon information from advertising. You may lament the rise of "instantaneous information" in the 30-second commercial spot, but it is a vital feature of the election campaign landscape, particularly aimed at less involved (but responsible) voters. This group needs to receive easily understood, straightforward information in a simple format.

However, not all negative ads are created equal. Up to this point, we have used a general umbrella term to cover a wide range of negative messages. Yet, not all negative attack ads work effectively. A poor ad can blow up in the face of the candidate who sponsored it. There are in fact "good" negative ads and "bad" ones, but you may be surprised at what constitutes each.

Good negative ads create all the desirable effects discussed earlier. Bad negative ads, however, produce something different—a backlash or boomerang. When a boomerang does occur, viewers have a strong, immediate reaction against the attacker and lots of empathy for the victim of the attack. It is fairly easy to recognize when an ad is attacking a candidate's stand on an issue versus when one is attacking a personal characteristic, such as likening someone to terrorist Osama bin Laden or dictator Adolf Hitler. Issues-based negative advertisements are more likely to elicit an instantaneous acceptance and less revulsion. Similarly, an ad that is considered below the belt or in poor taste (implied character assassination of a candidate's family member, for example) most likely will be condemned on the spot.

Good and Bad Negative Ads

A negative ad is not good or bad based exclusively on content, nor whether it is funny, entertaining, or well produced. The most important element is how useful the information is judged to be. For instance, conventional wisdom suggests an ad that alludes to the sexual exploits of a married candidate outside of marriage is inappropriate. If the criterion simply was "below the belt," the ad, based on this view, would be rejected and likely produce a backlash. In reality, though, the ad, which the attacker's campaign organization had predicted would have powerful effects, has virtually no impact since the extramarital activities of the attacked candidate were widely known. The information was old news and therefore judged not useful.

A second judgment enters voters' evaluation process of ads here as well: The attack must strike them as at least plausible. When viewing an attack ad, individuals certainly do not know if the information is true. Beyond the accuracy or perceived truthfulness, it seems to be quite important—if a message is going to work—that listeners would find the content within the realm of possibility.

Meanwhile, one component (Sec. 311) of the McCain-Feingold Campaign Finance Reform Law is popularly called the "stand by your ad" provision. As seen in the first negative attack ad that Pres. Bush's campaign levied against Sen. John Kerry (D.-Mass.), the President introduces the ad personally, saying, "I'm George W. Bush and I approved this message." Clearly, the logic behind the provision is that candidates and the independent organizations that sponsor ads for them will be less likely to "go negative" or to levy particularly vicious attacks if the candidates personally are tied to the message for fear of backlash or boomerang. Additionally, the provision does not allow soft money organizations to air any negative ads in the six weeks immediately preceding Election Day. Although it is too early to conclude that the provision is not working, there has been an early onslaught of attacks from both sides. As to the "softening" of attack ads, that, too, is difficult to assess, as it is impossible to know what ads might have been aired if the new regulations did not exist.

Moreover, the legislation may have an unintended effect. Since many of the attack ads will be restricted in the six weeks immediately prior to Election Day, the harshest will occur early on. By doing so, they are most likely to benefit from the sleeper effect, and, by November, many voters will forget where they heard it, but will remember the content of the attacks.

As protected political speech, negative campaign ads, regardless of any legislation, are here to stay. They can be informative, entertaining, interesting, and motivating. The best ones are. They also can be trashy, boring, and create a backlash. The worst ones do. Yet, an armed, informed audience—even one that claims "We can't stand all that mudslinging!"—is able to recognize that these messages have their place.

POSTSCRIPT

Is Negative Campaigning Bad for the American Political Process?

A 1996 Freedom Forum poll found that three-quarters of American voters believe that the press has a negative impact on U.S. presidential campaigns, detracts from a discussion of the issues, gives undue advantage to front-running candidates, is often confusing and unclear, and even discourages good people from running for president. Despite the criticism, these same voters rely heavily on journalists to provide the information needed to make informed voter decisions. They turn to journalists for information about the candidates, particularly their issue positions, and for information about how election outcomes will affect voters.

The implications of these findings for judgments about negativity in political campaigns are important. It seems clear that people are unhappy with current political coverage. People want more information, and they want it tailored to their questions and their needs. Political internet sites are perhaps one answer. They are proliferating; yet, even these suffer from the familiar problem of too much trivia and too little debate. It remains to be seen whether or not the advent of new technology will be able to fulfill its promise of creating a more positive dialogue between candidate and voter.

Lest a reader begin to feel too self-righteous about these issues, let us remember the complicity of the viewing public. Candidate debates attract a small number of viewers; political scandal sells. Just as in television entertainment, what the public gets is influenced by what the public selects from the available options. Certainly with the advent of cable niche programming, the public can select much more informative and less scandal-oriented programming than ever before. Thus, the critique that implicates the press and the politician also implicates the viewer.

A number of books try to analyze the consequences of negativity. One book that has specifically tackled the history and problem of campaign advertising is *Going Negative: How Attack Ads Shrink and Polarize the Electorate*, by Stephen Ansolabehere and Shano Iyengar (Free Press, 1997). Examining the consequences for the voter are Joseph Capella and Kathleen Hall Jamieson in *Spiral of Cynicism* (Oxford University Press, 1997). For an insight into the campaign planning process of the 2000 election, see *Electing the President, 2000: The Insiders' View* by Kathleen Jamieson and Paul Waldman (Editors) (University of Pennsylvania Press, 2001). For a journalistic take on the issue, see Mike McCurry, "Getting Past the Spin," *The Washington Monthly* (July/August 1999).

ISSUE 10

Do the Media Have a Liberal Bias?

YES: Bernard Goldberg, from *Bias: A CBS Insider Exposes How the Media Distort the News* (Regnery Publishing, 2002)

NO: Al Franken, *Lies, and the Lying Liars Who Tell Them: A Fair and Balanced Look at the Right.* Dutton, 2003

ISSUE SUMMARY

YES: Journalist Bernard Goldberg looks at the common phrase, "the media elite have a liberal bias," and gives examples of the way coverage becomes slanted, depending upon the reporter's or anchor's perception of the subject's political stance.

NO: Al Franken is a unique voice in American politics: a comedy writer and performer, Harvard fellow, and liberal political commentator. And he thinks the American media is anything but liberal. He faults the media for not fully exploring issues concerning tax changes that benefit the wealthy few.

T wo opponents square off on this issue: one takes up the traditional complaint that people in the media—the news makers and the on-air personalities—have a liberal bias, which presents the public with a critical view of the government and policies. The other decries the corporate and conservative bias of news media, which lacks the courage to call the establishment to account. Fundamental to this issue is a more central concept: whether or not a diversity of viewpoints is really available in the media so that the consumer can be informed appropriately and make up his or her mind depending upon the messages conveyed. Without media, accountability and openness of process may not be possible in contemporary government. Yet how do we evaluate the practices of the media?

Years of media analysis and theory underscore these issues and include such topics as "agenda setting," "status conferral features," "media functions," and "uses and gratifications." Research in any of these areas will shed greater light on the complexity of media content and audience interpretation of messages.

The selections by Goldberg and Franken also present a more "popular" approach to media commentary. Each is written from a distinctly personal viewpoint, which demonstrates that the "sender" of any message (in this case the author) can easily insert his or her own beliefs into a persuasive message. When viewed in this way, the question of whether or not the media can possibly present "neutral" messages takes on greater meaning. But while Goldberg and Franken both present their messages in print, the topic they are covering is journalism—which is subject to an even broader range of filters, gatekeepers, and audiences.

Goldberg writes from the perspective of a one-time CBS insider who criticized the media (and in particular, Dan Rather at CBS) for what he says are clearly liberal interpretations of information. He cites many examples, and seems to assume that his readers will agree with his interpretations. In doing so, he makes value judgments about issues that perhaps reveal a bias of his own.

Franken in his own humorous and hyperbolic manner castigates the press—and by implication the public—for their failure to expose the rhetoric of tax cuts. Bush, he argues, advocated a tax cut for the rich, and the press allowed him to sell it as a benefit for all citizens without the rigorous scrutiny that it deserved. His book cites many examples of how the press fails to investigate important information that might discomfort powerful corporate and political leaders. He, too, is polemical in his critique.

There is no shortage of combatants in this war over media bias. A selection of very popular books debate this issue—and often are very vitriolic in their analysis of oppositional pundits. See for example: *Slander: Liberal Lies About the American Right* by Ann H. Coulter (2002) or *Deliver Us from Evil : Defeating Terrorism, Despotism, and Liberalism* by Sean Hannity (2004). From the opposing side: *What Liberal Media? The Truth About Bias and the News* by Eric Alterman (2003) or *Big Lies: The Right-Wing Propaganda Machine and How It Distorts the Truth* by Joe Conason (2003). Whatever your political perspective, you will have no difficulty finding someone who agrees with you—and someone who doesn't. In fact, one possible outcome might be the return of the partisan press of the past. Would you be comfortable with a press system that abandoned the central tenet of impartiality?

One of the most important questions to consider as you read the following selections is whether or not any possible bias indicates a transmission of viewpoints or values. If the media lead us to think a certain way, then this may be an important issue to consider. If the media serve as one method among many for the socialization of the individual, then perhaps the topic is less important. Often the importance, and the bias, are in the eye of the beholder. By thinking and talking about this issue and news, you may find yourself having to take a position on the topic. Once you think you understand this concept, why not apply it to other forms of media, like music, film, or television?

The News Mafia

I can't say the precise moment it hit me, but I do know that it was on a Sunday night while I was watching the HBO series *The Sopranos*. That's when I started noticing that the wise guys in the mob and the news guys at the networks had the same kind of people skills.

Maybe Tony had somebody killed. Or maybe just roughed up. Or it might have been only words, something he said to his psychiatrist. I'm not sure. But the more I watched the more I saw how striking the similarities are between the Mafia and the media.

And, let the record show, I mean no disrespect to the Mafia.

In between hijacking trucks and throwing people off bridges, the wise guys are always going on about honor and loyalty and family, the holy trinity as far as guys with names like Tony Soprano and Paulie Walnuts are concerned. These are people who are exquisitely and monumentally delusional, of course. But it's this fundamental belief—that despite the bad PR, deep down where it really counts, they are just a bunch of honorable men who care about the important things in life and only hurt people who hurt them—that allows the wise guys to crush anyone who gets in their way.

It's the same with the News Mafia....

Trust me. I'm speaking from up-close-and-personal firsthand experience, from twenty-eight years on the inside as a news correspondent with one of the three big families, CBS News....

❧

February 13, 1996, was the day I committed my unpardonable sin and began to die....

I said out loud what millions of TV news viewers all over America know and have been complaining about for years: that too often, Dan [Rather] and Peter [Jennings] and Tom [Brokow] and a lot of their foot soldiers don't deliver the news straight, that they have a liberal bias, and that no matter how often the network stars deny it, it is true....

Actually I didn't *say* the networks were biased—I *wrote* it in one of the most important and widely read newspapers in the entire country, the *Wall Street Journal,* whose editorial page liberals love to hate. In an op-ed piece, I wrote, "There are lots of reasons fewer people are watching network news,

From *Bias: A CBS Insider Exposes How the Media Distort the News*, 2002, pp. 9-10, 12-21. Copyright © 2002 by Regnery Publishing. Reprinted by permission.

and one of them, I'm more convinced than ever, is that our viewers simply don't trust us. And for good reason.

"The old argument that the networks and other 'media elites' have a liberal bias is so blatantly true that it's hardly worth discussing anymore. No, we don't sit around in dark corners and plan strategies on how we're going to slant the news. We don't have to. It comes naturally to most reporters."

As my old buddy Wayne, who's never set foot in a newsroom in his life, put it, "What's the big deal; *everybody* knows that's true." Maybe, Wayne, but there's a big difference between when Rush Limbaugh or Bill Buckley says it and when a CBS News correspondent says it.

This was coming from the inside, from one of Rather's guys. Limbaugh could rave on about the liberal media all he wanted and the media elites would brush him off like a flake of dandruff on a blue suit. If William F. Buckley had written, word for word, what I had written, Dan Rather would have yawned and jumped in his limousine and headed for lunch at The Four Seasons.

Limbaugh and Buckley and all those other "right-wingers"—everybody to the right of Lenin is a "right-winger," as far as the media elites are concerned—were all a bunch of Republican partisans.

But I wasn't. I was a newsman. One of *their* newsmen! I had done a thousand stories for Walter Cronkite and Dan Rather on the *CBS Evening News* and later as the senior correspondent on *48 Hours*, the prime-time show Rather fronted. They don't let you stick around for more than two decades if you've got a political ax to grind. No, I was what The Dan and his nominal bosses in the front office call all of their reporters and producers: objective...fair...balanced.

I'll bet anything those are the exact words CBS News would have used to defend me if I had reported a story for the *Evening News* that came down hard on big business or the military or even the church. CBS News would have said, *Bernie has a well-deserved reputation for being objective, fair, and balanced, and we stand by Bernie and our story.*

But this piece I had written for the *Wall Street Journal* wasn't about business or the military or the church or any other safe target. Writing about the evils of business or the military or the church is like taking a walk in the park. I had just taken a stroll through a field of land mines. Taking on the pope is one thing. Taking on the media elites is quite another. And taking them on from the inside—violating their sacred code of *omerta*—is a sin.

A mortal sin.

◦⟨◉⟩◦

It's funny how some of the biggest, most dramatic changes in our lives happen almost by accident. If we hadn't gone to that particular drugstore to buy toothpaste and tissues on that particular day, we might not have met an old friend whom we hadn't seen in years, who invited us to a party where we met somebody's accountant, who walked us over to this schoolteacher whom we fell in love with and married. Go to a different drugstore and wind up with a different life.

Which brings us to Hurricane Andrew, the costliest natural disaster in the entire history of the United States, which just happened to blow through my house and thousands of others in South Florida in 1992. This brought me into contact for the very first time with a good ol' boy named Jerry Kelley, a chain-smoking, fifty-something building contractor who grew up in Enterprise, Alabama, and who makes Gomer Pyle sound like Laurence Olivier.

Without Hurricane Andrew there would have been no Jerry Kelley. And without Jerry Kelley there would have been no *Wall Street Journal* op-ed piece that changed my life forever.

Jerry Kelley saved my family and me. He repaired the damage the hurricane had done to our house. He was always there when we needed him. And we became friends, a kind of odd couple. We talked often, mostly about politics and current events, which he loved.

And on February 8, 1996, Jerry Kelley called me at home, wondering whether I had caught the *CBS Evening News* that night.

"Did you see that 'Reality Check' story on Dan Rather tonight?" he wanted to know, sounding even more like a cracker than he usually did, if that was possible. Jerry wasn't an angry kind of guy, but he was pretty hot that night. I told him I missed the Dan Rather newscast and asked what the problem was.

"The problem," he said, "is that you got too many snippy wise guys doin' the news, that's what the problem is." We went around like this for a while, and he told me to get a tape of the news and watch it. Then "you tell me if there's a problem."

Fair enough. The next day I went into the CBS News bureau in Miami to watch a videotape of the story that had Jerry so worked up.

The reporter was Eric Engberg, a Washington correspondent whose "Reality Check" was about presidential candidate Steve Forbes and his flat tax, which was the centerpiece of the Forbes campaign.

Not exactly a sexy subject. So what's the big deal, I wondered. But as I watched the videotape, it became obvious that this was a hatchet job, an editorial masquerading as real news, a cheap shot designed to make fun of Forbes— a rich conservative white guy, the safest of all media targets—and ridicule his tax plan.

Still, blasting the flat tax wasn't in the same league as taking shots at people who are against affirmative action or abortion, two of the more popular targets of the liberal media elites. How worked up was I supposed to get... *over the flat tax*?

But the more I watched the more I saw that this story wasn't simply about a presidential candidate and a tax plan. It was about something much bigger, something too much of big-time TV journalism had become: a showcase for smart-ass reporters with attitudes, reporters who don't even pretend to hide their disdain for certain people and certain ideas that they and their sophisticated friends don't particularly like.

Rather introduced Engberg's piece with the standard stuff about how it would "look beyond the promises to the substance" of the Forbes flat tax. Television news anchors enjoy using words like "substance," mostly because a half-hour newscast (about twenty-one minutes after commercials) has so little of it.

Engberg's voice covered pictures of Steve Forbes on the campaign trail. "Steve Forbes pitches his flat-tax scheme as an economic elixir, good for everything that ails us."

Scheme? Elixir? What the hell kind of language is that, I wondered? These were words that conjured up images of con artists, like Doctor Feel good selling worthless junk out of the back of his wagon.

But that was just a little tease to get us into the tent. Then Engberg interviewed three different tax experts. Every single one of them opposed the flat tax. Every single one! Where was the fairness and balance Rather was always preaching about? Wasn't there any expert—*even one*—in the entire United States who thought the flat tax *might* work?

Of course there was. There were Milton Friedman and Merton Miller, both of the University of Chicago and both Nobel Prize winners in economics. There was James Buchanan of George Mason University, another Nobel laureate. There were also Harvey Rosen of Princeton, William Poole of Brown, and Robert Barro of Harvard. All of them were on the record as supporting the flat tax to one degree or another.

Engberg could have found a bunch of economists to support the flat tax, *if he had wanted to.* But putting on a supporter of the flat tax would have defeated the whole purpose of the piece; which was to have a few laughs at Steve Forbes's expense.

There is absolutely no way—not one chance in a million—that Engberg or Rather would have aired a flat-tax story with that same contemptuous tone if Teddy Kennedy or Hillary Clinton had come up with the idea.

But even if you opposed the flat tax, even if you thought it was a bad idea that helped only the wealthiest Americans—fat cats like Steve Forbes himself—what about simple journalistic fairness? What about presenting two sides? Isn't that what Rather was always saying CBS News was about: objectivity, fairness, balance?

And then Engberg crossed that fuzzy little line that's supposed to separate news from entertainment. He decided it was time to amuse his audience. And who could blame him? The flat tax didn't have much pizzazz by showbiz standards. The audience might lose interest and, God forbid, change the channel. In the United States of Entertainment there is no greater sin than to bore the audience. A TV reporter could get it wrong from time to time. He could be snippy and snooty. But he could not be boring.

Which is why Eric Engberg decided to play David Letterman and do a takeoff of his Top Ten list.

"Forbes's Number One Wackiest Flat-Tax Promise," Engberg told the audience, is the candidate's belief that it would give parents "more time to spend with their children and each other."

Wacky? This was a perfectly acceptable word in the United States of Entertainment to describe, say, a Three Stooges movie. Or *Hamlet*, starring Jerry Lewis. Or *My Fair Lady*, with Chris Rock playing Professor Higgins.

But "wacky" seemed an odd word to describe a serious idea to overhaul America's ten-trillion-page tax code that enables lobbyists to donate tons of money to politicians who then use this same Byzantine tax code to hand out goodies to the very same special interests that just gave them all that money. If anything is "wacky," it's the *current* tax system, not an honest attempt to replace it with something new.

Besides, what Forbes meant is that since many Americans—not just the wealthy—would pay less tax under his plan, they might not have to work as many hours and might actually have more time to spend at home with their families. Maybe it's true and maybe it isn't, but is "wacky" the fairest and most objective way to describe it?

Can you imagine, in your wildest dreams, a network news reporter calling Hillary Clinton's health care plan "wacky"? Can you imagine Dan Rather or any other major American news anchorman allowing it?

And finally, the coup de grace, the knife to Steve Forbes's throat as Engberg went on camera to end his story. The "on camera," as we call it in the TV news business, is when the reporter gets to look the viewer in the eye and deliver a sermonette. This is when the reporter, if he hasn't been slanting the news up to this point, will often give you a little editorial just to make sure you know how you're supposed to think about the subject at hand. Eric Engberg ended his little vaudeville act thus: "The fact remains: The flat tax is a giant, untested theory. One economist suggested, before we put it in, we should test it out someplace—like Albania." Engberg flashed his signature smirk and signed off—"Eric Engberg, CBS News, Washington."

There is junk science, junk food, and junk bonds. This was junk journalism.

I don't believe for a second that Eric Engberg woke up that morning and said, "I think I'll go on the air tonight and make fun of Steve Forbes." The problem is that so many TV journalists simply don't know what to think about certain issues until the *New York Times* and the *Washington Post* tell them what to think. Those big, important newspapers set the agenda that network news people follow. In this case the message from Olympus was clear: We don't like the flat tax. So neither did Eric Engberg, and neither did anyone at CBS News who put his story on the air. It's as simple as that.

That the flat tax was a conservative idea only made the job of bashing it more fun. Yes, it's true that a number of conservative politicians came out against it. Lamar Alexander, for one, called it "a truly nutty idea." But Alexander, and some others who came out against Forbes's version of the flat tax—like Pat Buchanan, who said it was a plan that favored "the boys down at the yacht basin"—just happened to be running for president against Steve Forbes. That raises a few legitimate questions about their motives.

Make no mistake: the flat tax is fundamentally conservative. In *Newsweek,* George Will wrote, "In the 1990s conservatism had two genuinely radical proposals for domestic reform, proposals that would have fundamentally altered the political culture. Term limits for members of Congress would have ended careerism, today's strongest motive for entering, and for particular behavior in, politics. A flat tax would have taken the tax code out of play as an instrument for dispensing political favors, and would have put out of business a parasite class of tax lawyers and lobbyists in Washington."

By and large, the angst over the flat tax came from the Left. Which makes perfect sense. Liberals have an uneasy feeling about tax cuts in general and are downright hostile to the kinds of cuts that benefit the wealthy in particular, even if they also help a lot of other Americans. They may argue against the flat tax on economic grounds, which is fair enough since there are legitimate questions and concerns about a flat-tax rate. But much of the opposition from the Left had little to do with economics. It was visceral, from the same dark region that produces envy and the seemingly unquenchable liberal need to wage class warfare.

Paul Begala, the political strategist who worked on both the 1992 and 1996 Clinton-Gore campaigns, charmingly explained the Left's philosophy on people with money when, according to Bob Woodward's *The Agenda*, he told Treasury Secretary Robert Rubin, "F**k them [the rich]."

Karl Marx couldn't have said it better.

So the Left routinely uses words like "scheme" instead of the more neutral "plan" to describe tax cuts that favor "the wrong people." Sometimes they put the word "risky" before "scheme" to make it sound really scary. Al Gore did precisely that, about a hundred times a day, when he was running for president against George W. Bush. I understand why Al Gore and other liberals call something they don't like a "scheme." Politicians and partisans are allowed to do that. But should supposedly objective people like news reporters, people like Eric Engberg, use that kind of loaded language? Should a journalistic enterprise like CBS News—which claims to stand for fairness and objectivity—allow words like "scheme" and "wacky" in what is supposed to be a straight news story about a legitimate candidate running for president of the United States?

Engberg's piece—its strident, mocking tone, its lack of objectivity, its purposeful omission of anyone who supported the flat tax—was like a TV campaign commercial paid for by *Opponents of the Steve Forbes Flat Tax*.

From top to bottom the Engberg piece was breathtaking in its lack of fairness. So how could CBS put it on the air? Well, news fans, here's one of those dirty little secrets journalists are never supposed to reveal to the regular folks out there in the audience: a reporter can find an expert to say anything the reporter wants—*anything*! Just keep calling until one of the experts says what you need him to say and tell him you'll be right down with your camera crew to interview him. If you find an expert who says, "You know, I think that flat tax just might work and here's why..." you thank him, hang up, and find another expert. It's how journalists sneak their own personal views into stories in the guise of objective news reporting. Because the reporter can always say, "Hey, I didn't say the flat tax stinks—the guy from that Washington think tank did!"

It happens all the time.

I don't know Steve Forbes. I've never met him. I don't even buy his magazine. *And I had never voted for a Republican candidate for president in my entire life!* But he was a serious, intelligent man seeking the most important job in our country; and what CBS News had just done to him was shameful and not worthy of an important network news organization.

So I called Jeff Fager, who had just taken over as executive producer of the *CBS Evening News*. I had known Jeff for more than ten years. I asked him how in the world he could have put that story on the air. Fager didn't remember any details of the Engberg report. That's how *un*controversial it was to him.

I told Fager I had been complaining privately about bias at CBS News for years, that I always kept it in-house, but this time was different. This time, I told him, I was going to write about it, and then maybe he and the other people who decide what gets on the air would listen.

Jeff Fager is an interesting guy. Funny. Smart. Easygoing. But in some way he's *too* cool. Nothing fazes him. Jeff is the kind of guy who never suffers a crisis of confidence, not on the outside where you could tell, anyway. From what I could tell by working with him over the years, Jeff is someone who is more in touch with his "inner self" than all those self-esteem gurus who show up on PBS during a pledge drive *put together*. Which is probably why he wasn't upset with the Engberg hatchet job. So I sat down and started writing the op-ed piece.

The way I saw it, I wasn't taking on Engberg or Rather or CBS News for airing one snooty story about some politicians tax plan. For me, this was about a nagging problem that none of the big shots would take seriously. It was about the liberal biases that overwhelm straight news reporting.

NO

Al Franken

Lies and the Lying Liars Who Tell Them: A Fair and Balanced Look at the Right

Asking whether there is a liberal or conservative bias to the mainstream media is a little like asking whether al Qaeda uses too much oil in their hummus. The problem with al Qaeda is that they're trying to kill us.

The right-wing media tells us constantly that the problem with the mainstream media is that it has a liberal bias. I don't think it does. But there are other, far more important, biases in the mainstream media than liberal or conservative ones. Most of these biases stem from something called "the profit motive." This is why we often see a bias toward the Sensational, involving Scandal, and, hopefully Sex or Violence, or please, please, *pleeeze*, both.

And there's the Easy-and-Cheap-to-Cover bias, which is why almost all political coverage is about process and horse race and not about policy. Why have an in-depth report on school vouchers when two pundits who've spent five minutes in the green room looking over a couple of articles Xeroxed by an intern can just scream at each other about the issue on the air?

There's the Get-It-First bias. Remember the 2000 election? I believe there were some problems there associated with that one.

Pack Mentality. Negativity. Soft News. The Don't-Offend-the-Conglomerate-That-Owns-Us bias. And, of course, the ever-present bias of Hoping There's a War to Cover.

Does the mainstream media have a liberal bias? On a couple of things, maybe. Compared to the American public at large, probably a slightly higher percentage of journalists, because of their enhanced power of discernment, realize they know a gay person or two, and are, therefore, less frightened of them....

But to believe there is a liberal political bias in the mainstream media, you'd have to either not be paying attention or just be very susceptible to repetition. Yes, we've heard it over and over and over again. For decades. The media elite is an arm of the Democratic National Committee....

How about the 2000 presidential campaign? Remember in the first debate, Al Gore said he had gone down to a disaster site in Texas with Federal Emergency Management Agency director James Lee Witt? Actually, it turned out that he had gone to that disaster with a *deputy* of James Lee Witt. As vice president, Gore had gone to seventeen *other* disasters with James Lee Witt, but not that one. The press jumped all over him. There were scores of stories written about how Gore had *lied* about James Lee Witt....

Contrast that with the media's reaction to this Bush description of his tax cut in the very same debate. Bush said, "I also dropped the bottom rate from fifteen percent to ten percent, because, by far, the vast majority of the help goes to the people at the bottom end of the economic ladder."

"By far, the vast majority ... goes to the people at the bottom." That is what George W. Bush told America. The truth is that *the bottom 60 percent got 14.7 percent.* Gee, that's a pretty significant misstatement, don't you think? More important than whether a Texas fire was one of the seventeen disasters you went to with American icon James Lee Witt. So what was the reaction of the liberal mainstream press?

Nothing.

Do I believe that this was because the mainstream media has a *conservative* bias? No. I just think the attitude of the press was "He doesn't know! He doesn't know! Leave the man alone! He doesn't know!"

But, of course, he did. Which is why George W. Bush said he doesn't mind being "misunderestimated." Because by "misunderestimated," Bush means being underestimated for the wrong reason. The media thought he was kind of stupid. He isn't. He's just shamelessly dishonest.

The mainstream media does not have a liberal bias. And for all their other biases mentioned above, the mainstream media—ABC, CBS, NBC, CNN, *The New York Times*, the *Washington Post, Time, Newsweek*, and the rest—at least *try* to be fair.

There is, however, a right-wing media. You know who they are. Fox News. The *Washington Times*. The *New York Post*. The editorial pages of the *Wall Street Journal*. Talk radio. They are biased. And they have an agenda.

The members of the right-wing media are not interested in conveying the truth. That's not what they're for. They are an indispensable component of the right-wing machine that has taken over our country. They employ a tried-and-true methodology. First, they concoct an inflammatory story that serves their political goals. ("Al Gore's a liar.") They repeat it. ("Al Gore lies again!") They embellish it. ("Are his lies pathological, or are they merely malicious?") They try to push it into the mainstream media. All too often, they succeed. ("Tall Tales: Is What We've Got Here a Compulsion To Exaggerate?" *New York Times*, October 15, 2000.) Occasionally, they fail.... But even their failures serve their agenda, as evidence of liberal bias. Win-win. You got to admit. It's a good racket. And that's my point. We have to be vigilant.

And we have to be more than vigilant. We have to fight back. We have to expose those who bear false witness for the false witness bearers that they are. And we have to do it in a straightforward, plainspoken way. Let's call them what they are: liars. Lying, lying liars.

Hence the title of this book: *Al Franken Tells It Like It Is.*

"By Far the Vast Majority of My Tax Cuts Go to Those at the Bottom"

In the first debate with Gore then candidate Bush said of his tax cuts, "By far the vast majority of the help goes to those at the bottom end of the economic ladder." In the South Carolina primary debate with John McCain he said, "By far the vast majority of my tax cuts go to those at the bottom end of the spectrum." As you can see, he loved this line. He repeated versions of it everywhere.

Shall we parse this statement? Let's start at the end and work backward. "Bottom end of the spectrum." What's that gotta mean? At least the bottom 50 percent, right? Otherwise, the word "bottom" in this context is meaningless. He couldn't have meant the bottom 99 percent, could he? That would just be crazy.

How about "majority"? Well, that's unambiguous. It means more than 50 percent. So, so far, at the very least, the bottom half of the American people are getting 50 percent, plus a dollar, of Bush's tax cut.

Now let's add "vast." "Vast majority." "Vast" is big. Huge. Like the "vast" reaches of space. Very, very big. So, what's a *vast* majority?" 90 percent? 85? It's subjective, I admit. So let's go with a very conservative 70 percent. At this point in our parsing, the bottom 50 percent are getting 70 (give or take) percent of Bush's tax cut.

But wait. It's not just a "vast majority." It's *by far* a vast majority. Okay, let's think about that. What does "by far" mean? When you say a restaurant is "by far" the best steak house in town, you're really saying something. When you tell your spouse that sex with her or him is "by far" the best sex you've ever had, you may not be telling the truth—much in the same way that Bush wasn't in this case—but you are definitely trying to score some points. So I'm going to say that "*by far* the vast majority of my tax cuts go to those at the bottom" would mean that the poorest 50 percent were getting somewhere in the neighborhood of 85 to 99 percent of Bush's tax cut.

That's fair, right? That's a fair parsing.

As I said before, the bottom 60 percent got 14.7 percent of that tax cut.

On the *Hannity and Colmes* episode immediately following the last State of the Union address, Sean Hannity described the President's 2003 tax plan (which contained Bush's third tax cut) in his confident, unequivocal way: "Ninety-two million Americans will get $1,100 back in their pocket."

Of course, he was lying. Or was he? Maybe he was just confused. Sean may be evil, but he's not smart. I don't dispute that ninety-two million Americans were getting an *average* tax cut of $1,083. It's not the seventeen bucks I'm quibbling about. It's the *average* part. Hannity had left that out. Averages can be tricky. You and Bill Gates probably have an average net worth of $32 billion. My daughter and I have an average gender of half-male, half-female. My daughter, my *wife*, and I have an average gender of female.

In fact, less than twenty-five million Americans would be receiving a tax cut of $1,100 or more. Sixty-two million taxpayers would be getting tax cuts of less than a thousand dollars—averaging about $302. And fifty million households would get no tax cut at all....

Personally, I think the President, like most Americans, is smarter than Sean Hannity. So when Bush, who, after all, is President of the United States, repeatedly says something that isn't true, it's not confusion. It's a lie.

Take these remarks by the President at a 2001 "Tax Family Event," in which he introduced America to the Yahngs. Talking about his first tax plan, the President of the United States said,

> It is a plan that significantly reduces taxes for people at the bottom end of the economic ladder. If you're a family of four making $35,000, you'll receive a one hundred percent tax cut. It's an average tax relief for families of $1,600. The Yahng family under the plan I submit will receive actually more than that. They now pay $2,000 in taxes to the federal government. If this plan is enacted by the United States Congress, they'll end up paying $150 of taxes.

There are actually four lies crammed into this little paragraph. Lie #1 is the" one hundred percent tax cut" part of the second sentence. The President could have told the truth by saying, "one hundred percent *income* tax cut." You see, a family of four making $35,000 pays, on average, $5,355 in payroll taxes.[1] Seventy-four percent of Americans pay more in payroll taxes than in income taxes, so this is kind of important. Especially if you're "at the bottom end of the economic ladder."

Lie #2 is tricky, because the "average tax relief for families of $1,600" is technically accurate in the same way that it is accurate to say his 2003 plan would give families an average tax cut of $1,083. But in the previous sentence, he said, "if you're a family of four making $35,000," so I'm calling this a "sleight of hand" lie. If you don't want to count it, fine. I respect that.

Lie #3 is "They now pay $2,000 in taxes to the federal government." Again, he's forgetting (or, rather, omitting) their payroll tax. Lie #4—"They'll end up paying $150 of taxes"—comes from the same dishonest non-payroll-tax-acknowledging place in Bush's soul.

You may remember that, during the 2000 campaign, Bush held quite a few of these Tax Family Events to deflect criticism that his plan was a giant giveaway to the wealthy.

The first few of these events with "working families"... were disasters. After each one, the Gore campaign issued a press release showing how the working family would actually receive a larger cut under Gore's plan.

After a number of embarrassments, the Bush campaign realized it needed to take greater care in choosing its families. An e-mail sent out by the campaign to New Mexico Republicans seeking such a family laid out the criteria. A suitable family must make between $35,000 and $70,000, itemize its taxes, have no children in day care, no children in college, no one attending night school, no children younger than age one, and no substantial savings outside of 401(k).

No children in college? No one in night school? No children under one? No savings? Talk about living the American dream!

These highly selective criteria eliminated 85 percent of all couples in the income range. The 85 percent would have done better under the Gore tax plan. We can fairly conclude that a "vast majority" if not "*by far* a vast majority" of middle-income American families of four would be paying less taxes today if Gore had been inaugurated.

Rather than offering up an illuminating case of Mr. and Mrs. Joe Average, the Bush campaign was casting a political freak show in order to present a tiny minority as the norm.

The Bush campaign, however, would have had no problem finding families of four making between $350,000 and $700,000 who got a bigger tax cut under Bush's plan than under Gore's. In that income range, they all did....

The rationale for Bush's tax cuts was that, with a $4.6 trillion projected surplus, "I think it's fair, I think it's right that one quarter of the surplus go back to the people who pay the bills." (Not to quibble, but his tax cut was more than a *third* of the surplus. He was $450 billion off, enough to pay for all nonmilitary discretionary spending for a year.)

So, when we were expecting huge surpluses, Bush argued that it was our money, and if the government was taking more than it needed, we deserved to get some of it back. Specifically, we needed a $1.6 trillion tax cut, heavily tilted toward the wealthy.

But once evidence began to emerge that the economy was sputtering and the surplus was shrinking, this rationale no longer applied. There were new economic problems that needed new solutions. How could the economy be jump-started? Bush met with his top economic advisors and came back with an innovative answer: a $1.6 trillion tax cut, heavily tilted toward the wealthy.

It soon became apparent that we were headed back to deficit country. How would America's new fiscal discipline sheriff explain to the nation that he'd have to break his campaign promise never to go into deficit? The answer came on September 11, when terrorists struck the World Trade Center and the Pentagon, creating a national emergency and necessitating a war.

Not only did the tragedy provide a justification for deficit spending, it gave Bush a reliable laugh line for his speeches. Here's the joke. This is from a June 7, 2002, speech in Iowa. But he's told it on at least thirteen different occasions.

> I remember campaigning in Chicago and one of the reporters said, "Would you ever deficit spend?" I said, "Only—only—in times of war, in times of economic insecurity as a result of a recession, or in times of national emergency." Never did I dream we'd have a trifecta.

It got a laugh in Iowa. And a laugh in Georgia when he campaigned for Saxby Chambliss. It killed in Texas when he campaigned for gubernatorial candidate Rick Perry. They loved it at the Simon for Governor luncheon in Santa Clara. And he got laughter *and* applause at a meeting of the leaders of the Fiscal Responsibility Coalition in our nation's capital.

To me the joke itself is not as funny as the fact that it's based on a lie. He never said he'd allow a deficit" only in times of war, in times of economic security as a result of a recession, or in times of national emergency." He'd never said anything remotely like it during the campaign. On June 9, 2002, Tim Russert interviewed Budget Director Mitch Daniels on *Meet the Press.*

> RUSSERT: Now, we have checked everywhere and we've even called the White House as to when the President said that when he was campaigning in Chicago, and it didn't happen. The closest he came was when he was asked, "Would you give up part of your tax cut in order to ensure a balanced budget?" And he said, "No." But no one ever talked about a war, a recession, and an emergency, the trifecta.

Daniels responded that he was not "the White House librarian," so he didn't have a record of Bush saying this during the campaign. A few weeks later, Russert told me that he'd heard that Ari Fleischer was hopping mad the following Monday morning and wanted to "go after Russert" for questioning Bush's credibility. Apparently, Karl Rove then took Fleischer aside and explained that they might want to let this one slide.[2]

Even after Russert exposed the lie, Bush continued to tell it.

So now we have record deficits. But the good news is that, just as Bush promised, the 2001 and 2002 tax cuts have provided such a terrific stimulus to our economy that Congress passed another huge one in 2003.

Seriously, though, we have lost three million jobs in this country in the last two and a half years....

During the six-plus years that the two Bushes have been president, there has not been one new net job created. Not one. Extrapolating from that, if the Bushes had run this country from its very inception to the present day, not a single American would have ever worked.

The idea that tax cuts for those at the very top will stimulate job creation is called supply-side, trickle-down, or "voodoo" economics. The concept is simple. By giving those at the top, who are, in theory, the most productive Americans, a tax break, you will motivate them to work even harder and create more wealth, more jobs, and a bigger pie for everyone.

That reasoning explains why, when Bill Clinton wanted to raise taxes on the top 1 percent in 1993 to deal with the then-record deficit, Republicans said his plan would cause a recession. Here's a sampling.

> I believe this will lead to a recession next year. This is the Democrat machine's recession, and each one of them will be held personally accountable.
>
> —Newt Gingrich, August 5, 1993

> The Clinton plan is a one-way ticket to recession. This plan does not reduce the deficit ... but it raises taxes and it puts people out of work.
>
> Senator Phil Gramm, July 28, 1993

This plan will not work. If it was to work then I'd have to become a Democrat and believe that more taxes and bigger government is the answer.

Representative John Kasich, R-OH[3]
July 28, 1993

So every Republican in Congress voted against Clinton's Deficit Reduction Act. It passed in both houses by one vote. (Gore broke the tie in the Senate.) The next eight years saw the longest period of economic growth in American history. Also, bolstered by the U.S., most of the world experienced an economic boom.

It's taken as gospel by conservatives that everyone will work harder when they're paying a 33 percent marginal tax rate than when they are paying a 39.6 percent rate. I heard Rush Limbaugh make a point that attempted to illustrate their logic. He said that if we taxed people at a 100 percent marginal rate, the government would get no revenue because no one would work. And, for once, I had to agree with him. I think the marginal tax rate should be somewhere between zero and 100 percent.

Bush made a point that I didn't find quite as compelling in his acceptance speech at the 2000 Republican convention, the same speech in which he lied about the army divisions not being ready for duty. He said, "On principle, no one in America should have to pay more than a third of their income to the federal government."

The crowd went nuts.

It struck me as odd that there would exist *on principle* such a specific number for the optimum top marginal rate. And that this principle would somehow apply to every economic circumstance. I also thought it was lucky for Bush that this specific number was one third, rather than a messier or more complicated fraction. What if the Heritage Foundation had determined that the perfect top marginal rate was something slightly smaller than one third? Would Bush have gotten as rousing a cheer if he had said, "On principle, no one in America should have to pay more than nine twenty-ninths of their income to the federal government!"? Or worse, what if the optimum marginal rate were an irrational number, which cannot be expressed as a fraction?[4] How many digits beyond the decimal point would Bush have been willing to go?

No. I think the one third was actually kind of arbitrary. Also, I think people were cheering—not because of the principle of the thing—but because of the extra money they knew they'd be getting if Bush won.

Someone who seems to buy heavily into the supply-side ethos is my friend Bill O'Reilly. On his January 14,2003, *Factor,* O'Reilly explained, in his typically modest way, how an increase in income taxes would cause him to fire several of his employees. The explanation came in his Talking Points Memo segment of the show.

As far as the economy is concerned, "Points" continues to believe that putting more money back into the hands of Americans who earn it will help private enterprise. Raising taxes and increasing government spending is a surefire way to continue the economic doldrums. I'll back up that statement with my own story. Right now, I'm a busy guy, with TV, radio, books, a syndicated column, and a website. There are scores of people working with me, people who are making money and supporting their families. As I have mentioned, when my tax obligation is all added up, the government takes a bit more than 50 cents of every dollar I earn. And the Democrats want more. [I have no clue who he was talking about.] But I will tell you what. If my tax rate increases, I will cut back and do fewer things. It simply will not be worth my time, because I have enough money saved to live comfortably. I don't need to kill myself to pay the government. And if I do cut back, some of the people currently earning money under the *Factor* banner will stop earning that money.

The thought of O'Reilly cutting back is a frightening one. Not just for the employees he'd let go, and their families, who would suddenly have the wolf at their door. What scares me is the prospect that we could be deprived of thoughtful Talking Points like this one. Or that we'd see them only on TV, and not also get them on radio, in his syndicated column, and on his website. It's enough to make me want to fight for further tax cuts for the five-million-and-up bracket, even if it means that we'd have to cut back on Head Start and pre-natal care for the poor....

In fairness, Bill is probably working extra hard so that his children can inherit enough money to live extravagantly without ever having to work or challenge themselves. That, of course, is every parent's dream.

And now, thanks to the visionary who coined the terrifying phrase "death tax" to describe the eminently reasonable estate tax, more Americans than ever will be able to see that dream come true. In 2001, Congress endorsed the deeply American idea of a permanent aristocracy by passing a phase-out, and eventual repeal, of the estate tax.

As Bush said in his acceptance speech: "On principle, every family, every farmer and small business person should be free to pass on their life's work to those they love. So we abolish the death tax."

By this "principle," every elementary school teacher should be able to pass on their life's work to the people they love. They should be able to pass on the lives they've touched, the children they've inspired, the futures they've changed. Logistically speaking, that would be hard to do. It is, however, easy to pass down money. As you can see, this principle breaks down very quickly.

Yes, a family farmer should be able to pass his farm down to his children. Fortunately, that hasn't been a problem. As the law existed before Bush took office, family farms had a $2.6 million exemption. For family farms worth more than $2.6 million, the heirs had a grace period of up to fourteen years to pay the tax bill at low interest rates. The fact is that neither *The New York Times* nor the American Farm Bureau Federation could find a single family farm that has ever been lost to the estate tax.

That didn't stop the Republicans from running extremely ugly ads about the issue in both the 2000 and the 2002 campaigns. My favorite was this radio spot run against Paul Wellstone in Minnesota:

60 SECOND SPOT: DEATH TAX

SOUND EFFECTS: SOUND OF FARM IMPLEMENTS. CHICKENS CLUCK-
ING, COWS MOOING.

RUTH
Lloyd? We just got a letter from the IRS!

LLOYD
Ruth, what's wrong?

RUTH
They say we owe more taxes!

LLOYD
Bull! Dad always paid his taxes, even in the worst of times.

RUTH
We owe taxes 'cause he died?

LLOYD
He paid taxes when he worked! He paid taxes on this land, now he dies,
and he has to pay—*more*? Who the hell thought up that doozy?

RUTH
Senator Wellstone just voted to keep the death tax.

LLOYD
Paul Wellstone actually voted to tax people 'cause they died?

RUTH
What's going to happen?

LLOYD
We're going to have to sell the farm.

RUTH
No, Lloyd, we're going to call Paul Wellstone and tell him our folks paid
their fair share. And to keep his money-grubbing hands off our farm.

ANNOUNCER (V.O.)
Call Paul Wellstone. Tell him to protect small business and family farms,
and to stop taxing the dead. Paid for by Americans for Job Security.

Wellstone *had* voted against the full repeal of the estate tax. But he had also
voted to exempt family farms and small businesses, and to exempt all other
estates up to $8 million. You know, if anyone hated the small farmer, or, in
fact, the little guy in general, it was Paul "Moneygrubber" Wellstone. That's
why they had to plant the crowd for his memorial.

Bush used the death tax issue in practically every stump speech he gave, lamenting the devastation it visited on family farmers and small business owners. The Republicans pushed the estate tax repeal as a middle-class tax-relief issue. With some success. Seventeen percent of Americans thought the estate tax would apply to them. In fact, the tax affects less than 2 percent of estates—and nearly half of the revenue it produces comes from taxes on 0.16 percent of estates, worth an average of $17 million, belonging to about 3,300 families each year. In 1999, fully a quarter of the estate tax revenue came from just 467 estates. As David Brooks, who works at the *Weekly Standard* but is nonetheless a terrific guy, wrote in *The New York Times*, the estate tax is "explicitly for the mega-upper class."

Bush has said that it is immoral to tax people when they die. Since we are currently experiencing a $450 billion deficit, the amount of the revenue being lost by the phase-out and eventual repeal of the estate tax will have to be made up by taxes on you and me. It is arguably more moral to tax an incredibly rich person who is dead than a middle- or working-class person who is still alive. The living person might use the money for medical care, food, travel, or other things that dead rich people don't have to think about.

The other bogus argument put forth by opponents of the estate tax is that it amounts to "double taxation." The idea is that you pay taxes as you accumulate your fortune, and then your children have to pay taxes on it again when you die. There are two problems with this argument. First, everyone pays double taxes all the time. Sales taxes, for example, are taxes on already-taxed income. Fees on things like your driver's license, a fishing license, a hunting license, and other licenses—that's all double taxation. Also fees on things that aren't licenses. Like permits. Let's say you want to open a business selling licenses. You need a license permit! That's triple taxation. I think.

Import taxes, excise taxes, bridge tolls, car registration, taxes on alcohol, gasoline, and tobacco are all double taxes. So are property taxes, which tax assets bought with already taxed income.

However, the repeal of the estate tax will create a way to avoid not just double taxation, but also single taxation. Here's how to do it. Buy an enormous amount of stock or property. Let it accumulate value. Die. Now the money goes to your kids, who escape both estate *and* capital gains taxes. Thanks to Bush, by 2010, only one thing will be certain in life. And that thing is either death, or taxes.

This new tax loophole is not a trivial matter. For estates worth more than $10 million, over 56 percent of their value comes from unrealized capital gains. Capital gains come from money making money without anyone actually working. Thus, our nation's most generous tax laws will now apply to the children of the very rich inheriting money even their parents didn't earn.

Instead of giving $60 billion a year [5] to our country's heirs and heiresses, we could be paying for things like after-school programs, schools on military bases, child vaccinations in Third World countries, prosecution of polluters, health care for veterans—all things which Bush has cut.

Take your pick. Which is more important? Making sure that Ivana Trump will be able to live in the style to which she's grown accustomed even

NO / Al Franken   **217**

after The Donald has left our world? Or making sure that little Ivana Average can go to a school that has toilet paper in the bathrooms?

Funny thing happened at the end of the Senate debate on this issue. Republicans, who knew they had the votes to win, kept spouting off about family farms and small businesses. So the Democrats gave them a chance to prove their sincerity. Instead of abolishing the estate tax altogether, how about exempting the first $4 million per couple? Nope. How 'bout the first $8 million? Sorry.

Okay. Then how about this? Russ Feingold, Democrat of Wisconsin, offered an amendment that would exempt the first *on hundred million dollars* of a couple's net worth before a penny of estate taxes were paid. This would exempt all "family farms" and "small businesses" worth less than $100 million.

The amendment went down 48–51.[6]

In all this talk, one thing that gets lost is that there are forty-two million working Americans who have not gotten one cent in tax cuts. The *Wall Street Journal* refers to them as "lucky duckies" because they earn so little that they don't pay any income taxes. Many lucky duckies are deeply in debt to predatory lenders. Many of these lucky duckies couldn't afford college and cannot afford health insurance. Some of these lucky duckies, working Americans, will be homeless sometime during the year. Their children, the lucky ducklings, are far more likely than my kids, or Paul Gigot's, to be killed violently or die of a preventable disease.

Apparently, the *Wall Street Journal* thinks that the unluckiest thing in the world is paying taxes.

That's why they have been such vociferous supporters of the Bush tax cuts, more than half of which will eventually go to the top 1 percent of families.

In the last thirty years, those families saw their after-tax incomes rise 157 percent. The top one percent have incomes starting at $230,000. Their share of the national income has doubled, and is now as large as the combined income of the bottom 40 percent. The thirteen thousand families at the very top have almost as much income as the poorest twenty million households in America, which is like the population of Bemidji, Minnesota, (home of Paul Bunyan) having more income than the country's six largest cities—New York City, Los Angeles, Chicago, Houston, Philadelphia, and Phoenix—combined.

You know who I think the real lucky duckies are? The residents of Bemidji, Minnesota. I mean the ones in my analogy. So why are they the ones getting the sweetest deal from the tax cuts?

Anytime a liberal points out that the wealthy are disproportionately benefiting from Bush's tax policies, Republicans shout, "class warfare!"

In her book A *Distant Mirror: The Calamitous Fourteenth Century*, Barbara Tuchman writes about a peasant revolt in 1358 that began in the village of St. Leu and spread throughout the Oise Valley. At one estate, the serfs sacked the manor house, killed the knight, and roasted him on a spit in front of his wife and kids. Then, after ten or twelve peasants violated the lady, with the children still watching, they forced her to eat the roasted flesh of her husband and then killed her.

That is class warfare.

Arguing over the optimum marginal tax rate for the top one percent is not.

Notes

1. Like the Heritage Foundation and every other conservative think tank does when it computes tax burdens, I am including here the employer's portion of the payroll tax.

2. Funnily enough, one candidate *had* said something about a war, or a recession or a national emergency being an acceptable reason for running a deficit. It wasn't Bush, though. Or Nader. It was Al Gore, who said at the Economic Club of Detroit on May 8, 1998: "Barring an economic reversal, a national emergency, or a foreign crisis, we should balance the budget this year, next year, and every year."

3. Kasich, who is now presumably a Democrat, is substitute host on *The O'Reilly Factor*. Who says they aren't fair and balanced?

4. Examples include π or $\sqrt{2}$.

5. That's what the yield would be in 2011 if the tax were in place.

6. Kudos to Republicans who voted for the Feingold amendment: Chafee, Collins, Hutchison, McCain, Snowe, and Specter. Huge raspberries to the Democrats who crossed over: Baucus, Breaux, Cleland, Lincoln, Miller, Nelson of Florida, Nelson of Nebraska, and Wyden. Semi-kudos to Stevens of Alaska who did not vote.

POSTSCRIPT

Do the Media Have a Liberal Bias?

Media bias may seem to be a fairly simple, and perhaps not very powerful topic, but it shows how complex the relationship among senders and receivers of messages may be. The real issue has to do with whether the media tell us what to think or what to think about.

There is no doubt that the news audience is changing. People may be getting more information from the Internet or other sources, but the possibility of bias may become even more important. As news makers understand how audiences use news, we might well expect to see different values and approaches designed to reach different audiences. How do media transmit values from one generation to another? Why do we seek out opinions that often confirm what we already believe? Changes in human behavior are often so subtle that we take them for granted. But when we do this, we undermine how important the media are in helping us understand our relationships to our environment and to our social groups.

An important step in considering this issue is to try to understand the nature of news. As Goldberg and Franken have shown, messages in media have multiple purposes. As news and other media content become more available, we need to consider the possible bias of any message and ask several questions: Where does the message come from? Where did the information originate? What types of supporting evidence separate opinion from fact?

We also need to be aware of different styles of news over the years. In the 1970s "ambush journalism" was popular—journalists often appeared to be stalking subjects, and much criticism was given to the "hard news" approach. Presently, the issue tends to be more about the journalist's personality and role as a gatekeeper of information. In this case, any personal interests or biases of the journalist become very important.

In recent years, a few books, primarily memoirs of journalists have taken strong views on the role of the journalist and the way the field of journalism has grown over the years. Among some of the interesting sources in this area are Tom Wicker's *On the Record* (Bedford/St. Martin's, 2002) and Ted Koppel's *Off Camera* (Alfred A. Knopf, 2000), which are particularly good sources for a discussion of the topic of bias.

For other books that suggest changes in journalistic style and political differences in the United States, you may want to consult Nina J. Easton's *Gang of Five* (Simon & Schuster, 2000), about media use in the post-Reagan conservative era, or Lisa McGirr's *Suburban Warriors* (Princeton University Press, 2002), about the U.S. political shift toward conservatism.

On the Internet . . .

American Civil Liberties Union

This official site of the American Civil Liberties Union (ACLU) provides a general introduction of issues involving individual rights.

http://aclu.org

The Federal Communications Commission

This official site of the Federal Communications Commission (FCC) provides comprehensive information about U.S. federal media rules and guidelines.

http://www.fcc.gov

Student Press Law Center

The Student Press Law Center (SPLC) Web site provides the full text of *SPLC Report* magazine, news and information on laws and rulings that affect the student press, an online legal clinic, and the fill-in-the-blanks form for public records requests for each state.

http://www.splc.org

The National Freedom of Information Coalition

The National Freedom of Information Coalition is a coalition of various state First Amendment and open government organizations. This Web site provides information on the NFOIC as well as news articles pertaining to freedom of information.

http://www.nfoic.org

PART 4

Regulation

*F*or the media, the First Amendment entails both rights and responsibilities. How to ensure that these responsibilities will be met is the subject of much of communications law and legislative action. What are the valid limits of the rights of free speech and the press? How should society respond when First Amendment rights are in conflict with other individual rights? What changes will new technology force upon our operation of these rights? The issues in this section deal with who should be responsible for media content and with the rights of groups who find that content inappropriate.

- Should Internet Access Be Regulated?
- Should Freedom of Speech Ever Be Restricted?
- Should the FCC Liberalize Ownership Rules?

ISSUE 11

Should Internet Access Be Regulated?

✓ **YES: Michael A. Banks,** from "Filtering the Net in Libraries: The Case (Mostly) in Favor," *Computers in Libraries* (March 1998)

✓ **NO: American Civil Liberties Union,** from "Censorship in a Box: Why Blocking Software Is Wrong for Public Libraries," in David Sobel, ed., *Filters and Freedom: Free Speech Perspectives on Internet Content Controls* (Electronic Privacy Information Center, 1999)

ISSUE SUMMARY

YES: Author Michael A. Banks explains that as more people turn to libraries for Internet access, libraries and communities have been forced to come to grips with the conflict between freedom of speech and objectional material on the World Wide Web and in Usenet newsgroups. He adds that software filters are tools that help librarians keep inappropriate materials out of the library.

NO: The American Civil Liberties Union (ACLU) concludes that mandatory blocking software in libraries is both inappropriate and unconstitutional. Blocking censors valuable speech and gives librarians, educators, and parents a false sense of security when providing minors with Internet access, argues the ACLU.

This is an issue that becomes more complex the more one thinks about it. Should public libraries make adult pornography sites available to minor children? Obviously no would be most people's first response. Should software that blocks or filters objectionable material on the Internet be installed in public libraries? Obviously yes would again be the first response. So, is it okay to limit the sites available within a library for adults and children? Or, should only children be limited? Should children only be allowed access to terminals in the children's section? If so, then shouldn't children also be denied access to the many books in the library that cover the same topics?

Beyond these thorny philosophical questions of what constitutes censorship and what constitutes protection lurk some surprisingly practical issues. If software that filters out "unacceptable" sites is adopted, then who controls what children or adults can download from the "information superhighway"? Who determines what children should and should not access and what is offensive? In short, who writes the filtering programs, and what is eliminated? This is a case in which an easy solution—filtering software—has long-term consequences for repressing freedom of speech and access to information.

Teens present a particularly difficult age group when considering this issue. They are interested in many of the sites that would be blocked by filtering software, and most would agree that teens need to know information about sexual issues that would certainly be blocked by most existing filters.

Libraries face engrossing issues. Long the champion of freedom of speech, they have generally fought attempts to ban books. Although the Internet presents similar issues, libraries can lose big with their constituents by their actions. And the political climate that produced the Communications Decency Act, which made transmission of indecent material over the Internet a criminal act, has spawned many suits against libraries for decisions made in the online arena. Some have installed filtering software and have faced suits by the American Civil Liberties Union (ACLU). Others have kept access open and faced community outrage. Although the Communications Decency Act was declared unconstitutional by the Supreme Court, libraries do not know what liabilities they may face from patrons offended by what they see others access in public areas. In one case, a university library posted a notice that it could not control or censor what individual university students viewed but that those students should be aware that if other nearby library patrons found the material offensive, the viewer could be liable for charges of sexual harassment.

The case of libraries facing online access issues is only one specific example in the larger debate on the issues that we face as technology becomes more accessible in public institutions. In the following selection, Michael A. Banks argues for filtering the Internet; not everything there is appropriate for everybody. Some discrimination is called for, he asserts, and filtering software is the least intrusive manner of accomplishing that goal. The ACLU argues against filters as a voluntary alternative to government regulation of Internet content. Filters are now viewed as architectural changes that may facilitate the suppression of speech far more effectively than congressional lawmaking ever could.

Michael A. Banks

Filtering the Net in Libraries

The year is 1967. A patron finds a book in your library containing detailed instructions for making dynamite, and uses that information to build a bomb that he uses to destroy a neighbor's house. Now, you are being sued—and you may be charged with complicity in a crime.

Or, it's 1972, and last month you refused to allow a young patron to withdraw books from the "adult" section of your library. Despite the long-standing rule that anyone under 12 is restricted to the juvenile and reference sections, a lawsuit is brought, naming you, library staff, and trustees as defendants.

Absurd? Unthinkable? Indeed, yes—in those times. But such scenarios are possible now, with one major difference. Rather than allowing access to the "wrong" sort of books, or denying access to certain books, today's focus is on whether to allow Internet access. Asmore andmore people turn to local libraries for Internet access, the possibility of such conflicts becomes more probable. This situation has forced more than a few libraries to pass judgment on what Internet content is appropriate for adults and children to see. The task is simple in theory, but complex in practice. Exactly what should you permit, and what should you block? And why?

At the same time, some communities and/or individuals are demanding that libraries abstain from such judgment. For example, late in December 1997 a community group in Virginia filed suit against the public library system in Louden County in order to block an Internet usage policy. Among other things, the police specified that library computers used for Internet access be equipped with filtering software, to protect children from pornography and other objectionable material on the Web and in Usenet newsgroups. The lawsuit claims that the use of such software is a violation of free speech rights since material that adults may want to access is also blocked.

In short, even though you are not expected to have on hand every magazine and every book in the world, you are expected by many to provide access to the full Internet. Since, as the Virginia case proves, there are no hard and fast definitions of what constitutes community standards, the judgment calls are difficult, to say the least. Then there are the widely varying expectations of patrons as to their rights in using library equipment—often quite independent of any perceived community standards. All of this leaves some librarians try-

From Michael A. Banks, "Filtering the Net in Libraries: The Case (Mostly) in Favor," *Computers in Libraries*, vol. 18, no. 3 (March 1998). Copyright © 1998 by Information Today, Inc. Reprinted by permission of Information Today, Inc., 143 Old Marlton Pike, Medford, NJ 08055.

ing to answer the question: Do you prefer to be liable for "infringing" on freedom of speech, or do you prefer to be liable for the effects of exposure to objectionable text and images?

To Block, or Not to Block

The decision to apply blocks is an unfortunate situation, indeed, but one that many libraries will have to face over the next few years. With fewer than 40 percent of American households on the Internet, more and more people are turning to libraries for Internet access. Even patrons who have Internet access at home also use library computers to get online, a matter of convenience during library visits. This means that, sooner or later, someone is going to have a problem with what they or others can or cannot access on the Internet. So, what do you do? Allow everyone access to everything, or try to control what is available?

On the whole, I feel that it is simpler to opt for blocking or filtering Internet access. That way, you don't risk offending employees and patrons who don't want to see objectionable material. This is to say, the "liability" is less than if you permit wide-open Internet access because once that genie is out of the bottle, there is no turning back. If there are objections to blocking in your community, they can be sorted out and problems rectified (not the case if you don't block and minors are accessing Internet pornography through your system). The only questions that remain are what you filter out, and how.

No Newsgroups Is Good Newsgroups?

For those concerned about Internet security, I advise blocking all Usenet newsgroup access. Usenet newsgroups, in existence since 1979, are one of the oldest components of the Internet. Today, this venerable element is fast becoming all but useless. Why? Because nearly all of the 20,000-plus newsgroups are clogged and choked with "spam," mass advertising of useless moneymaking schemes, con games, and porno sites. In some newsgroups, it is impossible to sort out the worthwhile postings from the spam, thanks to the perpetrators' attempts to disguise the true nature of their postings. Also, many postings are literal traps and ambushes. As I'll show you below, the simple act of opening a newsgroup posting can cause your browser to be taken over completely. Certain Web pages can do the same thing but, fortunately, there are ways to defend against this happening—but only if you use Netscape.

This is why you might be wise to block all Usenet newsgroup access. Simply not installing the newsgroup reader element of your Web browser will do the trick. Or, you can rely on filtering software that blocks objectionable newsgroups. Remember, though, that almost any newsgroup can contain objectionable material—or the ambushes to which I referred above.

What About Filters?

I see filters as part of a complete Internet security program. There are a dozen or more good Web/newsgroup filters available, each as good as the next in certain respects. There's not enough room to cover all of them here, but I will provide an overview of a few of the better products. Before I do that, though, let's take a quick look at what filtering programs do.

Acting as a Web browser "supervisor," a filtering program prevents access to sites considered inappropriate for the person using the browser. The decision as to what is inappropriate is usually based on listings compiled by the software manufacturer or by one of the Internet rating services. (Some companies also accept recommendations from users for sites to be blocked or unblocked.) Most programs block "adult" or sexual material, as well as sites with racist or bigotry oriented themes. Sites promoting drug abuse are also blocked, along with adult online chat rooms. Various criteria are used to select sites to block, including the use of keywords, selective filtering of domains, and manual selection.

Unfortunately, filtering programs can be quite literal. At least one will not let you access a site or page carrying the surname or title "Sexton," because the word "sex" is contained in that name. However, if the software allows you to unblock sites manually, this problem can be overcome easily enough. With that in mind, you will want to ask yourself these questions when selecting a filtering program:

- Is the program updatable? Most filtering programs provide online updates of blocked site lists, sometimes by subscription. Relying on such updates is a good idea, as thousands of new potentially objectionable sites come online each month. The publishers that provide updates can catch almost all of these, and they do all the work for you.
- Can I unblock selected sites? Sometimes a filtering program mistakenly blocks a site that is not offensive. When this is the case, you should be able to unblock that site.
- Can I block selected sites? Despite all their efforts, the companies that publish blocking software cannot catch every objectionable site. Thus, you will want to be able to add sites to the blocked list.

In addition to altering lists of blocked sites, you may want to be able to alter the criteria that a filtering program uses to block sites on its own. This allows you to make up your own rules as to what is blocked, and why. The more versatility in this area, the better.

The following programs are among the better ones available. Since most blocking programs feature explanations of their blocking criteria at their Web sites, and some provide lists of blocked sites, I urge you to visit the Web site for each.

Cyber Patrol: Cyber Patrol is among the more successful Web filtering programs. It is used by America Online, AT&T WorldNet, Bell Atlantic, British Telecom, and CompuServe, among other online services and Internet service providers (ISPs), and it is bundled with some PCs. You can set up Cyber Patrol to control access to the Internet and newsgroups based on a variety of criteria. Or, you can grant access only to Cyber Patrol's list of approved sites (some 40,000) and block the rest of the Web. A particularly interesting feature of the program is an option that blocks users from typing in or viewing objectionable words or phrases, based in part on a default list of profanity. A special subscription service provides online updates to Cyper Patrol's blocked site lists. For more information, and to download a free trial version, visit http://www.cyberpatrol.com.

CYBERsitter: CYBERsitter is an interesting filtering/blocking program that runs in the background at all times and claims to be virtually impossible to detect or defeat. It works on several fronts. By default, it not only blocks access to adult-oriented Web sites, but also to newsgroups and images. In addition, Web pages and newsgroup posting are filtered to remove offensive language. Blocking and filtering are based on lists provided with the program, but you can add your own words to the lists. When filtering, CYBERsitter examines words and phrases in context, in order to eliminate some of the ambiguity of blocking. For more information about CYBERsitter, or to download a free trial version of the program, visit http://www.solidoak.com.

NetNanny: NetNanny is designed to manage Internet and computer access. You can use it to monitor, screen, or block access to anything that is on or running into, out of, or through a computer, online or off. The outgoing block can be useful in preventing users from using search engines to find and link to objectionable sites.

   The program comes with a list of blocked Internet sites and other parameters that it uses to block still more sites. The list and parameters can be updated at no charge at the NetNanny Web site, and you can add your own screening specifications. NetNanny is available forWindows or DOS. See http://www.netnanny.com for more information.

Net Shepherd: Net Shepherd is an Internet content rating service that filters the results of Alta Vista searches. Its PICS-compliant ratings database can be used with Microsoft Internet Explorer or Net Shepherd's own daxHOUND program, a content filtering tool. For additional information on Net Shepherd, visit http://www.netshepherd.com. Information about daxHOUND (and a download) can be found at http://www.netshepherd.com/products/daxHOUND2.0/daxhound.htm.

SurfWatch: SurfWatch is a filter that screens for unwanted material on the Internet. As with other filter and blocking programs, SurfWatch can be used with almost any Web browser. Various levels of access control are available, and the program cannot be easily disarmed by deleting it or by other means. SurfWatch screens Web sites, newsgroups, ftp and gopher sites, and Web chat rooms. Blocking is based on a list of sites generated by in-house research and customer reports. Online updates are available via subscription.

SurfWatch alone doesn't permit you to modify the list of sites, nor does it attempt to block sites that are violent in nature or include material that is hateful or otherwise potentially inappropriate. A free add-on called SurfWatch Manager lets you edit the list of blocked sites. Full information on SurfWatch, along with its list of blocked sites, is available at http://www.surfwatch.com.

X-STOP: The appropriately named X-STOP is a program designed for use by libraries and other institutions and businesses that provide Internet access. It selectively blocks and filters sites based on a variety of criteria. The program allows you to alter the criteria it uses for filtering. It also monitors outgoing words in order to prevent users from looking up objectionable sites with search engines. For more information, see http://www.xstop.com.

Ambushed by Java and JavaScript Risks

Even if you use a filtering program with your computer systems, you can still run into security problems, thanks to Java and JavaScript. You are probably aware of the many security risks associated with Java, a programming language that is used to transmit small computer programs, called "applets" to Internet users' computers, where they are free to run and do things like collect data from hard drives. Filtering programs cannot detect everything a Java program will do, so it is possible to transmit objectionable content with a Java applet. Thus, it is usually a good idea to disable Java on your browsers. It is true that Java-related risks are fewer since so many "loopholes" involving Java have been exposed. But you never know what someone is cooking up. Besides, the Javaless Web surfer usually misses nothing more than animations that slow down browsing anyway.

JavaScript can pose a slightly greater risk, for two reasons. First, there have been no warnings about problems created by JavaScript. Indeed, I expect this to be the first you've heard of such problems. JavaScript can be used to direct your browser to any page on the Web, alter its configuration, and pull other nasty tricks. This being the case, it is best to disable JavaScript when visiting Web sites unfamiliar to you, and when reading newsgroup messages, in which JavaScript can be used to take over browsers.

Second, the JavaScript language is far easier to use, and thus accessible to more people, than Java. This means that the risk of exposure to malevolent JavaScript code is greater. What can JavaScript do to your system? For openers, JavaScript can be used to take control of a browser from a Web page or a Usenet newsgroup posting in two different ways. With a simple line of code, someone can set up a page so that, should your mouse cursor pass over a link or an image (loaded or not), your browser will be forced to "go to" (load) a specified page on the Web. This happens without clicking on anything.

A more insidious JavaScript trick can take over your browser and re-open it without menus or controls, on top of all other applications. Here again, the perpetrator of this trick can put anything he or she wants to appear in your browser window. This not only forces you to look at the perpetrator's message or images, but also disrupts your browsing session. And it can get worse. I have seen this set up so that you are forced to see the same page—or a series of pages—over and over again. Even if you exit the browser, it will reopen and display whatever the perpetrator wants it to display. This has been used extensively by pornography site purveyors to force Web surfers to their sites and to keep them there. Worse, the code required to do the things just described can be hidden, so that you cannot see it even if you view a Web page's source.

The only defense against this is to disable JavaScript. This is easily done with Netscape. Unfortunately, you cannot disable JavaScript if you are using Microsoft Internet Explorer 4. Mircosoft does not "support" JavaScript, and so does not allow you to turn it off.

Summing up My Position

The arguments against restricting Internet access are many, and at times they sound shrill. However, the fact remains that not everything on the Internet is appropriate for everybody, just as not every book or magazine published is appropriate for everybody. This being the case, some discrimination is called for in choosing what a public institution makes available from the Internet. For example, even though libraries make many magazines available, they do not subscribe to *Hustler* because that would be an inappropriate addition to their collections. In this same vein, just because libraries provide access to the Internet, they do not need to provide access to the entire Internet.

I believe that much of the problem here stems from the differences between not subscribing to *Hustler* and not receiving Internet content that is pornographic, racist, or otherwise objectionable. In the former instance, you need do nothing to avoid a subscription; in the latter, action is necessary to keep pornographic content out of the library. The need to take action in order to avoid questionable Internet material unfortunately confuses some people into mistaking positive proaction for repressing action. No one demands that libraries subscribe to *Hustler*, and so I feel that no one should demand that libraries grant full and unrestricted access to the Internet to everyone.

Obviously, posted rules are not enough to limit access to pornography or other objectionable Internet content. Even those who do not want to access such content may have it forced on them. All this being the case, it behooves libraries to provide practical limits to Internet access. At present, filtering and/or blocking Internet content is the only means of even partially controlling access to offensive or objectionable material. Even though filtering sometimes results in legitimate sites being blocked—a problem that can be rectified manually—it is a practical action.

Those who might object on the basis of some specious "freedom of speech" issue should consider the Internet as an analog to real-world books and magazines. In this light, it is easy to see the absurdity of uncontrolled Internet access for children and other patrons. If the sort of content access that some advocate for the Internet were to be applied to conventional library content, *Hustler* magazine, neo-Nazi books and pamphlets, and worse objectionable material would have to be placed in juvenile and children's as well as general library collections. This is what uncontrolled access to the Internet in a public venue can be.

Censorship in a Box

Introduction

In libraries and schools across the nation, the Internet is rapidly becoming an essential tool for learning and communication. According to the American Library Association, of the nearly 9,000 public libraries in America, 60.4 percent offer Internet access to the public, up from 27.8 percent in 1996. And a recent survey of 1,400 teachers revealed that almost half use the Internet as a teaching tool. But today, unfettered access to the Internet is being threatened by the proliferation of blocking software in libraries.

America's libraries have always been a great equalizer, providing books and other information resources to help people of all ages and backgrounds live, learn, work and govern in a democratic society. Today more than ever, our nation's libraries are vibrant multi-cultural institutions that connect people in the smallest and most remote communities with global information resources.

In 1995, the National Telecommunications and Information Administration of the U.S. Department of Commerce concluded that "public libraries can play a vital role in assuring that advanced information services are universally available to all segments of the American population on an equitable basis. Just as libraries traditionally make available the marvels and imagination of the human mind to all, libraries of the future are planning to allow everyone to participate in the electronic renaissance."

Today, the dream of universal access will remain only a dream if politicians force libraries and other institutions to use blocking software whenever patrons access the Internet. Blocking software prevents users from accessing a wide range of valuable information, including such topics as art, literature, women's health, politics, religion and free speech. Without free and unfettered access to the Internet, this exciting new medium could become, for many Americans, little more than a souped-up, G-rated television network.

This special report by the American Civil Liberties Union [ACLU] provides an in depth look at why mandatory blocking software is both inappropriate and unconstitutional in libraries. We do not offer an opinion about any particular blocking product, but we will demonstrate how all blocking software censors valuable speech and gives libraries, educators and parents a false sense of security when providing minors with Internet access.

Like any technology, blocking software can be used for constructive or destructive purposes. In the hands of parents and others who voluntarily use it, it is a tool that can be somewhat useful in blocking access to some inappropriate material online. But in the hands of government, blocking software is nothing more than censorship in a box.

The ACLU believes that government has a necessary role to play in promoting universal Internet access. But that role should focus on expanding, not restricting, access to online speech.

Reno v. ACLU: A Momentous Decision

Our vision of an uncensored Internet was clearly shared by the U.S. Supreme Court when it struck down the 1996 Communications Decency Act (CDA), a federal law that outlawed "indecent" communications online.

Ruling unanimously in *Reno v. ACLU,* the Court declared the Internet to be a free speech zone, deserving of at least as much First Amendment protection as that afforded to books, newspapers and magazines. The government, the Court said, can no more restrict a person's access to words or images on the Internet than it could be allowed to snatch a book out of a reader's hands in the library, or cover over a statue of a nude in a museum.

The nine Justices were clearly persuaded by the unique nature of the medium itself, citing with approval the lower federal court's conclusion that the Internet is "the most participatory form of mass speech yet developed," entitled to "the highest protection from governmental intrusion." The Internet, the Court concluded, is like "a vast library including millions of readily available and indexed publications," the content of which "is as diverse as human thought."

Blocking Software: For Parents, Not the Government

In striking down the CDA on constitutional grounds, the Supreme Court emphasized that if a statute burdens adult speech—as any censorship law must—it "is unacceptable if less restrictive alternatives were available."

Commenting on the availability of user-based blocking software as a possible alternative, the Court concluded that the use of such software was appropriate for *parents*. Blocking software, the Court wrote, is a "reasonably effective method by which parents can prevent their children from accessing material which the *parents* believe is inappropriate." [Emphasis in the original]

The rest of the Court's decision firmly holds that government censorship of the Internet violates the First Amendment, and that holding applies to government use of blocking software just as it applied when the Court struck down the CDA's criminal ban.

In the months since that ruling, the blocking software market has experienced explosive growth, as parents exercise their prerogative to guide their children's Internet experience. According to analysts at International Data Corporation, a technology consulting firm, software makers sold an estimated $14 million in blocking software last year, and over the next three years, sales of blocking products are expected to grow to more than $75 million.

An increasing number of city and country library boards have recently forced libraries to install blocking programs, over the objections of the American Library Association and library patrons, and the use of blocking software in libraries is fast becoming the biggest free speech controversy since the legal challenge to the CDA.

How Does Blocking Software Work?

The best known Internet platform is the World Wide Web, which allows users to search for and retrieve information stored in remote computers. The Web currently contains over 100 million documents, with thousands added each day. Because of the ease with which material can be added and manipulated, the content on existing Web sites is constantly changing. Links from one computer to another and from one document to another across the Internet are what unify the Web into a single body of knowledge, and what makes the Web unique.

To gain access to the information available on the Web, a person uses a Web "browser"—software such as Netscape Navigator or Microsoft's Internet Explorer—to display, print and download documents. Each document on the Web has an address that allows users to find and retrieve it.

A variety of systems allow users of the Web to search for particular information among all of the public sites that are part of the Web. Services such as Yahoo, Magellan, Alta Vista, Webcrawler, Lycos and Infoseek provide tools called "search engines." Once a user has accessed the search service she simply types a word or string of words as a search request and the search engine provides a list of matching sites.

Blocking software is configured to hide or prevent access to certain Internet sites. Most blocking software comes packaged in a box and can be purchased at retail computer stores. It is installed on individual and/or networked computers that have access to the Internet, and works in conjunction with a Web browser to block information and sites on the Internet that would otherwise be available.

What Kind of Speech Is Being Blocked?

Most blocking software prevents access to sites based on criteria provided by the vendor. To conduct site-based blocking, a vendor establishes criteria to identify specified categories of speech on the Internet and configures the blocking software to block sites containing those categories of speech. Some Internet blocking software blocks as few as six categories of information, while others block many more.

Blocked categories may include hate speech, criminal activity, sexually explicit speech, "adult" speech, violent speech, religious speech, and even sports and entertainment.

Using its list of criteria, the software vendor compiles and maintains lists of "unacceptable" sites. Some software vendors employ individuals who browse the Internet for sites to block. Others use automated searching tools to identify which sites to block. These methods may be used in combination. (Examples of blocked sites can be found below.) ...

Typical examples of blocked words and letters include "xxx," which blocks out Superbowl XXX sites; "breast," which blocks website and discussion groups about breast cancer; and the consecutive letters "s," "e" and "x," which block sites containing the words "sexton" and "Mars exploration," among many others. Some software blocks categories of expression along blatantly ideological lines, such as information about feminism or gay and lesbian issues. Yet most websites offering opposing views on these issues are not blocked. For example, the same software does not block sites expressing opposition to homosexuality and women working outside the home.

Clearly, the answer to blocking based on ideological viewpoint is not more blocking, any more than the answer to unpopular speech is to prevent everyone from speaking, because then no viewpoint of any kind will be heard. The American Family Association [AFA], a conservative religious organization, recently learned this lesson when it found that CyberPatrol, a popular brand of blocking software, had placed AFA on its "Cybernot" list because of the group's opposition to homosexuality.

AFA's site was blocked under the category "intolerance," defined as "pictures or text advocating prejudice or discrimination against any race, color, national origin, religion, disability or handicap, gender or sexual orientation. Any picture or text that elevates one group over another. Also includes intolerance jokes or slurs." Other "Cybernot" categories include "violence/profanity," "nudity," "sexual acts," "satanic/cult," and "drugs/drug culture."

In a May 28th [1999] news release excoriating CyberPatrol, AFA said, "CyberPatrol has elected to block the AFA website with their filter because we have simply taken an opposing viewpoint to the political and cultural agenda of the homosexual rights movement." As one AFA spokesman told reporters, "Basically we're being blocked for free speech."

The AFA said they are planning to appeal the blocking decision at a June 9th meeting of CyberPatrol's Cybernot Oversight Committee, but expressed doubt that the decision would be overturned. The conservative Family Research Council also joined in the fight, saying they had "learned that the Gay Lesbian Alliance Against Defamation (GLAAD) is a charter member of CyberPatrol's oversight committee," and that "it was pressure by GLAAD that turned CyberPatrol around."

Until, now, AFA, FRC and similar groups had been strong advocates for filtering software, and AFA has even assisted in the marketing of another product, X-Stop. AFA has said that they still support blocking but believe their group was unfairly singled out.

Indeed, as the AFA and others have learned, there is no avoiding the fact that somebody out there is making judgments about what is offensive and controversial, judgments that may not coincide with their own. The First Amendment exists precisely to protect the most offensive and controversial speech from government suppression. If blocking software is made mandatory in schools and libraries, that "somebody" making the judgments becomes the government.

To Block or Not to Block: You Decide

According to a recent story in The Washington Post, a software vendor's "own test of a sample of Web sites found that the software allowed pornographic sites to get through and blocked 57 sites that did not contain anything objectionable."

And in a current lawsuit in Virginia over the use of blocking software in libraries, the ACLU argues that the software blocks "a wide variety of other Web sites that contain valuable and constitutionally protected speech, such as the entire Web site of Glide Memorial United Methodist Church, located in San Francisco, California, and the entire Web site of The San Francisco Chronicle."

Following are real-world examples of the kind of speech that has been found to be inaccessible in libraries where blocking software is installed. Read through them—or look at them online—and then decide for yourself: Do you want the government telling you whether you can access these sites in the library?

www.afa.net   The American Family is a non-profit group founded in 1977 by the Rev. Donald Wildmon. According to their website, the AFA "stands for traditional family values, focusing primarily on the influence of television and other media—including pornography—on our society."

www.cmu.edu   Banned Books On-Line offers the full text of over thirty books that have been the object of censorship or censorship attempts, from James Joyce's Ulysses to Little Red Riding Hood.

www.quaker.org   The Religious Society of Friends describes itself as "an Alternative Christianity which emphasizes the personal experience of God in one's life." Their site boasts the slogan, "Proud to Be Censored by X-Stop, a popular brand of blocking software."

www.safersex.org   The Safer Sex Page includes brochures about safer sex, HIV transmission, and condoms, as well as resources for health educators and counselors. X-Stop, the software that blocks these pages, does not block the "The Safest Sex Home Page," which promotes abstinence before marriage as the only protection against sexually transmitted diseases.

www.iatnet.com.aauw   The American Association of University Women Maryland provides information about its activities to promote equity for women. The Web site discusses AAUW's leadership role in civil rights issues; work and family issues such as pay equity, family and medical leave, and dependent care; sex discrimination; and reproductive rights.

www.sfgate.com/columnists/morse   Rob Morse, an award-winning columnist for The San Francisco Examiner, has written more than four hundred columns on a variety of issues ranging from national politics, homelessness, urban violence, computer news, and the Superbowl, to human cloning. Because his section is considered off limits, the entire www.sfgate.com site is blocked to viewers.

http://www.youth.org/yao/docs/books.html   Books for Gay and Lesbian Teens/Youth provides information about books of interest to gay and lesbian youth. The site was created by Jeremy Meyers, an 18-year-old senior in high school who lives in New York City. X-Stop, the software that blocks this page, does not block web pages condemning homosexuality....

In addition to these examples, a growing body of research compiled by educators, public interest organizations and other interested groups demonstrates the extent to which this software inappropriately blocks valuable, protected speech, and does not effectively block the sites they claim to block....

Teaching Responsibility: Solutions That Work...

Instead of requiring unconstitutional blocking software, schools and libraries should establish content-neutral rules about when and how young people should use the Internet, and hold educational seminars on responsible use of the Internet.

For instance, schools could request that Internet access be limited to school-related work and develop carefully worded acceptable use policies (AUPs), that provide instructions for parents, teachers, students, librarians and patrons on use of the Internet....

Successful completion of a seminar similar to a driver's education course could be required of minors who seek Internet privileges in the classroom or library. Such seminars could emphasize the dangers of disclosing personally identifiable information such as one's address, communicating with strangers about personal or intimate matters, or relying on inaccurate resources on the Net.

Whether the use of blocking software is mandatory or not, parents should always be informed that blind reliance on blocking programs cannot effectively safeguard children.

Libraries can and should take other actions that are more protective of online free speech principles. For instance, libraries can publicize and provide links to particular sites that have been recommended for children.

Not all solutions are necessarily "high tech." To avoid unwanted viewing by passers-by, for instance, libraries can place privacy screens around Internet access terminals in ways that minimize pubic view. Libraries can also impose content-neutral time limits on Internet use.

These positive approaches work much better than restrictive software that works only when students are using school or library computers, and teaches no critical thinking skills. After all, sooner or later students graduate to the real world, or use a computer without blocking software. An educational program could teach students how to use the technology to find information quickly and efficiently, and how to exercise their own judgment to assess the quality and reliability of information they receive.

...and Don't Work

In an effort to avoid installing blocking software, some libraries have instituted a "tap on the shoulder" policy that is, in many ways, more intrusive and unconstitutional than a computer program. This authorizes librarians to peer at the patron's computer screen and tap anyone on the shoulder who is viewing "inappropriate" material.

The ACLU recently contacted a library in Newburgh, New York to advise against a proposed policy that would permit librarians to stop patrons from accessing "offensive" and "racially or sexually inappropriate material." In a letter to the Newburgh Board of Education, the ACLU wrote: "The Constitution protects dirty words, racial epithets, and sexually explicit speech, even though that speech may be offensive to some." The letter also noted that the broad language of the policy would allow a librarian to prevent a patron from viewing on the Internet such classic works of fiction as Chaucer's Canterbury Tales and Mark Twain's Adventures of Huckleberry Finn, and such classic works of art as Manet's Olympia and Michelangelo's David.

"This thrusts the librarian into the role of Big Brother and allows for arbitrary and discriminatory enforcement since each librarian will have a different opinion about what is offensive," the ACLU said.

The First Amendment prohibits librarians from directly censoring protected speech in the library, just as it prevents indirect censorship through blocking software.

Battling Big Brother in the Library

In Loudoun County, Virginia, the ACLU is currently involved in the first court challenge to the use of blocking software in a library. Recently, the judge in that case forcefully rejected a motion to dismiss the lawsuit, saying that the government had "misconstrued the nature of the Internet" and warning that Internet blocking requires the strictest level of constitutional scrutiny. The case is now set to go to trial....

Earlier this year, the ACLU was involved in a local controversy over the mandatory use of Internet blocking programs in California's public libraries. County officials had decided to use a blocking program called "Bess" on every library Internet terminal, despite an admission by Bess's creators that it was impossible to customize the program to filter only material deemed "harmful to minors" by state law.

After months of negotiation, the ACLU warned the county that it would take legal action if officials did not remove Internet blocking software from public library computers. Ultimately, the library conceded that the filters presented an unconstitutional barrier to patrons seeking access to materials including legal opinions, medical information, political commentary, art, literature, information from women's organizations, and even portions of the ACLU Freedom Network website.

Today, under a new policy, the county provides a choice of an unfiltered or a filtered computer to both adult and minor patrons. No parental consent will be required for minors to access unfiltered computers.

The ACLU has also advocated successfully against mandatory blocking software in libraries in San Jose and in Santa Clara County, California. The ACLU continues to monitor the use of blocking software in many libraries across the nation, including communities in Massachusetts, Texas, Illinois, Ohio and Pennsylvania.

The Fight in Congress: Marshaling the Cyber-Troops Against Censorship

In February of this year, Senator John McCain (R-AZ) introduced the "Internet School Filtering Act," a law that requires all public libraries and schools to use blocking software in order to qualify for "e-rate," a federal funding program to promote universal Internet access. An amendment that would have allowed schools and libraries to qualify by presenting their own plan to regulate Internet access—not necessarily by commercial filter—failed in committee.

Another bill sponsored by Senator Dan Coats (R-IN) was dubbed "Son of CDA," because much of it is identical to the ill-fated Communications Decency Act.

The ACLU and others are lobbying against these bills, which have not yet come up for a vote as of this writing.

Censorship in the States: A Continuing Battle

Federal lawmakers are not the only politicians jumping on the censorship bandwagon. In the last three years, at least 25 states have considered or passed Internet censorship laws. This year, at least seven states are considering bills that require libraries and/or schools to use blocking software.

These censorship laws have not held up to constitutional scrutiny. Federal district courts in New York, Georgia and Virginia have found Internet censorship laws unconstitutional on First Amendment grounds in challenges brought by the ACLU. In April, the ACLU filed a challenge to an Internet censorship law in New Mexico that is remarkably similar to the failed New York law.

Conclusion

The advent of new forms of communication technology is always a cause for public anxiety and unease. This was as true for the printing press and the telephone as it was for the radio and the television. But the constitutional ideal is immutable regardless of the medium: a free society is based on the principle that each and every individual has the right to decide what kind of information he or she wants—or does not want—to receive or create. Once you allow the government to censor material you don't like, you cede to it the power to censor something you do like—even your own speech.

Censorship, like poison gas, can be highly effective when the wind is blowing the right way. But the wind has a way of shifting, and sooner or later, it blows back upon the user. Whether it comes in a box or is accessed online, in the hands of the government, blocking software is toxic to a democratic society.

Questions and Answers About Blocking Software

In the interest of "unblocking" the truth, here are answers to some of the questions the ACLU most often encounters on the issue of blocking software:

Q: Why does it matter whether Internet sites are blocked at the library when people who want to see them can just access them at home?

A: According to a recent Nielsen Survey, 45 percent of Internet users go to public libraries for Internet access. For users seeking controversial or personal information, the library is often their only opportunity for privacy. A Mormon teenager in Utah seeking information about other religions may not want a parent in the home, or a teacher at school, looking over her shoulder as she surfs the web.

Q: What about library policies that allow patrons to request that certain sites be unblocked?

A: The stigma of requesting access to a blocked site deters many people from making that request. Library patrons may be deterred from filling out a form seeking access, because the sites they wish to visit contain sensitive information. For instance, a woman seeking to access the Planned Parenthood website to find out about birth control may feel embarrassed about justifying the request to a librarian.

Q: But as long as a library patron can ask for a site to be unblocked, no one's speech is really being censored, right?

A: Wrong. Web providers who want their speech to reach library patrons have no way to request that their site be unblocked in thousands of libraries around the country. They fear patrons will be stigmatized for requesting that the site be unblocked, or simply won't brother to make the request. If public libraries around the country continue to use blocking software, speakers will be forced to self-censor in order to avoid being blocked in libraries.

Q: Isn't it true that libraries can use blocking software in the same way they select books for circulation?

A: The unique nature of the Internet means that librarians do not to have to consider the limitations of shelf space in providing access to online material. In a recent ruling concerning the use of blocking software in Virginia libraries, a federal judge agreed with the analogy of the Internet as "a collection of encyclopedias from which defendants [the government] have laboriously redacted [or crossed out] portions deemed unfit for library patrons."

Q: Doesn't blocking software help a librarian control what children see online?

A: The ability to choose which software is installed does not empower a school board or librarian to determine what is "inappropriate for minors." Instead, that determination is made by a software vendor who regards the lists of blocked sites as secret, proprietary information.

Q: Why shouldn't librarians be involved in preventing minors from accessing inappropriate material on the Internet?

A: It is the domain of parents, not librarians, to oversee their children's library use. This approach preserves the integrity of the library as a storehouse of ideas available to all regardless of age or income. As stated by the American Library Association's Office of Intellectual Freedom: "Parents and only parents have the right and responsibility to restrict their own children's access—and only their own children's access—to library resources, including the Internet. Librarians do not serve *in loco parentis.*"

Q: What do librarians themselves think about blocking software?

A: The overwhelming majority of librarians are opposed to the mandatory use of blocking software. However some, under pressure from individuals or local officials, have installed blocking software. The ALA has a Library Bill of Rights, which maintains that filters should not be used "to block access to constitutionally protected speech."...

Q: Are libraries required to use blocking software in order to avoid criminal liability for providing minors access to speech that may not be protected by the Constitution?

A: No. The First Amendment prohibits imposing criminal or civil liability on librarians merely for providing minors with access to the Internet. The knowledge that some websites on the Internet may contain "harmful" matter is not sufficient grounds for prosecution. In fact, an attempt to avoid any liability by installing blocking software or otherwise limiting minors' access to the Internet would, itself, violate the First Amendment.

Q: Would libraries that do not use blocking software be liable for sexual harassment in the library?

A: No. Workplace sexual harassment laws apply only to employees, not to patrons. The remote possibility that a library employee might inadvertently view an objectionable site does not constitute sexual harassment under current law.

Q: Can't blocking programs be fixed so they block only illegal speech that is not protected by the Constitution?

A: There is simply no way for a computer software program to make distinctions between protected and unprotected speech. This is not a design flaw that may be "fixed" at some future point but a simple human truth....

Q: What if blocking software is only made mandatory for kids?

A: Even if only minors are forced to use blocking programs, constitutional problems remain. The Supreme Court has agreed that minors have rights too, and the fact that a 15-year-old rather than an 18-year-old seeks access online to valuable information on subjects such as religion or gay and lesbian resources does not mean that the First Amendment no longer applies. In any case, it is impossible for a computer program to distinguish what is appropriate for different age levels, or the age of the patron using the computer.

Q: Is using blocking software at schools any different than using it in public libraries?

A: Unlike libraries, schools do act in place of parents, and play a role in teaching civic values. Students do have First Amendment rights, however, and blocking software is inappropriate, especially for junior and high school students.

   In addition, because the software often blocks valuable information while allowing access to objectionable material, parents are given a false sense of security about what their children are viewing. A less restrictive—and more effective—alternative is the establishment of content-neutral "Acceptable Use Policies" (AUPs).

Q: Despite all these problems, isn't blocking software worth it if it keeps some pornography from reaching kids?

A: Even though sexually explicit sites only make up a very small percentage of content on the Internet, it is impossible for any one program to block out every conceivable web page with "inappropriate" material.

When blocking software is made mandatory, adults as well as minors are prevented from communicating online, even in schools. According to a recent news story in the Los Angeles Times, a restrictive blocking program at a California school district meant coaches couldn't access the University of Notre Dame's website, and math instructors were cut off from information about Wall Street because of a block on references to money and finance.

POSTSCRIPT

Should Internet Access Be Regulated?

In the United States, we have been loath to create any system of information that would be restricted. For example, the First Amendment to our Constitution guarantees freedom of speech, and freedom of the press. The Internet is a unique communications medium, but for the most part, any type of restriction that has ever been considered with regard to the Internet has reflected a heated discussion of whether the First Amendment is absolute, or not. While the term "regulation" suggests something less drastic than "restricted," or "restrained," the words still bring to mind the guarantee of free speech that is at the heart of so many of our communications laws.

There will probably be many attempts to create some types of controls over content on the Internet, and these attempts will be controversial. While the initial concept of blocking technology was simple, its introduction into the realm of public institutions has raised many troubling questions. Here are a few that have emerged: If information is to be evaluated, who should do the evaluation—the authors/distributors, the public institution, the government, or the public? In a society barraged by information, how feasibly can a ratings system protect vulnerable audiences? Are there information sites that should be exempt from filtering, such as news organizations? What forms of assessment exist to test the effectiveness of such a filter? What should the criteria be for labeling a filtering experience a success or a failure? There is much material on the Internet that most of us would decry. In addition to graphic sexual images, one can find out how to make a bomb or how to join a hate group. Inmost cases, there are books in the library that contain the same information. It offends many people that individuals can go into a library and find hate groups online. Yet, anyone can check out books with similar information. Of course, the library can control its inventory in a way that cannot be done with unfiltered Internet access.

Extensive writing on this issue can be accessed by any Internet search engine. The ACLU volume from which the No-side selection was obtained can be further researched at the Electronic Privacy Information Center's Internet site: www.epic.org. Parents' organizations and child advocacy groups have argued for some form of protection for children. *Wired* magazine is an excellent resource for a number of perspectives on issues dealing with computers and the Internet. A different perspective is offered by Brian Kahin and James Keller, who have edited *Public Access to the Internet* (MIT Press, 1995), which features articles that focus on the benefits of Internet use.

Undergirding much of this debate is concern about pornography, which is an important topic for thought. How accessible is it, and should it be controlled on the Internet? Some recent publications dealing with this subject include Nicholas Wolfson's *Hate Speech, Sex Speech, Free Speech* (Praeger, 1997) and James M. Ussher's *Fantasies of Feminity: Reframing the Boundaries of Sex* (Rutgers University Press, 1997).

ISSUE 12

Should Freedom of Speech Ever Be Restricted?

YES: Eugene Volokh, from "Freedom of Speech, Cyberspace, Harassment Law and the Clinton Administration," www1.law. ucla.edu/~volokh/harass/cyberspa.htm, 1–7, 10–14.

NO: Edison and Jacobs Media Research, "Media Indecency Survey," www.edisonresearch.com/Edison_Jacobs_indecency_survey.htm.

ISSUE SUMMARY

YES: Law Professor Eugene Volokh examines several situations in which absolute freedom of speech would very likely conflict with the precedents that have been set in the realm of creating "hostile environment law." For example, if any offensive speech or images were transmitted in a public arena, the law would side with the more conservative approach toward restricting speech or images that would offend certain people, or that would create an uncomfortable atmosphere.

NO: Two media consulting firms collaborated on a survey of rock radio listeners to discover what might be offensive to them. The results, taken from the perspective of the audience who listens to rock, create an argument for restricting government involvement in censoring content, and a clear preference for allowing individuals to choose what they hear, or requiring parental involvement in the cases of radio content and audiences of children.

While there are many legal views about how inclusive our First Amendment "freedom of speech" should be, this issue examines content that often falls into the category of "offensive" content. One of the authors (Volokh) examines the perspective specifically from the use of the Internet (cyberspace) and how messages may offend, or create hostile environments for people who are using a linked "system" for communication. In the opposing view, two research companies that have undertaken a survey of rock radio listeners come up with a different approach for whom should make the decision of whether to listen to content that may be offensive.

Lawyer and law professor Eugene Volokh examines how offensive jokes, mocking racial or ethnic speech patterns, pornography in an office environment, on-line campus bulletin boards and public libraries may all pose problems that could or should see restrictions on freedom of speech. In particular, he looks at how creating hostile environments through the allowing of an atmosphere that demeans individuals has been upheld in recent harassment cases. While he agrees that restricting some speech in certain environments could have a chilling effect on free exchange of ideas, he argues that the rights of the individuals should take precedence over the general right of free speech. Among his most persuasive examples is the issue of hate speech, and whether that type of expression should be allowed to exist in settings where individuals must interact.

Edison Media Research and Jacobs Media surveyed 13,798 individuals who listen to rock radio to learn what, and when, those listeners might be offended by what they hear. Overwhelmingly, the respondents who chose to listen to rock were not offended by the content. While there was greater agreement that shock radio disc jockeys have gone too far these days, there was also an agreement that shock jocks should also have freedom of speech.

Also of importance was the Super Bowl 2004 event in which singer Janet Jackson's "costume malfunction" resulted in her baring a breast on national television at a time in which children could be watching. While most of the respondents were not personally offended by the action, they did express views that it was inappropriate, though most felt that the government should not be involved in restricting content. Rather, parents should exercise more control over what their children hear and watch.

This is an important issue because each of the authors focus on different examples that show how difficult it is to have one constitutionally guaranteed "right" (to free speech) that does not become complicated within specific situations. There may be times when rights and privileges have to be viewed within specific contexts. As you read these selections, please consider other situations in which the clarity of the law becomes more difficult to discern.

Eugene Volokh  **YES**

Freedom of Speech, Cyberspace, Harassment Law, and the Clinton Administration

During the height of the Clinton-Lewinsky scandal, many lawyer pundits talked about impeachment. Some talked about independent counsels and separation of powers. Some talked about the criminal law of perjury, or the rules of evidence, or whether indecent exposure constituted sexual harassment.

A few experts, though, focused on a more practical issue: Saying certain things about the scandal, they advised people, might be legally punishable. "Be careful what you say," one headline warned, when you discuss "the Starr report and Clinton/Lewinsky matter" in certain ways. "Talking about Clinton? Tread carefully," says another, pointing out the risk of "a lawsuit from an offended co-worker." Such discussions "ought to be avoided" because of the risk of legal liability. "[I]t's best to choose carefully who you share your remarks, your jokes, with....'Attorneys warn us about [legal liability]....' Office humor in particular 'is always quicksand'...." "There's no right [to make certain statements about the Clinton/Lewinsky affair] just because it's a public issue." "We had quite a few clients calling us when Lewinsky jokes...were making the rounds." "People think that if they hear something on TV or the radio they can say it at work [without fear of legal liability]. But that of course is not the case."

What body of law, one might ask, would suppress jokes about the President or discussion of the Starr Report? Not the most publicized free speech restriction of the Clinton years, the Communications Decency Act of 1996, (CDA) which was struck down 9-0 by the Supreme Court.

Rather, this remarkable speech restriction is hostile environment harassment law. Under this doctrine, speech can lead to massive liability if it is "severe or pervasive" enough to create a "hostile, abusive, or offensive work environment" for the plaintiff and for a reasonable person based on the person's race, religion, sex, national origin, disability, age, veteran status, and in some jurisdictions a variety of other attributes. And this rather vague and broad test has long been interpreted to cover not just face-to-face slurs or

From *Law and Contemporary Problems*, 2000. Copyright © 2000 by Eugene Volokh. Reprinted by permission of the author.

repeated indecent propositions, but also sexually themed jokes and discussions, even ones that aren't about co-workers or directed at particular co-workers. The prudent employer is wise to restrict speech like this, whether it is about President Clinton, Monica Lewinsky, Kenneth Starr, or anyone else—not just because of professionalism concerns (which some employers might care more about and others less), but because of the risk that this speech will be found to be legally punishable....

The words "in cyberspace" in the phrase "restrictions on free speech in cyberspace" are generally, in my view, not terribly significant; the medium by and large does not and should not affect the protection—or lack of protection—given to the content. The CDA and the Child Online Protection Act do pose some interesting cyberspace-specific questions, but even with these laws, most of the important issues are broader free speech questions: May speech be restricted if the restriction is in fact necessary to effectively serve a compelling government interest? What burdens may be placed on adults in order to shield children?...

The Hidden Communications Decency Act

In 1997, the Equal Employment Opportunity Commission filed a workplace harassment lawsuit, which is still pending, against the Federal Home Loan Mortgage Corporation, also known as Freddie Mac. The lawsuit alleged various misconduct by Freddie Mac employees, including the following item: Some employees allegedly sent to a department-wide distribution list "derogatory electronic messages regarding 'ebonics'"—a list of jokes mocking the black dialect, seemingly a response to the then-current Oakland School Board proposal to treat "ebonics" as a separate language. This, the EEOC claimed, contributed to a racially hostile work environment, and it was thus illegal for Freddie Mac to tolerate such speech; Freddie Mac had a duty to "take prompt and effective remedial action to eradicate" it.

Nor was this an isolated incident. In 1997, for instance, R.R. Donnelly, Morgan Stanley, and Citibank were all sued based in part on offensive jokes sent through e-mail. Newspaper articles reporting on these lawsuits featured headlines such as "Defusing the E-Mail Time Bomb...Establish Firm Workplace Rules to Prevent Discrimination Suits," "E-Mail Humor: Punch Lines Can Carry Price; Jokes Open Employers To Discrimination Suits," and "Firms Get Sobering Message; E-mail Abuses May Leave Them Liable." In a less widely reported case, the New Jersey Office of Administrative Law recently found a single incident of a long joke list being forwarded by e-mail to the whole department to be "sexual harassment," creating an "offensive work environment." The judge "f[ou]nd [that] the 'jokes' degrade, shame, humiliate, defame and dishonor men and women based upon their gender, sexual preference, religion, skin pigmentation and national and ethnic origin" and are thus illegal. Similarly, in *Trout v. City of Akron*, a jury awarded a plaintiff $265,000 based in part on coworkers viewing pornographic material on their computers....

Imagine how a cautious employer would react to a decision imposing liability in the Freddie Mac harassment case or even to the EEOC's decision to sue Freddie Mac. Though in theory individual offensive political statements are not actionable under harassment law unless they are aggregated with at least some other speech or conduct, in practice the employer can't just tell its employees, "It's fine for you to e-mail political statements that some may find racially, religiously, or sexually offensive, *unless* there have been other incidents in which other people have also been mistreating the offended worker in other ways—incidents of which you, the employee, might not even be aware." So long as constitutionally protected speech can be part of a hostile environment claim, the cautious employer must restrict each individual instance of such speech: After all, this particular statement might make the difference between a legally permissible, nonhostile environment, and an illegal hostile environment. The employer must say, "Do not circulate *any* material, even isolated items, that anyone might find racially, religiously, or sexually offensive, since put together such material may lead to liability."

This is exactly what employment experts are counseling employers to do. For instance, according to an article called *Employers Need to Establish Internet Policies*, "avoiding potential sex-harassment liability is a major incentive for companies to establish Internet policies." To prevent "incurring liability under state and federal discrimination laws," businesses should have written policies that bar, among other things, "download[ing] pornographic picture[s]"—not just distributing them but even simply downloading them — and sending "messages with derogatory or inflammatory remarks about an individual or group's race, religion, national origin, physical attributes, or sexual preference." The advice is, of course, not to "bar downloading pornographic pictures and sending messages with derogatory remarks when they are severe or pervasive enough to create a hostile, abusive, or offensive work environment"; rather, the advice is to bar any such downloading and any such messages.

The government, through threat of massive legal liability, is pressuring people to block access to material that it finds offensive. Obviously, private employers may, on their own, choose to restrict speech on their computers— just like private publishers may choose (and routinely do choose) not to publish profane, insulting, or politically offensive material, and just as Internet service providers may choose to restrict the material that they carry and to which they allow access. But when the law uses the threat of legal liability to pressure publishers or service providers into restricting speech on their property, the First Amendment is implicated. This is exactly what happens with harassment law.

True, the law isn't demanding a total ban: People whose Web access is blocked and whose e-mail is restricted because of the legal pressure can still read and write from home, though even from home they should not send e-mail to co-workers who might be offended, since a hostile environment at work may be created by speech sent from one employee's home e-mail address to another's. But the Communications Decency Act didn't impose a total ban, either—it would have still let people read and post what they wanted, so long as the material was difficult for minors to access, which probably meant that the sites would have had to charge for access using a credit card. The Supreme

Court correctly concluded that this burden, even though it wasn't a total ban, violated the First Amendment; the same should go for the burden imposed on speech by harassment law.

What's more, harassment law is in many ways broader than the CDA; the CDA, at least, didn't purport to cover allegedly racist, sexist, or religiously insulting statements. The CDA would not have imposed liability for ebonics jokes (unless they contained highly explicit sexual or excretory references), or for most Clinton-Lewinsky jokes. And the one other body of law that refers to "indecent speech"—the regime governing television and radio broadcasting—tolerates such jokes, as long as they aren't extraordinarily graphic.

But harassment law is not limited to indecency; it operates to generally suppress speech, whether or not sexually explicit or highly profane, that is potentially offensive based on race, religion, sex, and so on. And the evidence of harassment law's chilling effect on protected speech is much more concrete than the speculative (though plausible) evidence on which the Court relied in *Reno v. ACLU*. Harassment law goes where the CDA was forbidden to tread — and so far it hasn't been stopped....

The Hidden Campus Speech Code

In late 1994, the Santa Rosa Junior College newspaper ran an advertisement containing a picture of the rear end of a woman in a bikini. A student, Lois Arata, thought the advertisement was sexist; when the newspaper refused to let her discuss this concern at a staff meeting, she organized a boycott of the newspaper and wrote to the College Trustees to express her objections.

This led to a hot debate in a chat room on SOLO, a college-run online bulletin board for students, and some of the debate contained personal attacks on Arata and on Jennifer Branham, a female newspaper staffer. Some of the messages referred to Arata and Branham using "anatomically explicit and sexually derogatory" terms. Arata and Branham quickly learned of the messages (the two weren't chat room members themselves) and complained to the college, which put the journalism professor who had set up the bulletin board on administrative leave pending an investigation.

This suspension naturally intensified the controversy. Some of the new SOLO posts insulted Arata's personal appearance and said that she was protesting the ad because she was jealous. Others called Arata a "fascist" and a "feminazi fundamentalist." Branham, the newspaper staffer, was especially criticized. At two newspaper staff meetings, many of her fellow staffers "directed angry remarks at [her] and blamed her for the journalism professor's absence." Another staff member produced a parody "lampoon[ing] the newspaper's coverage of Branham's complaint, implying that the complaint was trivial."

I have no doubt that Arata and Branham were genuinely upset by this speech; but, especially on a college campus, such speech, warts and all, seems to be the sort of "uninhibited, robust, and wide-open" debate that we must expect when people debate issues that are important to them. Likewise, I had thought people were free to criticize classmates who organize boycotts or file complaints against a newspaper, bulletin board, or a respected community figure, even if the criticisms are unfair, personal, and intemperate.

The U.S. Department of Education Office for Civil Rights, however, took a different view. The students' speech, the OCR concluded, created a "hostile educational environment" for Branham based on her sex, and for Branham and Arata based on their actions in complaining about the original posts. What about the First Amendment? Well, the OCR reasoned,

> [s]tatutes prohibiting sexual harassment have been upheld against First Amendment challenges because speech in such cases has been considered indistinguishable from other illegal speech such as threats of violence or blackmail.... The Supreme Court has repeatedly asserted that the First Amendment does not protect expression that is invidious private discrimination. Thus, the First Amendment is not a bar to determining whether the messages...created a sexually hostile educational environment.

Moreover, the OCR had a plan to prevent such "illegal speech" in the future. "A new paragraph," the plan said, "shall be added to the [Santa Rosa Junior College] 'Administrative Computing Procedures,'" which shall bar (among other things) online speech that "harass[es], denigrates or shows hostility or aversion toward an individual or group based on that person's gender, race, color, national origin or disability, and...has the purpose or effect of creating a hostile, intimidating or offensive educational environment." And this prohibition shall cover "epithets, slurs, negative stereotyping, or threatening, intimidating or hostile acts...that relate to race, color, national origin, gender, or disability," including "acts that purport to be 'jokes' or 'pranks,' but that are hostile or demeaning." This is of course at least as broad as many of the campus speech codes that were struck down in the late 1980s and early 1990s—again, harassment law goes where the government has before been told it may not tread. Rather cryptically, the proposed speech code ends with "Nothing contained herein shall be construed as violating any person's rights of expression set forth in the Equal Access Act or the First Amendment of the United States Constitution."

The College settled the case by paying the complainants $15,000 each, and by adopting the OCR's policy. At a college run by the state government, and under pressure from the federal government, cyberspace communications containing "negative stereotyping," "denigrat[ion]," and "hostility or aversion" based on race or sex are now "illegal speech." And other administrators and legal experts agree; in the words of a New Jersey Law Journal article co-written by a computer science professor and a state court judge,

> [a]lthough a school [in context, referring to colleges and universities] by its very nature must provide for the guarantees of free speech as to classroom expression and assignment, the use of computers, [and] access to the Internet in open computer labs, should be appropriately regulated to avoid a hostile environment for offended students. Not to take such preventive actions at the... school is to place the... school at risk.

...First, the free speech issue here has little to do with the speech being in cyberspace. The Santa Rosa incidents started with online posts, but then went on to include a printed parody and oral comments at a newspaper staff meeting; the OCR correctly treated them similarly, because there was no real reason to treat them differently. And the hostile educational environment theory is already being used elsewhere to justify general speech codes that likewise apply equally to cyberspace speech and to other speech: Consider, for instance, a 1996 Kansas Attorney General Opinion, which argues that campus speech codes are constitutionally permissible, so long as they are written by analogy to hostile work environment law, or the Central Michigan University speech code, which prohibited any behavior creating a "hostile or offensive" educational environment and was struck down in *Dambrot v. Central Michigan University.*

Second, the Clinton Administration was mostly just tagging along for the ride. True, the Department of Education is pushing for speech restrictions. Besides the SOLO case, consider the Department of Education's *Sexual Harassment in Higher Education—From Conflict to Community*, which lists "sexist statements and behavior that convey insulting, degrading, or sexist attitudes" as examples of "sexually harassing behavior." Likewise, consider the OCR publication *Sexual Harassment: It's Not Academic*, which states that even in universities, "displaying or distributing sexually explicit drawings, pictures and written materials" may constitute harassment if it is unwelcome and "severe, persistent, or pervasive" enough.

Still, the OCR is only doing what the Kansas Attorney General, Central Michigan University, and others are doing. Maybe a more ideological Administration might have tried to lead some sort of anti-"hate-speech" crusade, but that's not what happened under Clinton. Rather, we have a specialist agency quietly trying to implement its own goal (protecting people against racist or sexist behavior) and seeing the First Amendment as largely an incidental barrier to be overcome if it's easy to do so.

Third, we see here how narrow speech restrictions beget broader ones. The OCR's argument starts with the uncontroversial assertion that threats and blackmail are punishable as "illegal speech." Then comes the assertion, which the OCR treats as uncontroversial, that harassing speech in workplaces (the subject of the statutes to which the OCR must have been referring) is likewise illegal speech. Then it follows that such speech in colleges is illegal speech.

Similarly, consider the OCR's argument that "The Supreme Court has repeatedly asserted that the First Amendment does not protect expression that is invidious private discrimination." It's true that the Court held that the First Amendment does not protect discriminatory acts, such as refusals to admit people into a school, university, or club, refusals to promote people, or the selection of a victim for a physical assault. It's also true that in *R.A.V. v. City of St. Paul*, the Court said in dictum that a "content-based subcategory of a *proscribable* class of speech" such as "sexually derogatory 'fighting words,' among other words" might be punishable by harassment law, without discussing whether harassment law may constitutionally punish otherwise nonproscribable, constitutionally protected speech. But from here the OCR makes an analogical jump, inferring from cases discussing bans on conduct and on constitutionally unprotected speech (such as fighting words) that the government may punish as "illegal speech" any expression that may create a "hostile, abusive, or offensive" environment and that thus supposedly constitutes "invidious private discrimination."

Analogy is a powerful force in our legal system. Supporters of workplace harassment law regularly use existing restrictions—such as obscenity law and bans on fighting words—as justification. It's hardly surprising that workplace harassment law would then itself be used as an analogy to justify educational harassment law....

Harassment by Library Internet Access

In 1997, the Loudoun County Public Library made the news by installing filters on all library computers. Such policies are usually justified by the desire to block children from accessing sexually explicit material, but here the stated rationale—reflected in the policy's title, *Policy on Internet Sexual Harassment*—was quite different:

> 1. Title VII of the Civil Rights Act prohibits sex discrimination. Library pornography can create a sexually-hostile environment for patrons or staff.... Permitting pornographic displays may constitute unlawful sex discrimination in violation of Title VII of the Civil Rights Act. This policy seeks to prevent internet sexual harassment [by installing software that blocks sexually explicit material, including "soft core pornography"]

The policy's author, library trustee (and lawyer) Dick Black, echoed this:

> The courts have said, for example, that someone can have materials — racist materials dealing with the Ku Klux Klan — in their home. However, the courts have upheld very strict limitations on having that in the workplace because of the racially discriminatory environment.

> Same thing applies here. People can do certain things in the privacy of their own homes that they cannot do in the workplace.

> Now this is not limited strictly to libraries. But the courts have said that whether it's a public state facility or whether it's a manufacturing plant, people cannot deprive women of their equal access to those facilities and their equal rights to employment through sexual harassment.

Nor is this an isolated incident; other libraries throughout the country have been doing the same thing, and offering the same justification. In the words of one article,

> [b]lue movie night in the computer lab [where users accessed sexually explicit material online] was not the end of the world as we know it. Left unaddressed, however, it could have become a problem of sexual harassment, with charges that such usage created an uncomfortable situation for many library users—not to mention library staff. Linked to other instances of insensitive, arguably sexist behavior, it could contribute to charges that a hostile environment existed—and could become evidence in a lawsuit.

> ...Playboy pinups in work areas invite sexual harassment suits. Why should the Internet be any different?

Again we see how some speech restrictions are used as analogies to support other ones, though here the analogy is not from workplaces to colleges or to service providers but the much more direct analogy from "normal" workplaces to libraries as workplaces. "Racist materials dealing with the Ku Klux Klan" are limited in workplaces generally; "same thing applies here" in libraries. Sexually suggestive materials are illegal in "a manufacturing plant"; same goes for libraries. "Playboy pinups in work areas invite sexual harassment suits. Why should the Internet be any different?"

The library case is different in an important way from the other three areas described above. Here, a government agency is acting as proprietor to restrict what is done with its own property, and thus may have far more authority than it would if it were acting as sovereign. It might be legitimate for the library board members as managers to try to shield library users or employees from involuntary exposure to offensive material, or even to entirely refuse to participate in disseminating material that they think offensive and harmful. Whether a government-owned library may install filters, quite apart from the harassment issues, remains an unsettled matter.

But the harassment question is nonetheless significant, because if libraries must filter to prevent harassment claims, then this rationale extends equally to private libraries and other private Internet access centers. A publicly accessible library at Duke University, for instance, would be obligated by state and federal law to install filters to prevent workplace harassment complaints by librarians and public accommodation harassment complaints by patrons; likewise for an Internet cafe. Here, the government would indeed be acting as sovereign controlling what private institutions do: Even if a private library wanted to provide unlimited access, it would face legal liability for doing so.

Judge Leonie Brinkema's decision in *Mainstream Loudoun v. Board of Trustees of the Loudoun County Library* struck an early blow against library Internet filtering. Such filtering, the decision held, violated the First Amendment (at least when it wasn't limited to child-only computers), notwithstanding the potential risk of harassment liability.

One of Judge Brinkema's rationales—that the defendants could point to very few harassment complaints that were brought as a result of patrons accessing sexually explicit materials—isn't promising for the long term, because such complaints are now piling in. For instance, seven librarians recently filed an EEOC complaint based on what they say is "repeated exposure to sexually explicit materials," and an environment "which is increasingly permeated by [pornographic] images on computer screens, [and] is also barraged by hard copies of the same, created on Library provided printers." Forty-seven of the 140 or so library employees signed a letter saying, in response to a library patron's complaint about other patrons accessing sexually explicit material, that "Every day we, too, are subjected to pornography left (sometimes intentionally) on the screens and in the printers. We do not like it either. We feel harassed and intimidated by having to work in a public environment where we might, at any moment, be exposed to degrading or pornographic pictures."

In response the library enacted a new policy that, among other things, bars even adult patrons from accessing material that is "harmful to minors"—a category of speech that includes material that's constitutionally protected as to adults—and also from otherwise "[e]ngag[ing] in any activity that...creates an intimidating or hostile environment." "The Library," the policy says, "is committed to providing its employees and patrons with an environment that is free from all forms of harassment, including sexual harassment, and prohibiting the display of obscene material, child pornography, and material that is harmful to minors."

Nor is the Minneapolis incident an isolated one; librarians in other places have likewise complained about patrons accessing material that they feel is sexually harassing. Judge Brinkema's argument that "[s]ignificantly, defendant has not pointed to a single incident in which a library employee or patron has complained that material being accessed on the Internet was harassing or created a hostile environment" thus seems to be no longer available. If that were the only argument in support of her decision, we would face the specter of harassment law being used to punish private and public libraries and Internet cafes that allow unfiltered access.

The judge's second justification—that the library could avoid harassment liability by placing computers in places where passers-by couldn't routinely see them, or installing privacy screens that make the screen visible only from the place where the user is sitting—seems, however, to be more robust. Such alternative solutions would not be perfect; a library patron may sit down to use a terminal and find that a pornographic site had been left on the screen by a previous patron, someone who's accessing a pornographic site might have technical trouble and ask a librarian for help, privacy screens may be imperfect, and patrons or librarians may see offensive material in a printer output bin. But courts might conclude that these situations are rare enough that when the proper measures are taken, technology does let libraries largely avoid the risk of harassment liability and at the same time provide unfiltered access.

Here, then, might be a case where the speech being in cyberspace does make a difference. To begin with, in the pre-cyberspace world, libraries generally did not stock illustrated pornography. Because buying and shelving books cost money, library decisions not to get a certain book were practically and perhaps even doctrinally immune from review, and to my knowledge few libraries decided to spend their funds on *Hustler.* They may have stocked a few "legitimate" books that included sexually explicit pictures, and it was possible that a patron might leave such a book open on the table, but I suspect this happened quite rarely.

On the other side of the ledger, computer technology makes it easier to decrease the risk that offended patrons or librarians will inadvertently see offensive material. Privacy screens on computers generally ensure that casual passers-by won't see what's going on. Any attempts to control offensive print materials (once the library had bought them) would probably be much less effective.

Conclusion

Forty years after the end of the Eisenhower Administration, what can we say about how it affected the freedom of speech? Not that much, probably, except of course for the way the Eisenhower appointees to the Supreme Court (and perhaps to lower courts) affected Free Speech Clause case law. Free speech concepts may have changed during the Eisenhower years, but little of that change comes from the legislative or executive agenda of the Eisenhower White House. This is true of many presidencies, and it will probably be true of the Clinton Administration.

Likewise, what can we say now about freedom of speech in movies, on telephones, via faxes, on television, in cyberspace, and in other media? By and large, the answer is that free speech jurisprudence has evolved to be comparatively medium-independent. Early holdings that movies are constitutionally unprotected have been reversed. In its very first cyberspace case, the Court refused to create a medium-specific test. While broadcast television and radio are still subject to different rules than other media, even this traditional distinction is now somewhat precarious. Medium does matter with regard to content-neutral distinctions that are justified by noncommunicative concerns, because different media raise different noncommunicative concerns—soundtrucks are loud, billboards block the view, cable television systems are often monopolies. As to content-based distinctions, though, medium is not terribly relevant.

But the basic concepts underlying the free speech exceptions remain important for decades. For instance, incitement, bad tendency, commercial speech, obscenity, libel, and now speech that creates a hostile environment are powerful concepts that can mold free speech thinking over a wide range of cases. Some of these free speech exceptions are eventually discarded (for instance, bad tendency). Others are changed (commercial speech, obscenity, libel), though many of the principles underlying them remain. Still others, such as "speech that creates a hostile environment," spread from their roots in narrow situations where they seem proper and even morally imperative into considerably broader areas, and can provide indirect precedential support for even broader restrictions.

Free speech law certainly must recognize exceptions to the core First Amendment principle that the government acting as sovereign generally may not restrict speech because of its content. But before endorsing any such exception, we should consider it carefully, and try to come up with principles that can limit its scope. The risk of speech restrictions growing by analogy in a legal system built on analogy is very real. And so far, the harassing speech exception has not gotten the judicial and academic scrutiny that it deserves, and that is needed to properly cabin the exception and to prevent its unchecked growth....

The Media Indecency Survey

Background

On February 1st, 2004, the singer Janet Jackson, in what she termed a "wardrobe malfunction" exposed her right breast during the television broadcast of the halftime of the Super Bowl. This incredibly high-profile event unleashed a firestorm of publicity and recriminations.

The backlash from the Jackson affair has been particularly strong in the world of radio. Politicians, eager to "clean up the airwaves" and to respond to various groups targeting "edgy" or "shocking" programming, have called radio executives in front of their committees and have chastised the FCC for not responding to public complaints and for not levying enough fines. Also, and perhaps most importantly, Congress has rushed through a variety of new laws that massively increase potential fines to broadcasters, as well as to threaten license revocations for repeat offenders.

Our two companies, Edison Media Research and Jacobs Media, have investigated the issues of "indecency" in the past, most notably in a survey performed in the fall of 2002 for Rock radio stations around the country. With the current level of interest in these issues, we felt it was time to talk to Rock radio listeners again, and to see if their feelings have changed. This survey furthers our inquiries into the topics and issues of indecency and adult material with regard to Rock radio listeners around the country.

Methodology

Jacobs Media and Edison Media Research collectively designed and administered this survey. We collected interviews via the Internet from a total of 13,798 respondents. In total, 40 Rock Radio stations around the United States invited their listeners to participate in the survey. The number of respondents who could come from any individual radio station was capped at 6% of the total sample. The interviews were conducted between March 12th and March 19th 2004.

As with all Internet-based research projects of this kind, the results reflect only those who choose to participate in the survey and do not necessarily represent the views of all Rock radio listeners in the country. Still, the 40 radio stations that invited their listeners are a broad cross-section of rock stations, with large and small markets, large and small stations, some stations with very edgy morning shows and some with very mild ones, and those that play the newest Rock music and those that play only Classic Rock.

According to audience estimates from Arbitron, just over 50 million people listen to Rock radio stations every week.

Sample Demographics

In total, there were 13,798 Rock radio listeners who completed our survey; these people were distributed as follows:

Men	61%
Women	39%
Under 18	5%
18-24	19%
25-34	28%
35-44	29%
45-54	17%
Over 54	2%
Democrat	26%
Republican	27%
Independent	34%
Attend Church Regularly	27%
Attend Church Few Times/Yr	19%
Rarely or Never Attend Church	54%
Listen to station with "Very Edgy" Morning Show	49%
Listen to station with "Moderately Edgy" Morning Show	24%
Listen to station with "Not Edgy" Morning Show	27%
Listen to "Alternative Rock" Station	24%
Listen to "Active Rock" Station	36%
Listen to "Classic Rock" Station	40%

Key Findings

- **Few Rock radio listeners are offended by what they hear on the radio.** We asked respondents: "Think about the radio station you listen to most often in the morning. How often does it offend you in some way?" More than half (55%) of respondents said "Never"; only 11% of respondents said more than "Rarely."

  Significantly, the answers are nearly identical among those who listen to stations with all kinds of shows, from the most "edgy" to the least. This implies that people choose a show that is unlikely to offend them.

  Women were only slightly more likely than men to be offended by what they hear (Women: 47% "Never Offended"; Men: 60%). Parents with children under 13 are no more likely to be offended than the group as a whole. Republican and Democrat Rock listeners have no significant difference between them with regard to this question.

  As one respondent pointed out, "I am the parent of a 13 year-old boy. If I hear something potentially offensive, I have the right to change the station with my own hand. I am disturbed that the government will 'parent' me by choosing what I can and cannot choose to listen to."

  One interesting twist—there was a sizeable minority of respondents who said, "Shock Jock radio personalities have gone too far." More than one-quarter of respondents (28%) agreed with this statement. Certain subgroups, such as women (32%), parents (32%), frequent church-goers (40%), Republicans (35%) and Classic Rock listeners (43%) agreed with this statement in larger numbers. Among those who listen to the mildest morning radio shows, 43% agreed with this statement.

- **While not personally offended by it, a majority finds the Janet Jackson/Super Bowl incident a "major issue."** Our respondents had interesting views on the Janet Jackson kerfuffle. Only 14% of respondents said that they were personally offended by it. Yet, just over half said it is an "important issue." We see the implication that our respondents can separate what is offensive to them and what is appropriate in different contexts.

  This is summarized by one of the web poll's participants who opines, "I believe in freedom of speech, and I believe that even shock jocks are entitled to this right. However, I think that programmers should be cognizant of what the expected audience will be. Without a doubt, the 'expected audience' for the Super Bowl halftime show included children. That act was totally inappropriate, and anyone who was privy to the planned exposure should be held responsible for abusing the broadcast."

Perhaps not surprisingly, men were much less likely to be offended by Ms. Jackson's "costume reveal" than women. But only 17% of our female respondents said they were personally offended by the stunt. Frequent church-goers (24%) and Republicans (20%) were slightly more likely than the group as a whole to have been personally offended—but clearly overwhelming majorities of these groups were also not offended.

Those who listen to the edgiest morning shows, as might be expected, were the most likely to say it was not an important issue (56%); among those who listen to the mildest morning shows only 39% thought the incident was "not important."

Well over half of all respondents, including many who thought the issue "not important," feel that someone should be punished or sanctioned for the Super Bowl incident. The entity most felt should be held accountable is Ms. Jackson herself (59%), followed by Justin Timberlake (50%), and MTV (21%). Only 34% of our respondents felt no one should be punished for what transpired.

- **Rock listeners overwhelmingly support Howard Stern.** Howard Stern is the rare radio personality who, because of his exposure across many media, is well known even in markets where his show doesn't run. Fully 98% of respondents (from a mix of markets where Howard is and isn't aired) said that they have heard of Howard Stern. More than 90% of those respondents were aware that Howard Stern's show had recently been taken off the air in a handful of radio markets because of indecency concerns.

Those who knew of Howard Stern's removal in these markets overwhelmingly believe that this was an unfair decision. When given the choice between two statements about Howard Stern's elimination, they answered as follows:

- They were right to take Howard Stern off the air   20%
- People who want to listen to Howard Stern
  should be allowed to do so   80%

In every subgroup a strong majority said that people who want to listen to Howard Stern should be allowed to do so. The groups most likely to say, "They were right to take Howard Stern off the air" were listeners to stations with mild morning shows (30%) and frequent church-goers (32%).

- **Rock listeners are extraordinarily sensitive to government involvement in programming.** We asked a series of questions to evaluate respondents' feelings about the government's role in overseeing programming on the radio. In pretty much every case, the group overwhelmingly felt negatively towards government involvement in programming. Even those who felt that the Janet Jackson incident was an "important issue" felt that the government should not overly restrict radio talent. Here are some example responses:

o "The FCC should take programs that it considers indecent off the air"

* Agree   12%

* Disagree   71%

* Neutral   17%

o "It angers you that the government is attempting to regulate the radio shows that you can listen to"

* Agree   72%

* Disagree   12%

* Neutral   15%

o "Radio personalities should be able to say whatever they please; if people don't want to listen they can change the station"

* Agree   58%

* Disagree   26%

* Neutral   16%

These findings were consistent among subgroups.

• **Respondents overwhelmingly feel that it is parents' responsibility to keep adult material away from children.** We asked respondents which of these statements best describes who is responsible when it comes to radio programming and listening:

   • It's the parents responsibility to keep material they find indecent away from their children   87%
   • It's the broadcasters' responsibility to eliminate indecent material from the airwaves so children can't hear it   13%

Every subgroup we looked at gave similar answers. Parents broke 86%/14% to parents' responsibility. Frequent church-goers were 81%/19%. Both Democrats and Republicans, who one might think would have differing opinions about the role of government, agreed with the first statement in similar numbers.

- **Rock radio listeners are suspicious of what's behind the current environment.** A strong majority of respondents says, "The investigation of some radio shows is an overreaction to the Janet Jackson/Super Bowl incident." Just under seven-in-ten agreed with this statement, and this held among all subgroups.

Further, a strong percentage were suspicious of the role of politicians in this situation:

o "The crackdown on radio personalities is clearly an election year ploy by politicians"

  - Agree   49%

  - Disagree   23%

  - Neutral   28%

Interestingly, this is the one place where we saw a large difference between Democrats and Republicans. A full 56% of Democrats thought that this is an election year ploy; only 38% of Republicans think so.

- **There is concern of a new "tyranny of the minority."** We asked if "small groups of people are having too much influence over whether radio programs should be fined or punished." Fully three-in-four (75%) agreed with this statement. Here, all subgroups gave responses within a similar range. One of our participants states, "I feel the vocal minority is the only groups that are ever heard from."

What's more, our Rock radio listening respondents don't approve of the new standard that seems to exist—where if anyone is offended then the show should be fined. The statement that received the most uniform response in our entire survey was to the following:

o "If even a small group of listeners is offended by a radio show's content, the FCC should take action against it."

  * Agree   5%

  * Disagree   81%

  * Neutral   14%

When one reads the comments that our respondents sent us, this stands out as one of the clear findings: Rock radio listeners feel that by dint of the size of the audience, they prove that these shows are meeting "community standards." The Rock radio listeners are saying, essentially, "50 Million Elvis Fans Can't Be Wrong."

- **It's shocking what Rock listeners want.** One cannot look at these results without coming to one easy conclusion: the people who are consuming shows that the government is investigating as being "indecent" or "offensive" are seldom offended by what they hear.

The relentless findings that these listeners are not offended by what they hear implies that those who are offended are *not listening*.

Conclusions and Recommendations

Based on this research, the following areas should be considered for further thought and discussion:

1. **"Shock" is often a matter of expectation.** This might explain why half the respondents believe the Janet Jackson incident is an important issue. When they sat down to watch the Super Bowl—an American tradition and a family television experience—they were expecting to see a good football game, and the typical music-oriented halftime show. Instead, they saw something altogether different—a violation of their expectations.

   This might also explain why the drumbeats weren't all that loud when Madonna and Britney Spears liplocked on the MTV Video Music Awards. That event almost always provides a controversial moment or two.

   Had the Janet Jackson/Justin Timberlake "costume malfunction" occurred on "Saturday Night Live," the reactions would have likely been muted. Why? SNL is a show that is famous for over-the-top behavior, and celebrities displaying out-of-character performance.

   When listeners listen to a show like Howard Stern's, however, most know what they're going to hear. The show's content and emphasis are not secret or surprising. There is an implicit "R" rating. Many morning radio shows have a reputation for shaking the tree, generating controversy, and making noise. This is why most of these shows rarely field listener complaints. Listeners are there not despite the controversial content, but *because* of it. On the other hand, those who are likely to be offended by "Shock Jock" antics typically don't listen. It is important also to point out that few teenagers are regular listeners to shows like Stern's.

2. **While there are listeners who feel that some morning radio shows have indeed gone "too far," they overwhelmingly are against the idea of government regulation of their content.** As the analysis clearly pointed out, an overwhelming majority feels that government control of radio content is not the way to address content issues. They also feel strongly that it is *their* responsibility to ensure

their children's media safety when it comes to radio content. Perhaps this is an outgrowth from years of more controversial content on television, be it on cable or broadcast network programs. Whether it's sex, violence, or other adult-oriented programming, parents of young children (who comprise nearly 40% of our respondents) told us they don't feel it is the job of broadcasters to censor programming. This says a great deal about how consumers have been able to handle the many media options that enter their lives. Most have a firm understanding of where there are "danger signs," and act accordingly. Again, this is probably why the Janet Jackson incident was so shocking—it was unexpected for something like it to occur during the Super Bowl.

It is interesting to see that while many people think some radio shows have gone too far—so few people say they are ever offended by what they themselves hear. This implies that in a radio market with so many options, most people are regulating themselves. This might explain why so many people who feel "Shock Jock radio personalities have gone too far" still say that the FCC should not regulate these shows nor do they personally get offended.

3. **Rockers are people, too.** One should not discount this survey as representative of a small faction. As noted in the analysis, 50 million listeners tune in Rock stations every week. In our sample, nearly half were over the age of 35, while over half are either married or living with a partner. Also 38% have children. These listeners are more likely to be exposed to controversial morning programming—and that's precisely the point. Because so much noise on this issue is coming from people and groups that *don't* listen to these shows, it is important to listen to the opinions of those who regularly consume them.

These facts also beg the question about community standards, and how to identify them. If indeed, the "community" for morning shows, or for radio programming in general, is comprised of those who actually listen, this study indicates that most are not surprised by what they hear. And an overwhelming majority tells us emphatically that they know what to do when they hear something that runs afoul of their tastes. This speaks to the issues the FCC is grappling with - defining community standards and acting accordingly.

4. **Research among fans of other formats should be conducted.** To get a full spectrum of how other radio listeners perceive some of the issues discussed in this study, follow-up projects should be conducted among partisans to other radio formats. Again, if the FCC and Congress hope to reflect the will of the people in decisions that have been or will be made, understanding how "end users"—in this case, radio listeners—feel is essential.

5. **Radio should consider adopting a ratings system.** With the superimposed letters that accompany every TV show from "SpongeBob SquarePants" to "N.Y.P.D. Blue," television viewers are given information to help them decide whether to watch, and whether to let their children watch. If radio broadcasters were willing, airing the

audio version of this type of rating system at every commercial break might provide the same type of information—or warning. If, for example, Howard Stern's listeners were clearly notified that the show is "intended for mature audiences," that might go a long way in dissuading listeners for whom his show is not targeted to go elsewhere.

6. **Small groups do not necessarily represent the larger population.** And listeners are very skeptical of the power and influence of certain small interest groups in the current radio regulatory controversy. Three-quarters are concerned about these groups and their potential to affect and impact radio programming. And as we clearly saw when given a choice, 97% of our sample would not contact the FCC if they heard something objectionable. Most understand they have the power to do the one thing that may hurt radio companies and so-called "shock jocks" the most—change stations.

We are hopeful that this unique view of a large number of radio listeners— including many of those who tune in some of these controversial morning shows—will stimulate discussion in both the radio, legislative, and regulatory communities.

POSTSCRIPT

Should Freedom of Speech Ever Be Restricted?

Sometimes it is easy to argue for a specific interpretation of the First Amendment until you personally become offended, or are made to feel uncomfortable by the unrestricted speech of others. Has this ever happened to you? This issue asks us to think not only about what we see and hear, but also what we do. Just as we are led to think about specific contexts for questionable content, we could also think of our own speech in professional, personal, and social environments, and how we might have different personal standards for what we might say at certain times, in specific places.

Considering whether the "audience" has any choice about attending to content is often one of the most critical issues in free speech cases. It may be true that we do often have choices of whether to listen to certain stations, personalities, or content, but sometimes technologies have programs associated with transmission that we don't willingly accept. If you've ever had the experience of computer pop-ups, spam, or unwanted advertsing when you use Internet services, you've probably dealt very specifically with the question of unwanted content.

There are many specific legal cases addressing the topics in this issue, such as *Reno v. the American Civil Liberties Union*, 521 U.S. 866 (1997) on the issues behind the short-lived Communications Decency Act; *Trout v. City of Akron*, No. CV-97-115879 (filed Nov. 17, 1997), on Internet pornography and harassment.

Newspapers have also treated these topics seriously over the years, and the titles of these articles give you a good sense of what contexts are addressed. See for example, "Online Jokes Can Lead to Serious Problems; Offensive Messages Might become Basis of Lawsuits," *Cincinnati Enquirer* (Sept. 14, 1998, B15); Michael Stetz, "E-Mail Humor in Eye of Beholder," *South Dakota Union-Tribune* (Nov. 29, 1998, A1); and Rick Anderson, "No Blonde Jokes," *Seattle Weekly* (June 3-9, 1999, 7).

ISSUE 13

Should the FCC Liberalize Ownership Rules?

YES: Michael K. Powell, "Yes, The FCC Should Relax Its Ownership Rules," *Congressional Digest,* October 2003.

NO: Robert W. McChesney and John Nichols, *The Nation;* Novemeber, 2003.

ISSUE SUMMARY

YES: Federal Communications Commission (FCC) Chairman Michael K. Powell in testimony before the Senate Committee on Commerce, Science and Transportation outlined the FCC proposal to relax ownership rules. He cites changes in the marketplace and argues that these changes will benefit the public interest through protecting viewpoint diversity, enhancing competition, and fostering localism.

NO: University professor McChesney and *The Nation* correspondent Nichols explore the unprecedented public outcry over the relaxation of ownership rules. Concern about the impact of consolidation crosses traditional political lines and reflects an increasing concern within the American public that media have become defined by commercial and corporate concerns.

Since the 1980s the U.S. media industries have undergone simultaneous shifts in the economy within which the media industry functioned, the technology through which media are distributed, and the regulatory philosophy through which media are viewed by government and the public. Since its inception, U.S. media has been based on the dual principles of private ownership and freedom from government interference with content. This libertarian philosophy was imported from Britain and was enshrined in the First Amendment to the Constitution. Freedom of the press and the public service expectations it engendered include serving as a watchdog of the government, providing fair and balanced coverage of political issues, and refraining from content that would harm children, inflame public passions, or increase social divisions. In the last quarter of the 20th century, theories about the public service responsibilities of the media began to change. FCC chairman Mark

Fowler famously remarked that television was no different from any other household appliance, "a toaster with pictures." The public interest began to be defined as what the public was interested in. Public "good" was increasingly defined as that which promoted the economic vitality and global competitiveness of the industry, including its ability to provide jobs, create wealth, and compete successfully in global markets.

At the same time, changing national and global economies were offering their own challenges. Even while media corporations were subjected to extreme pressures for financial performance, they were also losing substantial portions of their markets to increased competition. A decline in viewer loyalty and increased sources of media led to market fragmentation. Pressure to create larger corporate entities and changes in the ownership rules made by the Telecommunications Act of 1996 opened the market for substantial restructuring. Although the restructuring of the U.S. media industry is still very much underway, the effects are clear: the U.S. media is much more consolidated. It is easy to expect that the industry will continue to respond to financial performance demands by continuing efforts to consolidate, cluster properties, gain market power within local and regional operational areas, and capture synergies through vertical and horizontal integration.

As part of the 1996 Telecommunications Act, Congress mandated that the FCC review its broadcast ownership rules to determine "whether any of such rules are necessary in the public interest as a result of competition." In June of 2003 the FCC voted 3-2 to endorse six media ownership rule changes, including allowing a company to own both a newspaper and TV or radio station in the same market. It also proposed allowing a company to own 2 to 3 stations in a market, depending on market size. Another decision allowed a single company to own enough local stations to reach 45% of US households, up from 35% previously. Congress scaled this back to 39%.

There was a storm of protest over these proposed changes. As McChesney and Nichols describe, a grassroots protest emerged. Congress and the courts got involved, and the issue remains unresolved. The lines remain clearly drawn: Public interest groups say the ruling goes too far in giving big media corporations control over all the sources of information; media companies want to grow bigger and say the FCC hasn't gone far enough; and the FCC says it has reached a good balance.

Michael K. Powell  **YES**

Should the FCC Relax
Its Ownership Rules?

I am proud that this Commission and its staff can say that we conducted the most exhaustive and comprehensive review of our broadcast ownership rules ever undertaken. We have done so, obligated by our statutory duty to review the rules biennially and prove those rules are "necessary in the public interest." The Court of Appeals has interpreted this standard as placing a high hurdle before the Commission for maintaining a given regulation, and made clear that failure to surmount that hurdle, based on a thorough record, must result in the rule's modification or elimination.

Over the past 20 months we have been working tirelessly towards achieving three critically important goals in this proceeding: (1) reinstating legally enforceable broadcast ownership limits that promote diversity, localism, and competition (replacing those that have been struck down by the courts); (2) building modern rules that take proper account of the explosion of new media outlets for news, information, and entertainment, rather than perpetuate the graying rules of a bygone black and white era; and (3) striking a careful balance that does not unduly limit transactions that promote the public interest, while ensuring that no company can monopolize the medium.

To achieve these goals, however, the Commission needed to come face to face with reality. So, we faced the reality of the law and our responsibility to implement Congress's will, as interpreted by the courts. We faced the reality of having to compile and analyze a record unlike any other in our history. We faced the reality of the modern media marketplace. And by doing so, the Commission was able to craft a balanced package of enforceable and sustainable broadcast ownership limits.

Statutory Mandate and Court Decisions

In the Telecommunications Act of 1996, Congress established the biennial review mandate. In relevant part, Section 202(h) requires that the Commission review all of its broadcast ownership rules every two years and determine "whether any of such rules are necessary in the public interest as a result of competition." The Commission, as a consequence, is required to repeal or modify any regulation it cannot prove is necessary in the public interest. Congress gave the Commission a sacred responsibility, one that I do not take lightly.

Recent court decisions have established a high hurdle for the Commission to maintain a given broadcast ownership regulation. As interpreted by the U.S. Court of Appeals for the District of Columbia Circuit in the 2002 *Fox* [*Television Stations v. FCC* (2001)] and *Sinclair* [*Broadcast Group v. FCC* (2002)] cases, Section 202(h) requires the Commission to study and report on the current status of competition. Both decisions provide that the survival of any prospective broadcast ownership rules depends on this Commission's ability to justify those rules adequately with record evidence on the need for each ownership rule, and ensure that the rules are analytically consistent with each other. The implications of the court decisions were clear—fail to justify the necessity of each of our broadcast ownership regulations at the rules' and our sacred goals' peril.

The Modern Marketplace

Our fact-gathering effort demonstrated that today's media marketplace is marked by abundance. Since 1960, there has been an explosion of media outlets throughout the country. Even in small towns like Burlington, Vermont, the number of voices—including cable, satellite, radio, TV stations, and newspapers—has increased over 250 percent during the last 40 years. Independent ownership of those outlets is far more diverse, with 140 percent more owners today than in 1960.

What does this abundance mean for the American people? It means more programming, more choice, and more control in the hands of citizens. At any given moment, our citizens have access to scores of TV networks devoted to movies, dramatic series, sports, news, and educational programming, both for adults and children; in short, niche programming to satisfy almost any of our citizens' diverse tastes.

In 1960—the "Golden Age of Television"—if you missed the half-hour evening newscast, you were out of luck. In 1980, it was no different. But today, news and public affairs programming—the fuel of our democratic society—is overflowing. There used to be three broadcast networks, each with 30 minutes of news daily. Today, there are three 24-hour all-news networks, seven broadcast networks, and over 300 cable networks. Local networks are bringing the American public more local news than at any point in history.

The Internet is also having a profound impact on the ever-increasing desire of our citizenry to inform themselves and to do so using a wide variety of sources. Google news service brings information from 4,500 news sources to one's fingertips from around the world, all with the touch of a button. As demonstrated by this proceeding, diverse and antagonistic voices use the Internet daily to reach the American people. Whether it is the *New York Times* editorial page, or Joe Citizen using email to let his views be known to the Commission, or the use by organizations such as MoveOn.org to perform outreach to citizens, the Internet is putting the tools of democracy in the hands of speakers and listeners more and more each day.

I have not cited cable television and the Internet by accident. Their contribution to the marketplace of ideas is not linear, it is exponential. Cable and the Internet explode the model for viewpoint diversity in the media. Diversity-by-appointment has vanished. Now, the media makes itself available on our schedule, as much or as little as we want, when we want. In sum, citizens have more choice and more control over what they see, hear, or read than at any other time in history. This is a powerful paradigm shift in the American media system, and is having a tremendous impact on our democracy.

Public Interest Benefits

The marketplace changes mentioned above were only the beginning, not the end of our inquiry. The balanced set of national and local broadcast ownership rules we adopted preserve and protect out core policy goals of diversity, competition, and localism. Certain public interest benefits have clearly been documented in the record and the rules we adopted embrace and advance those benefits for the American public.

As an initial matter, the public interest is served by having enforceable rules that are based on a solid, factual record. For the last year, several of the Commission's broadcast ownership regulations have been rendered unenforceable—vacated or remanded by the courts.

Protecting Viewpoint Diversity.   In addition, the Commission, recognizing that "the widest possible dissemination of information from diverse and antagonistic sources is essential to the welfare of the public," introduced broadcast ownership limits that will protect viewpoint diversity. The Commission concluded that neither the newspaper-broadcast prohibition nor the TV-radio cross-ownership prohibition could be justified in larger markets in light of the abundance of diverse sources available to citizens to rely on for their news consumption.

By implementing our cross-media limits, however, the Commission will protect viewpoint diversity by ensuring that no company, or group of companies, can control an inordinate share of media outlets in a local market. We developed a Diversity Index to measure the availability of key media outlets in markets of various sizes. By breaking out markets into tiers, the Commission was able to better tailor our rules to reflect different levels of media availability in different sized markets. For the first time ever, the Commission built its data in implementing this rule directly from input received from the public on how they actually use the media to obtain news and public affairs information.

Furthermore, by instituting our local television multiple ownership rule (especially by banning mergers among the top-four stations, which the record demonstrated typically produce an independent local newscast) and our local radio ownership limit, the Commission will foster multiple independently owned media outlets in both broadcast television and radio—advancing the goal of promoting the widest dissemination of viewpoints.

Enhancing Competition.   Moreover, our new broadcast ownership regulations promote competition in the media marketplace. The Commission determined that our prior local television multiple ownership limits could not be justified as necessary to promote competition because it failed to reflect the significant competition now faced by local broadcasters from cable and satellite TV services. Our revised local television limit is the first TV ownership rule to acknowledge that competition.

This new rule will enhance competition in local markets by allowing broadcast television stations to compete more effectively not only against other broadcast stations, but also against cable and/or satellite channels in that local market. In addition, the record demonstrates that these same market combinations yield efficiencies that will serve the public interest through improved or expanded services such as local news and public affairs programming and facilitating the transition to digital television through economic efficiencies.

The Commission found that our current limits on local radio ownership continue to be necessary to promote competition among local radio stations and we reaffirmed the caps set forth by Congress in the 1996 Telecommunications Act. The Order tightens the radio rules in one important respect—we concluded that the current method for defining radio markets was not in the public interest and thus needed to be modified. We found that the current market definition for radio markets, which relies on the signal contour of the commonly owned stations, is unsound and produces anomalous and irrational results, undermining the purpose of the rule.

We therefore adopted geographic-based market definitions, which are a more rational means for protecting competition in local markets. For example, we fixed the case of Minot, North Dakota, which under our former rules produced a market with 45 radio stations. Under our reformed market definition, Minot would have only 10 radio stations included in the relevant geographic market.

By promoting competition through the local television and radio rules, the Commission recognized that the rules may result in a number of situations where current ownership arrangements exceed ownership limits. In such cases the Commission made a limited exception to permit sales of grandfathered station combinations to small businesses. In so doing, the Commission sought to respect the reasonable expectations of parties that lawfully purchased groups of local radio stations that today, through redefined markets, now exceed the applicable caps. We promote competition by permitting station owners to retain any above-cap local radio clusters but not transfer them intact unless such a transfer avoids undue hardships to cluster owners that are small businesses or promote the entry into broadcasting by small businesses— many of which are minority- or female-owned.

Finally, by retaining our ban on mergers among any of the top four national broadcast networks, the Commission continues to promote competition in the national television advertising and program acquisition markets.

Fostering Localism.   Recognizing that localism remains a bedrock public interest benefit, the Commission took a series of actions designed to foster localism by aligning our ownership limits with the local stations' incentives to serve the needs and interests of their local communities.

For instance, by retaining the dual network prohibition and increasing the national television ownership limit to 45 percent, the Commission promoted localism by preserving the balance of negotiating power between networks and affiliates. The national cap will allow a body of network affiliates to negotiate collectively with the broadcast networks on network programming decisions to best serve the needs of their local community, while at the same time allowing the networks to gain critical mass to prevent the flight of quality programs, such as sports and movies, to cable or satellite.

The record further demonstrated that by both raising the national cap to 45 percent and allowing for cross-ownership combinations in certain markets the Commission would promote localism. Indeed, the record showed that broadcast network owned-and-operated stations served their local communities better with respect to local news production—airing more local news programming than did affiliates. Furthermore, the record demonstrated that where newspaper-broadcast television combinations were allowed, those televisions stations have produced dramatically better news coverage in terms of quantity (over 50 percent more news) and quality (outpacing non-newspaper-owned television stations in news awards).

The Commission crafted a balanced set of broadcast ownership restrictions to preserve and promote the public interest goals of diversity, competition, and localism.

Conclusion

This critical review has been an exhaustive one. The Commission has struggled with a difficult conundrum: building an adequate record, satisfying the administrative burden of the Section 202(h) mandate, and ultimately justifying its rules before the courts that have expressed growing impatience with irrational and indefensible ownership rules.

Four years ago, in the last completed biennial review, I concluded "[i]t is indeed time to take a sober and realistic look at our broadcast ownership rules in light of the current competitive communications environment." With a full record in hand, it was appropriate to fulfill Congress's mandate of completing our broadcast ownership review. The extraordinary coverage of the issue and the comments and evidence on the record have allowed the Commission to make an informed judgment, and hopefully to resist claims of being both "arbitrary and capricious" before the courts.

NO

**Robert W. McChesney and
John Nichols**

Up in Flames

The Public Revolts Against Monopoly Media

Poor, poor, pitiful Michael Powell. His term as chairman of the Federal Communications Commission was supposed to be easy. He thought that like FCC
chairs before him, his job was to jet around the country meeting at swank
resorts with the CEOs of major media companies, take some notes and then
quietly implement their sweeping agenda for loosening the last significant
constraints on media consolidation in the United States. Nobody except
some corporate lobbyists and their political acolytes would know what was
going on. Then, when his term was *up,* he would get a cushy job with industry
or another plum political appointment. Look at his predecessor, William Ken-
nard, who now rakes in big money brokering telecommunications deals for
the Carlyle Group. It was supposed to be a win-win scenario for Powell and
the people he regulated.

Instead, everything went wrong. The FCC broke its traditional lockstep
and experienced a very public 3-to-2 split in June votes that narrowly endorsed
six media-ownership rule changes, including one that would allow a single network to control television stations reaching 45 percent of all American households and another that would allow one media company to buy *up* the daily
newspaper, as many as three television stations, eight radio stations and
(thanks to a separate court ruling) the cable system in a single market. Then,
despite the fact that Powell claimed he was acting under pressure from the judiciary, a federal appeals court blocked the changes until a full judicial review
could determine whether the public interest was being damaged. A few days
later, while Powell continued to insist he was relaxing the rules to meet the
Congressional mandate contained in the Telecommunications Act of 1996, the
Senate voted overwhelmingly to block implementation of the changes. All his
rationales have blown *up* in his face like a trick cigar.

And things could be getting worse for Powell. Even as the Bush White
House seeks to preserve the FCC chair's handiwork—presumably on the theory that it is payback time for big media companies, like Clear Channel, General Electric and Rupert Murdoch's News Corporation, that have supported
Bush's campaigns—the conservative leadership in the House is faced with an
unprecedented revolt among Republicans, who are signing on to a bipartisan

Reprinted with permission from the January 7, 2002 issue of *The Nation*, pp. 11-14. For subscription infromation, call 1-800-333-8536. Portions of each week's Nation magazine can be accessed
at http://www.thenation.com.

letter that demands a vote on whether the chamber should join the Senate in disapproving the rule changes.

Powell purports to know why things have gone awry. In a remarkable series of interviews with the New York Times, the Washington Post and CNBC, Powell said the normal rule-making process had been upset by "a concerted grassroots effort to attack the commission from the outside in." Seemingly unaware that a public agency like the FCC could, in fact, be addressed by the public, he expressed amazement that as many as 3 million Americans have contacted the FCC and Congress to demand that controls against media monopoly be kept in place. Capitol Hill observers say media ownership has been the second most discussed issue by constituents in 2003, trailing only the war on Iraq. Following Brecht's famous dictum, Michael Powell wants to fire the people.

Who are these attackers of the status quo who have so upset Powell's best-laid plans? Noam Chomsky and William Safire both came out against the rule changes. So did Common Cause and the National Rifle Association. Reformer Gene Kimmelman of the Consumers Union and conservative Brent Bozell of the Parents Television Council co-wrote an op-ed opposing Powell's rules relaxation. People who disagree on just about everything found themselves in agreement that in this debate over whether a handful of corporations should be allowed to dominate the discourse, the already fragile health of American democracy was at stake.

Powell's attempt to co-opt this anger by organizing public hearings on insuring local content on radio and TV failed miserably. The first hearing, on October 22, in Charlotte, North Carolina, drew an overflow crowd that cheered songwriter Tift Merritt when she told Powell, "To try to talk about localism without discussing media ownership is avoiding the issue." Independent Representative Bernie Sanders of Vermont, the leading Congressional critic of media monopoly, explains that "It is not a coincidence that everything blew up the way it did this year. The American people know they are getting less information than they had before about decisions that are being made in their name, and they know that we are passing some critical points where, if we don't act, citizens are not going to have the information they need to function in a democracy."

The diversity of the opposition confirms that the FCC rules have become a lightning rod for concerns not just about the specific issue of consolidation of media but also about a host of systemic flaws that have become evident as mass media have come increasingly to be defined by commercial and corporate concerns. People who have long felt shut out of the mainstream of American media—people of color, women, trade unionists and farmers—stood with families concerned about excessive violence and sexuality on television and in the movies. Journalists who found it harder and harder to do their job for reasons ranging from staffing cuts to inappropriate pressure to appear patriotic found common ground with activists still furious over the collapse of serious coverage of the 2000 election in general and the Florida recount fiasco. They were joined by masses of citizens who had watched with increasing disgust after September 11 as supine reporters unquestioningly accepted Administration contentions regarding the terrorist attacks and the Afghanistan and Iraq wars that followed.

Americans recognize that their media are experiencing digital Wal-Marti-zation. Like the chain that earns billions but cannot be bothered to pay employee health benefits, major media concerns in the United States brag about their profits to Wall Street but still cry poor when it comes to covering the news that matters to Main Street. A 2002 study by the Project on the State of the American Newspaper found that the number of reporters covering state capitols across the country full-time had fallen to just over 500, a figure the American Journalism Review described as "the lowest number we have seen, and probably the lowest in at least the last quarter century." Is this the market at work? Have citizens demanded, in the midst of a period of devolution that has made state governments more powerful than ever, that they get less state capitol coverage? Not at all. "It comes almost entirely as a consequence of newsroom budget cuts by companies seeking to bolster their shrinking profit margins during an eco-nomic downturn," says AJR. Those cuts parallel a decline in political coverage on television news programs, which fell in 2002 to the lowest level in decades. And what if one corporation owned the newspaper as well as TV and radio sta-tions in the same market? "It's a given that you'll see more cuts in staffing, fewer reporters covering city halls, state capitals, Washington and the world," says Newspaper Guild president Linda Foley. "And people know that. They know that if one company owns most of the media outlets—in their town, in their state or in the country as a whole—they are going to get a one-size-fits-all news that is a lot more likely to serve the people in power than it is the public interest and democracy."

To many Americans, it seems clear that the one-size-fits-all moment has already arrived. After years of decreasing international coverage—all the major television networks have shuttered foreign bureaus over the past decade in a wave of cutbacks that Pew International Journalism Program director John Schidlovsky refers to as "perhaps the single most negative development in journalism in my lifetime"—the United States found itself in March on the verge of launching a major invasion of a Middle Eastern country that most Americans could not locate on a map.

Indeed, it was the war on Iraq that triggered some of the most intense opposition to Powell's rules changes. At Bush's last prewar press conference, the White House press corps looked more like stenographers than journalists. Even some reporters were appalled; ABC News White House correspondent Terry Moran said the reporters looked "like zombies," while Copley News Ser-vice Washington correspondent George Condon Jr. told AJR that it "just became an article of faith among a lot of people: 'Look at this White House press corps; it's just abdicated all responsibility.'" Millions of Americans agreed. "I talked to people everywhere I went who said that if the media, espe-cially the television media, had done its job, there wouldn't have been a war," says Representative Jim McDermott.

Powell only poured gasoline on the *flames* when he declared that the "thrilling" TV coverage of the war proved there was nothing to be concerned about with regard to media consolidation. Antiwar groups like MoveOn.org and Code Pink, which did not share Powell's view, became prime movers in the burgeoning movement to block the rules changes, providing vehicles for communicating grassroots sentiment to the FCC and Congress via MoveOn's networks and organizing protests and petition drives across the country.

But Powell's problems involved far more than antiwar activism. Even inside the guarded palace that houses the FCC in Washington, the chairman faced opposition. Concerned that the rules changes threatened the public interest he was sworn to uphold, dissident FCC commissioner Michael Copps organized more than a dozen informal hearings around the country where academics, journalists, musicians and others spoke in virtual unanimity against the changes. Another FCC member, Jonathan Adelstein, often accompanied Copps. He too heard that rather than relaxation of the ownership rules, most people wanted them tightened. Copps and Adelstein went on to cast the two June votes against the changes. For his part, Powell refused to attend the hearings, claiming he was too busy. (Powell was indeed busy: The Center for Public Integrity revealed that the chairman, the two other GOP commissioners and their aides held dozens of closed-doors meetings with corporate lobbyists and CEOs.)

Another galvanizing force in the fight over the rule changes was the growing awareness of the damage done by the relaxation of radio ownership rules in 1996: Radio quickly came to be dominated by behemoths like the 1,200-station Clear Channel and the 272-station Cumulus Media. Musicians like Don Henley told Congress about what a disaster consolidated radio had been for popular music. And in town after town when Copps held his hearings, the standard complaint was about the elimination of local radio news, or local programming in any form. This issue struck a chord not just with liberal activists but also with conservatives, who dislike the lack of local ownership and content that come with media concentration. Conservatives also maintained that the level of vulgarity and obscenity in popular culture was being driven upward primarily by the media conglomerates. By the end of the summer, Trent Lott and Jesse Helms joined Bernie Sanders and Representative Barbara Lee in calling for overturning Powell's ownership-rules changes.

The strange-bedfellow coalitions that have developed are remarkable. But they have not yet been sufficient to win the fight. Though more than 200 Democratic and Republican members of the House have signed a letter calling for a vote to overturn the FCC rules changes, that initiative is being stalled by Speaker Dennis Hastert and majority leader Tom DeLay. MoveOn.org, Free Press and other media reform groups are conducting a major grassroots campaign to win enough signers to reach the "magic" 218 threshold that signals a majority of the House wants a vote—which could push leaders to let the House voice its disapproval. The Bush White House doesn't want that to happen, because if the overturn proposal passes, Bush's loyalty to the big media lobby would put him under pressure to use what could be his first veto to block a measure that is enormously popular. With his sliding poll numbers, that would play directly into the growing belief that Bush is an opportunist more concerned with aiding the bank accounts of his billionaire benefactors than representing the interests of the American majority.

Even if Bush backs off and the rules are overturned, however, a victory only locks in the rules that were in place on June 2. Indeed, as commissioner Copps notes, the changes represent "only the latest, although perhaps most radical step in a twenty-year history of weakening public-interest protections." Thus, win or lose, the great media reform fight of 2003 will have been less about reform than about preventing a corrupted, corporation-dominated status quo from growing even more corrupt and corporate.

It is important to win the fight against the FCC rule changes for both symbolic and practical reasons. But it is even more important to recognize that this is merely the beginning of a struggle for real media reform in America. Thus, when the first National Conference on Media Reform convenes November 7-9 in Madison, Wisconsin, the focus will be on the future. "If all we do is fight defensive battles, the best we'll ever be able to hope for is that things won't get any worse. But that's not enough," says Sanders. "What we need is an agenda to make things better." What are the pieces of that agenda?

- Representative John Conyers, the ranking Democrat on the House Judiciary Committee, is right to argue for a renewed look at antitrust initiatives. Competition and diversity have been under assault for more than two decades, and it is time to consider the effect on the marketplace of ideas when reviewing media mergers. It is time, as well, for the federal government to engage in a period of study and debate leading to agreed-on caps on media ownership that are considered appropriate for a democracy. The current system of case-by-case review of proposed mergers, which frequently results in the making of exceptions for individual firms and then whole sectors of media, is an abject failure.
- Congress should roll back the number of radio stations a single firm can own. Senator Russ Feingold is considering sponsoring such legislation. Congress should also be pushed to pass legislation prohibiting media cross-ownership and vertical integration. There are tremendous economic benefits to media conglomeration—but they accrue almost entirely to the media owners. The public gets the shaft.
- The regulatory process, which is in disarray and awash in corruption, must be reinvigorated. Commissioner Copps will hold a series of town meetings this fall designed to draw attention to the power that citizens still have to challenge the licenses of local broadcast outlets. "Most people do not even know that they can challenge the renewal of a local radio or television station if they believe that the station is not living *up* to its obligation due to a lack of local coverage, a lack of diversity, excessive indecency and violence, or for other concerns important to the community," says Copps. Activism needs to be directed at the hometown level, where broadcast licenses can be challenged.
- The promised expansion of access by not-for-profit groups to low-power FM radio-station licenses, which was scuttled by a back-room deal in Congress several years ago, must take place [see Kevin Y. Kim, page 22]. Parallel to this shift in policy, tax incentives should be cre-

ated to aid in the development of new, community-based, noncommercial broadcasting outlets.
- Funding for public broadcasting must expand dramatically. Only about 15 percent of funding for public radio and television comes from federal subsidies. And what funding does come from Congress is subject to great political pressures. Public broadcasting at the federal and state levels has the potential to provide a model of quality journalism and diversified cultural programming. But that won't happen if cash-starved PBS and NPR outlets are required, as some propose, to rely on the same sort of thirty-second spot advertising that dominates commercial broadcasting.

Broadcasters must be forced to give candidates free air time. Senators John McCain and Russell Feingold, the authors of the only meaningful campaign-finance-reform legislation of the past decade, are now proposing such a requirement. Their initiative is essential to making not just better campaigns but better media. Currently, media conglomerates are among the most powerful lobbyists against both campaign finance reform and media reform. The system works for them, even as it fails the rest of us.

Media conglomerates must not be allowed to impose their will on the United States and other countries via international trade deals. Media firms are currently lobbying the World Trade Organization and other multilateral organizations to accept a system of trade sanctions against countries that subsidize public broadcasting, that limit foreign ownership of media systems or that establish local content standards designed to protect national and regional cultures. They want similar assaults on regulation inserted into the proposed Free Trade Area of the Americas. Representative Sherrod Brown is right when he says Congress should not pass trade agreements that undermine the ability of Congress to aid public broadcasting and protect media diversity and competition.

Beyond specific regulatory and trade fights, the media reform movement must address what ails existing media. Still top-heavy with white middle-class men, TV news departments and major newspapers remain in thrall to official sources. Their obsessive focus on crime coverage and celebrity trials leaves no room for covering the real issues that affect neighborhoods and whole classes of people. Coverage of communities of color, women, gays and lesbians, rural folks and just about everyone else who doesn't live in a handful of ZIP codes in New York and Los Angeles is badly warped, and it creates badly warped attitudes in society.

Those attitudes shape the public discourse and public policy. Thus, media reformers must support the struggle to expand access to the airwaves and to assure that independent and innovative journalists, writers and filmmakers have the resources to create media that reflect all of America [see Makani Themba-Nixon and Nan Rubin, page 17].

This agenda is already long. And it is just the beginning. We have not even broached all the policies that will affect the Internet, such as copyright and access. That it is possible for a growing number of Americans to imagine these sorts of reforms being implemented provides a measure of recent progress. A year ago the conventional wisdom was that media reform was a nonstarter as a political issue—because even some activists feared it was too abstract for people to sink their teeth into, because the corporate lobbies owned the politicians and regulators, and because, for obvious reasons, there was next to no coverage of media policy fights. Now, the world looks very different. Media reform clearly registers with millions across the political spectrum. The range of issues being put into play provides rare opportunities for the forces of civil society to win tangible victories. Even small victories can have big meaning, but they won't come easily. Michael Powell may be shellshocked, but the people who have grown accustomed to running media policy in this country—the media conglomerates, their lobbyists and those politicians they still manipulate like channel clickers—aren't going to give up without a fight.

There is real work to be done. For a media reform movement that is sustainable enough, broad-based enough and powerful enough to forge real changes in media ownership patterns, and in the character of American media, it is essential to build upon the passionate base of activists who did so much to make media an issue in 2003. We have to make media policy part of the 2004 presidential debate and all the campaigns that will follow it. And we have to make it a part of the kitchen-table debates where the real course of America can, and should, be plotted. To do that, the media reform movement that captured the imagination of antiwar activists and others in 2003 must burrow just as deeply into labor, church, farm and community groups, which are only beginning to recognize how their ideals and ambitions are being damaged. If the initial challenge was one of perception—making media an issue—the next challenge is one of organization. "Media reform has become an issue for millions of Americans," says Bernie Sanders. "Now, we've got to make media reform more than an issue. We have to make it a reality for all Americans."

POSTSCRIPT

Should the FCC Liberalize Ownership Rules?

What are the consequences of consolidation for the role and responsibilities of media in society? Unfortunately, there is little research on the effects of media restructuring. Is media concentration a problem? We may not think so if economies of scale reduce the prices we pay for our media. We may, however, have problems if most of the media outlets in our community are owned by the same corporation. For example, is a chain owner more likely to impose a one-size- fits-all perspective on its coverage of local events, thus reducing diversity? The Telecommunications Act of 1996 has unleashed a torrent of mergers and acquisitions. Is the promise of erasing traditional monopolies, which will reduce prices for services, being recognized? Or, has the law opened the door for new forms of monopoly?

The tension between the historical public interest paradigm of media in the U.S. and the current focus on the industry's economics and financial performance may well be the fundamental question to be answered about the future of the U.S. media industry. How American policymakers and the public address that issue will have significant impact on the direction in which the industry develops in the next few decades. If media companies are viewed as private enterprises whose primary responsibility is to attract consumers and generate profits for stockholders, deregulation and consolidation in the industry will continue and media markets will be controlled by an ever-smaller number of players generating what types of content sells best. If, however, the pendulum of regulatory philosophy and public pressure begins swinging back towards the view that the media have a responsibility to serve the public interest commensurate with the special legal protections accorded media corporations, a return to more regulation on industry structure and behavior is likely to follow.

What is certain is that the media industry in the US is still in the midst of a period of rapid, transformational change, the outcome of which has significant implications for civic society and the global media economy. The realization of synergy from consolidation is elusive, which is why in general across all industries, approximately half of all mergers are undone within a decade

The issues of corporate restructuring are being played out daily in the pages of the business press and media trade publications. See for example the *Wall Street Journal, Broadcasting/Cable* magazine, and *Electronic Media* for discussions of the successes and failures in this realm. Recent national scandals involving corporate financial irregularities may have an impact on the financial performance pressures brought to bear on corporations. *The Business of*

Media: Corporate Media and the Public Interest by David Croteau and William Hoynes (Pine Forge Press, 2001) is an excellent exploration of the tensions between corporate ownership and traditional obligations of the press. See also *Media Ownership* by Gillian Doyle (Sage, 2002). For an overview of the issues of media and the economy, see *Media Economics: Theory and Practice* (Erlbaum, 2003). For further on the NO side of the issue see: *Our Media, Not Theirs: The Democratic Struggle Against Corporate Media* by John Nichols, Robert McChesney, Barbara Ehrenreich (Seven Stories Press, 2002). Finally, the classic author on media concentration is Ben Bagdikian and his newest book is titled *The New Media Monopoly* (Beacon, 2004).

On the Internet . . .

National Association of Broadcasters

The National Association of Broadcasters (NAB) is dedicated to promoting the interests of broadcasters. Some of the pages found at this site include information on television parental guidelines, laws and regulations, and research on current issues.

http://www.nab.org

The National Cable Television Association

The National Cable Television Association (NCTA) is dedicated to promoting the interests of the cable television industry. This site contains discussions of current issues and updates on issues of importance to the NCTA.

http://www.ncta.com

Telecom Information Resources

This Telecom Information Resources site has over 7,000 links to telecommunication resources throughout the world. At this site you will find information on service providers, government agencies, government policies, economic policies, and much more.

http://china.si.umich.edu/telecom/telecom-info.html

Television Bureau of Advertising

The Television Bureau of Advertising is a nonprofit trade association of the broadcast television industry. This Web site provides a diverse variety of resources to help advertisers make the best use of local television. Go to the "television facts" section for useful information.

http://www.tvb.org

PART 5

Media Business

*I*t is important to remember that media industries are businesses and that they must be profitable to be able to thrive. The changing face of media industries threatens established practices and firms. Digital technologies are changing delivery systems, enabling activities such as music downloading and satellite delivered radio. However, are there special standards to which we should hold media industries? How do we balance the needs of business and the obligations of freedom of speech and of the press? Are the structures of media industries responsive to the public's interest? Can we protect intellectual property and artistic copyright in the digital age? It is hard to know how to build a business plan for a future that is so unpredictable!

- Is Economics the Bottom Line in the Newsrooms of Today?

- Do the Media Introduce Us to New Ways of Thinking About Things?

- Can the Music Industry Survive, Despite Technologies that Facilitate Downloading?

ISSUE 14

Is Economics the Bottom Line in the Newsrooms of Today?

YES: Daniel Sutter, "Can the Media be so Liberal? The Economics of Media Bias," *Cato Journal*, Winter 2001

NO: "The State of the News Media 2004." Project for Excellence in Journalism. www.stateofthenewsmedia.org

ISSUE SUMMARY

YES: Daniel Sutter, Associate Professor of Economics at the University of Oklahoma, takes a unique approach to the study of the driving forces behind the production of news. He postulates three important forces: audience demand, ownership bias, and journalist socialization. Posing a liberal cartel as a rationale for news bias, he demonstrates the economic consequences of such a position.

NO: The Project for Excellence in Journalism produces an annual report on American Journalism. In evaluating the major trends in content, economics, ownership, and investment, they conclude that many forces are creating a transformation in journalism. These forces include fragmentation of audiences, variable journalistic standards, convergence of media, and economic forces. No single factor is the bottom line in the newsrooms of today.

One of the inalienable rights of the citizenry should be the freedom of the press. The founding fathers intended the media to have its voice protected by the government so that the public could have access to crucial information pertaining to society. Thus media organizations operate under a unique, dual system of obligations: the obligation to be a profitable business entity and the obligation to serve the public. The central question of these selections is the balance between economic necessity and journalistic practice.

Let's step back to ask how to judge journalistic practice. What should be the standards of media accountability—the standards we should expect from media businesses? In *Mass Communication Theory*, 4th ed. (Sage, 2000), Denis McQuail offers four central values: freedom, order, diversity, and information quality. Media freedom implies lack of constraint and is usually mea-

284

sured in terms of the degree of control over news content by government or by corporate owners. Editorial freedom from the outside is easier to measure than is the control exerted by managers or editors in the professional socialization process. Central to freedom are issues of editorial freedom, internal (journalistic) press freedom, and creative freedom. The value of order has sometimes been called the correlational function of media: Providing channels for communication by many groups for bringing the country together in times of crisis, and by supporting social and civic order, while also paying attention to the needs and concerns of minorities. Diversity presumes that the more different channels of communication there are, the better. That the information provided should be of high quality seems self-evident and important to creating a society of informed individuals ready to participate in democratic decision making. Central tenets of journalism designed to produce high-quality information are fairness and accuracy, impartiality, and comprehensive and relevant information.

Similarly, what should we expect from a business? A financial analyst would say that success should be measured by increasing shareholder wealth. If you can envision yourself as a small business owner, you would certainly want your business to provide a product or service that was needed in the marketplace and was also of high quality, to support you and your employees, and to turn a profit which could be used to allow the company to grow. What would an owner expect from a media business? The holding and increasing of consumers and their content; increasing advertising revenue; and a high quality product.

Reconciling these sometimes difficult "conflict aims" can be a difficult balancing act. Accusations can be quick to fly when journalists feel that economic issues are interfering with journalistic standards. Alternatively, owners note that journalists are often unconcerned with the "bottom line" and certainly won't be doing good journalism if the firm goes bankrupt.

In order to explore the question of where the power lies in the production of news, Sutton subjects the question of media bias to an economic analysis. Although he points to the strength of both ownership and journalistic standards, he finds a liberal cartel not an economically viable explanation of business practice. Despite his belief in the influence of journalistic practices, he is ultimately persuaded that ownership and the economic marketplace could solve the problem of bias if it were perceived as a major problem.

The State of the News Media 2004 examines changes in the media marketplace and product. According to their analysis, the news media is in a time of change where the interplay of audience, economic, and journalistic standards are creating a new system of news production and distribution. Despite the inevitable importance of economic factors and of journalistic practices, change is inevitable and cannot be attributed to a single force.

Daniel Sutter  **YES**

Can the Media Be So Liberal?
The Economics of Media Bias

The Challenge to the Presumption of Bias

Many conservatives charge that the national news media exhibit a liberal bias, despite surface appearances of impartiality. Charges of a liberal bias essentially require the existence of a news cartel. Is the structure of the news industry capable of sustaining a cartel? A liberal news cartel requires collusion among news organizations and constraint of maverick outlets. Cartels are always vulnerable to defection. Indeed, many critics who accuse the media of a liberal bias are likely skeptical of the ability of businesses to maintain stable cartels without government assistance. Competition usually forces firms to cater to their customer's preferences. Yet critics allege that all major national news organizations present the same biased coverage, which is more liberal than the median voter. A liberal media represents a failure in the news market.[1]

The documentation of media bias has become something of a cottage industry since Edith Efron's (1971) pioneering study. Critics accusing the media of either a liberal or conservative bias make use of surveys of working journalists, content analysis of stories covered, and anecdotes about stories killed or not pursued to make their case.[2] But a conclusive measure of political bias in the news has been elusive. That the Media Research Center and Fairness and Accuracy in Reporting respectively point to the same news as demonstrating liberal and conservative biases indicates that we lack such a measure. Unfortunately, we cannot simply "test" the news and determine once and for all if a liberal bias exists.[3] I adopt a different approach here. I do not attempt to document the existence of news bias. Rather, I ask what might generate and sustain a liberal news media. If we cannot measure bias directly, we should consider the conditions for its survival and whether the news industry meets these conditions. The parallel is the economist's approach to market power. Monopoly power can be difficult to measure directly. A firm with market power must face little current or potential competition. A successful cartel requires entry barriers and a mechanism to prevent defection by member firms. Economists will likely reject charges of monopoly power in a

From *Cato Journal*, Winter 2001, pp. 431-452. Copyright © 2001 by Cato Institute. Reprinted by permission.

contestable market, one with small sunk costs.[4] Scholars attempting to document liberal bias have not asked questions of this type.

Specifically I consider three questions concerning the liberal media charge. First, is the source of bias on the demand (news consumer) or supply side of the news market? Two potential supply-side sources can be distinguished, owners and journalists. Although owners have used their news organizations to further their favored political causes, corporate ownership of the media makes this less likely. Proponents of the liberal bias charge place great weight on the numerous surveys concerning journalists' personal political views and voting patterns, which suggests employees as the likely source of bias.

Biased news will alienate many potential customers with centrist or right-of-center views. A smaller audience reduces advertising revenues and profit. The second question then is, why do profit-maximizing owners allow their reporters to indulge their liberal views at the organization's expense? Professionalism gives journalists considerable leeway to set standards for the quality of their product. But if journalistic independence and professionalism only hurt the news organization's bottom line, owners could eliminate such independence.

The third question concerns entry of conservative news organizations into the market to undercut the liberal cartel. Entry could involve a change in programming at an existing organization, or creation of a new organization. If all current organizations present liberal news, a single right-of-center organization would have half of the political spectrum to themselves. The only conservative firm in a liberal-dominated market could likely draw larger audiences than possible as a member of the cartel. A liberal news cartel creates a profit opportunity for a news organization willing to listen to the conservative critics.

The probability of sustaining a news cartel diminishes as the number of firms in the market increases. Technology, and to a lesser extent regulation, have combined to keep the number of news organizations of any one type in the national news market relatively small. Until about 20 years ago there were basically only the three television networks, two weekly magazines, and perhaps four newspapers in the national media market. All but a handful of cities had only one daily newspaper and the three network affiliates with news operations; even multi-paper cities have only two or three dailies. As cable television, satellite printing, and the Internet increase the number of news organizations in a truly national news market, the profit incentive for product diversification will become overwhelming. I conclude that the conditions for sustaining a news cartel, while tenuous in the past, will vanish in the near future. The news industry will almost certainly feature organizations catering to a range of political perspectives.

Sources of a Liberal News Cartel

We require some means of defining the existence of bias in the news. Bias cannot merely be in the eyes of the beholder, because each of us would like news stories to confirm the validity of our views. Consequently, I apply the spatial model of politics to the news media's product.[5] The most reasonable way to define bias is relative to the views of the median voter. A liberal news organization would be located to the left of the median voter. And the deviation from the median voter's position must be nontrivial for bias to be a policy issue of significance.

I do not consider here the details of classifying a story or locating an organization on the spectrum based on their many stories.[6] A question of relevance, though, concerns charges of bias in the news media as a whole. Must all organizations share the same partisan orientation for the media to be biased? Or is the mean or median of organization positions the appropriate measure? Operation of the marketplace of ideas requires only that all views get a hearing before the court of public opinion, which suggests bias adversely affects this market only if it extends across all organizations. A situation where most organizations exhibit a left-of-center bias but at least one is located to the right of the median voter can result from product differentiation and a majority liberal audience. The rejection by citizens of partisan views of either the left or right does not represent inefficiency in the transmission of political views. As a practical matter, conservative critics charge that all the major news organizations share the liberal bias. Bozell and Baker (1990), for instance, do not attempt to make fine distinctions between the bias of the television networks. Consequently, I will assume that liberal news bias involves all the major national news organizations offering a product which deviates significantly from the median voter.[7]

If all news organizations must offer essentially the same left-of-center news to validate the critics' charges, then the liberal media charge requires a news cartel. Typically economists describe a cartel as restricting output to raise price and generate supra-competitive profits. Advertising is the dominant source of revenue for news organizations, so the media are not trying to raise the price they charge to customers (readers and viewers). Yet if all organizations supply left-of-center news, customer preferences are not being fully satisfied. Furthermore, a cartel is subject to defection by member firms; a firm can increase its sales and profits at the others' expense by lowering its price.

The following example illustrates that a liberal news media can be reasonably described as a cartel. Suppose for simplicity we distinguish three positions on the political spectrum: liberal, moderate, and conservative. Each consumer has a preferred position on this spectrum; for concreteness, let there be 300 moderates, 150 liberals, and 150 conservatives in the audience. Each news organization must adopt a position on the political spectrum for their news coverage. Consumers patronize the organization whose news coverage comes closest to their personal views; conservatives will choose the conservative outlet if one is available. A group of consumers divides equally among the competitors if two or more news organizations offer the closest match. Assume that all consumers consume news, even if their favored news is not provided.

One news organization, under these circumstances, could locate anywhere along the political spectrum and attain an audience of 600. A liberal news monopoly is not implausible. Suppose two or more organizations exist. If all organizations provided liberal news they will split the market, which is the same result as if all organizations provided moderate news. Yet a liberal news cartel is unstable. When two firms participate in a liberal cartel, each organization has an audience of 300. But one firm increases its audience to 450 if it shifts its news location to moderate, since it captures all the moderate and conservative news consumers. Firms have an incentive to defect from a cartel as the number of organizations increases. With two or three firms we would expect convergence to the middle; all organizations would provide moderate news and split the market. Once four firms were in the market, product differentiation could result: two firms with moderate news, one liberal and one conservative organization, each with an audience of 150. Although a firm might then present liberal news, a uniform liberal news media does not result. Given the nature of the strategic problem the affected firms face, we can reasonably characterize the liberal media charge as requiring a sustainable cartel.[8]

What is the source of bias? Political bias in the news media has three potential sources. On the demand side, a disproportionate number of consumers of the news might have liberal views with the news media merely providing the product their customers demand. Indeed, a demand side explanation does not imply market failure. Either owners or journalists could also be a supply-side source of biased news. A supply-side source of liberal bias would constitute a market failure, and raises the question of intentionality. Is the liberal media part of a conspiracy? A supply-side explanation of bias must address the stability of the liberal news cartel.

Viewers and the Media

The set of news consumers may differ from the set of voters. If liberals constitute a disproportionate percentage of news consumers, the median voter may regard the news media's programming as liberal. Yet the media are simply responding to their customers' preferences. News organizations serving their median customer will appear liberal from the perspective of the entire electorate. A demandside explanation does not imply that the news market fails.

Clearly, this is an empirical claim. Some evidence suggests that news consumers may be more liberal than voters. Robert Entman (1989: 141–43) provides evidence (drawn from the Michigan Current Population Survey) that nonvoters are more liberal than voters, which implies voters are not a representative sample of the population. Newspaper and newsmagazine subscription rates increase with education, and surveys typically show college graduates are more liberal than the population as a whole. Brian Goff and Robert Tollison (1990) show that newspaper circulation per capita across states increases with a measure of the liberalness of state voters. The available evidence, however, is far from conclusive in establishing news consumers as a source of bias.

Two important caveats apply even if the median news consumer were demonstrably more liberal than the median voter. First, not all viewers are to the left of the median voter. News organizations will engage in product differentiation when profitable. If the majority of news consumers are located to the left of the median voter, this might explain why most news organizations provide liberal news. But all organizations must locate left of the median voter to explain the liberal media. The audience must be quite skewed for profit-maximizing news organizations to all provide liberal news. Suppose we increase the proportion of consumers with liberal views in the previous model of program choice. If three organizations exist, 400 of the 600 consumers must be liberal so that no organization wishes to provide moderate news. The degree of divergence from the voting population required increases with the number of media organizations. With four news organizations at least 450 of the 600 consumers must prefer liberal news to sustain a liberal news cartel.

Second, even if we establish that the media and its viewership are left-of-center, this correlation does not determine the direction of causality. A demand-side explanation assumes that causality runs from audience to programming, that liberals disproportionately consume news and the media provide the product they demand. But causality could easily run in the other direction: the media's liberal bias could alienate conservatives, producing over time a liberal audience.... Certainly most people would prefer news which conforms with and reinforces their political beliefs, and should turn away from news which challenges these beliefs. I am considering a liberal national news market. Given the other sources of news, like local newspapers or television, disaffected conservatives might stop watching. A liberal news media could produce a liberal audience.[9] Because of the difficulties in explaining a news cartel based on a liberal audience, I turn now to supply-side explanations.

Bias in Ownership

Economists typically assume firms maximize profit, but owners as consumers wish to maximize utility. Utility maximization does not necessarily mean profit maximization since some amenities can be more easily acquired in production than through the market. Owners will generally be willing to trade some profit for other goals. Media owners can use their news organizations to advance their favored political causes. Owners' ideology is a potential supply-side source of bias in the media.[10]

Clearly many media owners over the years have been strongly identified with political parties or causes and used their organizations to achieve these goals.[11] Henry Luce, founder of *Time*, remarked of his magazine's coverage of the 1952 presidential election: "Eisenhower was right for the country for a large number of reasons, therefore, it was *Time's* duty to explain why the country needed Ike. Any other form of objectivity would have been unfair and uninvolved" (quoted in Halberstam 1979: 59). The Chandler family for many years ran the *Los Angeles Times* to benefit their favored (mostly Republican) candidates. Today media moguls Ted Turner and Rupert Murdoch are known for their strong and contrasting political views.

The political views of owners provide weak grounds for a liberal news cartel. The problem is not that owners will never sacrifice profits for political goals; many instances of this abound. Rather, all media owners must be willing to sacrifice profits for liberal political goals to sustain a news cartel. This assumption is open to two objections. First, although examples of liberal media owners can be found (Philip and Katherine Graham, Ted Turner), more often prominent media organizations have been used by owners to advance conservative causes. Many owners notable for their political views have right-of-center views: Luce of *Time*, Chandler of the *Los Angeles Times*, William Paley of CBS, and Robert McCormick of the *Chicago Tribune*. Proponents of the liberal media proposition have not established convincingly that all media owners are liberal.[12]

Second, contending that all media owners trade profits for liberal political goals clashes with evidence that profit maximization is an increasingly important goal for the media and the changing structure of media ownership. While we lack an objective measure of concern with the bottom line across organizations or over time, increased emphasis on profits following the acquisition of a newspaper or television station by a media conglomerate is a familiar refrain (Bagdikian 1997, Underwood 1993).... Most close observers of the media report a growing emphasis on the bottom line. And surveys of journalists report a perceived increase in emphasis on profit margins by management (Underwood 1993: 117–26, Weaver and Wilhoit 1996: 60–67). Unless these observations are entirely off the mark, owners must be less willing to trade profits for political goals now than in the past.

The growth of corporate ownership of the media strengthens the case for increased emphasis on profit as a goal....

Media outlets are...increasingly owned by widely held public corporations in contrast to family-owned or narrowly held corporations. The... concentration of ownership affects the likelihood of pursuit of goals other than profit maximization. Consensus on goals *besides* profit is more likely with a narrowly owned family business than with thousands of stockholders. Profit is a goal which everyone who invests in a business can agree on. Other goals are far less general. Even if all stockholders agree news organizations should champion causes, they will disagree about *which* causes to champion: environmental protection, the labor movement, protection of property rights, school choice, and so on. Some stockholders might desire a liberal bias and some a conservative bias, and others not interested in politics will wish to pursue only profit maximization....

Liberal Journalists and Media Bias

Journalists themselves are a second supply-side source of bias. Charges of a liberal bias in the news place great weight on surveys revealing the liberal views of a majority of journalists. The survey evidence is consistent and strong. In Robert Lichter, Stanley Rothman, and Linda Lichter's (1986: 20–53) 1979–80 survey of journalists at elite media organizations, 54 percent of respondents identified themselves as left-of-center, versus 17 percent right-of-center. The journalists who voted for a major party candidate in presidential elections between 1964 and 1976 overwhelmingly went for Democrats: Lyndon Johnson 94 percent, Hubert Humphrey 87 percent, and George McGovern and Jimmy Carter 81 percent each. David Weaver and Cleveland Wilhoit (1996: 15–19) in 1992 found that 47.3 percent of journalists identified themselves as left or left-leaning versus 21.7 percent right-of-center. In terms of party affiliation, 44 percent identified with the Democrats versus 16 percent Republicans and 34 percent Independents. Of the Washington journalists surveyed by Stephen Hess (1981: 87), 42 percent identified themselves as liberal versus 19 percent conservative.[13]

How did the journalism profession come to be dominated by liberals, and how is this domination maintained? An established partisan bias can be sustained through self-selection. The costs of membership in the organization for individuals with dissenting viewpoints can be extremely high. Colleagues will make statements about politics at the water cooler, on breaks, and at lunch which dissenters find objectionable. Saying nothing in response often involves a psychic cost, while responding brings potential social sanctions (Kuran 1995). A bias in the topics of media coverage provides dissenting individuals with inherently disconcerting assignments. Dissenters bear a higher cost of putting aside their feelings to do the story and do it well, and failure to do so results in lower quality job performance. Dissenters will tend to quit at a higher rate and have lower job performance, as measured by supervisors sharing the organization's dominant values.... And dissenting individuals might come to adopt the organization's dominant viewpoint, not out of strategic considerations but because of belief plasticity (Klein 1994). Individuals with the dominant view will find a career in the media more rewarding, and are more likely to invest in the training necessary to enter the field.

This leaves unresolved the establishment of bias. One possible answer could be the joint distribution of journalistic talent and political views across the population. People with the talent, temperament, and personality to be journalists might also be inclined toward liberal political causes....

A job which allows one to work toward changing the system, in however modest a fashion, provides higher nonpecuniary benefits for such a person. Journalists are intellectuals, a class long dominated by individuals hostile to business.

A third source of biased journalists lies in the screening function played by journalism schools which train an increasing fraction of reporters, particularly at leading news organizations.[14] As long as news organizations require the acquisition of these credentials, journalism programs choose the set of candidates available to employers. Surveys reveal that journalism students have even more pronounced liberal views than working journalists. Indeed, in 1982, 85 percent of Columbia Graduate School of Journalism students identified themselves as liberal, versus 11 percent conservative (Lichter, Rothman, and Lichter 1986: 48). Faculty could conceivably gear the curriculum to attract students with liberal leanings and repel young conservatives. Selection could extend to grades and recommendations.[15]

Journalists versus Owners in the Production of News

Conservative critics typically see the survey evidence, supported by some content analysis, as settling the issue. Objectivity in reporting is impossible; reporters cannot abandon their worldview in attempting to report on daily events. Examples of intentional bias, such as slanting stories to advance their views given the constraint of surface neutrality, are rare (see Efron 1971 for some examples, though). More generally, advocates of the liberal media hypothesis argue that bias is unintentional and unavoidable. Liberal reporters may simply know more liberal sources and find their explanations of events more persuasive....

The surveys establish though only an inherent tendency in journalists' reporting, if unchecked. Media owners and their agents (top editors and producers) could take steps to prevent journalists' personal views from biasing their reporting to prevent the content of news from being liberal. Critics of the liberal media proposition point to the incentive for the major news organizations to push their owners' conservative, pro-free-market politics.[16] The critics on the left properly point out a weak link in the liberal media argument. I believe, however, that these critics misidentify the media owners' motive for controlling journalists. Corporate media owners will be more interested in maximizing profits than pushing a political agenda. Being a member of a liberal news cartel costs individual media organizations (and perhaps the industry as a whole) potential profit. Corporations will try to control liberal journalists if liberal news reduces profit. Proponents of the liberal media thesis must explain why media owners fail to control their employees. Owners apparently are content to let journalists indulge their liberal views at the expense of the organization's profit.

A conflict of interest between employers and employees does not imply that workers will get their way. All owners want their employees to exert effort to achieve the organization's goal (profit). Effort is costly for employees to exert, and owners are residual claimants for (at least most of) the company's profits....

The question for the liberal media thesis then becomes why control of employees might be more of a problem for news organizations than other businesses. The nature of journalism provides a possible answer. Journalism is a profession; reviewing performance and detecting shirking requires a significant level of professional expertise. Professionalism creates certain standards that must be met in choosing sources and presenting a story. Only someone familiar with these standards can criticize a journalist's performance.... Objectivity provides reporters with a formula to use against critics of a story (Tuchman 1978, Miraldi 1990, Bennett 1996).

Owners, though, can hire editors or producers with knowledge of journalistic practices to control liberal bias in reporters. As an empirical matter, owners do not seem to be choosing top supervisory personnel to offset liberal reporters. Weaver and Wilhoit (1996: 17) find that 57.2 percent of executives (who supervise editorial personnel) at prominent news organizations describe themselves as left or left-leaning, compared to 59.4 percent of staffers at these organizations. But even an editor intent on controlling journalists would find the task daunting. News stories are not a standardized product; rather, each is unique. An editor very familiar with the techniques of reporting will typically lack the detailed knowledge necessary to criticize the choice of sources on a story or beat.... Print reporters particularly enjoy a great deal of autonomy... reporters initiated 69 percent of their stories in his study and 51 percent of stories were not edited by the home office at all (Hess 1981: 6, 8)....

The above arguments suggest that the cost of controlling reporters will be high. News organizations will closely control journalists only if the benefit of the effort exceeds the cost. The gain from controlling bias, the reduction in profit from liberal news, might be small for at least two reasons. First, allowing partisan news coverage could reduce the cost of producing news coverage. Individuals with strong political views will accept lower pay to do the type of reporting they believe in.[17] If the majority of journalists have left-of-center views, liberal news might cost less to supply than unbiased news. Traditionally salaries in the news industry have been modest. And the cost of trying to produce a right-of-center product with predominantly liberal reporters could be quite high. Profit-maximizing news organizations will trade off reduced revenue from a smaller audience if offset by a larger reduction in cost.

Second, the reduction in audience due to liberal news may be small. Americans have little interest in politics in general and foreign news in particular.... News coverage, particularly of politics, has traditionally been a financial drain (Schudson 1995). CBS established its distinguished news department to enhance the network's reputation, not because of a direct return on the investment (Halberstam 1979).[18] If lost revenue from biased coverage is $5 million a year instead of $500 million, news organizations have little incentive to crack the whip and keep their reporters in line. In terms of the programming model, some portion of consumers may not be able to discern the partisan position of an organization's coverage. These consumers might divide evenly among the different organizations regardless of their position on the spectrum. Also the number of organizations producing in a given news market determines the audience gain at stake. A news monopoly can indulge partisan news at a lower cost than an outlet which faces competition. Hence monopoly newspapers should exhibit more bias than magazines.

Maintenance of Bias: The Problem of Entrants

Even if existing news organizations did overcome their difficulties and maintain a liberal cartel, other organizations might enter the market and challenge the prevailing bias. An entrant could capture the moderate and conservative audience. Successful cartels must have means of punishing defectors and preventing entry. Yet proponents of the liberal media thesis offer little discussion of the barriers to entry and punishment mechanism which sustain the news cartel.

Licensing by the Federal Communications Commission constitutes a barrier to entry for radio and television. Indeed, for many years the FCC helped maintain the oligopoly position of the three over-the-air networks and delayed the development of cable television. The advent of cable, however, has reduced restrictions on entry, even though regulations still limit access to cable systems....The last two decades have nonetheless witnessed the success-full entry of CNN and Fox to the television market....

If barriers to entry prevent a new (conservative) organization from entering the news market, ideologues could always purchase an existing organization.[19] All three major television networks were sold in the 1980s. Only the news division need be modified in the organization; a television network's prime time and daytime lineups could be left intact. Given the alleged prevailing liberal bias, product differentiation could easily increase audience and advertising revenues. In addition to this profit incentive, the marginal benefit to conservatives of one countervailing source of news should be high. Further, wealthy conservatives willing to trade profits for political goals might invest in the takeover effort to break the liberal news cartel.

What prevents a change of orientation at an existing news organization, or how can cartel members punish a cheating firm? Professionalism provides journalists some ability to enforce their accepted practices on news organizations through peer evaluation.[22] If the new owners of a television network set about trying to impose a conservative perspective on the news product, other journalists could criticize the compromise of journalistic independence and deterioration of the quality of coverage. A reduction in the professional evaluation of the organization's product may adversely affect audience size and advertising revenue. Liberal journalists could themselves raise costs for a new conservative news orientation through work slowdowns and resignations. Indeed, more than 60 staff members of the *Chicago Sun-Times* took generous severance pay and resigned when Rupert Murdoch purchased the paper (Shawcross 1997: 175). In time new staff could be hired or trained, but a short-run increase in cost and deterioration of quality would be nearly inevitable.

Conclusion

Ultimately the reader must judge the strength of the liberal media thesis. I have taken a different approach to the topic and raised some economic objections. Liberal bias must have a source and maintenance of bias effectively requires a news cartel. The source of bias remains unclear, although journalists themselves are the most plausible source. Even if so, the establishment of ideological bias within the profession is a mystery. And two weak points still remain in the cartel argument: why media owners allow journalists to indulge their liberal views at the expense of potential profits, and what protects the cartel against defectors and entrants.

Journalistic professionalism and independence play a role in answering both objections. Professionalism and the uniqueness of each story make the reporter's judgments (regarding sources, a lead, and a frame) difficult to second-guess, creating an environment in which the journalist's political views could matter. A news organization which attempts to impose a conservative slant in its coverage will meet resistance from professional journalists who see independence from ownership as critical for good reporting. The larger question for the liberal media thesis then is why news organizations accept journalistic professionalism. Perhaps media owners do not have the will to battle their employees over money and working conditions, preferring to accommodate employees' demands to improve their public image. Yet news-papers (including the *Washington Post*) have battled their printers' unions to control costs. So a general unwillingness to oppose employee demands will not provide an answer. Professionalism must generate some benefit for news organizations. A higher quality product as judged by journalists could possi-bly translate into larger audiences and advertising revenues. Yet evidence casts doubt on this. Coverage of Watergate won Bob Woodward and Carl Bernstein and the *Washington Post* many accolades but did not increase profitability as measured by stock price (McChesney 1987). Many journalists decry the changes implemented by Gannett first in the *USA Today* and later in their chain papers to create a more reader-friendly product (Underwood 1993: 95–105). Budget cuts by CBS News in the 1980s lowered the quality of their prod-uct in the view of journalists. Are these organizations worse off financially as a result? Ownership is most likely to indulge professionalism if skilled journal-ists value independence and will trade salary in return. Competition among news organizations for the best journalists determines the value of their com-pensation package. The form of the package depends on journalists' prefer-ences and the cost to the organization of supplying types of compensation. Profit rises as long as the news journalists want to produce does not reduce the audience too much.

Two sources of potential barriers to entry or cost disadvantage to new organizations lie in the public sector: FCC limits on the number of television stations and government's public relations apparatus. Public-sector actions seem an inadequate basis on which to explain a liberal news cartel. Republicans held the presidency for 28 of the 40 years between 1952 and 1992. The White House could have directed scoops and interviews to conservative reporters and news organizations during these years. If FCC regulations were the source of a liberal news cartel, the Nixon administration could have knocked out a liberal news cartel via direct action instead of having Vice President Agnew speak out about bias.[21] Government regulation supported cartels in trucking, railroads, and airlines until the late 1970s; was news merely another example of govern-ment-sponsored cartelization? I suspect not. Support for trucking and airline cartels was less risky for politicians than a news cartel because politicians had no direct stake in the output of these industries.

Technology will likely eliminate any prospects of a liberal news cartel. A successful cartel typically requires a small number of firms. The cooperation necessary to maintain a cartel is more likely and the ability to identify and punish cartel violators greater with a modest number of firms. The past two decades have witnessed an increase in the number of national news organiza-tions; CNN and *USA Today* are just two examples. Many regional newspapers take on more of a national character due to web sites and satellite printing. Fox News is slowly becoming available to more cable systems.

As the number of news organizations increases, the incentive for parti-san differentiation by some becomes quite strong. Partisan media bias, as defined here as a deviation of the product of all news organizations from the position of the median voter, may be a thing of the past. The minimum efficient scale of production limited and then eliminated competition between papers in all but the largest metropolitan areas. And the rise of the three television networks combined with FCC regulation limited the number of television news organizations. But as the number of television networks and national newspapers expands, the potential for a successful news cartel diminishes. A proliferation of reporting techniques and partisan views should occur in the decades to come as the number of national news organizations increase. Fox News already attempts to differentiate its product from the perceived liberal media bias. At least some of the new organizations should find it profitable to cater to conservative viewers.

I have addressed the question of partisan political bias in the news, a bias in favor of the Democratic party or liberal issue positions at the expense of Republican candidates and conservative or libertarian causes. News gathering and reporting can have other effects on the news, biases which may be as significant as party bias. Coverage of government activities might be excessively positive because reporters fear retaliation (lack of access, complaints to superiors) from government officials over negative stories. Fairness in reporting always allows government officials to be quoted and thus to provide their spin on events. Academic critiques of journalism in fact focus more on these other biases. Analysis of a possible link between journalistic practices and the expansion of government, though, remains a subject for future research.

Notes

1. Charges of liberal bias typically concern the national news media, including the television networks, the major weekly newsmagazines, and leading papers like the *New York Times* and *Washington Post*. These organizations comprise only a portion of the news industry. Other portions of the industry, notably talk radio and local newspapers, have been accused of the conservative bias. Liberal bias in the national news market is of concern since the national media have a greater impact on the polital agenda than these other outlets do.

2. See Bozell and Baker (1190) and Baker (1994) for a sample of the types of evidence of liberal media bias.

3. Documentation of bias requires considering the impact of normal incentives and procedures on reporting. Washington reporters seek access to inside sources due to competition for stories. Reporters and sources engage in a repeated game, so mutual cooperation is likely to evolve; hostile reporters could see their administration sources dry up. If we observe reporters not being critical of Democratic administration, the behavior may not be a result of bias.

4. Although claims of both a liberal and conservative bias in the media must face these types of questions, this paper focuses on potential pitfalls of a liberal news cartel. Sutter (2000) considers the charge

that corporate ownership and advertising creates a conservative, pro-business bias in the media.

5. On the spatial model see Downs (1957). Goff and Tollison (1990) and Endersby and Ognianova (1997) have previously applied the spatial model to the political content of the news media.

6. Every organization runs many stories which will likely exhibit different points of view, and many stories will lack any partisan content. An organization may be located based on measure of central tendency (the median or mean story) or a measure of dispersion (variance or extreme stories). Different measures may produce different evaluations of an organization. I require only that some means of locating organizations exist.

7. Bias across a majority of organizations can affect policy outcomes. Suppose the median voter's preference helps determine policy outcomes. If two out of three television networks exhibit a liberal bias and voters likely to be influenced by bias are evenly distributed across the three networks, the median voter will end up more liberal than otherwise. Political parties trying to win elections would understandably be concerned about bias that changes even 1 or 2 percent of votes.

8. The exact outcome in models of this type depends on the assumptions made (Owen and Wildman 1992: 64–100). Allowing audience members not to consume news if no organization provides their most preferred news product would strengthen the incentive for a single firm to provide moderate news. Also a liberal cartel might have a smaller total audience than a moderate cartel. The difficulty of maintaining a liberal cartel would still result.

9. Of course, if we had a measure of media bias, we could examine the causality issue directly.

10. Media owners might also desire a large and activist government as a means of increasing demand for their product (Crain and Tollison 1997). The gains from such a strategy will likely be remote and modest, since rational ignorance limits citizens' demand for political information. I focus on ideological consumption by owners.

11. Prior to the rise of commercial media (the penny press) many newspapers were supported by political parties. I am concerned with the use of commercial media for political purposes.

12. Bozell and Baker (1990: 86–98) present evidence concerning the giving patterns of media organizations' charitable foundations.

13. Of journalists in the Brookings survey, 51 percent agreed that the Washington press corps had a political bias. Of those who believed a bias existed, 96 percent perceived a liberal bias versus 1 percent perceiving a conservative bias (Hess 1981: 87).

14. In 1992, of the working journalists surveyed by Weaver and Wilhoit (1996: 35), 82 percent had at least a four-year college degree, and 11.4 percent had a graduate degree. Furthermore, 40 percent of the journalists with college degrees had majored in journalism.

15. This impact need not involve conscious discrimination on the part of professors. Students who find a course interesting tend to work harder and do better. And professors tend to provide a higher evaluation of the abilities of protegés.

16. As Hertsgaard (1988: 85–6) puts it:

> The deeper flaw in the liberal-press thesis, however, was that it completely ignored those whom journalists worked for. Reporters could be as liberal as they wished and it would not change what news they were allowed to report or how they could report it. America's major news organizations were owned and controlled by some of the largest and richest corporations in the United States. These firms were in turn owned and controlled by individuals whose politics were, in general, anything but liberal. Why would they employ journalists who consistently covered news in ways they did not like?

For other examples of this argument see Bagdikian (1997), Parenti (1986), and Kellner (1990).

17. Frank (1996) presents survey evidence concerning students' willingness to accept lower pay for jobs offering greater intangible moral rewards.

18. This raises the question of why the TV networks provide news service at a loss. A combination of habit and the public service requirement imposed by government regulators probably explains this.

19. A group of conservatives did in fact attempt to buy CBS in 1985.

20. Efron (1971) suggests that members of the journalistic community who criticize the prevailing liberal bias face considerable ostracism from other professionals.

21. The Nixon administration did threaten not to renew the licenses of television stations owned by the Washington Post company

References

Bagdikian, B. (1997) *The Media Monopoly.* 5th ed. Boston: Beacon Press.

Baker, B.H. (1994) *How to Identify, Expose and Correct Liberal Media Bias.* Alexandria, Va.: Media Research Center.

Bozell, L.B., and Baker, B.H. (eds.) (1990) *That's the Way It Isn't: A Reference Guide to Media Bias.* Alexandria, Va.: Media Research Center.

Crain, W.M., and Tollison, R.D. (1997) "Expansive Government and the Media." Unpublished paper, George Mason University.

Downs, A. (1957) *An Economic Theory of Democracy.* New York: Harper and Row.

Efron, E. (1971) *The News Twisters.* Los Angeles: Nash Publishing.

Endersby, J.W., and Ognianova, E. (1997) "A Spatial Model of Ideology and Political Communication." *Harvard International Journal of Press/Politics* 2: 23–39.

Entman, R.M. (1989) *Democracy Without Citizens.* New York: Oxford University Press.

Frank, R.H. (1996) "What Price the Moral High Ground?" *Southern Economic Journal* 63(1):1–17.

Goff, B., and Tollison, R.D. (1990) "Why Is the Media So Liberal?" *Journal of Public Finance and Public Choice* 1:13–21.

Halberstam, D. (1979) *The Powers That Be*. New York: Alfred A. Knopf.

Hertsgaard, M. (1988) *On Bended Knee: The Press and the Reagan Presidency*. New York: Farrar, Straus Giroux.

Hess, S. (1981) *The Washington Reporters*. Washington, D.C.: Brookings Institution.

Kellner, D. (1990) *Television and the Crisis of Democracy*. Boulder, Colo.: Westview Press.

Klein, D.B. (1994) "If Government Is So Villainous, How Come Government Officials Don't Seem Like Villains?" *Economics and Philosophy* 10: 91–106.

Kuran, T. (1995) *Private Truths, Public Lies*. Cambridge Mass.: Harvard University Press.

Lichter, S.R.; Rothman, S.; and Lichter, L.S. (1986) *The Media Elite*. Bethesda, Md.: Adler and Adler.

McChesney, F.S. (1987) "Sensationalism, Newspaper Profits and the Marginal Value of Watergate." *Economic Inquiry* 25:135–44.

Miraldi, R. (1990) *Muckraking and Objectivity*. New York: Greenwood Press.

Owen, B.M., and Wildman, S.S. (1992) *Video Economics*. Cambridge, Mass.: Harvard University Press.

Parenti, M. (1986) *Inventing Reality*. New York: St. Martin's Press.

Schudson, M. (1995) *The Power of News*. Cambridge, Mass.: Harvard University Press.

Shawcross, W. (1997) *Murdoch: The Making of a Media Empire*. New York: Touchstone Books.

Sutter, D. (2000) *Political Bias in the News: A Skeptical Examination*. Unpublished book manuscript, University of Oklahoma.

Tuchman, G. (1978) *Making News*. New York: Free Press.

Underwood, D. (1993) *When MBAs Rule the Newsroom*. New York: Columbia University Press.

Weaver, D.H., and Wilhoit, G.C. (1996) *The American Journalist in the 1990s*. Mahwah, N.J.: Lawrence Erlbaum.

The State of the News Media 2004

Intro

Glance at some items in the news of late and it seems that many long-held ideas about journalism are unraveling.

President George Bush told ABC's Diane Sawyer in December that he preferred to get his news not from journalists but from people he trusted, who "give me the actual news" and "don't editorialize." After spending time at the White House, the New Yorker writer Ken Auletta concluded that senior staff members there saw the news media as just another special interest group whose agenda was making money, not serving the public—and surveys suggest increasingly that the public agrees.

Some argue that as people move online, the notion of news consumers is giving way to something called "pro-sumers," in which citizens simultaneously function as consumers, editors and producers of a new kind of news in which journalistic accounts are but one element.

With audiences now fragmented across hundreds of outlets with varying standards and agendas, others say the notions of a common public understanding, a common language and a common public square are disappearing.

For some, these are all healthy signals of the end of oligarchical control over news. For others, these are harbingers of chaos, of unchecked spin and innuendo replacing the role of journalists as gatekeepers over what is fact, what is false and what is propaganda. Whichever view one prefers, it seems everything is changing.

Or is it?

This study, the first in what is to be an annual report on the state of the news media in America, is an attempt to answer this question, to take stock each year of the state and health of American journalism.

The answer we arrive at in 2004 is that journalism is in the midst of an epochal transformation, as momentous probably as the invention of the telegraph or television.

Journalism, however, is not becoming irrelevant. It is becoming more complex. We are witnessing conflicting trends of fragmentation and convergence simultaneously, and they sometimes lead in opposite directions.

While audiences are fragmenting, we have greater capacity than ever to come together as a nation in an instant—for September 11, the Super Bowl or watching soldiers live on the battlefield in Iraq. While Americans are turning to more and varied sources for news, the media that they are relying on increasingly tend to be owned by a few giant conglomerates competing to cover what seem to be at any moment a handful of major stories.

Quality news and information are more available than ever before, but in greater amounts so are the trivial, the one-sided and the false. Some people will likely become better informed than they once could have been as they drill down to original sources. Other consumers may become steeped in the sensational and diverting. Still others may move toward an older form of media consumption—a journalism of affirmation—in which they seek news largely to confirm their preconceived view of the world.

The journalists' role as intermediary, editor, verifier and synthesizer is weakening, and citizens do have more power to be proactive with the news. But most people will likely do so only episodically. And the proliferation of the false and misleading makes the demand for the journalist as referee, watchdog and interpreter all the greater.

These conflicting movements toward fragmentation and convergence are not new to the culture in general or media in particular, but they have different consequences when they come to news. Journalism is how people learn about the world beyond their direct experiences. As our journalism fragments, it has consequences for what we know, how we are connected and our ability to solve problems.

Eight Major Trends

For now, the year 2004, the transformation is shaped by eight overarching trends:

- A growing number of news outlets are chasing relatively static or even shrinking audiences for news. One result of this is that most sectors of the news media are losing audience. That audience decline, in turn, is putting pressures on revenues and profits, which leads to a cascade of other implications. The only sectors seeing general audience growth today are online, ethnic and alternative media.
- Much of the new investment in journalism today—much of the information revolution generally—is in disseminating the news, not in collecting it. Most sectors of the media are cutting back in the newsroom, both in terms of staff and in the time they have to gather and report the news. While there are exceptions, in general journalists face real pressures trying to maintain quality.
- In many parts of the news media, we are increasingly getting the raw elements of news as the end product. This is particularly true in the newer, 24-hour media. In cable and online, there is a tendency toward a jumbled, chaotic, partial quality in some reports, without much synthesis or even the ordering of the information. There is also a great deal of

effort, particularly on cable news, that is put into delivering essentially the same news repetitively without any meaningful updating.

- Journalistic standards now vary even inside a single news organization. Companies are trying to reassemble and deliver to advertisers a mass audience for news not in one place, but across different programs, products and platforms. To do so, some are varying their news agenda, their rules on separating advertising from news and even their ethical standards. What will air on an MSNBC talk show on cable might not meet the standards of NBC News on broadcast, and the way that advertising intermingles with news stories on many newspaper Web sites would never be allowed in print. Even the way a television network treats news on a prime time magazine versus a morning show or evening newscast can vary widely. This makes projecting a consistent sense of identity and brand more difficult. It also may reinforce the public perception evident in various polls that the news media lack professionalism and are motivated by financial and self-aggrandizing motives rather than the public interest.

- Without investing in building new audiences, the long-term outlook for many traditional news outlets seems problematic. Many traditional media are maintaining their profitability by focusing on costs, including cutting back in their newsrooms. Our study shows general increases in journalist workload, declines in numbers of reporters, shrinking space in newscasts to make more room for ads and promotions, and in various ways that are measurable, thinning the product. This raises questions about the long term. How long can news organizations keep increasing what they charge advertisers to reach a smaller audience? If they maintain profits by cutting costs, social science research on media suggests they will accelerate their audience loss.

- Convergence seems more inevitable and potentially less threatening to journalists than it may have seemed a few years ago. At least for now, online journalism appears to be leading more to convergence with older media rather than replacement of it. When audience trends are examined closely, one cannot escape the sense that the nation is heading toward a situation, especially at the national level, in which institutions that were once in different media, such as CBS and The Washington Post, will be direct competitors on a single primary field of battle—online. The idea that the medium is the message increasingly will be passé. This is an exciting possibility that offers the potential of new audiences, new ways of storytelling, more immediacy and more citizen involvement.

- The biggest question may not be technological but economic. While journalistically online appears to represent opportunity for old media rather than simply cannibalization, the bigger issue may be financial. If online proves to be a less useful medium for subscription fees or advertising, will it provide as strong an economic foundation for newsgathering as television and newspapers have? If not, the move to the Web may lead to a general decline in the scope and quality of American journalism, not because the medium isn't suited for news, but because it isn't suited to the kind of profits that underwrite newsgathering.

• Those who would manipulate the press and public appear to be gaining leverage over the journalists who cover them. Several factors point in this direction. One is simple supply and demand. As more outlets compete for their information, it becomes a seller's market for information. Another is workload. The content analysis of the 24-hour-news outlets suggests that their stories contain fewer sources. The increased leverage enjoyed by news sources has already encouraged a new kind of checkbook journalism, as seen in the television networks efforts to try to get interviews with Michael Jackson and Jessica Lynch, the soldier whose treatment while in captivity in Iraq was exaggerated in many accounts.

These are some of the conclusions from this new study of the state of American journalism, a study that we believe is unprecedented in its comprehensive scope. The report breaks American journalism into eight sectors—newspapers, magazines, network television, cable television, local television, the Internet, radio, and ethnic and alternative media (which are distinct from each other).

For each of the media sectors, we tried to answer basic questions in six areas: the trends in content, audience, economics, ownership, newsroom investment and public attitudes. We aggregated as much publicly available data as is possible in one place and, for six of the sectors, also conducted an original content analysis. (For local television news, we relied on five years of content analysis the Project had previously conducted. For radio, ethnic and alternative media, no special content analysis was conducted.)

The study is the work of the Project for Excellence in Journalism, an institute affiliated with Columbia University Graduate School of Journalism. The study is funded by the Pew Charitable Trusts, whose leadership challenged us to take on this assignment. The chapters were written, with the exceptions of those on network television, cable, and newspapers, which had co-authors, by the Project's staff.

Our aim is for this to be a research report, not an argument. It is not our intention to try to persuade anyone to a particular point of view. Where the facts are clear, we hope we have not shied from explaining what they reveal, making clear what is proven versus what is only suggested. We hope, however, that we are not seen as simply taking sides in any journalistic debates.

We have tried to be as transparent as possible about sources and methods, and to make it clear when we are laying out data versus when we have moved into analysis of that data. We believe our approach of looking at a set of questions across various media differs from the conventional way in which American journalism is analyzed, one medium at a time.

We have tried to identify cross-media trends and to gather in one place data that are usually scattered across different venues. We hope this will allow us and others to make comparisons and develop insights that otherwise would be difficult to see. Across the six questions we examined we found some distinct patterns.

Content

The proliferation of new outlets and the increasingly instantaneous nature of newsgathering are creating three basic trends in the content of American journalism.

First, the content is more diverse. Network news, news magazines, and newspaper front pages carry a wider range of topics. But a good deal of the new diversity is in lighter fare—lifestyle, entertainment, consumer news—rather than news about diverse communities or populations. Some outlets are thriving as they reject the trend toward that lighter content. The success of NPR in radio, The Economist among magazines and The New York Times among newspapers suggest the possible rise of a growing elite niche across media sectors.

Second, as more outlets split up the audience and create more competition, financial pressures have led cable and broadcast to devote more of their news holes to branding efforts such as promotions and teases, and more commercials.

Third, to vie for audience in a more crowded 24-hour news environment, there is more pressure to run with stories more quickly—to get, as mentioned above, newsgathering in the raw, and to cover ad nauseam a few big blockbuster stories since it is cost efficient

Cable news channels have largely abandoned the traditional story-telling of written and edited packages in favor of live interviews and reporter stand-ups. This unscripted, extemporaneous approach to reporting does not lend itself to producing content that will move to the Web or that will survive beyond the moment. What is more, if the purpose behind the emphasis on live reports is to offer the most up-to-date information, the content often comes up short. News on cable, and on the Internet as well, is heavily repetitive.

The cable channels in the main follow a handful of stories each day on a fairly narrow range of topics, leaving the larger part of the news menu to anchor reads and the screen crawl.

At the risk of oversimplification, newspapers, the oldest medium, continue to have the strongest content, if for no other reason than that they still tend to have the most reporters. This also gives them an advantage in the transition to the Internet, at least for now, because the Web for the moment remains largely a text-based medium.

News Web sites on the whole are more like newspapers in their content and in their news agenda.

In news magazines hard news topics are losing space, while more is going to lifestyle matters like personal finance and diet. These are not strictly news magazines anymore so much as weekly general interest publications. Meanwhile, the growth in magazine titles is occurring in niche specialty publications about such topics as mountain biking and doll collecting.

Economics

For all the trouble with audiences, the economics of journalism in general are remarkably strong.

In the older media sectors, profitability remains robust. Newspapers made around a 20 percent profit in 2003. Local television news stations make roughly double that. Radio news, too, is a significant contributor to the bottom line for its owners, representing about 11 percent of the revenues of major radio companies.

Network television news is still a big revenue engine and in the late 1990s was perhaps the most reliably profitable part of the network television business, ahead of entertainment. But major news events like the war in Iraq cost so much to cover, network insiders say privately, that they whittled down profitability in 2003.

How can revenues be up for these media where audiences are down? In an era of fragmentation, these media continue to stand out as among the few places where advertisers can still attract a crowd. It may not be as big a crowd as it once was, but attracting any crowd has become harder.

Yet as other sectors attract more of the audience, they are attracting more and more advertising. Ad revenues for Spanish-language newspapers, for instance, have increased sevenfold between 1990 and 2001, from $111 million to $786 million, according to figures from the Latino Print Network.

The Internet, in turn, began to turn the corner on profitability in 2003, though the medium still relies largely on old media for its content and in many instances much of its costs. The overall profit numbers are small compared with traditional media, and some major Web sites are still not breaking even. Nonetheless, profits are growing at huge rates. If that continues, in a few years they will be significant contributors to company coffers.

What is less clear, however, is what economic model will work online. Will it be advertising based (like television), subscription based or some combination, and will those profits ever be enough to subsidize the kind of news gathering that newspapers and television did in their heyday. If the Internet is profitable, but not as profitable as old media, the result may be fewer resources for gathering news, spread over more outlets.

Ownership

As audiences fragment across more outlets, the corporate response has been to get bigger in order to deliver the audience for advertisers not in one place but under one corporate roof.

The effect of this on journalism is not as simple as the traditional arguments about consolidation might suggest. Critics have decried declining diversity of ownership and the rise of chains in media for 70 years. But the trend continues anyway.

Over the years, the Supreme Court has repeatedly upheld a core principle: out of a diversity of viewpoints, we are more likely to know the truth. Yet we are moving in conflicting directions where we have more outlets for news but fewer owners.

Bigness may give a company the means to provide high quality journalism, but it doesn't guarantee it. Bigness may also simply make journalism a less and less important part of a company's entertainment media portfolio and move it farther away from being a public trust.

As of 2004 here are the facts: In newspapers, 22 companies now represent 70 percent of the daily circulation (73 percent on Sunday), according to data from Editor and Publisher. In radio, the top 20 companies operate more than 20 percent of all the radio stations in the country; one, Clear Channel, dominates, operating stations in 191 of the 289 Arbitron-rated markets. In local television, the 10 biggest companies own 30 percent of all television stations reaching 85 percent of all television households in the United States. In network television, the owners are all giant corporations for whom television, let alone television journalism, represents only a small part of their revenues, less than 30 percent.

In magazines, while there has been consolidation, it is not on the same level as in other media. Many of the big players may be unfamiliar names to most readers of this report, and only four of the top ten magazine companies—Time Warner, Hearst, Advance and Primedia—are among the 25 largest media companies overall.

Online, big companies also prevail, at least when it comes to traffic as measured in aggregate by Nielsen and other ratings monitors. Today, more than half of the 20 most popular news Web sites are owned by one of the 20 biggest media companies. Yet it might be more accurate to say that there will always be two Internet worlds, one controlled by giant companies able to amass large audiences to a few Web sites, and the other populated by the world of citizen bloggers or niche web sites, where much of the innovation and energy may come from.

News Investment

Overall, the numbers reveal general declines in how much is invested in newsgathering in American journalism.

Newspapers today have about 2,200 fewer full-time professional newsroom employees than they did in 1990, according to data from the American Society of Newspaper Editors. Interpreting that decline is complicated. First the number of papers has declined. On the other hand, work once done by printers and composing room workers has migrated to the newsroom, adding more jobs in the newsroom related to production rather than newsgathering.

In network news, the number of correspondents since the 1980s has been cut by a third, according to data from Professor Joe Foote at Arizona State University. Correspondent workload has increased by 30 percent, according to Foote, and the number of foreign bureaus, our accounting finds, is down by half.

In local television, the Project's surveys suggest that the average workload increased 20 percent from 1998 to 2002. Fully 59 percent of news directors reported either budget cuts or staff cuts in 2002.

In radio, from 1994 through 2001, the number of full-time radio newsroom employees declined 44 percent and part-time employees declined 71 percent, according to survey data compiled by Professor Robert Papper of Ball State University.

In cable, only Fox appears to be building its news staff, but that is on a relatively small base.

In news magazines in the past 20 years, Time has reduced its staff by 15 percent and Newsweek by a full 50 percent, according to staff boxes published in the magazines. There has without question been some shuffling of names and job titles in these staff boxes. Nevertheless, overall declines are clearly evident. The number of listed foreign bureaus at the major news magazines also has fallen, by 27 percent at Time and 31 percent at Newsweek.

Online, the investment in newsgathering is growing, but for now much of the content is subsidized by the old media. These facts suggest a difficult environment—more pressure on people, less time to report stories and more reliance on technology, syndicated material and synthesizing second-hand information.

Some of these changes reflect more efficiency created by new technology and companies eliminating waste. Some of the investment in technology, moreover, is inevitable and necessary for modernization. In local television, the government has mandated the transition to fully digital technology within two years. But, technology can also be used to replace the newsgathering skills, homogenize the content, rely more on feed material and wires, which is cheaper than local or original reporting. It is difficult to see how news organizations can distinguish themselves and attract more audience in a more crowded environment if their content is more similar. There is a tendency for branding to be more focused around the style than the substance of reporting.

Conclusion

The larger trends we see in the data on content, audience, economics, ownership, and newsroom investment all could add to public distrust of the news media. There is something, in other words, of a vicious cycle in the public attitude data. As declining audience leads to newsroom cutbacks and other financial fixes, these reinforce the public's suspicions that news organizations are motivated more by economics than public service.

There is little sense in 2004 of a quick or simple way out. Some news organizations have clearly tried to respond, with efforts like civic journalism, or credibility initiatives by editors groups, or ethics training by television news directors groups, or attempts by news organizations to be more responsive to the public by inviting them into the newsroom.

These steps seem to address the problem, at least in small ways, that newsrooms can control. Yet they have not shown up in the numbers. Indeed, there is only one up-tick in the last 18 years in the general approval or attitudes toward the news media, in the survey data. That came in November 2001, after the terrorist attacks.[1] The only measurable differences in press performance during that period were these: the press had suddenly become far more serious in what it covered, and more factual and less interpretative in the way it covered it; the media suddenly devoted enormous resources to covering a story of paramount importance even if it cost them money; as a nation we faced a crisis that made the need for journalism more urgent.[2]

Those changes in news agenda, though, were not sustained. Within a few months, as the urgency of events subsided, studies found virtually no difference in the local news agenda and only a partial change in the agenda of nightly network news than before September 11.[3] And by August 2002, Pew Center Surveys found the rise in trust to have fallen back.[4]

It is possible that the public is simply of two minds. It wants a more entertainment-infused, more sensationalized, more interpretative style of news, and the media have given it to them. The public then feels repulsed and derides the messenger for delivering it.

It is also possible that this declining trust has only a little to do with the press, that these attitudes toward the news media are only a reflection of a declining trust in all institutions.

Brushing off these issues as a sign of public hypocrisy or general skepticism, however, seems too glib. The public attitudes aside, something is changing in the news media. Faced with declining audiences, many major news institutions have changed their product in a way that costs less to produce while still attracting an audience. The public senses this and says it doesn't like it.

Blaming the news media for these changes is too easy. Journalism faces more difficult economic circumstances than it once did. Yet the way the news industry responded has helped erode public trust. How long can the profession of journalism endure if people increasingly don't believe it? To reverse the slide in audience and trust will probably take a major change in press behavior, one that will make the news more relevant and customizable and at the same time suggest to the public, as it did briefly after September 11, that the news industry is more concerned with the public good than Americans suspect.

POSTSCRIPT

Is Economics the Bottom Line in the Newsrooms of Today?

The focus of these selections is on the different sources of change in the media news production business. Although "firewalls" are supposed to exist between the advertising and editorial sides, the effect of operating within a profit-oriented firm cannot be so simply solved. Nor can the power of journalistic socialization and practice be dismissed.

Often these clash, and the conflicts can be played out in the public eye. Journalists note the closing of news bureaus around the world. They decry the use of journalistic pools for coverage. The broadcast news industry points to the ratings of its news programs to support their news decisions—decisions that critics argue focus more on the entertainment value of news than on the important issues of our time. Journalists fondly consider an earlier time when news was supported, when cost didn't count, and when news, not entertainment, ruled the airwaves. Media businesses observe the increasing fragmentation of the market with cable channels and the Internet. They point to the demise of hundreds of local papers, when the marketplace would no longer support rival companies in the same market.

The answers are not easy. These writers concede the importance of both economic and journalistic power. They differ on where ultimate power resides. At the level of everyday reality, neither of these may be visible to the participants. A young journalist comes into the newsroom ready to take on the world; he or she quickly learns to make cogent arguments for his or her ideas and to pay their dues by covering whatever is assigned, learning from the copy editor, and being mentored by the old hands. The old hand is trying to find the time to cover the story that he or she finds of most interest. The section editors are vying for page space and reporter resources. The editor is trying be sure that all sections of the paper are excellent, and that the needs of the consumer are being met. And the publisher is trying to juggle resources to accomplish his or her goals, as well as those of the editor. (And that's on a good day!)

Judgement about the standards of media accountability or about the allocation of scarce resources within a business organization can seem distant in the harried newsroom. Yet practice and profit will be judged in any media organization. What then are the standards that should be applied to the practices of a media organization? What are the obligations that rights incur?

Since the FCC began lifting ownership restrictions, questions of whether money drives news, or whether news drives news, have been central topics for media professionals. Many inherently understand that our media institutions cannot exist if they, or some aspect of their corporate structures, are not profitable, but at the same time news fills a very important function for our understanding of daily life. In earlier days, it was never assumed that the news divisions of broadcast operations could make money, but since all major media organizations now often have news run by their entertainment divisions, the balance has changed. As we continue to see ownership issues and organizational structures change and evolve, we need to ask important questions about how these changes affect what we see and hear, and even more importantly, whether what we see and hear is enough to help us understand the world in which we live

ISSUE 15

Do the Media Introduce Us to New Ways of Thinking About Things?

YES: James Wolcott, "The Laptop Brigade," *Vanity Fair* (April, 2004)

NO: Jesse Sunenblick, "Little Murders," *Columbia Journalism Review* (January/February, 2004)

ISSUE SUMMARY

YES: Author James Wolcott examines the world of web logs (blogs) and calls them the "most vivifying, talent-swapping, socializing breakthrough in popular journalism..." As the newest form of journalistic speech, he sees the exchange of ideas as a backlash to the commercialism of traditional media, and he applauds the blog form as the best thing to happen to print journalism since the 18th century.

NO: Jesse Sunenblick criticizes traditional print media for becoming so conservative, and discusses the plight of the editorial illustrator, who, today, can't sell truly innovative, creative artwork because the owners of print media want non-offensive images that encourage audiences not to think or question the content of images.

The two selections in this issue ask readers to think about several questions. One series of questions deals with the changes in styles and forms of journalism—are traditional forms becoming obsolete? If they are not fading into obscurity, can we examine where the changes are taking place, and therefore have a sense of where the field is going in the future? Another series of questions focus on more basic issues. How do new forms of media evolve? How do audiences begin to use new forms, and in what ways do new forms challenge old assumptions about how media reflects and relates to society?

The question posed in this issue deals with how older forms of media adapt to change, and how new forms of media eventually become used for new purposes. To think about this issue, we could recall two statements by a popular media theorist from the 1960s, Marshall McLuhan; who wrote in his book *Understanding Media* (1964), that "all media is invented before we have a reason to use it," and, "the content of new media is that of old media." With McLuhan's warnings and Wolcott and Sunenblick's evidence, we can examine the current state of traditional print versus an emerging form, and critically evaluate the print industries at this time in history.

Wolcott's excitement about the use of blogs chronicles the evolution of personal communication over the Internet, and shows how any individual can express their points of view through the blog form. While he agrees that many blogs, especially in early stages of the form were "yapping" or a "refuge for nose-picking narcissists," he feels that as the form has developed, a new area for personal discourse has emerged that is highly democratic in nature. He also thinks blogs are increasingly effective as a means of giving individual citizens an opportunity to affect real political change through expressing views that mainstream media would never touch. As a challenge to traditional print journalism, blogs may well provide different voices that otherwise, could or would not be heard.

Sunenblick shares concerns that traditional print media have become too conservative, and criticizes mainstream print media for editorial choices that restrict controversial, new ideas. Citing massive censoring of editorial cartoons and artwork, Sunenblick bemoans the state of traditional print media and questions print forms that actually restrict new ideas or help the reader/viewer think about the nuances and subtleties of images.

It would be naïve to say that traditional print media have become passé, and that the only creative forms today are those offered by thoughtful individuals using the Internet for more direct communication—but there is a seed of truth to this statement. All forms of media change and evolve over time, but to paraphrase McLuhan's statements, it takes time for a new medium to evolve and be used for purposes other than that for which it was developed. When new, creative content is found, it often comes from an earlier form of media—in the case of blogging, we might be returning to the age of political discourse that was intensely personal, and persuasive. When we consider the fate of the editorial cartoon in traditional print media, we can see that the power the image once held, may not be in as widely distributed form as it once was.

As you read these selections, consider other popular forms of expression that also were intended to be persuasive. You might think about comic books, different styles of journalism (muckraking, alternative journalism, civic journalism), news magazine programs, or even infomercials! Over time, have they changed? If so, what elements (ownership restrictions, changing political climate, access to the forms) have influenced the media industries and the businesses that have supported their growth and development?

James Wolcott  **YES**

The Laptop Brigade

Are we in danger of drowning in blogorrhea? Of being swamped like Bob Hope and Jackie Gleason at the end of *How to Commit Marriage* in chin-high sludge? Only a few years ago blogs—short for Web logs, frequently updated journals that source other blogs and Web sites—were tiny blips on the computer screen, aquarium bubbles. Back then the buzz generators were nicely bankrolled online magazines such as *Salon, Slate, Nerve* (moody erotics for horny neurotics), and the now defunct *Inside*—many of whose contributors exuded cachet—and bare-bones rap sheets for news junkies such as Romenesko and the Drudge Report. Although a few "real writers"—such as Andrew Sullivan, the former editor of *The New Republic*, Mickey Kaus, also formerly of *The New Republic*, and Virginia Postrel, author of *The Future and Its Enemies*—opened blog hangouts, bloggers tended to be lumped in the amateur division and relegated to the drafty basement. Most were considered harmless hobbyists, like ham-radio operators and model-train enthusiasts, or personal diarists doodling on the laptop, hoping someday to get laid.

In a January 2004 edition of *Meet the Press*, journalist Roger Simon, a panelist on Tim Russert's political roundtable, voiced this attitude when he defined blogs for the Rip van Winkles in the audience. "Look, a true blog is 'I woke up this morning, I decided to skip chem class, now I want to write about the last episode of *Friends*.' That's what blogs are. You know, it's people talking to each other." Yapping, he made it sound like, which of course it often is. Nevertheless, Simon tripped over his mustache with his chem-class crack. His notion of a blog is as outdated as a Jack Carter comedy routine about kids today and their wiggy gyrations. Far from being a refuge for nose-picking narcissists, blogs have speedily matured into the most vivifying, talent-swapping, socializing breakthrough in popular journalism since the burst of coffeehouse periodicals and political pamphleteering in the 18th century, when *The Spectator, The Tatler*, and sundry other sheets liberated writing from literary patronage. If Addison and Steele, the editors of *The Spectator* and *The Tatler*, were alive and holding court at Starbucks, they'd be Wi-Fi-ing into a joint blog. If Tom Paine were alive and paroled, he'd be blog-jamming against the Patriot Act, whose very name he'd find obscene.

Papers like The Tatler *and* The Spectator *were written to be talked about. The essays enter a cultural debate that was highly oral and social rather than textual and academic, and coffeehouses were the chief sites of this debate....Coffeehouses were crucial arenas for the formation and expression of public opinion about plays and poetry, politics and finance, dress and manners.*
—From Erin Mackie's introduction to
*The Commerce of Everyday Life: Selections
from* The Tatler *and* The Spectator.

Blogs aren't written to be talked about, they're written to be written about. Conversation takes place on the screen, poppy fields of densely packed words issuing as far as the eye can scroll. Every variety and flavor of interest, enthusiasm, furtive itch, and crazed addiction breeds a squalling litter of blogs: nature blogs, fiction blogs, poetry blogs, fashion blogs, media blogs, music blogs, tech blogs, porn blogs, pet blogs, photography blogs, weather blogs, regional blogs, blogs that blog other blogs (such as Sully Watch, which applies a magnifying glass to Andrew Sullivan's performing-flea antics). Off-line magazines have their own online blogs, such as *The American Prospect's* Tapped (Matthew Yglesias's pithy summaries of weekend op-eds—"*George Will.* It's almost as if the president isn't very smart or something"—are a must-read), *The New Republic's* &c. column, and Gregg Easterbrook's Easterblogg, which nearly blew itself up in the cockpit when Easterbrook lambasted Miramax's Harvey Weinstein and Disney's Michael Eisner for behaving like money-hungry Jews in foisting Quentin Tarantino's ultra-violent *Kill Bill* on the culture—Easterbrook had some splainin' to do for that little outburst.

The poet Philip Larkin envisioned death as a void state of disconnection—nothing to think with, nothing to link with—and in the blogosphere thinking and linking are also co-dependent verbs. No blog can be an island entire unto itself. Visitors vote with their mouse clicks, and the vitality of a blog site derives from the rising number of hits it receives—the return visits. The higher the hit count, the heavier the hit traffic; the heavier the hit traffic, the larger the popularity; the larger the popularity, the greater the love. This is why there is no graver act than to remove a site from one's blog roll, eliminating the link. It can be a haughty kiss-off or a sad rebuke; either way, it's public notice that you no longer wish to be associated with this louse. By thy links they shall know thee, and the fact that neo-liberal blogger Mickey Kaus (Kausfiles at *Slate*) links to both Lucianne Goldberg, the right-wing Broom-Hilda of Monica Lewinsky infamy, whose comments section teems like a cauldron with racist, homophobic hate speech, and Ann Coulter, the She-Wolf of Sigma Chi, is evidence to his foes not of the Mickster's catholicity but of his scaly lizardry.

Just as 18th-century periodicals were often organs of the Whig and Tory Parties, blog sites cluster according to political outlooks. Internet space may appear to be an expanding universe of uncharted dimensions with no fixed center or hitching post, but a brain scan of the blogosphere would reveal the same hemispheric divide between left and right that prevails in the flesh realm. Not that there isn't some friendly fraternization. The Talking Points Memo blog of Joshua Micah Marshall, a journalist for the *Washington Monthly* and *The Hill*, is respected on both sides of the junction. Tacitus, a moderate-conservative blogger (that is, sane), is blog-rolled on some liberal sites. Sharing an opposition to the Sousa march of the American Empire, libertarian bloggers such as Lew Rockwell link to articles by anti-imperialistic lefties at Alexander Cockburn's Counterpunch site. But mostly liberals and conservatives congregate at their own tables in the cafeteria and shoot straw wrappers at each other, dirty looks. Sit them at the same table and huffiness can ensue.

On the January weekend before the New Hampshire primary, the Blogging of the President site—BOP, as it's more familiarly known—hosted a panel discussion about blogging, the Howard Dean phenomenon, and participatory democracy in the Internet Age that was broadcast on public-radio stations across the country. The BOP site is a group blog featuring one of the most cerebral, provocative, history-enriched ongoing symposia to be found on the Web. Its mainstays include Jay Rosen, Stirling Newberry, and Christopher Lydon, who are to political blogdom what Samuel Johnson and his fellow members of the Club were to London, only without the port and cold mutton. To bridge the hemispheric split, BOP invited a number of the leading bloggers from both left and right to join the jawfest, including Josh Marshall, Jeff Jarvis, Andrew Sullivan, and a mystery man who goes by the handle Atrios.

Bad blood simmered between the last two. Atrios once posted an open letter to *Salon* on his blog, Eschaton, deploring its hiring of Andycakes to whack out a weekly column on liberal idiocy. "I have a hard time believing that people are really going to pay to read essentially the same drivel—'LIBERALS STUPID AND BAD AND TREASONOUS'—that they can read for free over in his own little sandbox." For more than an hour the BOP confab was cordial, civilized, and nonconfrontational; then Sullivan, whom I picture biding his time and biting his lip, struck. He accused Atrios of hiding behind anonymity to lob garbage. "You attack personally but can't be attacked because no one knows who you are!," Sullivan complained. Take off your *Phantom of the Opera* mask, fiend! "I just choose to keep my personal and professional life separate," Atrios replied.

It wasn't exactly a rematch of the Norman Mailer–versus–Gore Vidal clash of titans on *The Dick Cavett Show*, but the issue percolated, coming to a boil with an article on *Salon* a week later. The author, Christopher Farah, lit into the whole pirate crew of "anonybloggers"—Josh Freelantzovitzes who get their rude jollies pumping raw sewage into the Internet about professional byliners whose jobs they probably covet. These masked marauders "have made names for themselves by having no names at all and by using the safety and security of their secret identities to spread gossip, make accusations and levy the most vicious of insults with impunity," Farah wrote. He cited Media Whores Online, as a major environmental polluter, and a mediasatire blog called the Minor Fall, the Major Lift. But public enemy No. 1 again was Atrios, whose graffiti slurs included calling Nicholas Kristof of *The New York Times* "human scum," and publishing an e-mail reputedly from a maid named Maria who claimed President Bush had taken cruel sexual advantage of her. Farah failed to register that the maid's woeful tale of seduction and betrayal was a parody of the *National Review Online's* house blog, which had been running anonymous e-mails from readers accusing John Kerry of unsubstantiated assaults on human decency, such as *trying to cut into line*. (Punk'd, *Salon* quickly edited that goof from the text, sparing Farah further embarrassment.) Feeling vindicated, Andrew Sullivan gave the article a hearty Cornfield County salute: "Anonyblogger Atrios recently called the New York Times' Nick Kristof 'human scum.' Welcome to the pond, Nick! Of course, Atrios is immune from personal attacks because he's anonymous."

The Farah article really got the frogs hopping in Bloggyville. Jonah Goldberg of *N.R.O.* sympathized with the anti-agonybloggers. He, too, had been taunted by strange kids on the playground. Pro-Atrios posters pointed out that Atrios isn't anonymous, but pseudonymous, a crucial distinction. There are practical reasons to deploy the secret identity of a pseud. Bloggers risk losing their jobs by posting under their real names, even if the blog isn't work-related. Adopting a pseud can also open up unexplored sides of a writer's persona, much as online role-playing does on game sites and in sex chat rooms. Online, reputation accrues much as it does in print. The blogger has blog cred to preserve and protect, and an inaccurate or bogus-arguing blogger faces backlash however faceless the blogger himself/herself may be. Most important, pseudonyms have a long, respectable history in pamphleteering, journalism, and fiction. The Federalist Papers were authored under the name Publius. Janet Flanner covered Paris for *The New Yorker* under the name Genêt. *The New Republic's* TRB column was written for decades by Richard L. Strout of *The Christian Science Monitor*. Philip Larkin wrote schoolgirl porn under the lesbian disguise of Brunette Coleman. (O.K., maybe not the best example.) And I would add, based on my own subjective impressions, the reason Andrew Sullivan attracts so many personal attacks isn't that he's recognizable and his attackers aren't, but that he makes it so easy and *fun*. He's like a bad tenor begging to be pelted with fresh produce.

On the surface the battle between Andy and Atrios is a minor spat between a drama queen and a shrinking violet, but it has deeper ripples. That Sullivan, a well-known byliner, television pundit, and former Gap model, felt impelled to pick a fight with a lesser-known blogger was a sign of insecurity—shaky status. It signifies the shift of influence and punch-power in the blogosphere from the right to the left. It is Atrios, not Andrew Sullivan, who is in ascendance in the blogosphere. Only a few years ago the energy and passion were largely the property of the right hemisphere, where Sullivan, Glenn "Instapundit" Reynolds, and *N.R.O.*'s Victor Davis Hanson fired up the neurons against the defeatism, anti-Americanism, and death's-head specter of Islamic terrorism billowing from the ruins of Ground Zero. Each morning, after subjecting myself to the depresso news in the daily papers and wishing I had a rabbit hole to dive into, I'd frequent these blogs for morale uplift, mentally applauding their jeers at matchstick figures on the left such as Susan Sontag, Noam Chomsky, and Edward Said (sentiments I'm ashamed of now), and saluting their bugle calls as the U.S. geared up to topple the Taliban. (Like millions of Americans, I lead a very active vicarious life—I get around a lot inside my head.) But I parted sympathies with the bugle boys when they repositioned their bombsights for Iraq. Honest, confused souls could disagree over the case for overthrowing Saddam Hussein. It was the ugly rhetoric, fathead hubris, and might-makes-right triumphalism that repulsed. Warbloggers hunkered into B-grade versions of the ideological buccaneers in the neoconservative camp. Punk-ass laptop Richard Perles, they excoriated dissenters as wimps, appeasers, and traitors, peddled every xenophobic stereotype (the French as "cheese-eating surrender monkeys," etc.), and brushed aside the plight of the Palestinians with brusque indifference or outright contempt. And the warbloggers behaved like they owned the legacy and sorrow of September 11, as if only they understood How Everything Changed and those who disagreed had goldfish bowls on their heads. "For the Clintonites, 9/11 didn't really happen," Sullivan preposterously claimed as recently as January 2004. When I stray into these sites now, it's like entering the visitors' center of a historical landmark. The rhododendrons need dusting, and the tour guide isn't listening to himself, having done his spiel endless times before.

Liberal blogs are now where the bonfires blaze. They set the tempo, push the debate, and crack the best jokes. TBogg, for example, with his continuing saga about America's Worst Mother and her four children, Leona, Hibiscus, Mandalay, and Grunion (the brats' names change with each installment). Atrios's Eschaton is a major stomping ground for anti-Bush information and anti-warblog humor. Josh Marshall's Talking Points Memo has always been essential, but over the last year he has surpassed himself with brilliant running analyses of the Valerie Plame scandal, lengthy Q&As with Wesley Clark and George Soros, and detective work on Bush's sketchy National Guard service (about which Kevin Drum at Calpundit has also done superb Sherlock Holmes sleuthing). Middle East scholar Juan Cole's blog has established itself as the go-to site for informed, incisive interpretations and info on what's unraveling in Iraq and the rest of the region. Economist Brad DeLong, when not defending Paul Krugman against his nitpickers, is the Harold Bloom of data crunching, finding secret harmonies hidden in the numbers. Bob Somerby blows his tiny ration of cool regularly at the Daily Howler, documenting the lies, flip exaggerations, and smarmy chumminess of the dominant media— their cackling incompetence. During the early Democratic primary contests, Al Giordano, who blogs out of South America for BOP and his own site, Big, Left, Outside, enjoyed the hottest streak of almost any handicapper, the first to hear John Kerry's hulking footsteps about to overtake Howard Dean.

Gracious in victory, Giordano gave a nod to Daily Kos, the blog site that had been a powerful transmitter of the Dean message. "My olive branch, and authentic praise, to a guy who dressed himself in glory," began Giordano's tribute to the namesake host of the Daily Kos. After Dean lost New Hampshire, Kos conceded that the Dean cause itself was probably lost. "I doubt that all my friends and readers here can understand how painful and hard that it was for Kos to admit. But, in the end, he chose truth over illusion. And I predict...that the Daily Kos will continue as the top blog on the Internet, as we pull on the Court Appointed President's arms and legs and quarter him in the months to come." Kos, the newly crowned king of Blogistan!

Who he?, as Harold Ross might ask. Kos is the army nickname of Markos Moulitsas Zuniga, who was born in Chicago in 1971 and raised in El Salvador, returning to the U.S. when his family fled that country's civil war. After high school, he enlisted in the army and was stationed in Germany, an artillery guy. After earning two bachelor's degrees, he moved to San Francisco and started Daily Kos in 2002. In those days of misty watercolor memories it took Daily Kos a month to get the number of hits that it now racks up in a day. The blog quickly differentiated itself from the gaggle. "I pounded my niche," he says, covering politics as an archipelago of anthills with his readers filing ant reports from the various colonies. It was political coverage from a bustling bottom-up perspective rather than a pundit's Olympian perch. Daily Kos's first spike in hitsville came during the summer of the 2002 midterm elections, when it provided exhaustive state-by-state breakdowns of each race. It was inside baseball with outsiders' enthusiasm—electoral sabermetrics. The second "huge spike," according to Kos, came during the buildup to the Iraq war, which Kos opposed. A military veteran, he couldn't be accused of being a weenie peacenik, and Daily Kos, along with antiwar.com and others, magnetized the Web opposition. The number of hits jumped from 20,000 a day to 100,000 plus. Kos and his partner, Jerome Armstrong, mapped out the online strategy of the Howard Dean campaign, which, whatever the spinout of Dean's candidacy, demonstrated blogging's efficacy as a fund-raising and enlistment tool. Kos's latest brainstorm is to use the blogosphere as a "farm system" to fund and groom the next wave of liberal writers and pundits, a counterforce to the conservative-think-tank infrastructure and its modeling academies, where juicy novices master the Ann Coulter Hair Toss and special tanning secrets.

From the outset Daily Kos was devised as a choral suite rather than a solitary squawk box. "Without the community, I wouldn't be anything," Kos says. He opened up the main column to some of the best posters from the comments section, and set up a diaries section for posters—blogs within his blog. Some of the most talented Daily Kossacks splintered off to start blogs of their own, listed on the Kos's blog roll under "Alumni." "The meritocracy of the blogosphere appeals I to me," Kos says. Age, race, sexual persuasion, wardrobe choices—none of these signify online, where no one knows what you, look like unless you post pictures of yourself with your cats. One Daily Kos grad is Steve Gilliard, a dynamo blogger whose posts about the insurgency in Iraq were more scarily prophetic than anything blathered by the military experts on cable news. It was Gilliard who threw down the dueling glove at the mainstream press which, he said, holds people accountable but freaks all over the car lot when accountability is expected of them. "I think it would be a really, really good idea to track reporters word for word, broadcast for broadcast, and print the results online," Gilliard proposed. "Keeping score of who's right and wrong, how many times they repeat cannards [sic] like Al Gore invented the internet and make obvious errors. Not accusations of ideology, but actual data and facts." It'll buggeth the journalists mightily, but it's also doing the press a favor. "If someone had actually checked Jayson Blair's work, the Times might have fired his ass years earlier." Gilliard's proposal has become more popularly known as the Adopt a Journalist program, debated and discussed on BOP, NPR's *On the Media*, and elsewhere. Al Giordano sees it as a stealthy insurrection: "The Internet, like Kerry, sneaks up on the frontrunner, Commercial Media, without letting its footsteps be heard, while it gets written off and underestimated by the very forces that seem to be in charge."

What the Adopt a Journalist program symptomizes is how fed up so many smart, informed, impassioned Internet newshounds are, how unwilling they are to play bystander and watch the media make another monster mash of the presidential election, as they did in 2000, or help stampede us into another misguided war. "Why Oh Why Can't We Have a Better Press Corps?" wails Brad DeLong on a regular basis on his site, and it's a question that resonates across the blogosphere. Because the press seems incorrigible. Paul Krugman writes a *Times* column urging political reporters not to repeat the gauche frivolity of 2000, driveling on about earth tones and alpha males, and what's happened so far? Bright chatter about Wesley Clark's sweaters and long eyelashes (really!—Jacob Weisberg of *Slate* found them a fetching detail), maunderings about Howard Dean's wife by such happy homemakers as Sally Quinn and Maureen Dowd, and much speculation about Botox deposits in craggy visages. Patti Smith's war cry about rock 'n' roll was "We created it—let's take it over." Journalism can't and shouldn't be taken over by bloggers, but they can take away some of the toys, and pull down the thrones.

Jesse Sunenblick

Little Murders

When Howell Raines quit *The New York Times,* Jerelle Kraus publicly called him Caligula, because he chopped off people's heads before they got to speak. Now she is telling me how Raines saw penises everywhere, in the most innocent, ridiculous places, making her job as op-ed art director difficult. "Nobody else would see it, but he would see it," she tells me, "and then I'd have to change it." What she remembers is a pencil. A Janusz Kapusta illustration of a round-erasered pencil, signing a peace treaty, which she had to square off, in 1993, because of Caligula. "Get it?" she says. "A round-erasered pencil?" I got it.

It was hard enough defending imagery that confronted religion or politics or race; to be on the lookout for accidental phalli was just another reminder of how far op-ed had fallen. Kraus knew better than anyone. No other art director had lasted more than roughly two years but she lasted thirteen years all told, 1979 to 1989 and 1993 to 1996, each year, in her view, more watered down than the last.

She was an artists' advocate up until the day Raines dropped her from op-ed in 1996. But you don't understand, Kraus would sometimes say, ugly is beautiful. Once an illustrator was on the other side of a doorway and he heard her fight for his piece, and he said to her, My God, I have never heard someone defend my work like that. How could Kraus tell an editor in the '90s that in the '70s and '80s ugly had been permissible on op-ed? Or that back then, editors actually believed artists inspired them?

Kraus is now art director of the Weekend sections and the Arts & Ideas section, a job she was happy to take. And op-ed is some other thing. When she looks at it, she can't help thinking rather morosely that her career maps out the decline. "I was able to do my job for a long time," she says. "I wanted metaphors. I wanted ideas. If the image repeats the words why run the story? The page has completely deteriorated, in terms of drawing. Things change, the world changes, but I get so many calls from artists who complain about how bad the art is, bad draftsmanship, pieces that don't have any substance."

A number of top illustrators told me the same thing: *All the heavy thinkers are gone. All the big ideas diminished. Not just pencils but anything requiring the slightest abstraction of thought.* Not just at the *Times,* they said, but all over the place; it was endemic. Opinion art was reduced to display. Cheap irony prevailed. A generation of artists had internalized the new parameters of the offense-o-meter. As Christoph Niemann, a frequent *Times* contributor, put it: "When I work for the *Times* on a constant basis, I don't even suggest certain ideas any more. Of course, you want to get your image printed."

It was funny, in a sense, to hear censorship complaints from a field that had all but been pronounced dead in the first place. Illustration has supposedly been killed off three times over the years, by photography, by television, and most recently by the computer. Illustrators survive on ten-year-old pay rates. I fought the feeling that these artists were irrelevant. But there is something timeless about pairing images with words, they told me, and they believe in it.

They also know that time to fight back is running out, which is why in 1999 they convened the first Illustration Conference. It was one thing to confront a new technology, like television; you could react to that, create alternative images. It was enough to worry about how huge caches of homogenous imagery were available to editors cheap over the Internet. But to worry about editors simply not getting it anymore, or being afraid to get it, to worry about the distinct possibility that their own art was considered offensive to the masses, that was dangerous. Some kind of shift had taken place. And so every other year they get together now, and discuss how best to continue doing work that matters.

In 1999 hundreds of illustrators convened in Santa Fe. That year the talk was of staying competitive in a changing marketplace: of avoiding unfair labor contracts that transferred ownership of an image to a newspaper or magazine into perpetuity; of integrating digital techniques into workmanship; of diversifying into children's books or animation. By last summer, at the third Illustration Conference, in Philadelphia, there was an undercurrent of fear. In a panel moderated by Steven Guarnaccia, *The New York Times* op-ed art director and a respected illustrator in his own right, some of the industry's more socially conscious editorial illustrators discussed the difficulties of getting artist-driven ideas published. It's one thing for artists to complain, but another thing entirely for an art director at our paper of record to share frustrations. Guarnaccia, choosing his words carefully, was one of the more vocal critics.

"As often as I can," he said, "I bring up artist-driven ideas. And unfortunately, they come in a trickle these days, partly because we've gotten a reputation for being timid for what we put on the page. Or I will push for a drawing that expresses a stronger idea than just the idea that's already in the piece. And the editors will love it, roll their eyes and say, 'We can never print that.'"

In October I started asking artists for their rejects, the kind of material that they couldn't seem to sell any more, or that had been substantially altered for publication. The examples came in slowly, huge JPEG files that ate up my e-mail space, and anecdotes from artists calling out certain publications for messing with their art. *The Wall Street Journal* for telling an illustrator he could draw a dead lobster for a food column, but he couldn't put the same dead lobster in a tank of hot water. *Business Week* for lobbying to make a pirate figure in an illustration female, although in the history of pirating females are very hard to find. *Rolling Stone* for asking an artist to remove a Gap reference in a Bill and Monica send-up.

When it comes to rejection stories I have an innate distrust of artists, especially illustrators. It is a unique form of torture, having one's ideas adjusted to fit someone else's imperative, and it can't help but breed cynicism. Artists can miss the mark. There is also the matter of individual taste—not all rejected art points to malfeasance—and the neurotic vigilance inherent in all good editors....

Most editorial illustrators work by commission, but in the fall of 2000, in the midst of a seemingly endless election quagmire in Florida, Ward Sutton got a jump on his competition. The author of the syndicated weekly *Sutton Impact* cartoon strip pitched an idea to the op-ed page at *The New York Times*, for a double portrait of the eventual winner, one face looking upward toward a rosy sky, the other looking down, morosely into shadowland, as if to say, yes, I am the victor, but was it really worth it?

The figures were fairly wooden save for two beads of sweat, expressing, said Sutton, "anxiety," on the forehead of the downcast face. Bush won. The *Times* accepted the illustration. It ran December 14, above a column by Richard Brookhiser touting the doggedness that came from "having been a frat boy Republican in the alien environment of late 1960s Yale." It ran, however, without the beads of sweat.

Because the thought of people putting their heads together to decide what to do about sweat seemed simultaneously amusing and significant, I called then-op-ed editor Terry Tang and asked her about it. Most editors are not inclined to discuss such things but she obliged. "The piece was about the ease with which Bush would surprise people who underestimated him," she said. "It wasn't about Bush sweating bullets."

"It ran as an illustration," she continued. "As art that accompanies what is primary, the opinion piece"—a response that implied a kind of literalism that, again, seemed simultaneously amusing and significant.

In the early days of the *Times* op-ed page, it is hard to imagine two beads of sweat causing this much hand-wringing. Created in 1970, the page was the first of its kind, a symbiosis of word and image where neither was subservient, where artists were encouraged to portray the essence of a text as opposed to literal interpretations, where their ideas were as essential as a writer's ideas. The result was opinioned, provocative art, often dark and unsettling, from upstarts like Brad Holland, Roland Topor, and Eugene Mihaesco that today in its audacity seems staggering. For the first anniversary of the Attica prison uprising Brad Holland drew the body of a black man with one arm cut off at the elbow, and in the darkness of night, above the ground where he lay dead, the amputated forearm rose to a clenched fist, the severed fist of black power....

The last renaissance for illustration in America followed the birth of the op-ed page, when magazines like *Esquire, Evergreen,* and *New York,* that catered to the so-called New Journalism, often opted for the kind of surrealist-inspired illustration found in the *Times,* rather than photography. Into the 1980s *Playboy, Rolling Stone,* and *The Atlantic Monthly* featured illustrated covers and used extensive in-text art. Weekend newspaper magazines at places like the Cleveland *Plain Dealer* and *The Boston Globe* won awards from *American Illustration*, an annual of the best of avant-garde art that made its debut in 1982. (Unlike the austere annuals of the Society of Illustrators, a venerable 103-year-old establishment based in New York, *American Illustration* featured a range of young conceptualists who learned from the tradition of the op-ed page.) Into the late 80s, *Time* magazine regularly hired four illustrators each week to compete to do the cover design, and often sent artists on site with writers to capture the essence of a place. Perhaps the most telling signal that illustration mattered could be found in the pages of magazines like *Seventeen*, or *Penthouse*, in which, if you browsed in 1982 you would find—amid the nakedness, the heavenly swoon—some interesting art: a Marshall Arisman illustration of the Reverend Jim Jones, the cult leader, his head and a handgun on a pillow; a Ralph Steadman caricature of Alexander Haig as some long-faced cat dripping blood from its paws; a terrifying Cristobal Toral oil painting of people wrapped like human cargo.

A few mainstays, like *The New Yorker*, remain loyal to illustration, but celebrity-driven photography and photomontage now dominate the covers of magazines that were once illustration-friendly. The rise of the computer and digital imagery, through Adobe Photoshop, has pushed many basic tasks in-house. Stock houses—companies that provide vast caches of homogenous imagery on the cheap, typically over the Internet—offer an easier and cheaper and quicker alternative to inventive illustration. Every month, it seems, magazines are changing their designs to incorporate more photography.

At the Illustration Conference, Milton Glaser, creator of the 'I ♥ New York' logo, gave a keynote speech about the decline. Glaser likes to talk about the death of nuance in general, and over the fall we had a few conversations in which he pointed to television as an instrument that has taken away our ability to form abstract thoughts. Concurrently, he sees a kind of lowering of the individual voice. "The corporate voice has become increasingly wary of individual expression," he told me. "Increasingly, editors want to control the nature of that voice, and conform it to some agreed-upon methodology."

In his speech, Glaser repeated his television mantra and then turned to the differences between photography and illustration. "Photography has another intrinsic characteristic that illustration lacks," he said. "The innate sense of capturing a 'real' moment in time, proving that the subject actually existed." Glaser insinuated that, because of its believability, photography is the best tool for creating consumer desire. "In a culture that values commerce above all other things," he continued, "the imaginative potential of illustration has become irrelevant.... Illustration is now too idiosyncratic." One might go a step further. Idiosyncrasy takes time to unravel. It takes an act of interpretation. There is danger implicit in interpretation. It gives the audience time to think, time to get upset, and, perhaps, to get offended....

The strange case of the collagist Stephen Kroninger underscores this kind of hypersensitivity. Kroninger, who had a solo show at the MoMA in 1992, was asked to do biweekly illustrations for the New York *Daily News*'s Ideas & Opinion page, beginning in the summer of 2001, an assignment that lasted only four months before he pulled out. It was an odd pairing in the first place, given Kroninger's famously acerbic political work. The second piece he did for the *Daily News* was inspired by a Labor Day speech by George Bush. "The slogan was about listening to the people," Kroninger told me. "He was somewhere in the Midwest talking about listening to the heartland, and it was like, yeah, sure, we know who you listen to."

His collage that week was a portrait of Bush with one big ear, for the rich, and one little ear, for the working people, and he lifted the speech's slogan as ironic text: "Listening to the American people." Kroninger sent it in and heard nothing. On Sunday he opened the paper to find someone else's art in its stead. He wasn't surprised. He'd been paid. He shrugged it off.

The next incident came after 9/11, when the Environmental Protection Agency publicly stated that the air quality in downtown Manhattan was fine, when people knew it wasn't fine. (It was later reported that the White House may have pressured the EPA into making such statements.) Kroninger has a friend, the artist Art Spiegelman, whose daughter attends Stuyvesant High School, five blocks from the ruins of the World Trade Center, where classes resumed, some said, too quickly, and where parents were already nervous. "He kept telling me stories about how everybody was saying there was nothing wrong with the air, about how he was trying to get a response from the city, the state, wherever, to say what he already knew, that the air wasn't fine. Maybe it was okay, but it wasn't fine. He told me I should do a piece about it, and I did."

It was an evolution-of-man motif, on a high school chalkboard, with modern man in gas mask and moonsuit and a teacher in the foreground (also wearing a gas mask), giving a science lecture to her students. Atop the collage was accompanying text about potentially "unacceptable" air inside Stuyvesant High School, pulled word-for-word from a *Daily News* article that had run on November 7. Editors cut that text, the only clue to the picture's meaning. What remained was a bizarre, indecipherable image that had lost its essence. Was the *Daily News* concerned about a too-specific reference in the art? Did the quote somehow become dangerous when affixed to art?

The suggestion that there are things people are willing to read, or look at in photographs and movies, that become circumspect in art was a common refrain as I was reporting this story. The classic example dates back to a 1983 drawing Marshall Arisman did for *Time*. Asked to illustrate a cover story on the death penalty, Arisman produced an image of a man strapped in the electric chair with a skull projecting sideways from his head. The image was cut. In its place ran a black page with "Death Penalty" in huge, white block lettering. Below those words were smaller words, a paragraph descending down and eventually cut off, that expressed the same jolting idea as Arisman's illustration: "The chair is bolted to the floor near the back of a 12-ft. by 18-ft. room. You sit on a seat of cracked rubber secured by rows of copper tacks. Your ankles are strapped into half-moon-shaped foot cuffs lined with canvas. A 2-in.-wide greasy leather belt with 28 buckle holes and worn grooves where it has been pulled very tight many times is secured around your waist just above..."

When I spoke with Arisman he volunteered the image immediately. Something an editor at *Time* had said stuck with him over the years: We're a society that's willing to read all sorts of things about violence, to look at photos about violence. But we're not willing to look at artwork about violence.

Arisman says he asked why that was so. The editor replied that when people look at photos, they think they're looking at reality, not a statement by the artist. But when people look at artwork, they think the artist invented it.

Again and again it was like this: the image that took the place of the original was so obviously weaker that no rationalization saved it. When I saw them side by side it often seemed comical, no more so than in the case of Mirko Ilic. Maybe it was that in his rough, Bosnian burr he caught the absurdity so well. "You can always sneak things in at the *Times*," he was fond of saying, "but that's not the point. I don't want to sneak anything in."

He fired away. "I was working in Yugoslavia, in the time of Communism. Never did I have to show a draft. I come to America, art directors start asking for drafts. I say first, What do you mean 'drafts'? And second, What do you mean 'art director?' Most art directors are females. I call them 'art secretaries' because editors are making the decisions. Move left. Move right. They've become messengers."...

It was weird: I didn't solicit stories about *The New York Times* but everyone I spoke with had one. Even Robert Grossman, who told me his own Howell Raines tale (involving a too-big nose, a former president, and a late-night emergency Photoshop session). Illustrators didn't exempt *The Washington Post* or the *Los Angeles Times* or anywhere else, but the *Times* stung the deepest, because of how influential its op-ed art had once been. One day in early November, with images still flooding in, I went there, to Forty-third Street, to visit the op-ed editor David Shipley. I negotiated the maze of the tenth-floor editorial offices and I found Shipley's room.

I had brought an image rejected by the *Times*. It was modest, a small picture set beside five letters to the editor about the grim prospects for peace between Israelis and Palestinians. But its circumstances seemed to sum things up. The artist, Cathie Bleck, had been commissioned to create something unspecific, something that would, in a general sense, depict the idea that peace in the Middle East had failed. She had a day to do it. She came up with a Humpty Dumpty motif. It was okayed by Steven Guarnaccia, but rejected by an editor. The image was not all that fresh—Bleck admits it—but what took its place was even less so: a broken peace sign, which was a wheel supporting a wheelbarrow, inside of which were the Star of David and a crescent moon. One obvious icon replaced another.

But we never got to discuss specific images anyway. We got sidetracked, somehow, me telling Shipley about this project, and him interrupting me at times to disapprove. "I have to say, that's tremendously naïve," he said. "If you're comparing an illustration in *Glamour* or *Rolling Stone* with one on the op-ed page or in *The New Republic*."

Shipley never smiled or frowned. Later I learned he'd written speeches for President Clinton. "I think it would be useful," he continued, "to make distinctions." His point is that doing illustration for a daily newspaper—with its tight deadlines and need to respond to breaking news—is often different from illustration done for monthly magazines. He told me about his passion for photography, how he was trying to visually surprise readers by adding things like puzzle pages, stand alone art, and charts and graphs. Then he moved on to caricature. "What's wrong with hinting at something rather than beating our readers over the head with a sledgehammer, resorting to the obvious?" We talked some more like that, and I believed him. He *was* opening up the page, and some illustrators I spoke with said he was easier to work with than his predecessor.

But in expanding the experience of the page, as he put it, it seemed to me that something had been lost. And when he then suggested that op-ed was still home to great art, I couldn't help but feel we were talking across some unbridgeable divide. Everything was fine to him. "Op-ed is one of the last places for black-and-white illustration," Shipley said. "It's something we cherish. I want people to think about illustration the same way they think about the articles. They don't have to get it in the first read."

Yes, that's what illustrators wanted, too. But that kind of nuance is rare today....

POSTSCRIPT

Do the Media Introduce Us to New Ways of Thinking About Things?

In 1948, Lyman Bryson edited a book titled *The Communication of Ideas* (Institute for Religious and Social Studies). In that book was a chapter by Harold D. Lasswell on "The Structure and Function of Communication in Society." In the article, Lasswell examined the classic question: "Who, says what, in which channel, to whom, with what effect?" From that time until now, we have continually asked the same question of any form of media. The simple "5-Ws" have been the model for analyzing how media works in society, and for how content may introduce ways of thinking to the audience.

Lasswell explained that media can give us an idea of the *surveillance* of the environment (meaning that we could understand how our surrounding environment worked); how it can explain the *correlation of the parts of society* (how the pieces fit together); and how there is a *transmission* function of the media (which helps every generation understand its history). Later, the function of *entertainment* was also added to our understanding of how media function in our lives. All together, these functions would indeed introduce us to new ideas and concepts, but also, they would create a more stable environment so that we could constantly evaluate and measure social issues.

Perhaps because formal studies of media were so new when Lasswell authored his key article, there had been little thought to how media industries would evolve, and therefore create new dynamics for some of the traditional functions. Lasswell probably could not envision how rapidly some of our media forms would evolve; as smaller, more portable forms of technology introduced new possibilities.

Perhaps changes to print media have been more carefully chronicled than any other form. Print is the oldest recorded form we have, but the reason for this is probably due more to the fact that journalists as writers tend to think carefully about how their craft has changed, and the effects of different styles of journalism on the public. A classic academic study of print media and technology is Elizabeth Eisenstein's *The Printing Press As An Agent of Change* (Cambridge University Press, 1979). A more contemporary, use-based study is Roger Streightmatter's *Mightier than the Sword: How the News Media Have Shaped American History* (Westview Press, 1998).

There are also interesting studies of journalists, and personal accounts of journalists and their views on the changing business of news gathering and dissemination. Former National Public Radio's *Morning Edition* anchor, Bob Edwards, has written a thoughtful account of one of the great radio pioneers in *Edward R. Murrow and the Birth of Broadcast Journalism* (John Wiley & Son, 2004).

The impact of images in the press also presents a fascinating subject for discussion. Indeed, the images contained in the following recommended books could be debated on-end. In reference to some of the most thought-provoking photographic images, *Life Magazine* has published an annual series with the title of *100 Photographs that Changed the World* (Editors of *Life Magazine,* most recent volume, 2003). Charles Brooks has edited a series of editorial cartoons every year since 1972, with annual editions each titled *Best Editorial Cartoons of the Year* (Pelican Publishing Co., most recent volume, 2004), and Robert Mankoff has edited *The New Yorker Book of Political Cartoons* (Bloomsberg Press, 2000).

ISSUE 16

Can the Music Industry Survive Despite Technologies That Facilitate Downloading?

YES: Kevin Kelly, "Where Music Will Be Coming From," *New York Times Magazine* (March 17, 2002).

NO: Statements of Sen. Orrin G. Hatch, Sen. Patrick J. Leahy, and Hank Barry, "Online Entertainment and Copyright Law: Coming Soon to a Digital Device Near You," Hearing before the Committee on the Judiciary, U.S. Senate (April 3, 2001).

ISSUE SUMMARY

YES: Author Kevin Kelly provides a brief history of music as it changed from live performer to recorded work. Stating that the most significant change has been the change from analog to digital recording, Kelly looks optimistically toward a future of music in which there will be greater varieties of music for discriminating fans.

NO: In a Senate Hearing to assess the matter of whether digitally recorded music could be protected by copyright, Senators Orrin Hatch and Patrick Leahy, and Napster Interim Chairman, Hank Barry, discuss the problems of trying to protect original ownership in an age of digital duplication.

The ethics of downloading music from the Internet, and sharing music with friends by file-swapping, has created a serious controversy ever since MP3 technology became available to the public. At the time, some companies facilitated downloading and file sharing. Napster, the brainchild of a young man named Shawn Fanning, created a tremendous controversy when it first appeared. Almost immediately, the Recording Industry Association of America (RIAA) filed complaints and legal proceedings against Napster and other, similar companies. In the summer of 2003, the RIAA began suing individuals whom they had tracked, who had accumulated very large data bases of downloaded music. In the first wave of suits, the RIAA pursued 216 individuals, and before the first year had concluded, the number of individuals for whom suits were pending increased to over 400.

A typical response from the person doing the downloading—who was usually young, and most often, a student—was that they didn't know they were engaging in an illegal activity when they downloaded music for free. A common position was that if the activity were illegal—why were technologies available that *could* download music for free? Still, many others continued to download music, even though they knew the action was illegal, but who claimed that they really weren't hurting anyone anyway, so what did it matter?

The original Napster company was put out of business, but Shawn Fanning was able to sell the Napster name to a company that re-emerged with the purpose of using the technology to sell downloaded music. In this issue, we see two sides of the question of the ethics and the business of downloading music. Kevin Kelly examines how the business of downloading music in a digital form could actually enable more musicians to get an audience for their music, and how the audience will actually be the beneficiaries of a wider range of music.

In the Senate Hearings dealing with all forms of on-line entertainment (including music, movies, television shows, and other software), we can see how the government is responding to the question of copyright and how the original works of authors can be protected even though we have technologies that can easily duplicate original material efficiently, effectively, and at low cost. While the remarks of Senators Hatch and Leahy actually encompass the wide range of digital duplication of many forms of content, the comments of Hank Barry, Interim Chairman of the newly organized Napster, reflect the effects of copyright specifically as they affect the music industry.

The fundamental issue here is whether artists should and can be paid for their works, even when technologies exist that can duplicate them with ease. Mr. Barry's argument for a Compulsory Licensing system would be similar to that which guaranteed profits to musical artists through radio play and juke box play. Do you think this system could work today in the world of downloading?

Though this issue really focuses on retaining ownership rights for musicians, we might also think about whom, in the traditional music marketing business, is affected by downloading. Certainly the merchants who sell recorded music, the manufacturers, the album/CD cover artists and all of the people who shrink-wrap and ship music to stores lose business. When the rights of the artists are juxtaposed against the way an industry has operated, do different sets of interests and financial concerns emerge?

Kevin Kelly  **YES**

Where Music Will Be Coming From

Technology is changing music. But then again, it always has. The invention of the piano 300 years ago centered Western music on the keyboard. Electricity's arrival in the late 19th century enabled the duplication of performances and, later, the amplification of instruments. With digitization, the pace of upheaval has further accelerated. Digital file-sharing technologies—Napster and its offspring—are now undermining the established economics of music. And everything we know about digital technologies suggests that Napster is only the beginning.

There is no music made today that has not been shaped by the fact of recording and duplication. In fact, the ability to copy music has been deeply disruptive ever since the invention of the gramophone. When John D. Smoot, an engineer for the European company Odeon, carted primitive recording equipment to the Indonesian archipelago in 1904 to record the gamelan orchestras, local musicians were perplexed. Why copy a performance? The popular local tunes that circulated in their villages had a half-life of a few weeks. Why would anyone want to listen to a stale rendition of an obsolete piece when it was so easy to get fresh music?

As phonographs spread throughout the world, they had a surprising effect: folk tunes, which had always been malleable, changing with each performer and in each performance, were transformed by the advent of recording into fixed songs that could be endlessly and exactly repeated. Music became shorter, more melodic and more precise.

Early equipment could make recordings that contained no more than four and a half minutes, so musicians truncated old works to fit and created new music abbreviated to adapt to the phonograph. Because the first sound recordings were of unamplified music, recording emphasized the loud sounds of singers and de-emphasized quiet instrumentals. The musicologist Timothy Day notes that once pianists began recording they tried, for the first time, to "distinguish carefully between every quaver and semiquaver—eighth note and sixteenth note — throughout the piece." Musicians played the way technology listened. When the legendary recordist Frederick Gaisberg arrived in Calcutta in 1902, only two decades after the phonograph was invented, he found that Indian musicians were already learning to imitate recorded music and lamented that there was "no traditional music left to record."

As the technologies of reproduction bloomed in the last century, consumerism boomed. What consumers consumed—whether in the form of a book, a CD or a can of Coke—were exact copies. The ability to make copies in mind-boggling quantities, ceaselessly and perfectly, was the chief ingredient of mass culture. Music rapidly adapted to the culture of the copy. Reproductions were made exact, while copies were multiplied vigorously. Music lived in its constant reproduction.

The grand upset that music is now experiencing—the transformation that Napster signaled—is the shift from analog copies to digital copies. The industrial age was driven by analog copies; analog copies are perfect and cheap. The information age is driven by digital copies; digital copies are perfect, fluid and free.

Free is hard to ignore. It propels duplication at a scale that would previously have been unbelievable. In only 10 months, 71 million copies of the music-sharing software Morpheus were downloaded. Of course, it's not just music that is being copied freely. It is text, pictures, movies, entire Web sites. In this new online world, anything that *can* be copied *will* be copied, free.

But the moment something becomes free and ubiquitous, its position in the economic equation is suddenly inverted. When nighttime electrical lighting was new, it was the poor who burned common candles. When electricity became easily accessible and practically free, candles at dinner became a sign of luxury.

In this new supersaturated online universe of infinite free digital duplication, the axis of value has flipped. In the industrial age, copies often were more valuable than the original. (Who wanted the "original" prototype refrigerator that the one in your kitchen was based on?) Most people wanted a perfect working clone. The more common the clone, the more desirable, since it would then come with a brand name respected by others and a network of service and repair outlets.

But now, in a brave new world of abundant and free copies, the order has inverted. Copies are so ubiquitous, so cheap (free, in fact) that the only things truly valuable are those *which cannot be copied*.

What kinds of things can't be copied? Well, for instance: trust, immediacy, personalization. There is no way to download these qualities from existing copies or to install them from a friend's CD. So while you can score a copy free of charge, if you want something authenticated, or immediately, or personalized, you'll have to pay.

In the domain of the plentifully free, music will do the only thing it *can* do: charge for things that can't be copied easily. A friend of a friend may eventually pass on to you the concert recording of a band you like, but if you pay, the band itself will e-mail it to you seconds after the performance. Sure, you can find a copy of that hit dance track, but if you want the mix approved by the legendary D.J., then you'll want to pay for it. Anyone can grab a free copy of Beethoven's Ninth, but if you want it customized for the audio parameters of your room or car, you'll pay for it. You may have downloaded that Cuban-Chinese rock band from the Morpheus site without paying, but the only way to get all that cool meta-information about each track, which lets you search for chords and lyrics, is to establish a relationship with the band by paying.

The quality least plentiful in a world of rampant free copies is attention. Each year more than 30,000 new music titles are released (or rereleased) into a very cluttered head space of new movies, new TV shows, new books, new games, new Web sites. No matter what your musical appetite, there are not enough hours in a lifetime to listen to but a tiny fraction of the global supply. People will pay simply to have someone edit the music and recommend and present selected material to them in an easy and fun manner. That is why producers, labels and the related ecology of reviewers, catalogers and guides will continue to make a living: they counter our natural lack of attention for the 10 million albums we can expect to see in another 50 years. In the end, an awful lot of music will be sold in the territory of the free because it will be easier to *buy* music you really like than to find it for free.

Free is overrated as a destiny. It is only the second phase of the three stages of copydom. The first phase—perfection—is experienced in both analog and digital. Perfect duplication made the modern world and modern music.

The second stage is freeness. Costless duplication made Napster possible and a music revolution thinkable.

Yet it is in the third level of digital copy-ness that the real revolution lies. This third power is liquidity, and it will take music beyond Napster.

Digital copies are not only perfect and free, they are also fluid. Once music is digitized it becomes a liquid that can be morphed and migrated and flexed and linked. You can filter it, bend it, archive it, rearrange it, remix it, mess with it. And you can do this to music that you write, or music that you listen to, or music that you borrow.

At first glance it seems audiences were drawn to online music because of the power of the free, but in reality the rush to online music came from digitized sound's ever-expanding power of liquidity. Once music could swirl around one's life unencumbered, the millions of people who downloaded peer-to-peer file-sharing software suddenly and simultaneously imagined a thousand ways to conjure with music's liquidity. It wasn't only that it was free; it was all the things you could do with it.

Once music is digitized, new behaviors emerge. With liquid music you have the power to reorder the sequence of tunes on an album, or among albums. To surgically morph a sound until it is suitable for a new use. To precisely extract from someone else's music a sample of notes to use oneself. To X-ray the guts of music and outline its structure, and then alter it. To substitute new lyrics. To rearrange a piece so that its parts yield a different voice. To re-engineer a piece so that it sounds better on a car woofer. To meld and marry music together into hybrid breeds. To shorten a piece, or to draw it out so that it takes twice as long to play.

With digitization, music went from being a noun, to a verb, once again.

If this third power of the digital copy were to play out in full, the world would be full of people messing around with sound and music much as they dabble in taking snapshots and shaping Web pages. The typical skepticism toward a scenario of ubiquitous creation and re-creation of music is that it is always easier to read than to write, to listen than to play, to see than to make. That is true. Yet 10 years ago, anyone claiming that ordinary people would flock to expensive computers to take time from watching TV in order to create three billion or more Web pages—well, that person would have been laughed out of the room as idealistic, utopian. People just aren't that creative or willing to take time to create, went the argument. Yet, against all odds, three billion Web pages exist. The growth of the Web is probably the largest creative spell that civilization has witnessed. Music could experience a similarly exuberant, irrational flowering of the amateur spirit.

Part of the reason people have been inspired to create text, graphics and action in the digital realm has been the arrival of new tools. Fans of music are already shuffling playlists, remixing tracks, sampling sounds, laying music with automatic drums and other instruments. They are already making music in the way that a camera makes an image—by starting with what is there and adding a unique view to it. Just as the introduction of the Brownie camera changed photography from an expert's art to a ubiquitous public expression, with the right tools in hand it is not a very long hop from now to a time when everyone makes music in a small, amateur way.

Much of the friction about Napster is cast as a question about the future of music. But no matter what happens, the world of the future will have lots of music, listened to by lots of people. The question is not about the future of music but about the future of *musicians*. The role of the professional musician is in flux. But again, it has always been so.

The rules for making a living making music have been remade over and over, from the first drumbeat. Until the 20th century, musicians in Western societies were generally held in contempt, their status approximating that of a vagabond. Even the most successful musicians were mistrusted.

Recording technology redeemed the professional musician. The machinery of recording and duplication steadily elevated the role of musicians during this century until many of them now have reached celebrity status and riches. This was a status only a handful of musicians could have dreamed of a few hundred years ago. Mozart never had it so good.

The arrival of perfect, free and liquid copies of music means that new economic models of making music will be forced upon musicians. Will the model of the future be to give away copies in order to sell out a performance? Or to rapidly issue new work from the studio faster than it can spread online? Or to release music in such wonderful packaging that it is cheaper to buy it than to copy it? The probable answer: all of the above and more.

If there is any lesson that should be taken from the online world, it is that options multiply. I am willing to bet that within the next 10 years a young band will come along that will be primarily and generously supported by a commercial sponsor. The band will write and play whatever music it feels like, but it will grant first option to the sponsor to use the sponsor's materials in commercials. The sponsor gets cool, hip music, and the band gets its stuff heard by millions, and anything the company doesn't use is the company's to pass out, free of charge.

Creating music is hard work. Creating music that is widely appreciated and constantly in demand is harder still. It may seem ludicrous to suggest to a working musician that in this new online world, music is becoming a commodity that is traded, cocreated and coproduced by a networked audience. How can an unskilled population create something that will be appreciated by many?

The partial answer is that most of us won't. It will still be a rare person who can write and play music that everyone swoons over. Those hit musicians will have their own economics. But most music, like most photography, needn't appeal to everyone. Most photographs taken in the world are taken by amateurs, and the images are of interest only to themselves or their families. Music does not have to be widely popular to be desired.

The future of music is unknown. But whatever it is, it will be swayed, as usual, by technology. Carver Mead, a computer-chip pioneer, advises us to "listen to the technology" to see where it is headed. If we listen to the technology of music, we might hear these possibilities:

- Songs are cheap; what's expensive are the indexable, searchable, official lyrics.
- On auction sites, music lovers buy and sell active playlists, which arrange hundreds of songs in creative sequences. The lists are templates that reorder songs on your own disc.
- You subscribe to a private record label whose agents troll the bars, filtering out the garbage, and send you the best underground music based on your own preferences.
- The most popular band in the world produces only very good "jingles," just as some of the best directors today produce only very good commercials.
- The catalog of all musical titles makes more money than any of the record companies.
- A generator box breeds background music tailored to your personal tastes; the music is supplied by third-party companies that buy the original songs from the artists.
- Because you like to remix dance tunes, you buy the versions of songs that are remix-ready in all 24 tracks.
- You'll pay your favorite band to stream you its concert as it is playing it, even though you could wait and copy it at no cost later.
- The varieties of musical styles explode. They increase faster than we can name them, so a musical Dewey Decimal System is applied to each work to aid in categorizing it.
- For a small fee, the producers of your favorite musician will tweak her performance to exquisitely match the acoustics of your living room.
- So many amateur remixed versions of a hit tune are circulating on the Net that it's worth $5 to you to buy an authenticated official version.
- For bands that tour, giving away their music becomes a form of cheap advertising. The more free copies that are passed around, the more tickets they sell.
- Musicians with the highest status are those who have a 24-hour Net channel devoted to streaming only their music.

- Royalty-free stock music (like stock photography), available for any use, takes off with the invention of a great music search engine, which makes it possible to find music "similar to this music" in mood, tempo and sound.
- The best-selling item for most musicians is the "whole package deal," which contains video clips, liner notes, segregated musical tracks, reviews, ads and artwork—all stored on a well-designed artifact in limited editions.
- Despite the fact that with some effort you can freely download the song you think you want in a format you think will work for your system, most people choose to go to a reliable retailer online and use the retailer's wonderful search tools and expert testimonials to purchase what they want because it is simply easier and a better experience all around.

In the end, the future of music is simple: more choices. As the possibilities of music expand, so do our own.

NO ↵   Orrin G. Hatch, Patrick J. Leahy, and Hank Barry

Opening Statement of Honorable Orrin G. Hatch, a U.S. Senator from the State of Utah

Chairman Hatch. Good morning, and welcome to this morning's hearing, "Online Entertainment: Coming Soon to a Digital Device Near You." That is kind of a long title. There have been a number of significant developments since the Committee's hearings last year on online entertainment and copyright law. Among many, let me mention three:

First, the Ninth Circuit has ruled that at least as a preliminary matter, Napster as we have known it cannot continue. For them, as Mr. [Don] Henley might say, it has been "The End of the Innocence." Even Napster acknowledges that this is so. And in its alliance with the forward-thinking Bertelsmann, Napster has pledged to reinvent itself so that the technology and music fan community it has unleashed can work together in a way that respects copyright law and the rights of creators. It has been suggested that this new Napster can be online in June, or at the latest, July [2001].

Second, MP3.com has settled its litigation with the large record labels and publishers, and yet, having paid damages and been granted licenses to go forward still cannot bring its service to the public. As Ms. Morisette might question, isn't it "Ironic"?

And, third, but by no means least, several significant market developments have been announced that seem to put us a step closer to the "celestial jukebox." One was reported in last Friday's Wall Street Journal that two of the five major labels, Vivendi-Universal and Sony, were moving toward launching a consumer online service called "Duet" which will bring their joint catalogs to consumers. And the second, and even more significant, announcement was yesterday's deal between three of the big labels—AOLTime Warner, Bertelsmann, and EMI—and the independent music service provider, Real networks, to bring a subscription music service to consumers over the Internet.

Pro-competitive marketplace solutions that provide for a significant online offering of popular music delivered to consumers through an entity not controlled by the labels has been the type of positive synergy I have long hoped to see. And I hope to learn more about the details of these developments and to hear more heartening information on this front. This Committee is here today, and will continue in the future, to monitor these and related developments in our ongoing efforts to ensure that our intellectual property laws keep pace with technology.

From Statements from the Hearing Before the Committee on the Judiciary, US Senate, April 3, 2001.

Technology has made our lives more convenient, but also made us more impatient. When a consumer drives up to a gas pump, she can insert her credit card, confirm that she has adequate funds in he account, her account is debited, and the oil company's account is credited, the transaction is completed, the consumer is thanked, and her tank is filled. All of this occurs within a matter of seconds, and the transfer of sensitive financial data is done so securely and with utter precision.

Now, while there are significant additional challenges in the context of a product that is delivered wholly online, most consumers think similar technological advances should allow them access to the music and movies they love whenever and wherever they want it. I believe it can, and that it can do so in a way that respects the rights of those who create the works we all want to enjoy in this new way. Instant access to an infinite offering of perfectly performed creativity on a portable device the size of a pen, or a phone, or in the car, or wherever I want it, without dragging cases of CDs, is more than a new way of delivering the same product. It is a transformation of our experience of entertainment and poses a revolution in the businesses that have delivered it. And I do appreciate the disconcerting panic that the uncertainty of new technology might cause established businesses such as the record labels....

Statement of Honorable Patrick J. Leahy, a U.S. Senator from the State of Vermont

...Music has been at the forefront of the online copyright battles, but the issue raised by the deployment of new software applications and new online services have even broader implications for other forms of copyrighted works.

For the copyright industries, to paraphrase a classic phrase: "It is the best of times, it is the worst of times; it is the age of wisdom, it is the age of foolishness."

These are certainly good economic times for our copyright industries. Computer software, motion pictures, television programs, music, publishing and other copyright-based industries have proven to be a critical engine for our economy. According to the latest edition of a report by Economists Incorporated, in 1999, American copyright industries accounted for almost 5 percent of our gross domestic product, or over $450 billion, and employment in this sector grew more than three times as fast as the remainder of the fast-growing U.S. economy.

In the same year, 1999, the U.S. copyright industry led all other major industry sectors with over $79 billion in foreign sales and exports. That is more than the automobile, the car parts, the aircraft, or the agricultural sector. That is a big change from when I came to the Senate.

The growth of these industries has been good for American workers. It has been good for our economy. And their continued success depends on strong copyright laws and effective enforcement of those laws.

Every year, the copyright industries lose billions of dollars in lost revenue to hard goods piracy around the world. According to Forrester Research, one pirated product is made for every three legitimate ones. Think of that. A quarter of the products are pirated.

Now, understandably, especially in a digital age, software manufacturers, the record companies, the movie producers, he retailers, whose business is selling licensed copies of these copyrighted works, are concerned that these losses are going to accelerate as digital works are downloaded freely and without consideration to the owners of these products....

Statement of Hank Barry, Interim CEO, Napster

...I think no one in this room—even those with whom we have disagreed vigorously—would contest that accessing music over the Internet is something that tens of millions of people, young and old, love to do. Over half of Napster's users are over 25, and they come from all walks of life. The question before us today—from all of our very different perspectives and responsibilities—is what does it take to make music on the Internet a fair and profitable business.

To realize this goal, I believe it will take an Act of Congress—a change to the laws to provide a compulsory license for the transmission of music over the Internet. And today I will tell you why I strongly believe such a change is necessary, an important step for the Internet, and why it will be good for artists, listeners and businesses.

Negotiation History

When I last testified before this Committee last July [2000], I did not believe this issue required a legislative solution. I believed that Napster should find a private contractual solution that the rights holders and the people who use Napster could all support. We said "let the marketplace work."

Since that time the Napster community has continued to grow. We then had 20 million members; we have grown to more than 60 million members today, even as we aggressively comply with the District Court's injunction.

Since people who use Napster buy more music than others and are very willing to pay for music over the Internet, I believed there was a basis for making an agreement with the record and music publishing companies. We built our business model around this idea: that the people using Napster want artists and songwriters to be paid, and that peer-to-peer Internet technology is the most efficient and convenient way ever devised to make music accessible.

I have tried for the last 9 months to make an agreement under which Napster can get a license from the record companies and the music publishers. I believed that any such agreement would serve as a precedent for other agreements and could serve as the basis for payments by the people using Napster to recording artists and songwriters. We were able to reach agreement with Bertelsmann on a business model for a new service and license terms for the sound recordings and the musical compositions they control. Yet I cannot today report that any other such agreement has been reached with a major label.

Perhaps I should not have been surprised at this result. Although the World Wide Web portion of the Internet has been around for 7 years, and billions of investor dollars have been spent founding and attempting to grow technology companies and consumer companies that would help all of us access music over the Internet, to this date no service has been able to provide a comprehensive offering of music on the Internet that is licensed by the major recording and publishing companies.

For the record companies, the promise of music over the Internet has always been "coming real soon now." Every time this Committee holds a hearing on these issues, new promises of imminent progress are made. Just last July, Fred Ehrlich from Sony told this Committee "we are in active conversations" with both eMusic and mp3.com. But, once again, these have turned out to be empty statements.

The DMCA was supposed to solve many of these problems. As Chairman Hatch said in the last hearing of this Committee on this issue:

"In short, it was believed that a stable, predictable legal environment would encourage the deployment of business models which would make properly licensed content more widely available. Sadly, this has not yet occurred to any great extent in the music industry, and the DMCA is nearly two years old."

Look at the facts. Where are the Internet businesses with clear and complete recording and music publishing licenses? There are none. Where are the emerging digital media companies with negotiated agreements with all rightsholders? There are none.

And of course these companies argue that this is Napster's fault. That argument might be granted some validity if there were even one fully-licensed business with anything approaching a comprehensive consumer offer. But there are none.

We might all well ask—why is this so complicated? Why can't the record companies and music publishing companies just issue licenses to eMusic, Liquid Audio, Listen.com, Yahoo, MSN and Napster, and everyone else, so consumers can pay money and have access to music over the Internet, while ensuring that artists and songwriters are paid? Why have the record and publishing companies continually said they are going to license, and then not followed through?

Well, one obstacle may have been a lack of will—the record companies have stated repeatedly that they believe that licenses of sales over the Internet will cut into physical goods sales and generally damage, not increase, their business. This fear, of course, has not been founded in reality to date. CD sales are stronger than other retail, even in the face of uncertain economic times. Internet music has increased interest in music as a whole. Like the VCR, the cassette, and every other major innovation, Internet music has been greeted by a chorus of doom from existing distributors. But let's assume that the will is there to license music over the Internet—certainly all of the record and publishing companies represented on this panel now say they want to move forward in this area.

Even if we assume that everyone agrees that licensing music for the Internet would be a good thing, my experience is that it is an almost impossibly complicated thing. And unfortunately I have to explain how complicated it is by going over the rights structure in this industry. So if you will let me do that...

Industry Overview

This background description here is for those of you who are not copyright lawyers....

As the members of this Committee know, when you buy a CD or tape, you are really getting copies of two separate works. The first is the sound recording that the artist and producers and musicians made in the studio. The second is the musical composition, the song that is being played. By law, each copy of the CD is also considered a reproduction of that musical composition. The complex part about this is that the sound recording and the musical composition that is sung on the sound recording (the "song"—the music) are almost always owned by different companies, even where, as in many cases, the recording artist is the same person who wrote the song.

Now if you are trying to make music available to the public on the Internet, whether for download or streaming or even for broadcast, and if you need a private contractual agreement to do that, then you have to negotiate with both sets of rightsholders—the record companies and the music publishers. First you have to go to the record companies (and if you want the good stuff, like polkas and Lithuanian folk songs, you have to go to many record companies—there are over 3,000 record companies in the US alone).

And when you have negotiated each of those 3,000 separate agreements, you are only half way there—because then you have to go and negotiate with all of the music publishers—and there are over 25,000 independent music publishers in the US alone. Mr. Murphy's organization represents many of them, but I believe Mr. Roberts from MP3.com would tell you that anything less than an overall comprehensive license to all compositions doesn't do you much good, because the likelihood is that rights you have and the rights you need will not match at all. And even one failure to match can bring down the whole structure.

This is further complicated by the fact that several of the largest music publishers, controlling millions of songs, are owned by the record labels, but the music publishing catalogs they control bear no relation to the sound recordings they control—they are not the same songs. For a final complication—the music publishers have two separate rights, the right to make a mechanical copy of the song and the public performance right, that may both be implicated in this type of licensing. And each of those rights is administered for them by a different rights organization....

Do they Work? Examples of Compulsory Licenses

As the RIAA says, compulsory licenses have a long history of success, allowing for the widespread implementation of a new technology while ensuring that rights holders are compensated. Congress has repeatedly used such licenses as a way of advancing public policy goals in the context of new and frequently inefficient marketplaces. Compulsory licenses have encouraged beneficial new technologies, and responded effectively to particular market failures—including excessive contracting costs and anticompetitive market structures.

Let's look at some examples:

In 1909, Congress created a right against the reproduction of musical compositions in mechanical forms (i.e., piano rolls), but limited this right through the creation of a mechanical compulsory license for musical works. The legislative history behind the mechanical compulsory license reveals that Congress enacted this provision, not only to compensate composers, but to prevent the Aeolian Company, which had acquired mechanical reproduction rights from all of the nation's leading music publishers, from limiting the dissemination of the music to the public through the creation of a monopolistic environment. Thanks to this, once a song has been recorded by anybody, it may be recorded by anyone else, without a further license from the music publisher, if the person making the new recording notifies the publisher and pays a statutorily mandated royalty based on the number of copies made. That's where "cover" songs come from—and only those of us who have heard different versions of "Louie Louie" can appreciate what that compulsory license has meant for American music.

Years later, Congress again enacted several additional compulsory licenses, this time related to consumers' ability to access broadcast transmissions via cable and satellite systems. In 1976, Congress passed a compulsory license for cable television systems that retransmit copyrighted works. Pursuant to the compulsory license provision, copyright owners are entitled to be paid prescribed royalty fees for a cable television company's secondary transmission of the copyrighted work embodied in television and radio broadcasts.

Then, in 1988, Congress passed the Satellite Home Viewer Act of 1988 (SHVA), which created a compulsory license system for satellite carriers that retransmit television broadcasts that operates similar to the cable compulsory license. Congress acted again in 1999 when it expanded the SHVA's scope to include local-into-local retransmission.

Congress recognized the ability of these then cutting edge technologies to further disseminate to the public television and radio content, and the need to ensure that rights holders remained adequately compensated. Congress understood, however, the inefficiencies inherent in forcing cable or satellite providers to negotiate individual licensing agreements, thereby resulting in the use of a compulsory license system.

Interestingly enough, considering the current controversy, Congress' next foray into compulsory licenses applied specifically to music. The Digital Performance Rights in Sound Recordings Act of 1995 created a limited performance right for sound recordings, subject to a compulsory license for certain digital audio deliveries of sound recordings. The compulsory license originally applied, in general, to non-interactive satellite and cable audio digital deliveries. The Digital Millennium Copyright Act amended the original law to explicitly include non-interactive webcasting of sound recordings within the compulsory license's scope.

At the time, Congress reasoned that these new technologies promised to encourage the widespread dissemination of this music to the public. Once again, Congress enacted the compulsory license mechanism as a means to ensure that artists and other rights holders were compensated, while not hindering the continued development and deployment of these digital delivery systems.

Finally, I think we can all agree that AM and FM radio have been good for recorded music. The benefits of radio have flowed from the effective compulsory license created by performing rights societies, such as ASCAP and BMI. They enforce songwriters' and music publishers' performance rights through a court created process that removes the need to negotiate with individual rights holders. While Congress did not create this procedure, it has implicitly endorsed it by recognizing these performing rights societies in recent legislation. Further, Congress repeatedly has refused requests to outlaw the use of these blanket licenses.

In all of these cases of compulsory licensing, creators benefit from, but do not completely control, the distribution of their product. A balance is struck—a balance that is at the heart of all intellectual property law. Remember, intellectual property is not the same as real property or personal property—copyright is a limited right. Copyright is not based on a private right of the individual, it is a creation of and a tool of public policy. It requires a constant balance between the public's interest in promoting creative expression and the public's interest having access to those works. This is a balance that has often proven impossible to find without the help of the Congress....

POSTSCRIPT

Can the Music Industry Survive Despite Technologies That Facilitate Downloading?

After reading these two selections, you may realize that the question of whether downloading technologies should be available is a moot point. Technological and ethical concerns have taken a permanent backseat to trying to protect the profits of an industry in other ways. While some say the RIAA has approached the problem inefficiently by suing kids who have no money or power for downloading activities, the industry organization has been effective enough to energize the government and other industry players to consider alternatives for protecting musicians and the exchange of music as a software.

It is also interesting to learn how big the media industry's profits are, by Senator Hatch's comments. This information also shows how the profits of the media industries influence the American economy. Media are not just small industries—they comprise a huge portion of our economic infrastructure.

In many ways, the controversy over downloading and the survival of the traditional recording industry has been played out on web pages and in trade magazines, far more than it has in the mainstream press. For industry positions, you may wish to access the RIAA's industry website, www.riaa.org; or look at government documents to see Congressional inquiry into the subject; www.govdocs.gov. Occasionally, the FCC also has a prepared statement on its home page, www.fcc.gov.

As mentioned, trade magazines have many columnists and commentaries on issues of digital duplication. In particular, *Record World, Variety,* and *Electronic News* devote considerable attention to this issue.

On the Internet . . .

Educause

The Educause Web site contains summaries of new technology news from various publications as well as links to many other resources. This site is designed to facilitate the use of technology in teaching, research, and learning.

http://www.educause.edu

The Electronic Frontier Foundation

The Electronic Frontier Foundation (EFF) is a nonprofit civil liberties organization that is working to protect free expression and access to public resources and information online. It also works to promote responsibility in the news media.

http://www.eff.org

The Journal of Computer-Mediated Communication

The Journal of Computer-Mediated Communication Web site has been maintained by the Annenberg School for Communication at the University of Southern California since 1995. Many issues are discussed in this electronic journal, including electronic commerce, law and the electronic frontier, Netplay, and designing presence in virtual environments.

http://www.ascusc.org/jcmc/

Yahoo International

This Yahoo International service contains resources on different countries, providing information about media systems and media programming available around the world.

http://dir.yahoo.com/regional/countries/index.html

Citizens Internet Empowerment Coalition

The Citizens Internet Empowerment Coalition (CIEC) is a broad group of Internet users, library groups, publishers, online service providers, and civil liberties groups working to preserve the First Amendment and to ensure the future of free expression. You will find discussions of the Communications Decency Act and Internet-related topics on this site.

http://www.ciec.org

PART 6

The Information Society

*P*redictions of a world that is increasingly reliant upon media and communication technologies have generally provided either utopian or dystopian visions about what our lives will be like in the future. But now the ability to communicate instantly around the world has become a reality. New media distribution technologies present new options for traditional ways of doing things. Not too many years ago, people were talking about the possibility of an information superhighway. Today, surfing the World Wide Web is common. Although we are still learning how electronic communication may change our lives and the ways we work and communicate, many questions have not changed. Will new ways of communication change the way individuals interact? Will the decision making of citizens change? Will everyone have access to the services and technologies that enable more immediate information exchange? What will new technologies mean to us as individuals as we enter the information age?

- Can Privacy Be Protected in the Information Age?
- Are People Better Informed in the Information Society?

ISSUE 17

Can Privacy Be Protected in the Information Age?

YES: Simson Garfinkel, from "Privacy and the New Technology," *The Nation* (February 28, 2000)

NO: Adam L. Penenberg, from "The End of Privacy," *Forbes* (November 29, 1999)

ISSUE SUMMARY

YES: Journalist Simson Garfinkel discusses how today's technology has the potential to destroy our privacy. He makes the case that the government and individuals could take steps to protect themselves against privacy abuse, particularly by returning to the groundwork set by the government in the 1970s and by educating people on how to avoid privacy traps.

NO: *Forbes* reporter Adam L. Penenberg discusses his own experiences with an Internet detective agency, and he explains how easy it is for companies to get unauthorized access to personal information. He specifically describes how much, and where, personal information is kept and the lack of safeguards in our current system.

Privacy, or the legal right "to be left alone," is something we often take for granted until we feel that our privacy has been violated. In the following selections, Simon Garfinkel and Adam L. Penenberg discuss the range of privacy issues with which we now are faced, due to the computer's ability to store and match records for virtually any transaction we make using a computer. Data companies are emerging that have various standards about seeking the permission to save and sell personal information. While Garfinkel discusses how we could protect our privacy by drawing from already existing laws and statutes, Penenberg explains that many companies have avoided any prior legislation or standards to become information brokers.

This issue brings up questions of what privacy is, and what it means to us, but it also reminds us that as we use newer technologies, there are often unavoidable problems caused by and related to their use. The "transparency," or lack of obvious technological control, is apparent in uses of the Internet and in the ability of high-speed computers to match check numbers, driver's license numbers, and other identifying bits of information. For those who wonder why their names appear on certain mailings, why they are contacted by telemarketers, or how secure their personal information is, this issue will bring up questions and uncover some of the answers.

Survey research reveals that many people feel that their privacy has been invaded at some time and that concerns about privacy are growing. But there are also some disturbing studies to indicate that young people are far less concerned about privacy issues than their parents. Could it be that younger people have not yet experienced the potential situations for privacy invasion, or, are we seeing a social value, in this case the right to privacy, in some type of transition?

Garfinkel advocates a position on privacy protection that would return us to a time in history when government was much more proactive in protecting the rights of citizens and residents. If his theory is correct, many agree that it would not be very expensive for the government to ensure safeguards about this basic right. However, trends in government involvement in businesses seem to be leading away from government oversight and toward giving greater control to businesses to monitor their own actions. Many of the companies discussed by Penenberg operate with few standards or guidelines at all. When the government itself is one of the primary repositories for personal information, could it, or should it, take the lead in defining certain standards and criteria for the protection of the innocent? Furthermore, if control should be exercised, would it be best left to the federal government, state, or local legislators?

Perhaps one of the key issues behind the privacy dilemma is the question of how and what people can do if they find that their privacy is invaded. With so many laws and statutes on the books, the legal wrangling over questions of privacy can be expensive and difficult to challenge. Many times people do not know how much information has been gathered about them until they find that the information is wrong, and it causes a problem. Consider the person who knows that he or she always pays bills on time, but for some reason, a credit reporting agency finds him or her negligent. Consequently, his or her new car loan or credit card application is denied because of the incorrect records. What recourse should that person have, and how long would it take to correct any misinformation? How could that person find out what other records might be inaccurate?

One of the growing areas of privacy concern is the collection and appropriate distribution of medical information about a person. Is it right to let others know the status of someone's confidential medical records? Should the results of voluntary or required drug testing, pregnancy tests, or AIDS tests be available to employers or anyone else without written authorization of the person being tested? Can those confidential records be used to prevent someone from buying insurance, getting a job, or getting a driver's license?

There are many questions related to issues of privacy, and we will undoubtedly see the courts debating exact parameters of privacy and information control in the near future. For now, we all need to think of the related issues of privacy and keep searching for answers to these important questions.

Privacy and the New Technology

You wake to the sound of a ringing telephone—but how could that happen? Several months ago, you reprogrammed your home telephone system so it would never ring before the civilized hour of 8 AM. But it's barely 6:45. Who was able to bypass your phone's programming?

You pick up the receiver, then slam it down a moment later. It's one of those marketing machines playing a recorded message. What's troubling you now is how this call got past the filters you set up. Later on you'll discover how: The company that sold you the phone created an undocumented "back door"; last week, the phone codes were sold in an online auction.

Now that you're awake, you decide to go through yesterday's mail. There's a letter from the neighborhood hospital you visited last month. "We're pleased that our emergency room could serve you in your time of need," the letter begins. "As you know, our fees (based on our agreement with your HMO) do not cover the cost of treatment. To make up the difference, a number of hospitals have started selling patient records to medical researchers and consumer-marketing firms. Rather than mimic this distasteful behavior, we have decided to ask you to help us make up the difference. We are recommending a tax-deductible contribution of $275 to help defray the cost of your visit."

The veiled threat isn't empty, but you decide you don't really care who finds out about your sprained wrist. You fold the letter in half and drop it into your shredder. Also into the shredder goes a trio of low-interest credit-card offers. Why a shredder? A few years ago you would never have thought of shredding your junk mail—until a friend in your apartment complex had his identity "stolen" by the building's superintendent. As best as anybody can figure out, the super picked one of those preapproved credit-card applications out of the trash; called the toll-free number and picked up the card when it was delivered. He's in Mexico now, with a lot of expensive clothing and electronics, all at your friend's expense.

On that cheery note, you grab your bag and head out the door, which automatically locks behind you.

This is the future—not a far-off future but one that's just around the corner. It's a future in which what little privacy we now have will be gone. Some

From Simson Garfinkel, "Privacy and the New Technology," *The Nation* (February 28, 2000). Adapted from Simson Garfinkel, *Database Nation: The Death of Privacy in the 21st Century* (O'Reilly, 2000). Copyright © 2000 by Simson Garfinkel. Reprinted by permission of O'Reilly & Associates, Inc. and the author.

people call this loss of privacy "Orwellian," harking back to *1984*, George Orwell's classic work on privacy and autonomy. In that book, Orwell imagined a future in which a totalitarian state used spies, video surveillance, historical revisionism and control over the media to maintain its power. But the age of monolithic state control is over. The future we're rushing toward isn't one in which our every move is watched and recorded by some all-knowing Big Brother. It is instead a future of a hundred kid brothers who constantly watch and interrupt our daily lives. Orwell thought the Communist system represented the ultimate threat to individual liberty. Over the next fifty years, we will see new kinds of threats to privacy that find their roots not in Communism but in capitalism, the free market, advanced technology and the unbridled exchange of electronic information.

The problem with this word "privacy" is that it falls short of conveying the really big picture. Privacy isn't just about hiding things. It's about self-possession, autonomy and integrity. As we move into the computerized world of the twenty-first century, privacy will be one of our most important civil rights. But this right of privacy isn't the right of people to close their doors and pull down their window shades—perhaps because they want to engage in some sort of illicit or illegal activity. It's the right of people to control what details about their lives stay inside their own houses and what leaks to the outside.

Most of us recognize that our privacy is at risk. According to a 1996 nationwide poll conducted by Louis Harris & Associates, 24 percent of Americans have "personally experienced a privacy invasion." In 1995 the same survey found that 80 percent felt that "consumers have lost all control over how personal information about them is circulated and used by companies." Ironically, both the 1995 and 1996 surveys were paid for by Equifax, a company that earns nearly $2 billion each year from collecting and distributing personal information.

Today the Internet is compounding our privacy conundrum—largely because the voluntary approach to privacy protection advocated by the Clinton Administration doesn't work in the rough and tumble world of real business. For example, a study just released by the California HealthCare Foundation found that nineteen of the top twenty-one health websites have privacy policies, but most sites fail to follow them. Not surprisingly, 17 percent of Americans questioned in a poll said they do not go online for health information because of privacy concerns.

꧁◉꧂

But privacy threats are not limited to the Internet: Data from all walks of life are now being captured, compiled, indexed and stored. For example, New York City has now deployed the Metrocard system, which allows subway and bus riders to pay their fares by simply swiping a magnetic-strip card. But the system also records the serial number of each card and the time and location of every swipe. New York police have used this vast database to crack crimes and disprove alibis. Although law enforcement is a reasonable use of this database, it is also a use that was adopted without any significant public debate. Furthermore, additional controls may be necessary: It is not clear who has access to the database, under what circumstances that access is given and what provisions are being taken to prevent the introduction of false data into it. It would be terrible if the subway's database were used by an employee to stalk an ex-lover or frame an innocent person for a heinous crime.

"New technology has brought extraordinary benefits to society, but it also has placed all of us in an electronic fishbowl in which our habits, tastes and activities are watched and recorded," New York State Attorney General Eliot Spitzer said in late January [2000], in announcing that Chase Manhattan had agreed to stop selling depositor information without clear permission from customers. "Personal information thought to be confidential is routinely shared with others without our consent."

Today's war on privacy is intimately related to the recent dramatic advances in technology. Many people today say that in order to enjoy the benefits of modern society, we must necessarily relinquish some degree of privacy. If we want the convenience of paying for a meal by credit card or paying for a toll with an electronic tag mounted on our rearview mirror, then we must accept the routine collection of our purchases and driving habits in a large database over which we have no control. It's a simple bargain, albeit a Faustian one.

This trade-off is both unnecessary and wrong. It reminds me of another crisis our society faced back in the fifties and sixties—the environmental crisis. Then, advocates of big business said that poisoned rivers and lakes were the necessary costs of economic development, jobs and an improved standard of living. Poison was progress: Anybody who argued otherwise simply didn't understand the facts.

Today we know better. Today we know that sustainable economic development depends on preserving the environment. Indeed, preserving the environment is a prerequisite to the survival of the human race. Without clean air to breathe and clean water to drink, we will all die. Similarly, in order to reap the benefits of technology, it is more important than ever for us to use technology to protect personal freedom.

Blaming technology for the death of privacy isn't new. In 1890 two Boston lawyers, Samuel Warren and Louis Brandeis, argued in the *Harvard Law Review* that privacy was under attack by "recent inventions and business methods." They contended that the pressures of modern society required the creation of a "right of privacy," which would help protect what they called "the right to be let alone." Warren and Brandeis refused to believe that privacy had to die for technology to flourish. Today, the Warren/Brandeis article is regarded as one of the most influential law review articles ever published.

Privacy-invasive technology does not exist in a vacuum, of course. That's because technology itself exists at a junction between science, the market and society. People create technology to fill specific needs and desires. And technology is regulated, or not, as people and society see fit. Few engineers set out to build systems designed to crush privacy and autonomy, and few businesses

or consumers would willingly use or purchase these systems if they understood the consequences.

⁕

How can we keep technology and the free market from killing our privacy?
One way is by being careful and informed consumers. Some people have
begun taking simple measures to protect their privacy, measures like making
purchases with cash and refusing to provide their Social Security numbers—or
providing fake ones. And a small but growing number of people are speaking
out for technology with privacy. In 1990 Lotus and Equifax teamed up to create a CD-ROM product called "Lotus Marketplace: Households," which would
have included names, addresses and demographic information on every
household in the United States, so small businesses could do the same kind of
target marketing that big businesses have been doing since the sixties. The
project was canceled when more than 30,000 people wrote to Lotus demanding that their names be taken out of the database.

Similarly, in 1997 the press informed taxpayers that the Social Security
Administration was making detailed tax-history information about them
available over the Internet. The SSA argued that its security provisions—requiring that taxpayers enter their name, date of birth, state of birth and mother's
maiden name—were sufficient to prevent fraud. But tens of thousands of
Americans disagreed, several US senators investigated the agency and the service was promptly shut down. When the service was reactivated some months
later, the detailed financial information in the SSA's computers could not be
downloaded over the Internet.

But individual actions are not enough. We need to involve government
itself in the privacy fight. The biggest privacy failure of the US government has
been its failure to carry through with the impressive privacy groundwork that
was laid in the Nixon, Ford and Carter administrations. It's worth taking a
look back at that groundwork and considering how it may serve us today.

The seventies were a good decade for privacy protection and consumer
rights. In 1970 Congress passed the Fair Credit Reporting Act, which gave
Americans the previously denied right to see their own credit reports and
demand the removal of erroneous information. Elliot Richardson, who at the
time was President Nixon's Secretary of Health, Education and Welfare, created a commission in 1972 to study the impact of computers on privacy. After
years of testimony in Congress, the commission found all the more reason for
alarm and issued a landmark report in 1973.

The most important contribution of the Richardson report was a bill of
rights for the computer age, which it called the Code of Fair Information Practices. The code is based on five principles:

- There must be no personal-data record-keeping system whose very
  existence is secret.
- There must be a way for a person to find out what information about
  the person is in a record and how it is used.

- There must be a way for a person to prevent information about the person that was obtained for one purpose from being used or made available for other purposes without the person's consent.
- There must be a way for a person to correct or amend a record of identifiable information about the person.
- Any organization creating, maintaining, using or disseminating records of identifiable personal data must assure the reliability of the data for their intended use and must take precautions to prevent misuse of the data.

✦

The biggest impact of the Richardson report wasn't in the United States but in Europe. In the years after the report was published, practically every European country passed laws based on these principles. Many created data-protection commissions and commissioners to enforce the laws. Some believe that one reason for Europe's interest in electronic privacy was its experience with Nazi Germany in the thirties and forties. Hitler's secret police used the records of governments and private organizations in the countries he invaded to round up people who posed the greatest threat to German occupation; postwar Europe realized the danger of allowing potentially threatening private information to be collected, even by democratic governments that might be responsive to public opinion.

But here in the United States, the idea of institutionalized data protection faltered. President Jimmy Carter showed interest in improving medical privacy, but he was quickly overtaken by economic and political events. Carter lost the election of 1980 to Ronald Reagan, whose aides saw privacy protection as yet another failed Carter initiative. Although several privacy-protection laws were signed during the Reagan/Bush era, the leadership for these bills came from Congress, not the White House. The lack of leadership stifled any chance of passing a nationwide data-protection act. Such an act would give people the right to know if their name and personal information is stored in a database, to see the information and to demand that incorrect information be removed.

In fact, while most people in the federal government were ignoring the cause of privacy, some were actually pursuing an antiprivacy agenda. In the early eighties, the government initiated numerous "computer matching" programs designed to catch fraud and abuse. Unfortunately, because of erroneous data these programs often penalized innocent people. In 1994 Congress passed the Communications Assistance to Law Enforcement Act, which gave the government dramatic new powers for wiretapping digital communications. In 1996 Congress passed two laws, one requiring states to display Social Security numbers on driver's licenses and another requiring that all medical patients in the United States be issued unique numerical identifiers, even if they pay their own bills. Fortunately, the implementation of those 1996 laws has been delayed, thanks largely to a citizen backlash and the resulting inaction by Congress and the executive branch.

◦❀◦

Continuing the assault, both the Bush and Clinton administrations waged an all-out war against the rights of computer users to engage in private and secure communications. Starting in 1991, both administrations floated proposals for use of "Clipper" encryption systems that would have given the government access to encrypted personal communications. Only recently did the Clinton Administration finally relent in its seven-year war against computer privacy. President Clinton also backed the Communications Decency Act (CDA), which made it a crime to transmit sexually explicit information to minors—and, as a result, might have required Internet providers to deploy far-reaching monitoring and censorship systems. When a court in Philadelphia found the CDA unconstitutional, the Clinton Administration appealed the decision all the way to the Supreme Court—and lost.

One important step toward reversing the current direction of government would be to create a permanent federal oversight agency charged with protecting privacy. Such an agency would:

- Watch over the government's tendency to sacrifice people's privacy for other goals and perform governmentwide reviews of new federal programs for privacy violations before they're launched.
- Enforce the government's few existing privacy laws.
- Be a guardian for individual privacy and liberty in the business world, showing businesses how they can protect privacy and profits at the same time.
- Be an ombudsman for the American public and rein in the worst excesses that our society has created.

Evan Hendricks, editor of the Washington-based newsletter *Privacy Times*, estimates that a fifty-person privacy-protection agency could be created with an annual budget of less than $5 million—a tiny drop in the federal budget.

Some privacy activists scoff at the idea of using government to assure our privacy. Governments, they say, are responsible for some of the greatest privacy violations of all time. This is true, but the US government was also one of the greatest polluters of all time. Today the government is the nation's environmental police force, equally scrutinizing the actions of private business and the government itself.

At the very least, governments can alter the development of technology that affects privacy. They have done so in Europe. Consider this: A growing number of businesses in Europe are offering free telephone calls—provided that the caller first listens to a brief advertisement. The service saves consumers money, even if it does expose them to a subtle form of brainwashing. But not all these services are equal. In Sweden both the caller and the person being called are forced to listen to the advertisement, and the new advertisements are played during the phone call itself. But Italy's privacy ombudsman ruled that the person being called could not be forced to listen to the ads.

There is also considerable public support for governmental controls within the United States itself—especially on key issues, such as the protection of medical records. For example, a 1993 Harris-Equifax survey on medical privacy issues found that 56 percent of the American public favored "comprehensive federal legislation that spells out rules for confidentiality of individual medical records" as part of national healthcare reform legislation. Yet Congress failed to act on the public's wishes.

The Fair Credit Reporting Act [FCRA] was a good law in its day, but it should be upgraded into a Data Protection Act. Unfortunately, the Federal Trade Commission and the courts have narrowly interpreted the FCRA. The first thing that is needed is legislation that expands it into new areas. Specifically, consumer-reporting firms should be barred from reporting arrests unless those arrests result in convictions. Likewise, consumer-reporting firms should not be allowed to report evictions unless they result in court judgments in favor of the landlord or a settlement in which both the landlord and tenant agree that the eviction can be reported. Companies should be barred from exchanging medical information about individuals or furnishing medical information as part of a patient's report without the patient's explicit consent.

❧◉☙

We also need new legislation that expands the fundamental rights offered to consumers under the FCRA. When negative information is reported to a credit bureau, the business making that report should be required to notify the subject of the report—the consumer—in writing. Laws should be clarified so that if a consumer-reporting company does not correct erroneous data in its reports, consumers can sue for real damages, punitive damages and legal fees. People should have the right to correct any false information in their files, and if the consumer and the business disagree about the truth, then the consumer should have a right to place a *detailed* explanation into his or her record. And people should have a right to see all the information that has been collected on them; these reports should be furnished for free, at least once every six months.

We need to rethink consent, a bedrock of modern law. Consent is a great idea, but the laws that govern consent need to be rewritten to limit what kinds of agreements can be made with consumers. Blanket, perpetual consent should be outlawed.

Further, we need laws that require improved computer security. In the eighties the United States aggressively deployed cellular-telephone and alphanumeric-pager networks, even though both systems were fundamentally unsecure. Instead of deploying secure systems, manufacturers lobbied for laws that would make it illegal to listen to the broadcasts. The results were predictable: dozens of cases in which radio transmissions were eavesdropped. We are now making similar mistakes in the prosecution of many Internet crimes, going after the perpetrator while refusing to acknowledge the liabilities of businesses that do not even take the most basic security precautions.

We should also bring back the Office of Technology Assessment, set up under a bill passed in 1972. The OTA didn't have the power to make laws or issue regulations, but it could publish reports on topics Congress asked it to study. Among other things, the OTA considered at length the trade-offs between law enforcement and civil liberties, and it also looked closely at issues of worker monitoring. In total, the OTA published 741 reports, 175 of which dealt directly with privacy issues, before it was killed in 1995 by the newly elected Republican-majority Congress.

Nearly forty years ago, Rachel Carson's book *Silent Spring* helped seed the US environmental movement. And to our credit, the silent spring that Carson foretold never came to be. *Silent Spring* was successful because it helped people to understand the insidious damage that pesticides were wreaking on the environment, and it helped our society and our planet to plot a course to a better future.

Today, technology is killing one of our most cherished freedoms. Whether you call this freedom the right to digital self-determination, the right to informational autonomy or simply the right to privacy, the shape of our future will be determined in large part by how we understand, and ultimately how we control or regulate, the threats to this freedom that we face today.

NO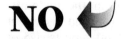

Adam L. Penenberg

The End of Privacy

The phone rang and a stranger cracked sing-songy at the other end of the line: *"Happy Birthday."* That was spooky—the next day I would turn 37. "Your full name is Adam Landis Penenberg," the caller continued. "Landis?" My mother's maiden name. "I'm touched," he said. Then Daniel Cohn, Web detective, reeled off the rest of my "base identifiers"—my birth date, address in New York, Social Security number. Just two days earlier I had issued Cohn a challenge: Starting with my byline, dig up as much information about me as you can. "That didn't take long," I said.

"It took about five minutes," Cohn said, cackling back in Boca Raton, Fla. "I'll have the rest within a week." And the line went dead.

In all of six days Dan Cohn and his Web detective agency, Docusearch.com, shattered every notion I had about privacy in this country (or whatever remains of it). Using only a keyboard and the phone, he was able to uncover the innermost details of my life—whom I call late at night; how much money I have in the bank; my salary and rent. He even got my unlisted phone numbers, both of them. Okay, so you've heard it before: America, the country that made "right to privacy" a credo, has lost its privacy to the computer. But it's far worse than you think. Advances in smart data-sifting techniques and the rise of the massive databases have conspired to strip you naked. The spread of the Web is the final step. It will make most of the secrets you have more instantly available than ever before, ready to reveal themselves in a few taps on the keyboard.

For decades this information rested in remote mainframes that were difficult to access, even for the techies who put it there. The move to desktop PCs and local servers in the 1990s has distributed these data far and wide. Computers now hold half a billion bank accounts, half a billion credit card accounts, hundreds of millions of mortgages and retirement funds and medical claims and more. The Web seamlessly links it all together. As e-commerce grows, marketers and busybodies will crack open a cache of new consumer data more revealing than ever before.

It will be a salesman's dream—and a paranoid's nightmare. Adding to the paranoia: Hundreds of data sleuths like Dan Cohn of Docusearch have opened up shop on the Web to sell precious pieces of these data. Some are ethical;

some aren't. They mine celebrity secrets, spy on business rivals and track down hidden assets, secret lovers and deadbeat dads. They include Strategic Data Service (at datahawk.com) and Infoseekers.com and Dig Dirt Inc. (both at the PI Mall, www.pimall.com).

Cohn's firm will get a client your unlisted number for $49, your Social Security number for $49 and your bank balances for $45. Your driving record goes for $35; tracing a cell phone number costs $84. Cohn will even tell someone what stocks, bonds and securities you own (for $209). As with computers, the price of information has plunged.

You may well ask: What's the big deal? We consumers are as much to blame as marketers for all these loose data. At every turn we have willingly given up a layer of privacy in exchange for convenience; it is why we use a credit card to shop, enduring a barrage of junk mail. Why should we care if our personal information isn't so personal anymore?

Well, take this test: Next time you are at a party, tell a stranger your salary, checking account balance, mortgage payment and Social Security number. If this makes you uneasy, you have your answer.

"If the post office said we have to use transparent envelopes, people would go crazy, because the fact is we all have something to hide," says Edward Wade, a privacy advocate who wrote *Identity Theft: The Cybercrime of the Millennium* (Loompanics Unlimited, 1999) under the pseudonym John Q. Newman.

You can do a few things about it. Give your business to the companies that take extra steps to safeguard your data and will guarantee it. Refuse to reveal your Social Security number—the key for decrypting your privacy—to all but the financial institutions required by law to record it.

Do something, because many banks, brokerages, credit card issuers and others are lax, even careless, about locking away your records. They take varied steps in trying to protect your privacy. Some sell information to other marketers, and many let hundreds of employees access your data. Some workers, aiming to please, blithely hand out your account number, balance and more whenever someone calls and asks for it. That's how Cohn pierced my privacy.

"You call up a company and make it seem like you're a spy on a covert mission, and only they can help you," he says. "It works every time. All day long I deal with spy wannabes."

I'm not the paranoid type; I don't see a huddle on TV and think that 11 football players are talking about me. But things have gone too far. A stalker would kill for the wealth of information Cohn was able to dig up. A crook could parlay the data into credit card scams and "identity theft," pilfering my good credit rating and using it to pull more ripoffs.

Cohn operates in this netherworld of private eyes, ex-spooks and ex-cops, retired military men, accountants and research librarians. Now 39, he grew up in the Philadelphia suburb of Bryn Mawr, attended Penn State and joined the Navy in 1980 for a three-year stint. In 1987 Cohn formed his own agency to investigate insurance fraud and set up shop in Florida. "There was no shortage of work," he says. He invented a "video periscope" that could rise up through the roof of a van to record a target's scam.

In 1995 he founded Docusearch with childhood pal Kenneth Zeiss. They fill up to 100 orders a day on the Web, and expect $1 million in business this year. Their clients include lawyers, insurers, private eyes; the Los Angeles Pension Union is a customer, and Citibank's legal recovery department uses Docusearch to find debtors on the run.

Cohn, Zeiss and 13 researchers (6 of them licensed P.I.s work out of the top floor of a dull, five-story office building in Boca Raton, Fla., sitting in cubicles under a flourescent glare and taking orders from 9 a.m. to 4 p.m. Their Web site is open 24 hours a day, 365 days a year. You click through it and load up an online shopping cart as casually as if you were at Amazon.com.

The researchers use sharp sifting methods, but Cohn also admits to misrepresenting who he is and what he is after. He says the law lets licensed investigators use such tricks as "pretext calling," fooling company employees into divulging customer data over the phone (legal in all but a few states). He even claims to have a government source who provides unpublished numbers for a fee, "and you'll never figure out how he is paid because there's no paper trail."

Yet Cohn claims to be more scrupulous than rivals. "Unlike an information broker, I won't break the law. I turn down jobs, like if a jealous boyfriend wants to find out where his ex is living." He also says he won't resell the information to anyone else.

Let's hope not. Cohn's first step into my digital domain was to plug my name into the credit bureaus—Transunion, Equifax, Experian. In minutes he had my Social Security number, address and birth date. Credit agencies are supposed to ensure that their subscribers (retailers, auto dealers, banks, mortgage companies) have a legitimate need to check credit.

"We physically visit applicants to make sure they live up to our service agreement," says David Mooney of Equifax, which keeps records on 200 million Americans and shares them with 114,000 clients. He says resellers of the data must do the same. "It's rare that anyone abuses the system." But Cohn says he gets his data from a reseller, and no one has ever checked up on him.

Armed with my credit header, Dan Cohn tapped other sites. A week after my birthday, true to his word, he faxed me a three-page summary of my life. He had pulled up my utility bills, my two unlisted phone numbers and my finances.

This gave him the ability to map my routines, if he had chosen to do so: how much cash I burn in a week ($400), how much I deposit twice a month ($3,061), my favorite neighborhood bistro (the Flea Market Cafe), the $720 monthly checks I write out to one Judith Pekowsky: my psychotherapist. (When you live in New York, you see a shrink; it's the law.) If I had an incurable disease, Cohn could probably find that out, too.

He had my latest phone bill ($108) and a list of long distance calls made from home—including late-night fiber-optic dalliances (which soon ended) with a woman who traveled a lot. Cohn also divined the phone numbers of a few of my sources, underground computer hackers who aren't wanted by the police—but probably should be.

Knowing my Social Security number and other personal details helped Cohn get access to a Federal Reserve database that told him where I had deposits.

Cohn found accounts I had forgotten long ago: $503 at Apple Bank for Savings in an account held by a long-ago landlord as a security deposit; $7 in a dormant savings account at Chase Manhattan Bank; $1,000 in another Chase account.

A few days later Cohn struck the mother lode. He located my cash management account, opened a few months earlier at Merrill Lynch & Co. That gave him a peek at my balance, direct deposits from work, withdrawals, ATM visits, check numbers with dates and amounts, and the name of my broker.

That's too much for some privacy hawks. "If someone can call your bank and get them to release account information without your consent, it means you have no privacy," says Russell Smith, director of Consumer.net in Alexandria, Va., who has won more than $40,000 suing telemarketers for bothering him. "The two issues are knowledge and control: You should know what information about you is out there, and you should be able to control who gets it."

How did Cohn get hold of my Merrill Lynch secrets? Directly from the source. Cohn says he phoned Merrill Lynch and talked to one of 500 employees who can tap into my data. "Hi, I'm Dan Cohn, a licensed state investigator conducting an investigation of an Adam Penenberg," he told the staffer, knowing the words "licensed" and "state" make it sound like he works for law enforcement.

Then he recited my Social Security, birth date and address, "and before I could get out anything more he spat out your account number." Cohn told the helpful worker: "I talked to Penenberg's broker, um, I can't remember his name...."

"Dan Dunn?" the Merrill Lynch guy asked. "Yeah, Dan Dunn," Cohn said. The staffer then read Cohn my complete history—balance, deposits, withdrawals, check numbers and amounts. "You have to talk in the lingo the bank people talk so they don't even know they are being taken," he says.

Merrill's response: It couldn't have happened this way—and if it did, it's partly my fault. Merrill staff answers phoned-in questions only when the caller provides the full account number or personal details, Merrill spokesperson Bobbie Collins says. She adds that I could have insisted on an "additional telephonic security code" the caller would have to punch in before getting information, and that this option was disclosed when I opened my CMA [cash management account]. Guess I didn't read the fine print, not that it mattered: Cohn says he got my account number from the Merrill rep.

Sprint, my long distance carrier, investigated how my account was breached and found that a Mr. Penenberg had called to inquire about my most recent bill. Cohn says only that he called his government contact. Whoever made the call, "he posed as you and had enough information to convince our customer service representative that he was you," says Russ R. Robinson, a Sprint spokesman. "We want to make it easy for our customers to do business with us over the phone, so you are darned if you do and darned if you don't."

Bell Atlantic, my local phone company, told me a similar tale, only it was a Mrs. Penenberg who called in on behalf of her husband. I recently attended a conference in Las Vegas but don't remember having tied the knot.

For the most part Cohn's methods fly below the radar of the law. "There is no general law that protects consumers' privacy in the U.S.," says David Banisar, a

Washington lawyer who helped found the Electronic Privacy Information Center (www.epic.org). In Europe companies classified as "data controllers" can't hand out your personal details without your permission, but the U.S. has as little protection as China, he contends.

The "credit header"—name, address, birth date, Social Security—used to be kept confidential under the Fair Credit Reporting Act. But in 1989 the Federal Trade Commission exempted it from such protection, bowing to the credit bureaus, bail bondsmen and private eyes.

Some piecemeal protections are in place: a 1984 act protecting cable TV bills; the 1988 Video Privacy Protection Act, passed after a newspaper published the video rental records of Supreme Court nominee Robert Bork. "It's crazy, but your movie rental history is more protected under the law than your credit history is," says Wade, the author.

Colorado is one of the few states that prohibit "pretext calling" by someone pretending to be someone else. In July James Rapp, 39, and wife Regana, 29, who ran info-broker Touch Tone Information out of a strip mall in Aurora, Colo., were charged with impersonating the Ramseys—of the JonBenet child murder case—to get hold of banking records that might be related to the case.

Congress may get into the act with bills to outlaw pretext calling. But lawyer Banisar says more than 100 privacy bills filed in the past two years have gone nowhere. He blames "an unholy alliance between marketers and government agencies that want access" to their data.

Indeed, government agencies are some of the worst offenders in selling your data. In many states the Department of Motor Vehicles was a major peddler of personal data until Congress passed the Driver's Privacy Protection Act of 1994, pushing states to enact laws that let drivers block distribution of their names and addresses. Some states, such as Georgia, take it seriously, but South Carolina has challenged it all the way up to the U.S. Supreme Court. Oral arguments are scheduled....

As originally conceived, Social Security numbers weren't to be used for identification purposes. But nowadays you are compelled by law to give an accurate number to a bank or other institution that pays you interest or dividends; thank you, Internal Revenue Service. The bank, in turn, just might trade that number away to a credit bureau—even if you aren't applying for credit. That's how snoops can tap so many databases.

Here's a theoretical way to stop this linking process without compromising the IRS' ability to track unreported income: Suppose that, instead of issuing you a single 9-digit number, the IRS gave you a dozen 11-digit numbers and let you report income under any of them. You could release one to your employer, another to your broker, a third to your health insurer, a fourth to the firms that need to know your credit history. It would be hard for a sleuth to know that William H. Smith 001–24–7829–33 was the same as 350–68–4561–49. Your digital personas would converge at only one point in cyberspace, inside the extremely well guarded computers of the IRS.

But for now, you have to fend for yourself by being picky about which firms you do business with and how much you tell them. If you are opening a bank account with no credit attached to it, ask the bank to withhold your

Social Security number from credit bureaus. Make sure your broker gives you, as Merrill Lynch does, the option of restricting telephone access to your account, and use it. If a business without a legitimate need for the Social Security number asks for it, leave the space blank—or fill it with an incorrect number. (Hint: To make it look legitimate, use an even number between 10 and 90 for the middle two digits.)

Daniel Cohn makes no apologies for how he earns a living. He sees himself as a data-robbing Robin Hood. "The problem isn't the amount of information available, it's the fact that until recently only the wealthy could afford it. That's where we come in."

In the meantime, until a better solution emerges, I'm starting over: I will change all of my bank, utility and credit-card account numbers and apply for new unlisted phone numbers. That should keep the info-brokers at bay for a while—at least for the next week or two.

POSTSCRIPT

Can Privacy Be Protected
in the Information Age?

When issues of privacy originally surfaced during the formation of the United States, the key features had to do with what people did in their own homes as opposed to in public. The Bill of Rights and our Constitution guarantee "security of person" to everyone. But when our country was formed, no one could have foreseen the type of technologies we have today that are capable of processing information for individuals in any private or public setting, through terminals and other technologies that blur the distinctions between what goes on in the privacy of home, and what private activities can actually take place in a public arena.

Today the issues of privacy have attained greater complexity. For example, who owns your e-mail? If you're sending personal messages through a system that is owned and maintained by an employer, a school, or even a subscription system provider—does the system administrator have access to your personal messages? Almost universally, the answer is "yes" because the administrator needs to be able to monitor the system. When you use a computer in a public library, do you create a record of messages and deletions that can be tracked by someone else? Again, the answer is usually "yes."

Without a doubt, different cultures have various attitudes, laws, and values with regard to issues of personal privacy. In the United States, the definition of privacy has been handed down from the Supreme Court. Challenges to privacy often are debated in our highest court, and therefore, are influenced by legal precedent. New technology challenges the court to examine those precedents and see if a balance among the right to know, the right to privacy, and the technological capability to share information can coexist.

In many other countries, however, there are different cultural attitudes and concepts of what is "private" and what is not. Both the UN Declaration of Human Rights and the World International Property Organization (WIPO) have considered the right to privacy as a basic human need for all people. It is the role of governments then, to come up with national and regional policies to enforce these various beliefs with regard to their specific cultures. An excellent collection of issues such as these can be found in James R. Michael's *Privacy and Human Rights: An International and Comparative Study With Special Reference to Development in Information Technology* (UNESCO, 1994).

A number of studies further illuminate how broad a concept privacy may be for individuals. Ann Cavoukian's *Who Knows: Safeguarding Your Privacy in a Networked World* (McGraw-Hill, 1997) takes a practical approach toward understanding how we can control information about ourselves.

ISSUE 18

Are People Better Informed in the Information Society?

YES: Wade Roush, "The Internet Reborn," *Technology Review* (October, 2003).

NO: Matthew Robinson, "Party On, Dudes!," *The American Spectator* (March/April 2002).

ISSUE SUMMARY

YES: *Technology Review* senior editor Wade Roush reflects on the way we currently use the architecture of the web. She outlines the likely scenario for the future of the Internet, with global networks connected to "smart nodes" which will be able to store all of our files, and allow us to access them from remote sites with only small, hand-held devices. The improvements in technology will then lead to a more dynamic use of the web, and will make the Internet more-user friendly, as well as more secure.

NO: Author Matthew Robinson warns that no matter what technologies we have available, human beings seem interested in fewer subjects and know even less about politics and current events. He warns that even though we may call it an "information" society, there is evidence to suggest that we actually know less than in earlier years. His examples are humorous as well as sobering.

Many people feel that as we move toward a more technologically oriented lifestyle, we, as a nation, and as participants in the new information society, are inevitably moving toward a better quality of life. It almost seems logical that better technology is the result of moving from more primitive forms of communicating to more sophisticated, faster, and efficient means. But an age-old question is whether the ability to communicate equals a quality communication experience. Without a doubt, messages that can be sent, retrieved, and enhanced may all appear to be technological breakthroughs, and positive transactions. But there is another side to this scenario in which we must address whether an excess of information truly informs.

In this issue we examine two selections that ask the same question, but propose different ways to answer the question. The Roush article challenges our assumptions about the Internet as we now know it. Despite the rapid growth of the Internet, Roush compares it to a "1973 Buick refitted with air bags and emissions controls." Because the basic infrastructure of the Internet was built on trust and was originally designed to serve fewer people, it is vulnerable to viruses and worms caused by pranksters who hack into services and disrupt operations. The Roush article also reminds us that even though we may think that our current technologies are "state-of-the-art," they too may have structural limitations.

But Roush does not necessarily criticize the developers of our current Internet—instead, he describes how computer scientists and engineers have begun to design and implement an overlay to help protect computer users by better, more sophisticated nodes that will not only improve the Internet's functions, but will provide a plethora of new services that will indeed help the average user. His article, while critical of the original architecture of the Internet, is very optimistic about overcoming our current problems and embracing the freedom provided by a stronger, more flexible system that will enhance information flow and storage. In many ways, he looks optimistically toward improvements that perpetuate the argument that more technology equals better services.

Matthew Robinson, on the other hand, tackles the question of whether people are more informed today, despite the number of sources and technologies available to them. His statistics are at the same time humorous yet frightening. If Robinson is correct, there is much evidence to support the idea that as time goes by, the public's knowledge of basic civics and politics becomes even weaker. If this is the scenario of the future, we must question whether the information society really does represent a better world, or a world in which we've lost much of what we already have.

Robinson's article is reminiscent of the predictions of many forms of media. When radio was invented, some predicted that people would stop reading newspapers and magazines; when television was invented, some feared that people would stop going to films, listening to radio, and reading newspapers or books. And in many ways, there is evidence to demonstrate that *some* of these predictions were at least partially true.

As a concluding issue to this book, these selections ask the reader to make real decisions about how they feel about new technologies and the quality of our lives. The author Neil Postman wrote about predicting what our future would be like in his book, *Amusing Ourselves To Death* (Penguin, 1985). Postman recalled earlier authors, like George Orwell, who, in 1949, wrote a futuristic book called *1984* (Harcourt, Brace), and Aldous Huxley, who, in 1932, wrote *Brave New World* (London, Chatto, & Windus). Each of these authors focused on the most common form of media available to them—print media in the form of their book, and each dealt with the future in a different way. Orwell foretold of a time in which people couldn't read because they had no books. Huxley's world envisioned a world with books, but the people chose not to read. We will conclude this volume by asking you, our readers—does a new, improved Internet help transfer and store information that helps you lead a better quality of life?

Wade Roush  **YES**

The Internet Reborn

If you're like most cyber-citizens, you use the Internet for e-mail, Web searching, chatting with friends, music downloads, and buying books and gifts. More than 600 million people use these services worldwide—far more than anyone could have predicted in the 1970s, when the Internet's key components were conceived. An estimated $3.9 trillion in business transactions will take place over the Internet in 2003, and the medium's reach is increasingly global: an astonishing 24 percent of Brazilians, 30 percent of Chinese, and 72 percent of Americans now go online at least once per month.

Still, despite its enormous impact, today's Internet is like a 1973 Buick refitted with air bags and emissions controls. Its decades-old infrastructure has been rigged out with the Web and all it enables (like e-commerce), plus technologies such as streaming media, peer-to-peer file sharing, and videoconferencing; but it's still a 1973 Buick. Now, a grass-roots group of nearly 100 leading computer scientists, backed by heavyweight industrial sponsors, is working on replacing it with a new, vastly smarter model.

The project is called PlanetLab, and within the next three years, researchers say, it will help revitalize the Internet, eventually enabling you to

- forget about hauling your laptop around. No matter where you go, you'll be able to instantly re-create your entire private computer workspace, program for program and document for document, on any Internet terminal;

- escape the disruption caused by Internet worms and viruses—which inflicted an average of $81,000 in repair costs per company per incident in 2002—because the network itself will detect and crush rogue data packets before they get a chance to spread to your office or home;

- instantly retrieve video and other bandwidth-hogging data, no matter how many other users are competing for the same resources;

- archive your tax returns, digital photographs, family videos, and all your other data across the Internet itself, securely and indestructibly, for decades, making hard disks and recordable CDs seem as quaint as 78 RPM records.

From *Technology Review* October 2003, pp. 28-32, 36-37. Copyright © 2003 by *MIT Technology Review*. Reproduced with permission of *MIT Technology Review* in the format Textbook via Copyright Clearance Center.

These predicted PlanetLab innovations—with the potential to revolutionize home computing, e-commerce, and corporate information technology practices—can't be incorporated into the existing Net; that would be too disruptive. Instead, the PlanetLab researchers, who hail from Princeton, MIT, the University of California, Berkeley, and more than 50 other institutions, are building their network on top of the Internet. But their new machines—called smart nodes—will vastly increase its processing power and data storage capability, an idea that has quickly gained support from the National Science Foundation and industry players such as Intel, Hewlett-Packard, and Google.

Since starting out in March 2002, PlanetLab has linked 175 smart nodes at 79 sites in 13 countries, with plans to reach 1,000 nodes by 2006. It's the newest and hottest of several large-scale research efforts that have sought to address the Internet's limitations... "The Internet has reached a plateau in terms of what it can do," says Larry Peterson, a Princeton computer scientist and the effort's leader. "The right thing to do is to start over at another level. That's the idea behind PlanetLab."

The Network *Is* the Computer, Finally

Like many revolutions, PlanetLab is based on a startlingly simple idea that has been around for a long time, advanced most notably by Sun Microsystems: move data and computation from desktop computers and individual mainframes into the network itself.

But this can't be done with today's Internet, which consists of basic machines, called routers, following 1970s-era procedures for breaking e-mail attachments, Web pages, and other electronic files into individually addressed packets and forwarding them to other machines. Beyond this function, the routers are dumb and inflexible: they weren't designed to handle the level of computing needed to, say, recognize and respond to virus attacks or bottlenecks elsewhere in the network.

PlanetLab's smart nodes, on the other hand, are standard PCs capable of running custom software uploaded by users. Copies of a single program can run simultaneously on many nodes around the world. Each node is plugged directly into a traditional router, so it can exchange data with other nodes over the existing Net. (For that reason, computer scientists call PlanetLab an "overlay" network.) To manage all this, each node runs software that divides the machine's resource—such as hard-drive space and processing power—among PlanetLab's many users (see "Planetary Pie," below). If the Internet is a global, electronic nervous system, then PlanetLab is finally giving it brains.

The payoff should be huge. Smarter networks will foster a new generation of distributed software programs that preempt congestion, spread out critical data, and keep the Internet secure, even as they make computer communications faster and more reliable in general. By expanding the network as quickly as possible, says Peterson, the PlanetLab researchers hope to restore the sense of risk-taking and experimentation that ruled the Internet's early days. But Peterson admits that progress won't come easily. "How do you get an innovative service out across a thousand machines and test it out?"

It helps that the network is no longer just a research sandbox, as the original Internet was during its development; instead, it's a place to deploy services that any programmer can use and help improve. And one of the Internet's original architects sees this as a tremendously exciting trait. "It's 2003, 30 years after the Internet was invented," says Vinton Cerf, who codeveloped the Internet's basic communications protocols as a Stanford University researcher in the early 1970s and is now senior vice president for architecture and technology at MCI. "We have millions of people out there who are interested in and capable of doing experimental development." Which means it shouldn't take long to replace that Buick.

Baiting Worms

The Achilles' heel of today's Internet is that it's a system built on trust. Designed into the Net is the assumption that users at the network's endpoints know and trust one another; after all, the early Internet was a tool mainly for a few hundred government and university researchers. It delivers packets whether they are legitimate or the electronic equivalent of letter bombs. Now that the Internet has exploded into the cultural mainstream, that assumption is clearly outdated: the result is a stream of worms, viruses, and inadvertent errors that can cascade into economically devastating Internet-wide slow-downs and disruptions.

Take the Code Red Internet worm, which surfaced on July 12, 2001. It quickly spread to 360,000 machines around the world, hijacking them in an attempt to flood the White House Web site with meaningless data—a so-called denial-of-service attack that chokes off legitimate communication. Cleaning up the infected machines took system administrators months and cost businesses more than $2.6 billion, according to Computer Economics, an independent research organization in Carlsbad, CA.

Thanks to one PlanetLab project, Netbait, that kind of scenario could become a thing of the past. Machines infected with Code Red and other worms and viruses often send out "probe" packets as they search for more unprotected systems to infect. Dumb routers pass along these packets, and no one is the wiser until the real invasion arrives and local systems start shutting down. But in theory, the right program running on smart routers could intercept the probes, register where they're coming from, and help administrators track—and perhaps preempt—a networkwide infection. That's exactly what Netbait, developed by researchers at Intel and UC Berkeley, is designed to do.

This spring, the program showed how it can map a spreading epidemic. Brent Chun, Netbait's author, is one of several senior researchers assigned to PlanetLab by Intel, which helped launch the network by donating the hardware for its first 100 nodes. Chun ran Netbait on 90 nodes for several months earlier this year. In mid-March, it detected a sixfold spike in Code Red probes, from about 200 probes per day to more than 1,200—a level of sensitivity far beyond that of a lone, standard router. The data collected by Netbait showed that a variant of Code Red had begun to displace its older cousin.

As it turned out, there was little threat. The variant turned out to be no more malignant than its predecessor, for which remedies are now well known. But the larger point had been made. Without a global platform like PlanetLab as a vantage point, the spread of a new Code Red strain could have gone undetected until much later, when the administrators of local systems compared notes. By then, any response required would have been far more costly.

Netbait means "we can detect patterns and warn the local system administrators that certain machines are infected at their site," says Peterson. "That's something that people hadn't thought about before." By issuing alerts as soon as it detects probe packets, Netbait could even act as an early-warning system for the entire Internet.

Netbait could be running full time on PlanetLab by year's end, according to Chun. "Assuming people deem the service to be useful, eventually it will get on the radar of people at various companies," he says. It would then be easy, says Chun, to offer commercial Internet service providers subscriptions to Netbait, or to license the software to companies with their own planetwide computing infrastructures, such as IBM, Intel, or Akamai.

Traffic Managers

Just as the Internet's architects didn't anticipate the need to defend against armies of hackers, they never foresaw flash crowds. These are throngs of users visiting a Web site simultaneously, overloading the network, the site's server, or both. (The most famous flash crowd, perhaps, formed during a 1999 Victoria's Secret lingerie Web broadcast that had been promoted during the Super Bowl. Within hours, viewers made 1.5 million requests to the company's servers. Most never got through.) Such events—or their more malevolent cousins, denial-of-service attacks—can knock out sites that aren't protected by a network like Akamai's, which caches copies of customers' Web sites on its own, widely scattered private servers. But the question is how many copies to make. Too few, and the overloads persist; too many, and the servers are choked with surplus copies. One solution, described in papers published in 1999 by the researchers who went on to found Akamai, is simply to set a fixed number.

In the not-too-distant future, PlanetLab nodes will adjust the number of cached copies on the fly. Here's how it works. Each node devotes a slice of its processor time and memory to a program designed by Vivek Pai, a colleague of Peterson's in the computer science department at Princeton. The software monitors requests for page downloads and, if it detects that a page is in high demand, copies it to the node's hard drive, which acts like the memory in a typical Web server. As demand grows, the program automatically caches the page on additional nodes to spread out the load, constantly adjusting the number of replicas according to the page's popularity. Pai says that simulations of a denial-of-service attack on a PlanetLab-like network showed that nodes equipped with the Princeton software absorbed twice as many page requests before failing as those running the algorithms published by the Akamai founders.

This new tool, known as CoDeeN, is already running full time on PlanetLab; anyone can use it, simply by changing his or her Web browser's settings to connect to a nearby PlanetLab node. It's a work in progress, so service isn't yet fully reliable. But Pai believes the software can support a network with thousands of nodes, eventually creating a free "public Akamai." With this tool, Internet users would be able to get faster and more reliable access to any Web site they chose.

But banishing flash crowds won't, by itself, solve Internet slowdowns. Other PlanetLab software seeks to attack a subtler problem: the absence of a decent "highway map" of the network. Over the years the Internet has grown into an opaque tangle of routers and backbone links owned by thousands of competing Internet service providers, most of them private businesses. "Packets go in, they come out, and there's very little visibility or control as to what happens in the middle," says Thomas Anderson, a computer scientist at the University of Washington in Seattle.

One solution is software known as Scriptroute. Developed by Anderson and his colleagues at the University of Washington, it's a distributed program that uses smart nodes to launch probes that fan out through particular regions of the Internet and send back data about their travels. The data can be combined into a map of the active links within and between Internet service providers' networks—along with measurements of the time packets take to traverse each link. It's like having an aerial view of an urban freeway system. Anderson says operators at Internet service providers such as AOL and Earthlink, as well as universities, could use Scriptroute's maps to rapidly diagnose and repair network problems in one to three years.

Sea Change

Keeping data intact can be just as tricky as transmitting it: ask anyone who has left a personal digital assistant on a train or suffered a hard-drive crash. What's needed, says Berkeley computer scientist John Kubiatowicz, is a way to spread data around so that we don't have to carry it physically, but so it's always available, invulnerable to loss or destruction, and inaccessible to unauthorized people.

That's the grand vision behind OceanStore, a distributed storage system that's also being tested on PlanetLab. OceanStore encrypts files—whether memos or other documents, financial records, or digital photos, music, or video clips—then breaks them into overlapping fragments. The system continually moves the fragments and replicates them on nodes around the planet. The original file can be reconstituted from just a subset of the fragments, so it's virtually indestructible, even if a number of local nodes fail. PlanetLab nodes currently have enough memory to let a few hundred people store their records on OceanStore, says Kubiatowicz. Eventually, millions of nodes would be required to store everyone's data. Kubiatowicz's goal is to produce software capable of managing 100 trillion files, or 10,000 files for each of 10 billion people.

To keep track of distributed data, OceanStore assigns the fragments of each particular file their own ID code—a very long number called the Globally Unique Identifier. When a file's owner wants to retrieve the file, her computer tells a node running OceanStore to search for the nearest copies of fragments with the right ID and reassemble them.

Privacy and security are built in. An owner who wants to retrieve a file must first present a key that has been generated using now common encryption methods and stored in a password-protected section of her personal computer. This key contains so many digits that it's essentially impossible for others to guess it and gain unauthorized access. The key provides access to OceanStore directories that map human-readable names (such as "internet.draft") to fragment ID codes. The ID codes are then used to search OceanStore for the nearest copies of the needed fragments, which are reassembled and decrypted. And there's one more layer of protection: the ID codes are themselves generated from the data's contents at the time the contents are saved using a secure cryptographic function. Like encryption keys, the codes are so long (160 binary digits) that even today's most advanced supercomputers can't guess or fake them. So if data retrieved from OceanStore has an unaltered ID, the owner can be sure the data itself hasn't been changed or corrupted.

Kubiatowicz would like to see OceanStore become a utility similar to DSL or cable Internet service, with consumers paying a monthly access fee. "Say you just got back from a trip and you have a digital camera full of pictures," he suggests. "One option is to put these pictures on your home computer or write them to CDs. Another option is that you put those pictures into OceanStore. You just copy them to a partition of your hard drive, and the data is replicated efficiently on a global scale." That option could be available within three to five years, he predicts, but in the interim, two things need to happen. First, his team needs to produce sturdier versions of the OceanStore code. Second, someone needs to provide enough nodes to enlarge the system to a useful scale. That someone is likely to be a private company looking to enter the distributed-storage business, predicts Peterson. "I could imagine OceanStore attracting the next Hotmail-like startup as its first customer," he says.

Beyond providing distributed, secure storage, OceanStore could eventually make every computer your personal one. At its next level of development, it could store your entire computing environment—your PC desktop, plus all of the applications you're running and all the documents you have open—across the network and reconstitute it on demand, even if you popped up at an Internet terminal halfway around the world. This capability would be useful to the businessperson on the road, to a doctor who suddenly needs to review a chart, or to a contractor who wants to tweak a blueprint from home. Several companies are working to realize this vision. Intel calls it Internet Suspend/Resume, and Sun researchers are testing several approaches to "desktop mobility." But PlanetLab could provide the infrastructure that makes such technology possible, by offering a means to manage the large amounts of data—perhaps tens of gigabytes—that personal-computer users might regularly rely on.

Laundry List

Such ideas may seem radical. Then again, just a decade ago, so did e-commerce. The question now is which big idea will evolve into the Google or Amazon.com of the new, smarter Internet. By charter, PlanetLab can't be used for profit-making enterprises, but businesses may soon spring from the platform it provides. "We want it to be a place where you leave services running long-term—which brings us much closer to the point where someone commercial might want to adopt it or replicate it for profit," Peterson says. That could happen if the experiments running now, along with the methods being developed to keep the network operating smoothly, provide a reliable model for future intelligent networks. "We don't know where that next big idea is going to come from," says Peterson. "Our goal is just to provide the playing field."

PlanetLab's early industry sponsors, such as Intel and Hewlett-Packard, may be among the first to jump in. HP Labs in Palo Alto, CA, for example, installed 30 PlanetLab nodes in June and plans to use the network to road-test technologies that could soon become products. One example: software developed by researcher Susie Wee that uses a CoDeeN-like distribution network to deliver high-resolution streaming video to mobile devices. The goal is to avoid wasting bandwidth, and Wee's software would do just that by streaming, say, video of a major-league baseball game to a single local node, then splitting the data into separate streams optimized for the screen resolutions of different viewers' devices—whether desktop PCs, wireless laptops, PDAs, or cell phones. HP or its licensees could bring such a service to market within two years, Wee says. Projects like this one, says Rick McGeer, HP Labs' scientific liaison to a number of university efforts, means that PlanetLab is "not only a great experimental test bed, it's a place where you can see the demonstrable value of services you don't get on today's Internet."

Of course, researchers' enthusiasm about smart networks doesn't keep them from pondering the new problems they could create. Until now, viruses and worms have always been launched from machines at the Internet's edges; imagine how much more damage an attack could do if it originated from a trusted node inside the network. And there's no centralized authority to force local PlanetLab machines to meet security standards, as there is with Akamai and other private networks. But researchers at Princeton and other PlanetLab member institutions say they're already working on ways to avoid these hazards.

While it's impossible to know which blockbuster new technology and business paradigms will emerge from smarter networks, projects like Planet-Lab virtually ensure that the Internet will eventually fulfill some of its long-unrealized potential in areas like broadband access, security, shared storage, and reliable video, text, and other content delivery. "There is a long laundry list of things we can and should do better on the Internet," Internet pioneer Cerf says. "Why didn't we do it before? Well, some of it is that they are hard problems; some of it is because the technology wasn't capable enough—we needed more brute-force computing capability than we had 20 years ago. And in some cases, it's because nobody cared."

That's now changing. Peterson expects that ultimately PlanetLab and similar networks will bring about a wholesale reinvention of the Internet. As smart nodes are installed at more of the Internet's existing hubs, these networks could multiply to the point that they cease to be add-ons at all and simply *become* the next generation's Internet. As Peterson puts it, "This is exactly the Internet all over again." The results could be as different from e-mail and Web browsing as those technologies are from the telephone—or a 1973 Buick is from a low-emissions, fuel-efficient Toyota—with impact to match.

PARTY ON, DUDES! Ignorance Is the Curse of the Information Age

Almost any look at what the average citizen knows about politics is bound to be discouraging. Political scientists are nearly unanimous on the subject of voter ignorance. The average American citizen not only lacks basic knowledge, but also holds beliefs that are contradictory and inconsistent. Here is a small sample of what Americans "know":

Nearly one-third of Americans (29 percent) think the Constitution guarantees a job. Forty-two percent think it guarantees health care. And 75 percent think it guarantees a high school education.

Forty-five percent think the communist tenet "from each according to his abilities, to each according to his needs" is part of the U.S. Constitution.

More Americans recognize the Nike advertising slogan "Just Do It" than know where the right to "life, liberty and the pursuit of happiness" is set forth (79 percent versus 47 percent).

Ninety percent know that Bill Gates is the founder of the company that created the Windows operating system. Just over half (53 percent) correctly identified Alexander Hamilton as a Founding Father.

Fewer than half of adults (47 percent) can name their own representative in Congress.

Fewer than half of voters could identify whether their congressman voted for the use of force in the Persian Gulf War.

Just 30 percent of adults could name Newt Gingrich as the congressman who led Republican congressional candidates in signing the Contract with America. Six months after the GOP took congress, 64 percent admitted they did not know.

A 1998 poll by the Pew Research Center for the People and the Press showed that 56 percent of Americans could not name a single Democratic candidate for president; 63 percent knew the name "Bush," but it wasn't clear that voters connected the name to George W. Bush.

According to a January 2000 Gallup poll, 66 percent of Americans could correctly name Regis Philbin when asked who hosts *Who Wants to Be a Millionaire*, but only 6 percent could correctly name Dennis Hastert when asked to name the speaker of the House of Representatives in Washington.

Political scientists Michael X. Delli Carpini and Scott Keeter studied 3,700 questions surveying the public's political knowledge from the 1930s to the present. They discovered that people tend to remember or identify trivial details about political leaders, focusing on personalities or simply latching onto the politics that the press plays up. For example, the most commonly known fact about George Bush while he was president was that he hated broccoli, and during the 1992 presidential campaign, although 89 percent of the public knew that Vice President Quayle was feuding with the television character Murphy Brown, only 19 percent could characterize Bill Clinton's record on the environment.

Their findings demonstrate the full absurdity of public knowledge: More people could identify Judge Wapner (the long-time host of the television series *The People's Court*) than could identify Chief Justice Warren Burger or William Rehnquist. More people had heard of John Lennon than of Karl Marx. More Americans could identify comedian-actor Bill Cosby than could name either of their U.S. senators. More people knew who said "What's up, Doc;" "Hi ho, Silver;" or "Come up and see me sometime" than "Give me liberty or give me death;" "The only thing we have to fear is fear itself;" or "Speak softly and carry a big stick." More people knew that Pete Rose was accused of gambling than could name any of the five U.S. senators accused in the late 1980s of unethical conduct in the savings and loan scandal.

In 1986, the National Election Survey found that almost 24 percent of the general public did not know who George Bush was or that he was in his second term as vice president of the United States. "People at this level of inattentiveness can have only the haziest idea of the policy alternatives about which pollsters regularly ask, and such ideas as they do have must often be relatively innocent of the effects of exposure to elite discourse," writes UCLA political science professor John R. Zaller.

All of this would appear to be part of a broader trend of public ignorance that extends far beyond politics. Lack of knowledge on simple matters can reach staggering levels. In a 1996 study by the National Science Foundation, fewer than half of American adults polled (47 percent) knew that the earth takes one year to orbit the sun. Only about 9 percent could describe in their own words what a molecule is, and only 21 percent knew what DNA is.

Esoteric information? That's hard to say. One simple science-related question that has grown to have major political importance is whether police ought to genetically tag convicted criminals in the hopes of linking them to unsolved crimes. In other words, should police track the DNA of a convicted burglar to see if he is guilty of other crimes? Obviously, issues of privacy and government power are relevant here. Yet how can a poll about this issue make sense if the citizenry doesn't understand the scientific terms of debate? Asking an evaluative question seems pointless.

The next generation of voters—those who will undoubtedly be asked to answer even tougher questions about politics and science—are hardly doing any better on the basics. A 2000 study by the American Council of Trustees and Alumni found that 81 percent of seniors at the nation's 55 top colleges scored a D or F on high school-level history exams. It turns out that most college seniors—including those from such elite universities as Harvard, Stanford and the University of California—do not know the men or ideas that have shaped American freedom. Here are just a few examples from *Losing America's Memory: Historical Illiteracy in the 21st Century*, focusing on people's lack of knowledge about our First Citizen—the man whose respect for the laws of the infant republic set the standard for virtue and restraint in office.

Barely one in three students knew that George Washington was the American general at the battle of Yorktown—the battle that won the war for independence.

Only 42 percent could identify Washington with the line "First in war, first in peace, first in the hearts of his countrymen."

Only a little more than half knew that Washington's farewell address warned against permanent alliances with foreign governments.

And when it comes to actually explaining the ideas that preserve freedom and restrain government, the college seniors performed just as miserably.

More than one in three were clueless about the division of power set forth in the U.S. Constitution.

Only 22 percent of these seniors could identify the source of the phrase "government of the people, by the people, and for the people" (from Lincoln's Gettysburg Address).

Yet 99 percent of college seniors knew the crude cartoon characters Beavis and Butthead, and 98 percent could identify gangsta rapper Snoop Dogg.

Apparent ignorance of basic civics can be especially dangerous. Americans often "project" power onto institutions with little understanding of the Constitution or the law. Almost six of 10 Americans (59 percent) think the president, not Congress, has the power to declare war. Thirty-five percent of Americans believe the president has the power to adjourn Congress at his will. Almost half (49 percent) think he has the power to suspend the Constitution (49 percent). And six in 10 think the chief executive appoints judges to the federal courts without the approval of the Senate.

Some political scientists charge that American ignorance tends to help institutions and parties in power. That is hardly the active vigilance by the citizenry that the founders advocated. Political scientists continue to debate the role of ignorance and the future of democracy when voters are so woefully ignorant. As journalist Christopher Shea writes, "Clearly, voter ignorance poses problems for democratic theory: Politicians, the representatives of the people, are being elected by people who do not know their names or their platforms. Elites are committing the nation to major treaties and sweeping policies that most voters don't even know exist."

Professors Delli Carpini and Keeter discovered, for example, that most Americans make fundamental errors on some of the most contested and heavily covered political questions. "Americans grossly overestimate the average profit made by American corporations, the percentage of the U.S. population that is poor or homeless, and the percentage of the world population that is malnourished," they write. "And, despite 12 years of anti-abortion administrations, Americans substantially underestimate the number of abortions performed every year."

With most voters unable to even name their congressperson or senators during an election year, the clear winner is the establishment candidate. Studies by Larry Bartels at Princeton University show that mere name recognition is enough to give incumbents, a 5-percentage-point advantage over challengers: Most voters in the election booth can't identify a single position of the incumbent, but if they've seen the candidate's name before, that can be enough to secure their vote. (In many cases, voters can't even recognize the names of incumbents.)

Media polls are typically searching in vain for hard-nosed public opinion that simply isn't there. Polls force people to say they are leaning toward a particular candidate, but when voters are asked the more open-ended question "Whom do you favor for the presidency?" the number of undecided voters rises. The mere practice, in polling, of naming the candidates yields results that convey a false sense of what voters know. When Harvard's "Vanishing Voter Project" asked voters their presidential preferences without giving the names of candidates, they routinely found that the number of undecided voters was much higher than in media polls. Just three weeks before the 2000 election, 14 percent of voters still hadn't made up their minds.

Even when polling covers subjects on which a person should have direct knowledge, it can yield misleading results because of basic ignorance. The nonpartisan Center for Studying Health System Change (HSC) found that how people rate their health care is attributable to the type of plan they *think* they are in, more than their actual health insurance. The center asked 20,000 privately insured people what they thought of their coverage, their doctor and their treatment. But instead of just taking their opinions and impressions, the center also looked at what coverage each respondent actually had.

Nearly a quarter of Americans mis-identified the coverage they had. Eleven percent didn't know they were in an HMO, and another 13 percent thought they were in an HMO but were not. Yet when people believed they were in a much-maligned HMO (even when they actually had another kind of insurance), their perceived satisfaction with their health care was lower than that of people who believed they had non-HMO coverage (even when they were in an HMO). Similarly, on nearly all 10 measures studied by the center, those HMO enrollees who thought they had a different kind of insurance gave satisfaction ratings similar to those who actually had those other kinds of insurance.

Once center researchers adjusted for incorrect self-identification, the differences between HMO and non-HMO enrollees nearly vanished. Even on something as personal as health care, citizens display a striking and debilitating ignorance that quietly undermines many polling results.

After looking at the carnage of polls that test voter knowledge rather than impressions, James L. Payne concluded in his 1991 book *The Culture of Spending:*

Surveys have repeatedly found that voters are remarkably ignorant about even simple, dramatic features of the political landscape. The vast majority of voters cannot recall the names of congressional candidates in the most recent election; they cannot use the labels "liberal" and "conservative" meaningfully; they do not know which party controls Congress; they are wildly wrong about elementary facts about the federal budget; and they do not know how their congressmen vote on even quite salient policy questions. In other words, they are generally incapable of rewarding or punishing their congressman for his action on spending bills.

Ignorance of basic facts such as a candidate's name or position isn't the only reason to question the efficacy of polling in such a dispiriting universe. Because polls have become "players in the political process," their influence is felt in the policy realm, undercutting efforts to educate because they assume respondents' knowledge and focus on the horse race. Is it correct to say that Americans oppose or support various policies when they don't even have a grasp of basic facts relating to those policies? For instance, in 1995, Grass Roots Research found that 83 percent of those polled underestimated the average family's tax burden. Taxes for a four-person family earning $35,000 are 54 percent higher than most people think. Naturally, when practical-minded Americans look at political issues, their perceptions of reality influence which solutions they find acceptable. If they perceive that there are fewer abortions or lower taxes than there really are, these misperceptions may affect the kinds of policy prescriptions they endorse. They might change their views if introduced to the facts. In this sense, the unreflective reporting on public opinion about these policy issues is deceptive.

The Wall Street Journal editorial page provides another example of how ignorance affects public debate. Media reports during the 1995 struggle between the Republicans in Congress and the Clinton White House continually asserted that the public strongly opposed the GOP's efforts to slow the growth of Medicare spending. A poll by Public Opinion Strategies asked 1,000 Americans not what they felt, but what they actually knew about the GOP plan. Twenty-seven percent said they thought the GOP would cut Medicare spending by $4,000 per recipient. Almost one in four (24 percent) said it would keep spending the same. Another 25 percent didn't know. Only 22 percent knew the correct answer: The plan would increase spending to $6,700 per recipient.

Public Opinion's pollsters then told respondents the true result of the GOP plan and explained: "[U]nder the plan that recently passed by Congress, spending on Medicare will increase 45 percent over the next seven years, which is twice the projected rate of inflation." How did such hard facts change public opinion about Medicare solutions? Six of 10 Americans said that the GOP's proposed Medicare spending was too *high*. Another 29 percent said it was about right. Only 2 percent said it was too *low*.

Indeed polling and the media may gain their ability to influence results from voter ignorance. When a polling question introduces new facts (or any facts at all), voters are presented with a reframed political issue and thus may have a new opinion. Voters are continually asked about higher spending, new programs, and the best way to solve social ills with government spending. But how does the knowledge base (or lack of knowledge) affect the results of a polling question? That is simply unknown. When asked in a June 2000 *Washington Post* poll how much money the federal government gives to the nation's public schools, only 31 percent chose the correct answer. Although only 10 percent admitted to not knowing the correct answer, fully 60 percent of registered voters claimed they knew, but were wrong. Is there any doubt that voters' knowledge, or lack thereof, affects the debate about whether to raise school spending to ever higher levels?

Reporters often claim that the public supports various policies, and they use such sentiment as an indicator of the electoral prospects of favored candidates. But this, too, can be misleading. Take, for instance, the results of a survey taken by The Polling Company for the Center for Security Policy about the Strategic Defense Initiative. Some 54 percent of respondents thought that the U.S. military had the capability to destroy a ballistic missile before it could hit an American city and do damage. Another 20 percent didn't know or refused to answer. Only 27 percent correctly said that the U.S. military could not destroy a missile.

What's interesting is that although 70 percent of those polled said they were concerned about the possibility of ballistic missile attack, the actual level of ignorance was very high. The Polling Company went on to tell those polled that "government documents indicate that the U.S. military cannot destroy even a single incoming missile." The responses were interesting. Nearly one in five said they were "shocked and angry" by the revelation. Another 28 percent said they were "very surprised," and 17 percent were "somewhat surprised." Only 22 percent said they were "not surprised at all." Finally, 14 percent were "skeptical because [they] believe that the documents are inaccurate."

Beyond simply skewing poll results, ignorance is actually amplified by polling. Perhaps the most amazing example of the extent of ignorance can be found in Larry Sabato's 1981 book *The Rise of Political Consultants*. Citizens were asked: "Some people say the 1975 Public Affairs Act should be repealed. Do you agree or disagree that it should be repealed?" Nearly one in four (24 percent) said they wanted it repealed. Another 19 percent wanted it to remain in effect. Fifty-seven percent didn't know what should be done. What's interesting is that there was no such thing as the 1975 Public Affairs Act. But for 43 percent of those polled, simply asking that question was enough to create public opinion.

Ignorance can threaten even the most democratic institutions and safeguards. In September 1997, the Center for Media and Public Affairs conducted one of the largest surveys ever on American views of the Fourth Estate. Fully 84 percent of Americans are willing to "turn to the government to require that the news media give equal coverage to all sides of controversial issues." Seven-in-10 back court-imposed fines for inaccurate or biased reporting. And just over half (53 percent) think that journalists should be licensed. Based on sheer numbers—in the absence of the rule of law and dedication to the Bill of Rights—there is enough support to put curbs on the free speech that most journalists (rightly) consider one of the most important bulwarks of liberty.

In an era when Americans have neither the time nor the interest to track politics closely, the power of the pollster to shape public opinion is almost unparalleled when united with the media agenda.

For elected leaders, voter ignorance is something they have to confront when they attempt to make a case for new policies or reforms. But for the media, ignorance isn't an obstacle. It's an opportunity for those asking the questions—whether pollster or media polling director—to drive debate. As more time is devoted to media pundits, journalists and pollsters, and less to candidates and leaders, the effect is a negative one: Public opinion becomes more important as arbiter for the chattering classes. But in a knowledge vacuum, public opinion also becomes more plastic and more subject to manipulation, however well intentioned.

Pollsters often try to bridge the gap in public knowledge by providing basic definitions of terms as part of their questions. But this presents a new problem: By writing the questions, pollsters are put in a position of power, particularly when those questions will be used in a media story. The story—if the poll is the story—is limited by the questions asked, the definitions supplied, and the answers that respondents are given to choose from.

The elevation of opinion without context or reference to knowledge exacerbates a problem of modern democracies. Self-expression may work in NEA-funded art, but it robs the political process of the communication and discussion that marries compromise with principle. Clearly "opinion" isn't the appropriate word for the mélange of impressions and sentiment that is presented as the public's belief in countless newspaper and television stories. If poll respondents lack a solid grasp of the facts, surveys give us little more than narcissistic opinion.

As intelligent and precise thinking declines, all that remains is a chaos of ideologies in which the lowest human appetites rule. In her essay "Truth and Politics," historian Hannah Arendt writes: "Facts inform opinions, and opinions, inspired by different interests and passions, can differ widely and still be legitimate as long as they respect factual truth. Freedom of opinion is a farce unless factual information is guaranteed and facts themselves are not in dispute."

If ignorance is rife in a republic, what do polls and the constant media attention to them do to deliberative democracy? As Hamilton put it, American government is based on "reflection and choice." Modern-day radical egalitarians—journalists and pollsters who believe that polls are the definitive voice of the people—may applaud the ability of the most uninformed citizen to be heard, but few if any of these champions of polling ever write about or discuss the implications of ignorance to a representative democracy. This is the dirtiest secret of polling.

Absent from most polling stories is the honest disclosure that American ignorance is driving public affairs. Basic ignorance of civic questions gives us reason to doubt the veracity of most polls. Were Americans armed with strongly held opinions and well-grounded knowledge of civic matters, they would not be open to manipulation by the wording of polls. This is one of the strongest reasons to question the effect of polls on representative government.

Pollsters assume and often control the presentation of the relevant facts. As a blunt instrument, the pollster's questions fail to explore what the contrary data may be. This is one reason that public opinion can differ so widely from one poll to another. When the citizens of a republic lack basic knowledge of political facts and cannot process ideas critically, uninformed opinion becomes even more potent in driving people. Worse, when the media fail to think critically about the lines of dispute on political questions, polls that are supposed to explore opinion will simplify and even mislead political leaders as well as the electorate.

When the media drives opinion by constant polling, the assumption of an educated public undermines the process of public deliberation that actually educates voters. Ideas are no longer honed, language isn't refined, and debate is truncated. The common ground needed for compromise and peaceful action is eroded because the discussion about facts and the parameters of the question are lost. In the frenzy to judge who wins and who loses, the media erodes what it is to be a democracy. Moments of change become opportunities for spin, not for new, bold responses to the exigencies of history.

Not only are polls influenced, shaped, and even dominated by voter ignorance, but so is political debate. The evidence shows that ignorance is being projected into public debate because of the pervasiveness of polls. Polls are leading to the democratization of ignorance in the public square by ratifying ill-formed opinions, with the march of the mob instigated by an impatient and unreflective media. Polls—especially in an age marked by their proliferation—are serving as broadcasting towers of ignorance.

Political science professor Rogan Kersh notes, "Public ignorance and apathy toward most policy matters have been constant (or have grown worse) for over three decades. Yet the same period has seen increasing reliance on finely tuned instruments for measuring popular opinion and more vigorous applications of the results in policy making." And here is the paradox in the Age of Polls: Pollsters and political scientists are still unclear about the full consequences of running a republic on the basis of opinion polls. The cost of voter ignorance is high, especially in a nation with a vast and sprawling government that, even for the most plugged-in elites, is too complicated to understand. Media polling that does not properly inform viewers and readers of its limitations serves only to give the façade of a healthy democracy, while consultants, wordsmiths and polling units gently massage questions, set the news agenda and then selectively report results. It is like the marionette player who claims (however visible the strings) that the puppet moves on his own.

POSTSCRIPT

Are People Better Informed in the Information Society?

It would be wonderful if we could predict the future with certainty, but unfortunately, even predictions are subject to change. It is interesting to note that virtually every new form of technology, especially media, has often been greeted with a mixed sense of optimism and pessimism. New technologies challenge us to think of new practices, new values, and new structures. Sometimes the combination of those elements suggest comfort, ease, and security—other times the threat to what we already know can be a disconcerting feeling of change, without control. We might be able to look back at the evolution of media and think that the variety of content available is great, but it would also be possible to see how our media forms have changed in negative ways too. Your parents were of the generation who knew free television and radio—when media in the airwaves was delivered to the home without a hefty cable bill. Today, unless you live in a part of the country where broadcast signals can still be received in your home, you may not have any choice in your delivery service, or the charges affixed by your program provider.

One of the pleasures of science fiction is that there is usually enough evidence in any portrayal of the future that elements of the story appear to be plausible. There are many futuristic novels like *1984* and *Brave New World* which, in their day, sent chills down the spines of readers. Today's equivalent of these novels would be a film like *The Matrix*.

To read more accounts of how media and technology can and do affect the quality of our lives by facilitating changes within our major institutions— such as education, government, and through popular culture, we suggest a number of readings from a variety of viewpoints. As mentioned above, Neil Postman's classic, *Amusing Ourselves To Death* looks at the impact of television on our lives. His thesis is that even news has to be packaged to be entertaining, and the desire to be entertained stretches to other institutions as well, like schools and within our political arena. Postman's later books, *Technopoly* (Vintage, 1992) and *Building a Bridge to the 18th Century* (Alfred A. Knopf, 1999) also deal with the subtle changes we often experience, but never critically question, as we venerate science and technology, and exclude very human traits such as morality and common sense.

Former Secretary of Labor, Robert Reich has written a very enjoyable, readable book focusing on social change in America, with some reference to the role of media and technology. See Reich, The Future of Success (Alfred A. Knopf, 2001). And for more specific references to media, see John Naughton's *A Brief History of the Future: From Radio Days to Internet Years In a Lifetime* (Overlook Press, 1999).

Contributors to This volume

EDITORS

ALISON ALEXANDER is professor and head of the Department of Telecommunications in the Grady College of Journalism and Mass Communication at the University of Georgia. Prior to becoming department head, she was a faculty member for 11 years at the University of Massachusetts. She received her Ph.D. from Ohio State University, her M.A. from the University of Kentucky, and her B.A. from Marshall University. She was editor of *The Journal of Broadcasting & Electronic Media* from 1989-1991. She is past president of both the Association for Communication Administration and the Eastern Communication Association. She has served on the board of directors of the Broadcast Education Association. Dr. Alexander's research examines audiences and media content, with a focus on media and the family. She is the author of over 40 book chapters, reviews, and journal articles. She is coeditor of *Media Economics: Theory and Practice,* 3ed. (Lawrence Erlbaum, 1997) and *How to Publish Your Communication Research* (Sage Publications, 2001).

JARICE HANSON is professor of Communication at the University of Massachusetts, Amherst, and was the founding Dean of the School of Communications at Quinnipiac University. She received a B.A. in speech and performing arts and B.A. in English at Northeastern Illinois University in 1976. She also received an M.A. and Ph.D. from the Department of Radio-Television Film at Northwestern University in 1977 and 1979, respectively. She is the author of *Understanding Video: Applications, Impact and Theory* (Sage, 1987), *Connections: Technologies of Communication* (Harper-Collins, 1994), and coauthor, with Dr. Uma Narula, of *New Communication Technologies in Developing Countries* (Lawrence Erlbaum, 1990). She is also author of over 30 articles in academic, professional, and popular publications. Her research focuses on media technology, policy, and media images.

STAFF

Larry Leoppke   Managing Editor
Jill Peter   Senior Developmental Editor
Nichole Altman   Develop,ental Editor
Beth Kundert   Production Manager
Jane Mohr   Project Manager
Tara McDermott   Design Coordinator
Bonnie Coakley   Editorial Assistant
Kari Voss   Lead Typesetter
Jean Smith   Typesetter
Sandy Wille   Typesetter
Karen Spring   Typesetter

AUTHORS

THE AMERICAN CIVIL LIBERTIES UNION (ACLU) is an advocacy organization dedicated to the preservation of individual rights as outlined in the Bill of Rights. It is involved in litigating, legislating, and educating the public on a broad array of issues affecting individual freedom in the United States.

GEORGE J. ANNAS is the Edward R. Utley Professor of Law and Medicine at Boston University's Schools of Medicine and Public Health in Boston, Massachusetts. He is also director of Boston University's Law, Medicine, and Ethics Program and chair of the Department of Health Law. His publications include *Judging Medicine* (Humana Press, 1988) and *Standard of Care: The Law of American Bioethics* (Oxford University Press, 1993).

ERICA WEINTRAUB AUSTIN (Ph.D., Stanford University) is a Professor, Edward R. Murrow School of Communication, Washington State University.

RUSS BAKER is a freelance writer based in New York City who often writes on issues of media and press policy.

MICHAEL A. BANKS is the author of 40 books, including *The Internet Unplugged: Utilities and Techniques for Internet Productivity ... Online and Off* (Information Today, 1997) and many magazine articles for the general and computer press. He writes about Internet criminals and privacy threats and how to protect against them.

HANK BARRY is currently interim chairman of Napster, the second incarnation of the the company started by Shawn Fanning, but now owned by Bertlesmann.

DONALD BOGLE is an author and professor at the University of Pennsylvania and at New York University. The author of *Toms, Coons, Mulattoes, Mammies, and Bucks: An Interpretive History of Blacks in American Films* (Continuum International Publishing Group, 2001), Bogle is also the author of numerous other books on blacks and the media.

ERIK P. BUCY is an assistant professor in the Department of Telecommunications at Indiana University, Bloomington. He conducts research on electronic democracy and the psychological effects and nonverbal issues within political news.

JOHN E. CALFEE is a resident scholar at the American Enterprise Institute in Washington, D.C. He is a former Federal Trade Commission economist, and he is the author of *Fear of Persuasion: A New Perspective on Advertising and Regulation* (Agora, 1997).

MICHELLE COTTLE is a staff editor for The Washington Monthly, for which she occasionally writes key features.

JOSEPH R. DIFRANZA is an M.D. in the Department of Family Practice at the University of Massachusetts Medical School in Fitchburg, Massachusetts. He and his colleagues have written several articles on the effects of tobacco advertising on children.

EDISON MEDIA RESEARCH is an organization that conducts survey research to develop strategic information for media organizations. The company is based in Somerville, N.J.

JIB FOWLES is professor of communication at the University of Houston-Clear Lake. His previous books include *Why Viewers Watch* (Sage Publications, 1992) and *Advertising and Popular Culture* (Sage Publications, 1996). His articles have also appeared in many popular magazines.

AL FRANKEN is the best-selling author of *Rush Limbaugh is a Big Fat Idiot and Other Observations, Oh, the Things I Know!,* and *I'm Good Enough, I'm Smart Enough, and Doggone It, People Like Me!* In 2003, he served as a Fellow with Harvard's Kennedy School of Government

SIMSON GARFINKEL is a columnist for the *Boston Globe* and fellow at the Berkman Center for Internet and Society at Harvard Law School. He is author of *Database Nation: The Death of Privacy in the 21st Century* (O'Reilly & Associates, 2000).

MICHAEL GARTNER, former president of NBC News, is editor of the *Ames Daily Tribune,* a daily newspaper near Des Moines, Iowa. His 36-year-long career in print journalism includes 14 years with the *Wall Street Journal.* He received a J.D. degree from New York University and is a member of the bar associations in New York and Iowa.

JAMES W. GENTRY is a professor in the Department of Marketing, College of Business Administration, at the University of Nebraska-Lincoln. He received his Ph.D. from Indiana University.

BERNARD GOLDBERG was a CBS newsman for 30 years during which he won seven Emmy Awards. He now reports on HBO's *Real Sports* and writes for the *New York Times* and the *Wall Street Journal.*

KIMBERLY S. GREGSON is a Ph.D. candidate in the Department of Telecommunications at Indiana University, Bloomington, where she researches framing of political campaigns and virtual communities.

ORRIN HATCH is a U.S. Senator from Utah. He is Chair of the Committee on the Judiciary for Online Entertainment and Copyright Law.

MARJORIE HEINS is the former director and staff counsel to the American Civil Liberties Union Arts Censorship Project. She is the author of *Sex, Sins, and Blasphemy: A Guide to American Censorship,* 2d ed. (New Press, 1998) and *Not in Front of the Children: "Indecency" in History, Politics, and Law* (Hill and Wang, 2001).

PAUL M. HIRSCH is a professor at the Kellogg School of Management at Northwestern University. He is the author of many articles on management practices and mass media organizations. His research interests include organization theory and media industries.

JACOBS MEDIA is a radio-consulting firm specializing in Rock radio. Founded by Fred Jacobs, the organization conducts research for a variety of radio clients, including National Public Radio.

KEVIN KELLY is a writer whose most recent book is *New Rules for the New*

Economy: 10 Radical Strategies for a Connected World.

BRENDAN I. KOERNER occasionally writes for the *Washington Monthly*. He is a Markle Fellow at the New America Foundation.

RUTH ANN LARISCY is professor of public relations at the University of Georgia. She studies political campaigning, with a focus on negative advertising.

PATRICK J. LEAHY is a U.S. Senator from the state of Vermont.

MARY C. MARTIN is an assistant professor in the Department of Marketing, Belk College of Business Administration, at the University of North Carolina at Charlotte. She received her Ph.D. from the University of Nebraska-Lincoln.

ROBERT W. MCCHESNEY is the author of eight books on media and politics, Professor, communication at the University of Illinois at Urbana-Champaign and host of the weekly talk show, Media Matters, on WILL-AM radio.

JOHN MCWHORTER teaches linguistics at the University of California at Berkeley and is the author of *Losing the Race: Self-Sabotage in Black America* (Free Press, 2001).

HORACE NEWCOMB is director of the Peabody Awards and Lambdin Kay Professor at the Grady College of the University of Georgia. He is the editor of *Museum of Broadcast Communications Encyclopedia of Television* (Fitzroy Dearborn Publishers, 1997).

JOHN NICHOLS is a Washington correspondent for *The Nation* and has authored *Jews for Buchanan: Did You Hear the One About the Theft of the American Presidency?* (The New Press, 2001).

DIANE OWEN is an alumnus of the Civic Education Organization. She writes on law and democracy.

ADAM L. PENENBERG writes for *Forbes*. He is a journalist who writes on issues of privacy and security.

BRUCE E. PINKLETON (Ph.D., Michigan State University) is an Associate Professor, Edward R. Murrow School of Communications, Washington State University.

KATHA POLLITT, a poet and an essayist, is associate editor for *The Nation*. Best known for her book of poetry, *Antarctic Traveller* (Alfred A. Knopf, 1982), she has also written about the legal and moral ramifications of important social practices and decisions.

W. JAMES POTTER is a professor of communication at Florida State University. He has conducted research on media violence and has served as one of the investigators on the National Television Violence Study. Recent books include *Media Literacy* (Sage Publications, 1998) and *An Analysis of Thinking and Research About Qualitative Methods* (Lawrence Erlbaum, 1996).

MICHAEL K. POWELL is Chairman of the Federal Communications Commission. He was designated Chairman by President Bush. Mr. Powell, a Republican, was nominated to the FCC by President Clinton.

HOWELL RAINES was executive editor and worked for the *New York Times* for twenty-five years. He is the author of three books, and won the Pulitzer Price for feature writing in 1992.

WADE ROUSH lives in San Francisco and is a senior editor of *Technology Review.*

MATTHEW ROBINSON is managing editor of *Human Events*, and the author of *Mobocracy: How the Media's Obsession with Polling Twists the News, Alters Elections and Undermines Democracy.*

HERBERT SCHILLER was Professor Emeritus of Communication at the University of California, San Diego upon his death in 2000. He was the author of a dozen books on the media, information and culture, and a foremost proponent of the critical/cultural perspective in the United States.

PAUL SIMON (D-Illinois, retired) is currently director of the Public Policy Institute and faculty member at Southern Illinois University. As senator, he spearheaded the drive to curb television violence.

JESSE SUNENBLICK writes for the *Columbia Journalism Review*, and is a recent graduate of New York University's Department of Journalism's Portfolio Program.

DANIEL SUTTER is Associate Professor of Economics at the University of Oklahoma. He studies public policy and public choice.

SPENCER TINKHAM is a professor of advertising at the University of Georgia. He studies political campaigns and negative advertising.

NAM-HYUN UM (MA, Washington State University) is an Account Executive, Cheil Communications, Seoul, Korea.

EUGENE VOLOKH is an attorney and professor at UCLA Law School in California.

JAMES WOLCOTT regularly contributes to *Vanity Fair* and other publications dealing with issues of the media and media content.

Index